MONETARY ECONOMICS

MONETARY ECONOMICS

Institutions, Theory and Policy

SURAJ B. GUPTA

Former Professor of Monetary Economics

Delhi School of Economics

University of Delhi

S Chand And Company Limited

(ISO 9001 Certified Company)

S Chand And Company Limited

(ISO 9001 Certified Company)

Head Office: D-92, Sector–2, Noida – 201301, U.P. (India), Ph. 91-120-4682700

Registered Office: A-27, 2nd Floor, Mohan Co-operative Industrial Estate, New Delhi – 110 044, Phone: 011-49731800

www.**schandpublishing.com;** e-mail: **info@schandpublishing.com**

Marketing Offices:

Chennai	:	Ph: 23632120; chennai@schandpublishing.com
Guwahati	:	Ph: 2738811, 2735640; guwahati@schandpublishing.com
Hyderabad	:	Ph: 40186018; hyderabad@schandpublishing.com
Jalandhar	:	Ph: 4645630; jalandhar@schandpublishing.com
Kolkata	:	Ph: 23357458, 23353914; kolkata@schandpublishing.com
Lucknow	:	Ph: 4003633; lucknow@schandpublishing.com
Mumbai	:	Ph: 25000297; mumbai@schandpublishing.com
Patna	:	Ph: 4011400; patna@schandpublishing.com

First Edition 1982
Subsequent Editions and Reprints 1984, 85 (Twice), 96, 97, 98, 99, 2000, 2001, 2002, 2003, 2004, 2006 (Twice), 2007, 2009 (Twice), 2011, 2012, 2013, 2014, 2018, 2019, 2020 (Twice), 2021, 2022

Reprint 2025

ISBN: 978-81-219-0434-6 **Product Code:** H5ECM41ECON10ENAD0XR

PRINTED IN INDIA

By Vikas Publishing House Private Limited, Plot 20/4, Site-IV, Industrial Area Sahibabad, Ghaziabad – 201 010 and Published by S Chand And Company Limited, A-27, 2nd Floor, Mohan Co-operative Industrial Estate, New Delhi – 110 044.

To the memory of my parents

Preface to the Fourth Edition

I am very happy at the continued warm response to the book. Its present edition has been thoroughly revised and updated. In recent years, several important changes have taken place in the monetary scene in India. I have tried to capture them at appropriate places throughout the book, especially in Chapters 2 to 9, 19, 20 and Appendix H.

In the end, I am very happy to record my sense of gratitude and appreciation to my wife, Manorama for valuable assistance in completing the revision of the book for the present edition.

SURAJ B. GUPTA

Preface to First Edition

This is a text book on monetary economics which combines within its folds a systematic discussion of institutions, theory and policy concerning money and credit in India. It is addressed to the teachers and students of monetary economics at master's and B.A./B.Com. honours' levels of Indian universities. The guiding principle in the selection of topics included in the book and their discussion has been their relevance to contemporary Indian experience and planning needs. Accordingly, besides monetary theory and policy, much of the discussion relates to credit institutions, credit allocation at various levels. The theory of inter-borrower allocation of credit discussed in Chapter 16 deserves special mention in this context.

Since India became free in 1947, the institutional credit scence has undergone a sea change. New public-sector financial institutions such as development banks have come up in a big way and old types of financial institutions such as commercial banks and insurance companies, both life and general, have been nationalised, greatly strengthened and expanded. The Reserve Bank of India, the central bank of the country, nationalised with effect from 1 January, 1949 has been playing a wide-ranging role in financial matters. The launching of the Five Year Plans from 1951-52 and the government's effort to step up the rate of all- round economic development of the country, the problems of inflation, poverty, unemployment, inequality, and imbalances of several kinds have all made monetary and credit planning matters of great importance. For success in this field, a correct understanding of the working of the powerful and complex forces of money and finance, the market and non-market institutional processes through which they operate, the forces behind these processes and their interconnection is essential.

This is the perspective from which money and credit have been studied in this book. The sub-title of the book emphasises the threefold aspects of institutions, theory and policy that have served as the organizing principles for the discussion. Accordingly, the book has been divided into three parts : Institutions (Part One), Theory (Part Two) and Policy (Part Three). If in the field of money and credit institutional processes dominate the market processes, no study of money and credit in the abstract can be meaningful. To be both enlightening and meaningful, it must be based on a careful study of the monetary and credit institutions. Since these institutions are time and place specific, we have studied the forces of money and credit with specific reference to post-independence India. If the study of theory and policy concerning money and credit must be informed by a correct understanding of the related institutions, the study of the latter, too, must be equally informed by theory and policy concerns. Such an *inter-related* study of institutions, theory and policy is the key distinguishing feature of the book.

The book has been designed to serve as a university-level text. While it incorporates selectively several new developments within each part, it leaves out such dead-wood topics as the gold standard, the history of Indian currency, etc. I have also left out deliberately detailed discussion of such topics as theories of portfolio choice or the term structure of interest rates despite their popularity in western monetary economics, because much of such theorising has little relevance for understanding the working of financial forces in India. The Indian market in government debit is a statutorily captive market on the demand side and under monopoly control of the RBI on the supply side, with only a few brokers and no dealers. The organised stock exchanges for other marketable securities are still narrow, shallow and underdeveloped. They handle only a small part of the total credit outstanding as well as the credit raised and disbursed annually in the economy. The bulk of the organized- sector credit is still provided in the form of direct loans and advances and not through marketable financial instruments such as equity shares, bonds, bills etc. Such allocation of credit is weighed greatly by considerations of risk of default (see Chapter 16) and policy directives of the government and the RBI. Consequently, western monetary theory based on the functioning of stock markets (as prime examples of financial markets) and concentrating on expected yield and uncertainty of capital values (of marketable assets) to the neglect of the risk of default and non-marketable custormer loans, is wide of the mark and hence dispensable. I have also not discussed international monetary institutions and problems, because, in my personal opinion, they are best taken up in courses on international economics. The space thus saved has been used to discuss intensively the role of financial intermediaries in the saving-investement process (Chapter 2) and financial markets and concrete financial institutions, as they operate in India (Chapters 3-10).

While writing this book I have taken special care to make the discussion of the subject-matter covered reasonably self-sufficient and easily intelligible, without sacrificing the quality of treatment. The discussion of some topics of monetary theory of either specialised or somewhat-advanced nature has been given in the form of appendices. Notes to the main text are brief and have been placed at the end of individual chapters. References are listed at the end of the book.

The courses in monetary economics in India do not follow a uniform pattern. Some might also need revision and updating. This book should cover most of the topics of any well-rounded course in monetary economics. Appropriate selections of chapters (or even sections) can also be made to suit the course requirements of individual universities. I shall consider my labours well rewarded if the book serves well the needs of teaching monetary economics in Indian universities.

Several friends, colleagues and students had prompted me from time to time to write this book. Several others have helped me in the actual writing of it. Foremost among them have been my wife Manorama and my daughter Vandana. As always, my younger brother O.P. Aggarwal has been a constant source of information on institutional practices and arrangements. My loving thanks to each one of them. I am also happy to acknowledge with thanks the friendly service readily provided by the staff of the Rattan Tata Library (Delhi School of Economics). In writing a text book, one draws upon the contributions of so many other authors that separate acknowledgement of each one of them, apart from some references, is an impossible task, Therefore. I make no attempt at it.

SURAJ B. GUPTA

ABBREVIATIONS

CAS	Credit Authorisation Scheme
CCB	Central Co-operative Banks
CRR	Cash Reserve Ratio
FIs	Financial Intermediaries
GIC	General Insurance Corporation
ICICI	Industrial Credit and Investment Corporation of India
IDBI	Industrial Development Bank of India
IFCI	Industrial Finance Corporation of India
IMF	International Monetary Fund
IRCI	Industrial Reconstruction Corporation of India
IOU	I Owe You
LDCs	Less Developed Countries
LICI	Life Insurance Corporation of India
MEI	Marginal Efficiency of Investment
NABARD	National Bank for Agricultural and Rural Development
NBFIs	Non-Bank Financial Intermediaries
NLR	Net Liquidity Ratio
PACS	Primary Agricultural Credit Societies
PCs	Participation Certificates
QTM	Quantity Theory of Money
RBC	Reserve Bank Credit
RBI	Reserve Bank of India
RBM	Reserve Bank Money
RRBs	Regional Rural Banks
SBI	State Bank of India
SCB	State Co-operative Banks
SCC	Selective Credit Controls
SFC	State Financial Corporation
SIDC	State Industrial Development Corporation
SIIC	State Industrial Investment Corporation
SLDB	State Land Development Banks
SLR	Statutory Liquidity Ratio
UK	United Kingdom
USA	United States of America
UTI	Unit Trust of India

Contents

Preface

Abbreviations

Part One : Institutions **1—176**

1. *Money and the Payments System*
   - 1.1 What is Money ? 3
   - 1.2 Functions of Money ? 3
   - 1.3 Kinds of Money 6
   - 1.4 The Payments System 9
   - 1.5 Deposits 11
   - 1.6 Measures of Money Supply 15
2. *Credit and the Financial System*
   - 2.1 What is Credit ? 19
   - 2.2 What is a Financial System ? 20
   - 2.3 Financial Intermediaries 23
   - 2.4 Functions and Importance of the Financial System 28
   - 2.5 Kinds of Credit 37
3. *Financial Markets*
   - 3.1 Introduction 43
   - 3.2 The Structure of Financial Markets 43
   - 3.3 Call Money Market 48
   - 3.4 Treasury Bill Market 49
   - 3.5 Commercial Bill Market 52
   - 3.6 The New Bill Market Scheme 56
   - 3.7 The Stock Market 58
   - 3.8 The Gilt-edged Market 64
4. *The Reserve Bank of India*
   - 4.1 Introduction 67
   - 4.2 RBI as Currency Authority 68
   - 4.3 RBI as Banker to Government 70
   - 4.4 RBI as Banker's Bank and Supervisor 71
   - 4.5 Controller of Money Supply and Credit 73
   - 4.6 Exchange Management and Control 73

	4.7	Monetary Data and Other Publications	74
	4.8	RBI's Promotional Role	75
5.	*Commercial Banks—I*		
	5.1	What is a Bank ?	82
	5.2	Classification of Commercial Banks	84
	5.3	The Regional Rural Banks	84
	5.4	Liabilities and Assets of Banks	86
	5.5	Evaluation of the Cash Credit System	94
	5.6	A New Simplified Loan System	96
6.	*Commercial Banks—II*		
	6.1	Development of Commercial Banking before Independence (1947)	97
	6.2	Major Developments in Commercial Banking after Independence	98
	6.3	Sectoral Allocation of Commercial Bank Credit	104
	6.4	Some Further Developments	112
7.	*Co-operative Banks*		
	7.1	Introduction	113
	7.2	The Structure of Co-operative Banks	115
	7.3	State Co-operative Banks (SCBs)	118
	7.4	Central Co-operative Banks (CCBs)	119
	7.5	Primary Agricultural Credit Societies (PACs)	120
	7.6	Primary Co-opertive Banks (PCBs)	125
	7.7	The RBI/NABARD and Co-operative Banking System	126
8.	*Development Banks*		
	8.1	What are Development Banks?	129
	8.2	Industrial Development Banks for Large Industries (All-India)	131
	8.3	All-India Industrial Development Banks-Main Features with Evaluation	133
	8.4	State-level Industrial Development Banks	140
	8.5	Export-Import (or Exim) Bank of India	142
	8.6	National Bank for Agricultural and Rural Development (NABARD)	142
	8.7	Land Development Banks	144

9. *Non-Bank Financial Intermediaries*

9.1	Introduction	145
9.2	The Life Insurance Corporation of India	146
9.3	General Insurance Companies	148
9.4	The Unit Trust of India (UTI) and other Mutual Funds	149
9.5	Provident/Pension Funds	151
9.6	Post Offices	151
9.7	Other 'Non-Bank Financial Companies' (NBFCs)	152

10. *Unregulated Credit Markets*

10.1	Introduction	159
10.2	Types of Unregulated Credit Agencies	160
10.3	The Hundi	161
10.4	Indigenous Bankers	161
10.5	Indigenous Bankers—An Evaluation and Suggestions for Reform	165
10.6	Finance Brokers	169
10.7	Money Lenders	170
10.8	Other Lenders—The Informal Loan Market	173
10.9	Unregulated Credit and Black Money	174
10.10	Unregulated Credit Markets and Credit Policy	175

Part Two : Theory **177—335**

11. *The Demand for Money*

11.1	Introduction	179
11.2	Nominal versus Real Cash Balances	180
11.3	The Neoclassical Theory	181
11.4	Keynes' Theory	184
11.5	The Transactions Demand for Money	191
11.6	Friedman's Theory	195
11.7	Empirical Evidence	197

12. *Money and Prices*

12.1	Introduction	200
12.2	Fisher's Transactions Approach to the QTM	201
12.3	The Quantity Equation in Income Form	203
12.4	The Cambridge Cash-Balances Approach	205

12.5	The QTM as a Theory of Money Income	207
12.6	The QTM as a Theory of P	211
12.7	Modern QTM	212
12.8	The QTM—An Appraisal	217
13.	*Money, Interest and Income*	
13.1	Introduction	224
13.2	Keynes' Monetary Theory	224
13.3	Keynes' Theory of the Rate of Interest	226
13.4	Rate of Interest and Investment	231
13.5	Investment and Income	234
13.6	Income, Output, Employment and the Marginal Productivity of Labour	239
13.7	Marginal Productivity of Labour and the Price Level	240
13.8	Hicks' IS-LM Model	242
14.	*Inflation*	
14.1	Introduction	250
14.2	Demand-Pull Inflation	250
14.3	Quantity Theory of Money (QTM) Excess Demand and Inflation	254
14.4	Cost-Push Inflation	255
14.5	Income-Shares Inflation	260
14.6	Demand-Shift Theory of Inflation	261
14.7	The Phillips Curve	261
14.8	Structural Inflation in the LDCs	264
14.9	Money and Inflation	268
15.	*Theory of Money Supply*	
15.1	Introduction	270
15.2	The H Theory of Money Supply	271
15.3	The Money-Multiplier Process	280
15.4	Determinants of the Money Multiplier	286
15.5	Factors affecting H	286
15.6	Adjusted H	289
15.7	Is H an autonomous Policy-determined Variable ?	290
15.8	Reserve Bank's Analysis of Money Supply	292
16.	*The Supply of Credit and its Allocation*	
16.1	Introduction	297
16.2	The Theory of Bank Credit and Bank Deposits	297

16.3 The Allocation of Institutional Credit as an Institutional Process 300
16.4 Financial Factors in the Allocation of Institutional Credit 302
16.5 Non-Financial Factors in the Allocation of Institutional Credit 314

17. *Interest Rates*
17.1 Introduction 316
17.2 The Loanable Funds Theory 316
17.3 Heterogeneity of Interest Rate Determination 321
17.4 Interest Rate Differentials 324
17.5 Equalising and Non-equalising Differences in Interest Rates 330
17.6 Deficiencies in the Prevailing System of Administered Interest Rates 331

Part Three : Policy **337—384**

18. *Goals, Targets and Indicators*
18.1 Introduction 339
18.2 Goals, Targets, Indicators and Instruments 340
18.3 Goals of Monetary Policy 342
18.4 Targets of Monetary Policy 350
18.5 The Indicator-Problem 353

19. *Instruments of Control*
19.1 Introduction 355
19.2 Open Market Operations 356
19.3 Variations in Reserve Requirements 358
19.4 Changes in the Cost and Availability of Reserve Bank Credit to Banks 361
19.5 Changes in the Cost and Availability of Reserve Bank Credit to Development Banks 364
19.6 The Statutory Liquidity Ratio 365
19.7 Moral Suasion 366
19.8 Selective Credit Controls 367
19.9 Credit Monitoring Arrangement (CMA) 369

20. *Monetary-Credit Policy of the Reserve Bank of India*
20.1 Introduction 371

20.2	Monetary Policy	371
20.3	Monetary Policy Measures	377
20.4	Some Aspects of Credit Theory	378
Appendix A	The QTM, Monetary Velocity and the Commodity Market	385
Appendix B	The Real-Balance Effect	390
Appendix C	Monetary Transmission Mechanism	392
Appendix D	Inflationary Expectations	395
Appendix E	The Phillips Curve, Expectations and Other Factors	399
Appendix F	Chakravarty Committee Recommendations	406
Appendix G	M_1 or M_3?	424
Appendix H	New Financial Developments	427
References		449
Index		455

Part One : Institutions

Monetary forces operate through myriad of channels— market and non-market, institutional and others. The study of financial institutions, instruments, and markets is, therefore, of the first importance to understand the working of monetary forces, to analyse their effects, to plan policy measures and evaluate their consequences. This gains in further importance, because these institutions are peculiar to each country; they are the products of its history, traditions, the genius of its people and the government; they also change over time. In India, much has happend on this front over the short span of 34 years after it became free of the foreign rule. Compressing of all the major developments in a systematic framework and bringing out their implications for the working of the economy and monetary and credit policies is the task attempted in this Part of the book under ten chapters (1–10).

The first three chapters discuss money, credit, financial system, financial intermediaries, and financial markets and instruments in general terms and as they are found in India. A detailed discussion of the banking system of India is offered in the next four chapters (4–7), beginning with a study of the functions and promotional role of the Reserve Bank of India (Chapter 4), going on to commercial banks in the next two chapters and to co-operative banks in Chapter 7. In each of these fields of banking, several important structural and policy developments have taken place. These developments represent in concrete terms institutional response to complex problems of finance, which mere theorising cannot easily envisage or even comprehend.

Development banks are specialised institutions for the provision of development finance and associated services to designated sectors of the Indian economy. They are studied in Chapter 8, followed by a study of several non-bank financial intermediaries operating in India in Chapter 9. Any study of the Indian financial system will be incomplete without a discussion, howsoever brief and impressionistic, of the unregulated credit markets and their functionaries. The task is attempted in the closing chapter (10) of this Part.

CHAPTER 1

Money and the Payments System

1.1 What is Money?

Money is anything that is generally acceptable as a means of payment in the settlement of all transactions, including debt. It is the commonly-used medium of exchange or means of transferring purchasing power. General acceptability as a means of payment or as a medium of exchange is the unique feature of money. This makes money and money alone general purchasing power, *i.e*, the power to buy things directly in all markets. It does not require to be converted into something else before it can be spent or used for the settlement of debt. What makes money money is the belief held by everyone that it will be accepted as such by all others in the economy. General acceptability as the common means of payment is the *sine qua non* or the differentia of money.

Various things have served as money at different times and places. They have varied from courie shells, goats, cows, and rice to silver and gold pieces and coins, paper currency notes and demand (or chequing) deposits of banks. At present, in India, money, commonly defined, comprises coins and paper currency and demand deposits of banks. More on this later in this chapter.

1.2 Functions of Money

The functions of money have been well summed up in a couplet:

Money is a matter of functions four:
A medium, a measure, a standard, a store.

(1) Money as a Medium of Exchange

The primary and unique function of money is that of acting as a medium of exchange. This function of monev is so important and unique that, in the previous section, we have defined it in terms of this sole function. Later in the book also we shall use it as the distinguishing characteristic of money, a characteristic that will help separate money from other (near-money or non-money) assets. It is this function alone which can help identify money as money. All other attributes or functions of money are derived from this primary function. But they do not help distinguish money uniquely from other assets. Needless to say that to be a successful medium of exchange, money must be commonly-accepted as such by all in all transactions.

The use of money as a common medium of exchange has facilitated exchange greatly. Without money, exchange will involve a direct barter of goods and services for goods and services. But most of the time, for such exchange to take place, there must occur a double coincidence of wants. That is, each party to the exchange must have precisely what the other party requires, and in appropriate quantity and at the time required. Speaking dramatically, hungry weavers have to search for naked farmers and *vice versa* to exchange their surplus cloth with farmers' surplus food. This would involve tremendous waste of time and resources in search effort and in making bargains. Alternatively, barter will require a series of transactions in completing the desired exchange. Each individual must accept payment in kind (of goods offered), consume what he wishes and store or try to sell the excess to someone else, who, in turn, does the same. This would also be highly wasteful of time and resources in a large, complex society. The use of money as medium of exchange avoids much of this waste by economising on the use of scarce real resources in carrying out exchanges. This is said to promote transactions efficiency in exchange. In addition, the use of money also promotes allocational efficiency by making it possible to exploit potential gains from specialisation in trade and production and emergence of specialised markets (dealers) in every type of goods and services. Without money, in certain spheres of economic activity, it will be difficult to organize exchange at all, and hence production. For example, think of selling a film show in Delhi to a wide variety of viewers and payable in kind in terms of the produce of each viewer! And how should the film stars and others engaged in the production of films be awarded?

Not all barter transactions, however, need be difficult to arrange or inefficient purely as methods of conducting exchange. And hence they may survive even in a money-using system. For example, in parts of Indian agriculture, hired labour is still paid in kind, invariably foodgrains. Similarly, under share-cropping arrangements, landlords usually get rent of land as a portion of the total produce of land. But the area of barter transactions is surely limited and diminishing over time.

(2) Money as a Unit of Account

Money customarily serves as a common unit of account or measure of value in terms of which the values of all goods and services are expressed. This makes possible meaningful accounting systems by adding up the values of a wide variety of goods and services whose physical quantities are measured in different units. Important examples of value totals are the national income estimates of a country, total money cost of a project, total sale proceeds of a multi-product firm, *etc.* This makes comparisons of various kinds across time and across regions (even countries with different national moneys but at given exchange rates among them) possible. It has been truly said that it has been possible for economics to grow as a science, because it analyses social behaviour concerned with the production, exchange, distribution and consumption of goods and services whose values can be measured in a common unit, money. Prices, with which so much of economic theory is concerned, are only values per unit of goods and services expressed in terms of money. These prices, being expressed in a common unit, can be directly compared with each other and the ratio of exchange between any pair of goods easily computed. In the absence of money as a common denominator, the number of exchange ratios among goods to be reckoned with will be bewilderingly large—several times larger than the number of money prices.[1]

However, money as a measure of value is not perfect. For its own value (in terms of goods and services) does not stay constant. It varies from time to time. This is not true of physical measures such as measures of distance (a meter), weight (a kilogram), time (an hour), *etc.* These measures stay invariant over time and across regions/countries. The variability of the value of money raises several important socio-economic problems. We shall discuss them later in the book.

(3) Money as a Standard of Deferred Payment

Money also serves as a standard or unit in terms of which deferred or future payments are stated. This applies to payments of interest, rents, salaries, pensions, insurance premia, *etc.* Loans, interest, rents, wages, *etc.* stipulated in kind are not unknown. We have already spoken of wages and land rents in kind still prevailing in large parts of Indian agriculture. Similarly, commodity loans, especially seed loans, have also been prevalent. But, in a money-using system, the bulk of deferred payments are stipulated in money terms.

Large fluctuations in the value of money (*i.e.*, inflation or deflation of prices) make money not only a poor measure of value, but also a poor standard of deferred payment. This is because the value of money is not something intrinsic to it, but a social phenomenon. This makes monetary management for the stable value of money socially very important.

(4) Money as a Store of Value

Money also serves as a store of value, *i.e.*, members of the public can hold their wealth in the form of money. This function is derived from the use of money as a medium of exchange in a two-fold manner. First, the use of money as a medium of exchange decomposes a single barter transaction into two separate transactions of purchase and sale. Under barter, purchase and sale are necessarily simultaneous operations. The use of money necessarily separates the two transactions in time. This will require that the medium of exchange also serve as a store of value. Then, in a money-using system, incomes in the form of wages, salaries, rent, interest and profits are money payments received discontinuously. They may be spent either immediately or over the time interval of the receipt of two incomes. When the latter option is exercised, at least a part of the receipt is held in the form of money for varying period. All this is encouraged by a unique feature of money—that it is generalized purchasing power, and assuch the only perfectly liquid asset. No doubt, money is not the only store of value. There are other assets of all kinds which also serve as stores of value and compete with money in this capacity. But money is unique as a store of value in that it alone is perfectly liquid. That is, it alone serves as a generally acceptable means of payment. The fluctuations in the value of money that affect its functions as a measure of value and as a standard of deferred payment also influence its role as a store of value.

1.3 Kinds of Money

Money has had several incarnations. These have varied over time and space. A study of the evolution of money, the related circumstances, the working of various monetary standards is fascinating. But we resist the temptation and restrict ourselves to the present.

At present in India money consists of coins, paper currency, and deposit money.

Coins are an example of metallic money. They are not full-bodied, but only token money, because the intrinsic (metallic) value of token coins is less than their face value.

Currency notes are merely pieces of paper that have no intrinsic value of their own. They are not convertible into anything of value at a fixed rate. The issuing authority does not stand ready to buy them back against gold or silver or full-bodied gold or silver coins of equal value at a pre-determined price. Thus, all paper currency is inconvertible. The legend carried on the face of a Reserve Bank of India (RBI) currency note of (say) ten rupees that 'I promise to pay the bearer the sum of ten rupees' (signed by the Governor, the RBI) is a carry-over from the past when currency notes were convertible into full-bodied silver rupees. Now it simply means that notes can be converted into other notes or token coins of equal value.

Deposit money is not like coins or currency notes that can be passed on from hand to hand for a transfer of purchasing power. Deposits are only entries in the ledgers of banks to the credit of their holders. We are treating only demand deposits of banks on which cheques can be drawn as money. The cheques are an instrument through which these deposits can be transferred from the payer to the payee. Only when the ownership of these deposits has been so transferred is the medium-of-exchange or the means-of-payment function of these deposits completed. The transfer is completed by debiting the amount of the cheque to the account of the drawer of the cheque and crediting it to the account of the drawee. This transfer is a simple affair if both the drawer and the drawee of the cheque are account holders in the same bank (branch). It involves the use of a specially-organized clearing arrangement, when the drawer and the drawee belong to two different banks.

A *clearing-house* is an association of banks operating in a particular locality. It serves as a meeting place for the representatives of member banks at appointed hours on each working day to settle payments of cheques and other transfer orders on each other by their customers. This is done by cancellation of equal amounts of credits and debits of each bank against every other bank, taken singly and settling the balance by drawing a cheque of the appropriate amount on its account with the clearing house or the RBI in favour of the surplus bank. In the cse of out-of-town cheques on other banks, a similar process works. The local branch of the drawee's bank takes over from its counterpart in another place. For an out-of-town cheque on another branch of the same bank, collection of the amount of a cheque is effected through a process of internal clearing.

The clearing-house facility is of great importance for the successful working of any banking system and of the use of bank money as a medium of exchange. Clearing arrangements economise greatly the use of cash, since the mutually offsetting transfers of funds among banks are settled merely through double entries in the books of the clearing-house without any actual transfer of cash and since such transfers constitute a large bulk of total transfers executed through deposit money. Bank clearings facilitate transfers of funds quickly, safely, and at low cost. The advantages accrue to the users of cheques. They encourage the use of bank money in place of currency For businesses specially, quick clearings are very important as they affect the day-to-day cash-flow or liquidity positions of the cheque-using firms.

The clearing houses are run by the RBI at places where it has its offices and by the State Bank of India (SBI) and its subsidiaries elsewhere. At the end of March 1988 there were 729 clearing houses in the country, of which 14 were managed by the RBI, and the rest by the SBI and its 7 associated banks.

We have explained above the clearing arrangement of banks, because it is central to the working of any payments system that uses deposit (bank) money. Chequing deposits serve as means of payment only when they are transferred from one depositor to another. When cheques are encashed, that is converted into currency, demand deposits of equal amount are extinguished. In a sense, the demand deposits have still effected the payment. But, in the process, they have died. Temporarily, their place has been taken by currency. But, this is not the end of the matter. The loss of currency to a bank depletes its cash reserves and will lead to a multiple contraction of deposits (see Chapter 15).

All the three components of present-day money have one feature in common. All of them are *fiduciary (credit) money:* money that circulates as money on the basis of the trust commanded by its issuers. This illustrates very well the truth of the statement that 'money is what the public believes to be money.' The essential property of money is that it should be generally acceptable as means of payment. For this, it is not at all necessary that money should be something that has utility (or productivity) of its own independent of its services yielded as money. The members of the public accept it in payment because they are confident that they can similarly pay it further in settlement of transactions of all kinds. Fiduciary money exploits this confidence to the full. Looked at differently, the use of fiduciary money is highly economical : it releases precious metal embodied in coins under full-bodied metallic standards for non-monetary uses.

Looking back, all metallic standards were wasteful. (But we reserve judgment on the important issue whether complete dependence on fiduciary money is the major source of inflationary trends.)

Another useful distinction is between *(a)* legal tender or fiat money and *(b)* non-legal tender or credit money proper. Coins and currency notes are *fiat money*. They serve as money on the fiat (order) of the government. Though all currency notes of the value of rupees two and above are issued by the Reserve Bank of India, this is done on behalf and authority of the Government of India. Technically, they are guaranteed by the latter. This simply means that they are *legal tender*. So are other coins and currency notes. Being legal tender means that, under the law of the land, the money in question must be accepted or cannot be refused in settlement of payments of all kinds. This is not true of demand deposits of banks, which are fiduciary money proper, as they are accepted as money on trust. They are not legal tender. A payee can legally refuse to accept payment in demand deposits (made through a cheque), and insist on payment in cash. This is because there is no guarantee that a cheque will be honoured at the issuer's bank.

Legal tender money may be limited or unlimited legal tender. Small coins are usually limited legal tender. That is, they are legal tender for payments upto only a certain maximum amount. Beyond this amount, for a single payment, they cease to be legal tender. In India, small coins, including one-rupee coins and notes, are limited legal tender. All other currency are unlimited legal tender.

1.4 The Payments System

The payments system is the set of institutional arrangements through which purchasing power is transferred from one transactor in exchange to another. Specialisation in production necessitates exchange. For efficient exchange, a common medium of exchange or means of payment is necessary. We have already seen in Section 1.1 above that such a common medium of exchange is what we call money. Thus the payments system is organized around the use of money. An efficient organization of the monetary system is the *sine qua non* of an efficient payments system.

Payments are made locally as well as across places, within the same country using one national money (say rupees), or across countries involving the use of foreign monies. In making local payments also physical distance is important. Then, payments are made in small, medium, or large amounts. An efficient payments system should permit all kinds of payments to be made with utmost convenience, expeditiously, safely, and at very low costs to the economy and the transactors.

For making small local payments (mostly arising in retail trade and daily wage payments), currency has proved to be the best means of payment. For making large and out-of-town payments, the use of chequing deposits and bank drafts is more popular. For faster payments, telegraphic transfers of money are also made. Other modes of payment used are money orders and postal orders sold by post offices and hundis of indigenous bankers. For making foreign payments, banks again come into the picture. Thus the banking system plays a dominant role in the organization and running of the payments system. The spread of banking in the country is important not only for the mobilisation of savings and for allocation of credit but also as a dominant component of the payments system. We should remember that the banking system includes the Reserve Bank of India, which acts as the currency authority in the country and is responsible for meeting all the currency needs of the public.

Given the public's demand for each kind of means of payment, an efficient payments system must meet this demand in full. Shortages of particular kinds of money as, for example, of small coins (which occurred during the Second World War or in the early 70s) should be avoided. Bank clearings have come to play a very important role in settling payment. Any disruption of such clearings (as occurs, for example, during a strike or go-slow agitation of bank employees) disrupts the flow of payments in the economy, creates liquidity problems for all, and slows up the rate of economic activity. Interestingly, the importance of the smooth functioning of the payments system is recognized only when such a system is disrupted.

The speed with which payments are completed is also important. Speedy payments mean that funds do not remain tied up in transit for too long. Therefore, speedy payments make for more efficient utilisation of funds and thereby of resources. As a result, the speed (or rate) of production also goes up. This kind of intangible benefit of an efficient payments system is generally not well appreciated. The slow speed of payments cannot be made good by larger amounts of the means of payment (money). Given the real stock of money (that is, the nominal stock of money deflated by the price level), the speed of payments can be faster or slower. This speed impinges on the flow of funds through the economy, the cash flow positions of individual units, and their capacities to go ahead with planned spendings of all kinds, final and intermediate, which affects the flow of production.

The organization and running of the payments system involves costs—costs to transactors and to the economy. Individual transactors have to pay banks, post offices, indigenous bankers, or others for the transfer of funds. These agencies, in turn, incur costs in creating and maintaining such transfer facilities. The more efficient the payments system, the lower the cost of transfer of funds per rupee. The gain of lower costs accrues to the whole economy.

There is another kind of cost of maintaining the payments system which the economy as a whole incurs. This concerns the production and maintenance of currency. (The cost of producing and maintaining checking deposits of banks has already been covered in the previous paragraph.) In regimes of full-bodied metallic currency (whether of gold or silver or some other metal), such costs were quite high. The paper currency system, in this sense, is much more economical.

1.5 Deposits

In the next section we shall study alternative measures of money supply. As a preparation to that discussion we describe various kinds of deposits, some of which will be found to be hot candidates for the status of money.

Deposits are moneys accepted by various agencies from others to be held under stipulated terms and conditions. In India deposits are accepted by banks, post offices, and non-bank companies.[2] In this section we shall explain briefly only the deposits accepted by the first two agencies, as they alone have been proposed as constituents of alternative measures of money supply.

1.5.1 Bank Deposits

Banks accept mainly three kinds of deposits .

(i) Current Account Deposits. Deposits in current account are payable on demand. They can be drawn upon by cheque without any restriction. These deposits are mostly held by business firms, which use them for making business payments. No interest is paid on these deposits. But, in return, the banks render various kinds of customer services to their account holders on a modest charge. The most important service, of course, is the cheque facility, *i.e.*, making payment to the party specified in the cheque. Then, collections are made of cheques, drafts, dividend warrants, postal orders, *etc.* on behalf of the account holder. For local cheques, drafts, *etc.*, no fee is

charged. Some commission is charged only for making collections for out-station cheques, drafts, *etc.* The bank keeps regular account of all the transactions made in a particular account and submits statements of the same to the account-holder at regular intervals.

(ii) Fixed (-Term) Deposits. They are deposits for a fixed term, which may vary from a few days to a few years. They are not payable on demand and do not enjoy chequing facilities. That is, cheques cannot be issued against them for making payments. Legally, the moneys deposited in them become payable only on the maturity of the fixed term (period) for which the deposit was initially made. In practice, however, banks allow a depositor to withdraw funds from his deposit prematurely in case of need, provided the depositor is willing to lose some interest. Normally, the depositor is paid 1–2 per cent less than the rate of interest applicable for the period the deposit remained with the bank. (Alternatively, the bank allows the depositor to borrow funds against his fixed deposit as security at its normal lending rate. This ensures the encashability of a fixed deposit in time of need, though at some interest cost to the deposit-holder.)

Fixed deposits are interest-earning deposits, the rate of interest rising with the term of the deposit. However, banks in India are prohibited by the RBI from making interest payments on deposits for periods upto 14 days. For other periods, the rates of interest are fixed by the RBI. For example, currently, the one-year-deposit rate is 8.5 percent, but for deposits of 5 or more years, the rate is 11 per cent per year.

A variant of fixed deposits are *recurring* (or *cumulative time) deposits.* For such an account, a depositor makes a regular deposit (say, per month) of an agreed sum of money over an agreed period. Generally, the duration of such deposits ranges from 2 to 7 years. The monthly deposit is in multiples of Rs. 5. Interest is credited on the accumulated monthly balance (inclusive of interest). That is, compound interest is paid on recurring deposits. Such deposits are designed to induce small savers to save regularly and accumulate their savings with banks for a certain period.

(iii) Savings Account Deposits. These deposits combine features of both current account deposits and fixed deposits. They are like the former in that they are payable on demand and also withdrawable by cheque. But the chequing facilities are not unrestricted. A savings account cannot be used very actively, that is, banks do not allow too many cheques to be drawn on it in a short period. For this reason, these deposits are supposed to be held only by households for holding their

short-term savings. For the same reason, savings accounts cannot be opened in the name of business firms. An individual owner of a business firm holding a savings account in his/her name is not supposed to use it (its chequing facility) for business purposes.

Savings-account deposits, like fixed deposits, are interest-earning. The current annual rate of interest paid by large scheduled commercial banks is 5 per cent per annum, payable on the minimum monthly balance held from the 11th day of a month till its end.

Reclassification of All Bank Deposits into Demand Deposits and Time Deposits

In monetary analysis, only a two-fold classification of bank deposits into *(a)* demand deposits and *(b)* time deposits is made. Demand deposits are defined as deposits payable on demand through cheque or otherwise. It is important to note that among deposits it is only demand deposits which serve as a medium of exchange, for their ownership can be transferred from one person to another through cheques and clearing arrangement explained in the previous section. If they could not be so used, though they were fully payable in cash on demand, they themselves would not serve as a medium of exchange. They would only be instantly convertible into cash, which alone would serve as a medium of exchange. All other deposits which are not payable on demand and on which cheques cannot be drawn have a fixed term to maturity. They are, therefore, called time deposits.

For monetary analysis, the publication of monetary data, and for policy regulations, the RBI reclassifies various kinds of bank deposits described above under two heads: demand deposits and time deposits. All current account deposits are obviously demand deposits and fixed deposits (including recurring deposits) are time deposits. The problem of classifying savings deposits is not that simple, because they combine the features of both demand deposits and time deposits. The RBI distinguishes between (what it calls) *(a)* the demand liability portion of savings deposits and *(b)* the time liability portion of savings deposits. Till August 1978 the former used to be defined as 'the portion of savings deposits freely withdrawable.' This portion was included (along with current account deposits) under demand deposits. The rest of the savings deposits were included under time deposits. The actual division was left to banks, which report to the RBI twice a year (at the end of June and December) the proportion of their savings deposits to be classified as demand deposits. At the end of March 1978, for scheduled commercial banks, the demand deposit portion of savings deposits was 87 per cent. In the past, this portion has fluctuated sharply—from 64.3 per cent at the end of March 1963 to 86.9 per cent a year after, and 93.2 per cent at the end of March 1968.

From August 1978 the RBI amended the ground rule for apportioning savings deposits into demand and time deposits. Under the new rule 'the average of the monthly minimum balances in a savings account on which interest is being credited to the account shall be regarded as a time liability and the excess over the said amount as a demand liability.' Earlier, what was included in demand deposits was that portion of savings deposits that was freely withdrawable. With the amendment, what is included is the portion of savings deposits that is *actually* freely drawn upon by the depositors, while that portion which remains with the banks earning interest is being taken under time deposits. As a consequence of the above-mentioned amendment, the demand liability portion of savings deposits had come down from 87 per cent at the end of March 1978 to 60 per cent at the end of March 1979. Such classificatory changes have thus introduced an element of arbitrariness and artificial fluctuations in the measurement of money supply.

The rationale of the above amendment is questionable, because what imbues the demand deposit portion of savings deposits with the quality of money (narrowly defined) is their withdrawability by cheque and without notice and not their actual withdrawal.

On this consideration, all (and not a part) of savings deposits should be treated as demand deposits. Such a practice will simplify greatly the task of measurement of money supply and also eliminate a certain arbitrariness currently being practiced in this task.

1.5.2 **Post Office Deposits**

Post Offices also accept deposits from the public. Broadly speaking, they are of two kinds: *(a)* savings deposits and *(b)* time deposits. The latter also include recurring deposits and cumulative time deposits. Savings deposits are withdrawable on demand, but only by withdrawal slips. The chequeable portion of these deposits is negligibly small. Moreover, there is a restriction on the number of withdrawals per month, and also a maximum limit on a single withdrawal. For a large withdrawal, an advance notice is required. Thus, encashability of post-office savings deposits is not perfect. More importantly, they do not serve as a medium of exchange, because, for lack of chequing facilities, they are not used for transferring purchasing power from one party to another.

1.6 Measures of Money Supply

Money is something measurable. Once we have settled on a theoretical definition of money, we can identify empirically the things that serve as money in an economy. Then, the total stock of moneys of various kinds at a particular point of time can be computed. By repeated measurements at different points of time, a whole time series of money supply can be constructed. This will show the time behaviour of money supply. Coupled with other data and helped by theory, this information can be used to throw light on the effect of changes in the supply of money on several key variables such as income, prices, wages, employment, rate of interest, balance of payments, *etc.*, and how to control changes in the supply of money to attain certain policy goals.

At the outset, we must note two things about any measure of money supply. First, that the supply of money refers to its *stock* at any point of time. This is because money is a stock variable in contrast with a flow variable, such as real income, which refers to its rate per unit time (say, per year). It is the change in the stock of money (say) per year, which is a flow.

Second, the stock of money always refers to the stock of money *held by the public.* This is always smaller than the total stock of money in existence. The term public is defined to include all economic units (households, firms and institutions) except the producers of money (such as the government and the banking system). For the most common definition of money, the government means the Central Government plus all state governments; the banking system means the RBI plus all banks which accept demand deposits. This means that the word public is inclusive of all local authorities, non-bank financial institutions, and non-departmental public-sector undertakings (such as Hindustan Steel, Indian Airlines, *etc.*) and even the foreign central banks and governments and the International Monetary Fund who hold a part of Indian money in India in the form of deposits with the RBI. In other words, in the standard measures of money, money held by the government and the banking system is not included.

The primary reason for measuring the stock of money in this way is that this separates the producers or the suppliers of money from the holders or the demanders of it. For both monetary analysis and policy formulation, such a separation is essential, as we shall see later in the book.

The measurement of money supply is an empirical matter. We study the various measures of money supply published by the RBI. Till 1967–68 the RBI used to publish only a single measure of money supply (M) defined as the sum of currency and demand deposits, both held by the public. Following convention, we call it the narrow measure of money supply. From 1967–68 the RBI started publishing additionally a 'broader' measure of money supply, called 'aggregate monetary resources' (AMR). It was defined empirically as money narrowly defined plus the time deposits of banks held by the public. From April 1977 yet another change was introduced. Since then the RBI has been publishing data on four alternative measures of money supply in place of the earlier two. The new measures are denoted by M_1, M_2, M_3, and M_4. The two earlier measures were represented by M and AMR. The respective empirical definitions of these measures are given below.

M or M_1 = C + DD + OD.
M_2 = M_1 + savings deposits with post office savings banks,
AMR or M_3 = M_1 + net time deposits of banks,
M_4 = M_3 + *total* deposits with the Post Office Savings Organization (excluding National Savings Certificates).

In the above definitions,
C = currency held by the public,
DD = net demand deposits of banks,
OD = 'other deposits' of the RBI.

The contents of each of the components of M to M_4 are explained briefly below.

Currency consists of paper currency as well as coins. Paper currency is predominant in the form of Reserve Bank of India currency notes of the denomination of rupees two and above (rupees five, ten, twenty, fifty, and one hundred notes). In addition, we also have small amounts of Government of India rupee one notes. Though made of paper, they are counted as rupee one coins. Together with rupee one coins and other small coins, they constitute the small-coins component of money supply. They are direct monetary liability of the Government of India. However, they are put into circulation by the RBI as the agent of the Central Government. The RBI does this by holding stocks of government currency on hand and by maintaining full convertibility of this currency into the rest of the country's currency and *vice versa.*

We have already explained in the previous section the meaning, nature and the composition of demand deposits. What get included in any measure of money supply are the *net* demand deposits of banks, and not their total demand deposits. This is because we have defined money (and any one of its components) as something held by the 'public' only and total deposits include both deposits from the public and inter-bank deposits. The latter are deposits which one bank holds with others. Since they are not held by the public, they are netted out of the total demand deposits to arrive at net demand deposits. We may remind the readers that demand deposits comprise the current-account deposits and the demand deposit portion of savings deposits, all held by the public.

'Other deposits' of the RBI are its deposits other than those held by the government (the Central and state governments), banks, and a few others. They include demand deposits of quasi-government institutions (like the IDBI), foreign central banks and governments, the IMF and the World Bank, *etc.* Empirically, whatever the measure of money supply, these 'other deposits' of the RBI constitute a very small proportion (less than one per cent) of the total money supply. Therefore, no harm will be done, if in our future discussion we ignore these 'other deposits.'

The following additional points about the new measures of money supply *vis-a-vis* the old measures need to be noted.

(1) M is only a revised measure of M—the RBI's old measure of money supply. The revision is not conceptual, but only in terms of coverage. The new series gives a better coverage of the co-operative banking sector (chapter 7). Formerly, only the *demand liabilities* of the State co-operative banks were included in money supply. Other tiers of the co-operative banking sector were neglected on account of the non-availability of data. In the new series *net (i.e.,* excluding inter-bank) demand deposits of State co-operative banks, Central co-operative banks and a segment of primary co-operative banks consisting of *(i)* urban co-operative banks and *(ii)* salary earners' credit societies are included. Similarly, M_3 is the revised version of the series on AMR with extended coverage for the co-operative banking sector.

(2) The new series M_2 and M_4 have been devised to accommodate Post Office deposits. We have already explained the nature of these deposits in the previous section.

(3) The RBI views the four new measures of money stock to represent different degrees of liquidity. It has specified them in the

descending order of liquidity, M_1 being the most liquid and M_4 the least liquid of the four measures.

Which of the alternative measures of money supply to choose and why ? We cannot attempt an answer here, as it will involve going into questions of monetary theory, policy, and empirical testing (However, see Appendix G on this subject). It should suffice to say at this state that the most common measure of money supply is that provided by M or M_1.

Till 1978 the RBI also used to concentrate most of its accounting analysis on this narrow measure of money supply. But things have changed since. Due to the introduction of a change in 1978 in the division of savings deposits of banks as between demand deposits and time deposits (Section 1.5.1), the data on M for post-1978 years are no longer comparable with those for the previous years. So, the RBI has shifted its accounting analysis of changes in money supply in terms of M_3.

But whatever the measure of money supply used, one thing clearly stands out about its time profile in India—that its rate of growth has accelerated over time[3]. Thus in the case of M_1 (narrow definition), the annual average rate of growth was 3.6% during the 1950s, 7.6% during the 1960s, 11.75% in the 1970s and 13.16% in the 1980s. The corresponding rates of growth for M_3 (broad definition of money) were 6%, 8.9%, 14.7% and 14.7%, respectively.

At this stage we do not have any basis to either explain the sources of increase in M (or M_1) or AMR (or M_3) or to evalute such increases as socially beneficial or injurious. But they are very important questions of monetary theory and policy; we shall take them up in Parts Two and Three.

NOTES

1. The number of exchange ratios under barter will be n (n – 1)/2, where n is the number of goods. With money, there will be only n money prices to contend with

2. For deposits with non-bank companies, see Section 9.7.

CHAPTER 2

Credit and the Financial System

2.1 What is Credit?

The term credit may be defined broadly or narrowly. Speaking broadly, credit is finance made available by one party (lender, seller, or shareholder/owner) to another (borrower, buyer, corporate or non-corporate firm). The former may be a pure lender (a financial institution or a private money-lender), a seller supplying goods against the buyer's promise of future payment or a shareholder /owner of a corporate/non-corporate firm making funds available to the firm viewed as a separate entity.

More generally, the term credit is used narrowly for only debt finance. In this book, we shall also use the term in this sense. Thus defined, credit is simply the opposite of debt. Debt is the obligation to make future payments. Credit is the claim to receive these payments. Both are created in the same act of borrowing and lending. This act is a special kind of exchange transaction, which involves future payments. In an exchange transaction, to every sale there is an equal purchase since, by definition, sale and purchase are two sides of the same transaction. Similarly, in a credit transaction, the amount loaned is equal to the amount borrowed (and the interest paid is equal to the interest received). At any time, the total volume of debt is equal to the total amount of credit.

Credit is a stock-flow variable. At any point of time, there is a certain amount of credit (of any one kind or all kinds) outstanding. It is a revolving stock. Once a loan is repaid, the amount received can be advanced to the same party or some other party or parties. Any increment (decrement) in the stock of credit per period represents a positive (negative) flow of credit per period.

Credit should be carefully distinguished from money. Even bank credit is not the same thing as money. Their nature and functions are not the same. Money is an asset of the holding public. It is a liability of the banking system (including the RBI) and the government. However, it is not all the liabilities of the banking system that are money, but only those that serve as media of exchange, namely currency and the demand deposits. Bank credit, on the other hand, is a liability of the borrowing public (or the government) to banks and an asset of banks. Then, money serves as the commonly-accepted medium of exchange and the unit of account. Bank credit itself does not serve as bank money. What serves as bank money (in the narrow sense) is the demand deposit of a bank on which cheques can be drawn in the settlement of payments. Bank credit only allows the borrower a claim to such a deposit (or bank money) upto a certain sanctioned amount. All this will be discussed in some detail in section 15.3.

Then, bank credit is only one form of credit. In a modern economy, there exist several other sources of credit as well. Collectively they constitute the financial system.

In a credit economy, that is economy with borrowing and lending, each spending unit (whether a household, a firm, or the government) can be placed in any one of the three categories: deficit spenders, surplus spenders, and balanced spenders, according as its total expenditure is greater than, less than, or equal to its total (owned or internal) receipts, respectively. We shall have several occasions to use these terms or concepts in the book. The chief function of credit is to relax the constraint of balanced budgets. As we shall study later, it is through this chief function that the financial system is able to promote savings, investment, better allocation of resources, and growth in the economy. It is also worth remembering that if credit is not well managed, it can cause inflation or deflation and unemployment. It can also lead to malutilisation of resources, excessive concentration of income and wealth in a few hands, and exploitation of the weak and the poor.

2.2 What is a Financial System?

A financial system should be distinguished from a payments system. In Section 1.4, we had defined the latter as the set of institutional arrangements through which purchasing power is transferred from one transactor in exchange to another. The payments system is, thus, concerned with payments in cash. The financial system is much broader than a payments system in that it covers both cash and credit transactions. importantly, ntly, the financial system is a set of institutional arrangements through which financial surpluses (or commands over real resources) in the economy are mobilised from surplus units and transferred to deficit spenders. The institutional arrangements include all conditions and mechanisms governing the production, distribution, exchange, and holding of financial assets or instruments of all kinds and the organization as well as the manner of operation of financial markets and institutions of all descriptions. In concrete terms, financial assets, financial markets, and financial institutions are the three main constituents of any financial system.

Financial assets or claims are generally subdivided under the two heads of primary (or direct) securities and secondary (or indirect) securities. The former are financial claims against real-sector units. The examples are bills, bonds, equities, book debts, *etc.* They are created by real-sector units as ultimate borrowers for raising funds to finance their deficit spending. The secondary securities are financial claims issued by financial institutions or intermediaries against themselves to raise funds from the public. The examples are such diverse financial assets as the Reserve Bank currency, bank deposits, life insurance policies, UTI units, IDBI bonds, *etc.*

In the present-day Indian economy important financial assets are currency, bank deposits (current, savings, and fixed), post office savings deposits, life insurance policies, provident fund contributions, bonds (government and corporate), bills, hundis, corporate shares (ordinary and preference), units of the UTI, company deposits, compulsory deposits, deposits with investment companies/trusts, nidhis, chit funds and similar other organizations. The list is not meant to be exhaustive. Nor is any asset listed above homogeneous. Thus, currency includes both coins and paper currency notes, which are further of different denominations. Ordinary shares or bonds of no two corporations are identical. Nor are any two insurance policies. The products of the financial industry are truly heterogeneous. We have already studied about currency, bank deposits of various kinds, and post office savings deposits in the previous chapter. We shall study more about other financial assets and various financial institutions and markets operating in India in later chapters.

To have some idea of the relative magnitudes of major financial assets held by the public about which data are available, we give below their money value in Table 2.1.

Table 2.1
Major Financial Assets Held by the Public
(last Friday/end of March 1995)

(Rs. crores at current prices)

	Financial Asset	*Value*	*Percentage Share of Total*
	(1)	(2)	(3)
1.	Currency	1,00,000	9.44
2.	Demand deposits	87,000	8.22
3.	Time deposits with banks	3,39,000	32.01
4.	Post office deposits and other small savings	83,000	7.84
5.	Non-banking Company deposits	2,11,000	19.92
6.	LIC	56,000	5.29
7.	Provident and Pension funds	1,23,000	11.61
8.	UTI units	60,000	5.67
	Total	**10,59,000**	**100.0**

SOURCE: The values of assets in the above table have been taken from the RBI, *Report on Currency and Finance*, 1994-95, Vol. II, various statements.

Besides the financial assets included in the above table, the public also holds corporate equities and bonds and debentures. These assets are also held by banks and other financial institutions. Estimates of their values in the hands of non-financial public are not available. So, we have not included them in Table 2.1. We have also left out government securities, most of which are held by financial institutions. For record, we may note that at the end of March 1995, the total internal government debt was of about Rs. 2,75,000 crore, of which 91-day treasury bills were of Rs. 36,000 crore and special securities were of the value of Rs. 94,000 crore, giving a total amount of Rs. 1,30,000 crore. The rest of Rs. 1,45,000 crore was in the form of market loans and bonds. Of the latter, the state governments owed about Rs. 31,000 crore. In addition, the state governments had borrowed about Rs. 1,17,000 crore from the Central Government in the form of loans and advances.

In a modern industrial economy, a wide variety of financial institutions, more popularly called financial intermediaries (FIs) have grown. We shall study about their role and common services and features in the next section. Financial markets and associated financial instruments as they operate in India will be described in the next chapter.

FIs are generally classified under two main heads: (a) banks and (b) non-banks or non-bank financial intermediaries (NBFIs). The dichotomous classification shows the special position banks occupy in a country's financial structure. Banks in India will be the subject of our study in Chapters 4 to 7. In the next three chapters thereafter we shall study development banks, other NBFIs, and unregulated credit markets.

2.3 Financial Intermediaries

Financial Intermediaries (FIs) are institutions or firms that mediate or stand between ultimate lenders and ultimate borrowers or between those with budget surpluses and those who wish to run budget deficits. The examples are banks, insurance companies, unit trusts (or mutual funds), investment companies, provident funds, *etc.* The central function of all FIs is to collect surpluses (savings) of other economic units and to lend them on to deficit spenders. Both the surplus units and the deficit spenders belong to the real sector of the economy. Their principal economic activity is to buy and sell productive factors and current output, whereas the principal economic activity of financial institutions is the purchase and sale of financial assets.

In the previous section we have already introduced the distinction between primary securities and secondary securities. The former are bought by both surplus real-sector units and FIs. When surplus units buy these securities, they are said to provide 'direct finance' to ultimate borrowers. A part of the total surpluses of surplus units is provided to deficit spenders in this way. But this is only a part of the story in a modern money-using system. A large and growing part of the savings of individual units are now placed in secondary securities and thereby make them available to ultimate borrowers. The ultimate lenders are still the surplus units. But they lend to ultimate borrowers indirectly through FIs and not directly. Therefore, in such cases the finance provided by them is called indirect finance.

Thus the FIs are dealers in securities. What they buy are primary securities, what they sell are secondary securities. By absorbing primary securities in their asset portfolios and producing secondary securities to finance them, they virtually transmute primary securities into secondary securities. The essence and the success of financial intermediation lie in this asset transformation. This is the alchemy which only the FIs possess. They alone are able to produce securities that are, in general, far more acceptable to surplus units than the primary securities produced by deficit spenders. The latter themselves cannot produce financial claims that meet as well the asset preferences (in terms of risk, liquidity, convenience, *etc.*) of the wealth-holding public as the secondary securities manufactured by the FIs. The latter embody innovations in financial technology whereby disparate asset-debt preferences of lenders and borrowers are reconciled and satisfied to the satisfaction of both the parties.

One simple example of the asset-transmutation role of the FIs will throw further light on it. Consider a farmer who wants a crop loan against his promissory note supported by the crop sown in his field. The local village moneylender has been the traditional source of finance to him. But an urban household will not be willing to lend to the farmer because of high risk and inconvenience involved. Normally, there will be no point of contact between the two in the first instance. It will be different with a bank (or a cooperative credit society). The bank may be having several such borrowers among its customers and organizational links and staff to service such loans. The urban household may be operating a savings account with this bank and thereby entrusting a part of its surpluses to the bank. The bank will be lending a part of the savings of the urban household to the farmer. Yet the urban household does not care so long as it has confidence in the bank's ability to pay cash on demand. Thus, the secondary security in the form of savings deposits has enabled the bank to mobilise savings of households which can be used to lend even to a distant farmer, who could not otherwise borrow directly from an urban household on the strength of his own promise to pay.

2.3.1 Gains to Lenders and Borrowers

Talking generally, why do surplus units prefer to lend to FIs rather than directly to deficit spenders? In other words, why do they prefer secondary securities to primary securities? The main advantages to ultimate lenders are summed up below.

(1) Low risk. Other things being the same, lenders are interested in minimising all kinds of risk of capital and interest loss on loans or financial investments they make. These risks may arise in the form of risk of default or risk of capital loss on stock-market assets. Such risks on secondary securities are far less than on primary securities for individual lenders. How FIs are able to reduce such risks even though they themselves hold primary securities will be explained later. Besides, government regulation of the organization and working of major FIs helps in reducing risks of their creditors. Any strengthen-

ing of the financial system that goes to inspire public confidence in it reduces further any psychological risk suffered by lenders.

(2) *Greater Liquidity.* FIs offer much greater liquidity on their secondary securities to their lenders. Consider a few examples. Demand deposits of banks are prefectly liquid. They can be drawn upon without notice. Banks allow even time deposits to be drawn upon subject to certain conditions involving only some loss of interest. They, of course, always stand ready to lend against them. Units of the UTI can be sold back to it. Savings embodied in life insurance policies are not equally liquid, but loans can always be arranged against them from banks or the LIC itself. Primary securities do not carry any of these features, because primary borrowers need funds for agreed periods to finance their expenditures. For reasons to be explained later, FIs can offer much greater liquidity to their creditors, and yet lend on a much longer term to their debtors.

(3) *Convenience.* Secondary securities sold by FIs are easy to buy, hold, and sell. The information cost and transaction cost involved are very low. Banks run branches in all urban areas and several semi-urban and rural areas. The deposits they sell are standardised and information about them easily available. So the choice about bank deposits, life insurance policies, UTI units is not as difficult as about (say) corporate equities (primary securities). Much, however, depends on the quality of customer service provided by the FIs, which in the case of public-sector FIs in India is deplorably poor. This has hampered greatly the growth of financial intermediation in the country.

(4) *Other Services.* Each of the FIs specialises in selling special kinds of secondary securities and other services associated with them. Thus, banks specialise in selling deposits with particular features. In addition, they transfer funds, collect cheques for their clients, offer safe-deposit vaults, and, most important of all, are the dominant lender. All these and several other services attract the public to banks and induce it to hold deposits with them. The UTI sells units (shares) of a balanced asset protfolio of marketable corporate securities to the investing public. The LIC collects long-term savings of the public by selling life insurance. These other services can be had only when particular kinds of secondary securities carrying them are bought.

Borrowers also have a preference for FIs due to the following reasons :

1. FIs have big pools of funds, so that big individual demands for funds can be satisfied only by the FIs;

2. There is much greater certainty of the availability of funds with the FIs at all times'

3. The rate of interest charged by the FIs is generally lower than that charged by other lenders; and

4. Regulated FIs do not fleece small borrowers in the manner moneylenders do. On the contrary, as a matter of official policy, banks and other official lending agencies are required to give small borrowers preferential treatment both in the grant of credit and in the rate of interest charged by them. The actual implementation of policy leaves much to be desired.

2.3.2 The Economic Basis of Financial Intermediation

In view of the above, the question arises how are the FIs able to offer better financial facilities both to the lenders and borrowers? What is the economic basis of their success or of the financial alchemy whereby they purchase and hold primary securities, which are much riskier and far less liquid than the secondary securities they sell as their liabilities to the general public and yet earn handsome profits on their activities? The answer will help us understand better the source of social gain accruing from improvements in financial technology.

The true economic basis of financial intermediation lies in the economies of scale in portfolio management and in the law of large numbers. This is explained below.

1. *Law of large numbers.* Banks, insurance companies, unit trusts, and all other FIs operate on the assumption, supported by statistical law of large numbers, that not all the creditors will put forward their claims for cash at the same time. Add to this the fact that if some creditors are withdrawing cash, some others (whether old or new) are paying in cash. Besides, FIs receive regularly interest payments on loans and investments made and repayments of loans due. Fortified by this knowledge, banks keep in cash only a small fraction of even their demand liabilities and invest or lend the rest. For the same reason, unit trusts can also afford to keep most of their funds (liabilities) invested in securities and yet offer to buy back all the units the unitholders like to sell at any time. Life insurance companies also operate on the actuarial fact that a determinable fraction of lives insured will actually expire in a normal year, so that they need keep only an estimated fraction of their total life funds in cash and near-cash and the rest of them can be invested on long-term basis. Thus FIs can afford to manufacture liabilities (secondary securities) that are far more liquid than the primary securities they buy as

earning assets.

2. *Economies of Scale in Portfolio Management.* The average size of the asset portfolios of banks, insurance companies and other organized-sector FIs is quite large in value. So, these FIs can reap several economies of scale in portfolio management, which improve significantly their *net* rates of return from their asset holdings. These economies accrue in the following main forms:

(a) Reduction of risk through portfolio diversification. Lending/investing is always risky. It carries risk of default and of capital loss on marketable assets. One common way of reducing risk is through pooling of independent risks by placing funds in a diversified portfolio. Thereby what the investor may lose in a few directions may more than make up in other directions. But for adequate diversification, the size of the portfolio must be reasonably large, otherwise the cost of portfolio management will become excessively high. An average wealthowner cannot afford the degree of portfolio diversification and the resulting reduction of risk an average FI can. Then a large FI can schedule maturities of its loans to match anticipated outflows and thereby safeguard its liquidity.

(b) Professional Management. The large size of the asset portfolios to be managed allows FIs to employ professional managers, who are well-versed in the complexities of modern finance, in appraising loan proposals, in evaluating investment opportunities, in monitoring their loans and investments, in analysing consequences of market and other developments for the health of their businesses. Individual wealth owners cannot afford the cost of professional management and other support staff. They do not in general have the expertise, time, or even the desire to manage financial asset portfolios comprising of primary securities.

(c) Indivisibilities and market imperfections. Some loans and investments are of very large size individually. Average household wealth-owner cannot handle them. In certain cases even FIs have to come together in consortia, pool their resources, and spread their risks to finance them. The per rupee administration cost of large loans borne by FIs is quite low.

In certain cases, such as purchase of treasury bills or placement of call funds, only sums above a certain minimum amount too large for an average householder are accepted by the borrower to save transactions costs. Thus, FIs with large asset portfolios can earn interest even on very short-term funds and construct the maturity structure of their assets as desired. Small assetholders cannot do so.

(d) Other cost economies. Because of the large volume of business, the fixed cost of establishment, cost of information and various transactions costs are lower per unit of transaction to a FI than to an average household wealthowner.

2.3.3. FIs and the Economy

FIs play a very important role in the functioning of a modern complex economy, in promoting economic development, and in the working of monetary-credit policy. This role inheres in the separation of saving and investment, so characteristic of modern capitalist economies. In most cases savers are different from investors. In India the bulk (75 to 80 percent of the total) of savings is done by households. About half of it is invested directly by them in physical assets, but the rest is committed to financial assets. In industrially-developed western economies, the proportion of financial investment of household savings is much higher. Corporate firms and the government are everywhere net deficit spenders. Financial assets are the vehicles through which the savings of surplus spenders are mobilised and allocated among deficit spenders. Some part of this mobilisation-allocation is accomplished through primary securities acquired directly by the savers. But the bulk of financial savings is handled by the FIs. The more numerous, varied, well-organized, geographically well-distributed, and efficient the FIs, that is the more developed the financial infrastructure of an economy, in general, the more economically developed will also be that economy. This is discussed in the next section.

2.4 Functions and Importance of the Financial System

The financial system helps production, capital-accumulation, and growth by *(i)* encouraging savings, *(ii)* mobilising them, and *(iii)* allocating them among alternative uses and users. Each of these functions is important and the efficiency of a given financial system depends on how well it performs each of these functions.

2.4.1 Inducement to save

Savers require stores of value to hold their savings in. The financial system promotes savings by providing a wide array of financial assets as stores of value, aided by the services of financial markets and intermediaries of various kinds. For wealth holders, all this offers ample choice of portfolios with attractive combinations of income, safety and yield. With financial progress and innovations in financial technology, the scope of portfolio choice has also improved. Therefore, it is widely held that the savings-income ratio is positively elastic with respect to both financial assets and financial institutions. That is, financial progress generally induces larger savings out of the same level of real income.

As stores of value, financial assets command certain advantages over tangible assets (physical capital, inventories of goods, *etc.*) : they are convenient to hold or easily storable, more liquid, that is, more easily encashable, more easily divisible, and less risky. The pecuniary yield from money is zero. But, as a generalized means of payment, it gives convenience yield to its holders and users. Non-money financial assets yield money returns to their holders. In addition, some of them render other specific services as well. For example, life insurance policies also provide cover against risk of loss of life over the currency of the policy. Corporate equities serve as a hedge against inflation.

A very important property of financial assets is that they do not require regular management of the kind most tangible assets do. Factories, farms, and shops need to be run by their owners in order to earn income. Owners of financial assets are completely absolved of this responsibility, so that they can devote their full time and energy to whatever other pursuits they like to follow. Owners of financial assets are only the ultimate (or indirect) owners and not the immediate (or direct) owners (except for equity shareholders) of tangible assets. The latter are the borrowers of funds who are responsible for the actual management of tangible assets. They assume all the risks of production. Thus, financial assets have made possible the separation of ultimate ownership and management of tangible assets. In the case of corporations even the immediate owners, the shareholders, do not run the management. This separation of savings from management has encouraged savings greatly. With the availability of financial assets as stores of value, the public can save and hold its savings in these assets without the necessity of converting these savings into tangible assets and then managing these assets. On the other hand, management can be professionalised, that is, the management of tangible assets can be entrusted to professional managers (without requiring them to own these assets), which improves productivity.

Savings are done by households, businesses, and government. Following the official classification adopted by the Central Statistical Organization (CSO), Government of India, we reclassify savers into the household sector, domestic private corporate sector, and the public sector. The household sector is defined to comprise individuals, non-Government, non-corporate entities in agriculture, trade and industry, and non-profit making organizations like trusts and charitable and religious institutions. The public sector comprises central and state governments, departmental and non-departmental undertakings, the RBI, *etc.* The domestic private corporate sector comprises non-government public and private limited companies (whether financial or non-financial) and cooperative institutions. Of these three sectors, the dominant saver is the household sector, followed by the domestic private corporate sector. The contribution of the public sector to total net domestic savings is relatively small. The RBI's provisional estimates for net domestic savings for the year 1990-91 are given in Table 2.2.

Table 2.2
Estimates of Gross Domestic Savings (1994-95)
(Provisional)

(Rs. crores at current prices)

		Value	*Percentage of GNP at current market prices*
1.	Household sector	1,78,700	18.9
2.	Public sector	16,000	1.7
3.	Domestic private corporate sector (including cooperatives)	36,000	3.8
4.	Total Gross Domestic Savings (1+2+3)	2,30,700	24.4

SOURCE: RBI *Report on Currency and Finance.* 1994-95 Vol. II. Statement 12.

Both the public sector and the private corporate sector are net deficit spenders who draw upon the savings of the houschold sector (the dominant saver in the economy) to finance their spendings. The household sector also borrows from other sectors, which include mainly banks, co-operatives, term-lending institutions, and the government. In 1990–91, its gross savings in financial assets were about Rs. 56,000 crore, financial liabilities (borrowings) were about Rs. 11,000 crore, giving the net figure of Rs. 45,000 crore. Besides this, the household sector had also saved in the form of physical assets of the gross value of about Rs. 27,000 crore. Thus, of its gross savings, about two-thirds were held in the form of financial assets. The composition of these assets is given in Table 2.3 (where figures have been liberally rounded off).

Table 2.3
Composition of Savings of the Household Sector in the form of Financial Assets (Gross) (1994-95)

(Rs. crores,at current prices)

Item	*Value*	*Per cent of total financial assets*
1. Currency	16,000	12.64
2. Deposits	57,000	45.02
3. Insurance (Life)	11,300	8.93
4. Provident funds/Pension funds	20,600	16.27
5. Claims on government	11,000	8.69
6. Corporate and Co-operative shares and debentures, including units of the UTI	11,600	9.16
7. Trade Debt (Net)	– 900	– .71
Total	**1,26,600**	**100.0**

SOURCE: RBI *Report on Currency and Finance,* 1994-95, Vol. I. Table II. 6 P. 7.

The following points about the information given in Table 2.3 may be noted:

1. The percentage shares of various financial assets in the total are not stable, but vary substantially from year to year;

2. Deposits are predominantly savings deposits and fixed deposits of households with commercial and cooperative banks. They also include deposits with non-banking companies;

3. Savings in the form of insurance are measured by changes in the 'life fund' of the LIC, State Insurance Funds and Postal Insurance.

Such savings along with savings through provident funds are contractual savings;

4. Provident funds include the Employees Provident Fund, State (central and state governments) Provident Funds and 'Other Provident Funds'. More than one half of the total accruals under these funds is attributable to the Employees Provident Fund.

5. Claims on government include small savings collections from households, the household sector's direct investment in government securities and the deposits made under the Compulsory Deposit Scheme. Small savings include mainly post office savings bank deposits, time deposits, and national savings certificates.

Savings by households are done for several reasons. The motives to save may be to provide for known future needs, such as old age, education and marriage of children the desire to own property, to buy high-value consumer durables, or simply to satisfy the urge to grow wealthy. The motive may also be to build up capacity to meet better uncertain future needs such as sickness or accident, that is, to provide for the rainy day. Household and business savings also arise due to lack of synchronisation between income stream and expenditure stream, the latter following the former.

Different kinds of financial assets are required and have come to be produced to meet diverse needs and preferences of different categories of savers. Yet there is vast scope for introducing known kinds of financial assets not yet available in India such as shares or deposits of building societies that specialise in providing loan finance to their members for constructing residential houses, for developing mortgage market, for innovating with new kinds of financial assets, and in making available more widely, especially in semi-urban and rural areas, the financial assets which are already being produced, such as life insurance and UTI units. For improving further the financial system's influence on the public's willingness to save, measures should be taken to reduce the risk of default and market riskiness of financial assets, to improve their liquidity and rates of return, and to maintain price stability to avoid real-value depreciation of monetary financial assets.

It may be noted in passing that not all tangible assets are inferior o financial assets as *passive* stores of value. By a passive store of value we mean something which does not require regular management as does a farm or a factory. Important examples of such tangible assets in the Indian context are gold and silver ornaments or bullion. They are attractive stores of value for the public. This is especially so during periods of inflation when the real value of most financial assets (except equity shares) goes down and gold and silver appreciate in money value along with inflation. Some time this appreciation is greater than the average rate of inflation, making these precious metals highly attractive stores of value. This again emphasises the importance of price stability.

2.4.2 Mobilisation of Savings

Financial assets separate the act of saving from the act of real (physical) investment. Savings are done by millions of individual households and firms. They may be in large or small amounts, long term or short term. All these individual savings need to be collected or mobilised before they can be spent by deficit spenders. A financial system is a highly efficient mechanism for mobilising savings. In a fully-monetised economy this is done automatically when, in the first instance, the public holds its savings in the form of money. However, this is not the only way of instantaneous mobilisation of savings. Other financial methods used are deductions at source of the contributions to provident fund and other savings schemes. More generally, mobilisation of savings takes place when savers move into financial assets, whether currency, bank deposits, post office savings deposits, life insurance policies, bills, bonds, equity shares, *etc*.

As already said, financial assets are broadly divisible into two categories: *(a)* primary securities and *(b)* secondary securities. The former are securities issued by the ultimate borrowers such as bills, bonds, equity shares, company deposits, *etc*., while secondary securities are securities issued by financial institutions (also called financial intermediaries), such as banks, insurance companies, *etc*. When the public buys primary securities, it makes its surpluses available directly to deficit spenders. It represents direct mobilisation as well as allocation of credit, though it is also through the mediation of financial assets and markets. When the public buys secondary securities, it entrusts its savings to financial institutions who allocate it further among competing borrowers. This represents financial intermediation. A part of saving does not go through the financial system. It is that part which is invested directly by savers in tangible assets, whether houses, businesses, or precious metals.

For financial planning and control institutionalisation of savings is important, because it is easier to control lending/investing policies of financial institutions than of millions of direct lenders or direct investors in physical assets.

2.4.3 Allocation of Funds

Another important function of a financial system is to arrange smooth, efficient, and socially equitable allocation of credit. Money-lenders and indigenous bankers have been providing finance to their borrowers since long. But their finance suffers from several defects (see Chapter 10). With modern financial development, new financial institutions, assets and markets have come to be organized, which are playing an increasingly important role in the provision of credit. In the previous sub-section, we have already spoken about direct purchase of primary securities by the public. Such direct lendings by the general public have been made possible by the organization of stock markets and marketable financial assets, such as corporate bonds and equities. Besides, there are banks, insurance companies, and other financial institutions. They serve as financial intermediaries between the ultimate lender and the ultimate borrower. They mobilise savings of the former by selling their own liabilities (deposits, insurance policies, *etc.*) and make these funds available to deficit spenders at their own risk. So, many savers find the secondary securities of financial institutions much more acceptable than the primary securities of all sorts of borrowers.

The allocative role of financial institutions is very important. Only corporations can go to the stock market for raising funds through public issue of equity shares and bonds. Even there the support of financial institutions as buyers of securities is important. But non-corporate borrowers cannot issue marketable liabilities. Therefore, they depend on bank finance or private finance. In the market for funds there is generally credit rationing. This makes the availability of credit important to all potential borrowers. Financial institutions (subject to the policy of the government and the RBI) determine how institutional finance will get allocated among various sectors of the economy and among competing borrowers.

In the allocative function of financial institutions lies their main source of power. By granting easy and cheap credit to particular firms, they can shift outward the resource constraint of these firms and make them grow faster. On the other hand, by denying adequate credit on reasonable terms to other firms, financial institutions can restrict the growth or even normal working of these other firms substantially. Thus, the power of credit can be used highly discriminately to favour some and to hinder others. Realizing this early in the day, all important business houses in India had either started or otherwise controlled individual banks and/or insurance companies. For the same reason, all major financial institutions, called picturesquely as 'commanding heights' of the economy, have been either nationalised or set up in the public sector from the very beginning. Thereby the direct control of financial institutions by business houses has been eliminated. But these houses do continue to enjoy substantial influence on the actual credit allocation by these institutions. Organized credit to weaker sections is still inadequate.

2.4.4 Serving Production, Trade, and Investment

All the above services of savings promotion, mobilisation, and allocation are essential for production, capital formation and growth. Investment obviously requires that there is corresponding amount of saving. If at individual firm level all investment were to be financed by internal savings only, the aggregate rate of investment in the economy will be pitiably small, because a major portion of savings is done by non-investors. What the financial system does is to break the straight jacket of internal finance (or balanced budget). It places at the disposal of entrepreneurs resources saved by others. This enlarges greatly the aggregate rate of investment.

Earlier we had said that the financial system enlarges greatly the aggregate rate of savings and their mobilisation by offering savers a wide variety of financial assets to suit their needs and preferences. There is a comparable service offered to investors (and producers) to induce them to absorb the savings the system generates. As borrowers they are facilitated to produce a wide range of financial liabilities to suit their needs and preferences. Thus, for example, they can borrow short term or long term, issue bills or bonds, ordinary shares, or preference shares; bonds may be convertible into equity shares, or not. Then, corporate shares are limited liability documents, that is, the liability of a shareholder is limited only to the face value of shares he holds. The sources of funds are also several : open market, banks, insurance companies, indigenous bankers and moneylenders, trade credit, *etc.* All this brings into contact a much larger number of ultimate borrowers and ultimate lenders than would be possible otherwise. It bears repetition to say that this promotes specialisation of the functions of saving and investment. Those who have the capacity and willingness to save, but not to undertake production, may only save and entrust their savings to others, either directly or indirectly through financial intermediaries. These other persons may have both the competence and willingness to organise production, but may not have enough resources of their own to make the required investments. The financial system makes it possible for them to make use of their entrepreneural skills by providing them credit. Apart from encouraging investment, this makes possible better use of scarce entrepreneural and technical skills in the country.

A well-developed financial system is able to mobilise and allocate all kinds of savings, howsoever small or short-term. This helps in the maximum utilisation of savings. It also facilitates flow of savings throughout the economy and thereby the flow of funds in directions where returns are presumably highest. This supposedly helps in the maximisation of returns from resources.

Production requires various kinds and amounts of capital (funds): long-term capital for making fixed investment in physical plant (land, buildings and machinery); medium term capital for buying other tools and equipment; and short term working capital to finance current operations of business. Shortage of any kind of capital with any firm can hurt badly its productive activity and growth. The financial system helps firms in raising funds for meeting its various requirements. Of course, every firm must have some equity funds of its own to start business. For big projects requiring large amounts of capital, no single firm or house is usually in a position to raise all the required funds internally. It has, therefore, to depend upon outside sources. Even in the case of big corporations, promoters' equity is usually a small proportion of total equity capital. The rest of the equity capital and all long-term debt capital are raised in the open market by the public issue of shares and bonds. Thus, a corporation is not only a new form of business organization, more importantly, it is a financial innovation which makes it possible to collect financial surpluses of far-flung surplus-spenders through open-market sale of shares and bonds. Small firms suffer greatly from the paucity of funds. Their needs for credit are met inadequately and at very high cost.

In usua discussions there is a presumption that mobilisation of surpluses and their allocation among deficit spenders by a financial system are always to the good of the society as a whole. This is not necessarily true. The financial system can work to the detriment of savers in a variety of ways. Public sector monopoly and official regulation tend to help in the process. For example, the deposit rates of banks can be kept artificially low; the premia rates of insurance companies can be kept artificially high and their bonus rates to policy holders deplorably low. On the lending side, too, the financial system (at least in parts) can be a vehicle of exploitation of the weak and the expropriator of the small, as has been largely true of moneylenders' credit. Small borrowers can be starved of bank credit and big borrowers surfeited with it. Excess credit to government to finance its ever-growing deficits is a major source of inflation and all its ills and inequities. Thus, the equity of the financial system cannot be taken for granted.

2.5 Kinds of Credit

Credit is not one homogeneous good or asset. It is of various kinds. To understand better the nature, scope and complexity of credit and its problems, we look at the several kinds of credit.

There is no unique way of classifying credit. It can be, and need to be, classified in more than one way, each way specialising in only one aspect or dimension of credit. Thus, we classify credit from five different angles: *(a)* source, *(b)* end-use, *(c)* users, *(d)* term, and *(e)* cost. The problems of credit need to be studied from each of these angles.

2.5.1 The Sources of Credit

In the present-day Indian economy credit is provided by a wide variety of sources. These sources may be conveniently classified as in Figure 2.1.

Figure 2.1
Sources of Credit

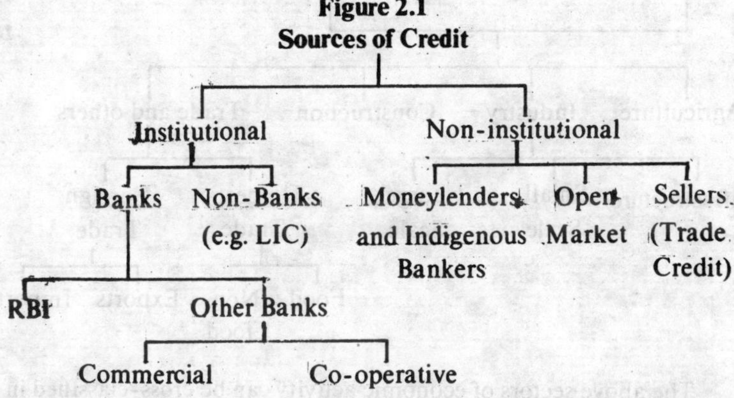

Each source can be further subdivided into various sub-classes. We shall study each major source in later chapters. Here, we are presenting only a skeletal picture of them.

2.5.2 The End-uses of Credit

Real credit is a scarce resource. Therefore, its proper allocation among competing uses and users is of great importance for the attainment of whatever social objectives a society sets before itself. Credit is required and used, less or more, in all spheres of economic activity. So, we may classify credit by its end-use by way of major areas of economic activity. This is done schematically in Figure 2.2. This provides the basis for the distinction between agricultural credit, industrial credit, export credit, *etc.*

The classification in Figure 2.2 is neither rigorous nor exhaustive. Its categories are not necessarily mutually exclusive,nor their boundaries well-defined. Yet some such broad classification is essential for evaluating the prevailing credit arrangements in the country and for any meaningful credit planning. This is because the credit needs, their nature, and the problems of organizing credit supply are likely to differ from one sector to the other, according to their own structural features.

Figure 2.2
End-Uses of Credit

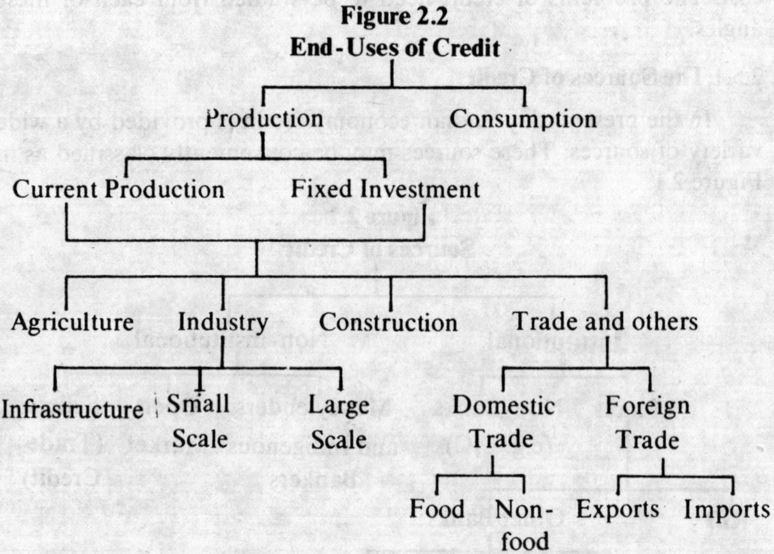

The above sectors of economic activity can be cross-classified in a number of ways. One cross-classification adopted by the RBI for regulating the allocation of bank credit is that between the priority and non-priority sectors (see Chapter 4). Another cross-classification is that between rural-urban credit. It is based on the location of economic activity. The categories of rural credit and urban credit are self-explanatory.

The end-use classification of credit is particularly important for evaluating the allocation of credit from a particular source. For example, this is particularly important in the case of commercial bank credit as these banks are the largest single source of institutional credit in India. For comprehensive credit planning, the end-use classification of non-bank institutional credit will also be important. This knowledge, however, will only be a first-step in credit planning. We must also develop social criteria for the optimal allocation of credit, know the factors responsible for the prevailing allocation of credit, identify the difficulties involved in changing this allocation and the remedial measures necessary for the realization of the desired allocation of credit.

2.5.3 The Users of Credit

The classification of credit by its users is not common. But, this dimension of credit allocation, especially of the allocation of institutional credit, is of much social importance. The most important proclaimed social objective of the nationalisation of major commercial banks has been to reallocate bank credit in favour of the weaker sections of the community. This kind of social concern relates to the users of bank credit and not to the nature of its use. We shall study about inter-borrower allocation of credit in Chapters 16 and 20.

2.5.4 The Term of Credit

Yet another dimension of credit is the length of time for which it is extended. The term of credit is important for both the borrower and the lender. A borrower needs credit for various uses, some of which will pay themselves back over a short period and some over a medium or a long period. For example, the loan taken by a manufacturer to buy raw materials for his products can normally be repaid after a short period. The actual time-length will depend upon the time-length of the production-sale cycle, that is, the time it takes to manufacture the raw materials into finished products, sell them, and realize the sale proceeds. On the other hand, the credit taken to instal a machine will normally pay itself back over the expected life of the machine. Suppose this life is 20 years, which is a long period by common reckoning. Then, the manufacturer will need long-term credit for buying the machine. Similarly, in agriculture, a farmer needs short-term credit for buying seeds and fertiliser for a crop and long-term credit for making permanent improvements on land. The former will pay itself back once the given crop is harvested and sold, the latter will pay itself back over a long period so long as the improvement lasts.

From the lenders' side, too, the term of credit is important. For financial institutions that raise funds by issuing their own liabilities to the public, the determining factor is the nature of their liabilities: whether they are short-term liabilities or long-term liabilities. For example, a commercial bank raises funds by selling deposits of various kinds to the public. Most of these deposits are short-term liabilities. Only time deposits of a maturity of more than a year are medium-term liabilities. Therefore, such a bank generally prefers to make short-term advances. On the other hand, life insurance companies get long-term funds. The insurance policies which they sell are, in general, for long periods. Therefore, they can afford to lend for long periods. They also prefer to do so in order to ensure steady interest income from their investments and to keep the task of reinvestment of funds to the minimum. This task will increase manifold if insurance companies make only short-term investments. Similar considerations hold regarding the expected time-lengths of the financial surpluses of surplus spenders and the credits expected by them.

The financial industry is a service industry. It's *raison d'etre* lies in servicing the real sector, which is responsible for the production and distribution of real goods and services. The real system for its efficient working requires credit of various time-lengths. The financial system has to see how best it can meet these needs without endangering either its own health or that of the real system it is supposed to serve. For this, the financial system devises ways and means whereby short-term funds can be transformed into long-term funds and *vice versa*.

We cannot go into the intricacies of all the financial devices for the aforesaid transformations. But one general point does need to be made. In financial matters liquidity is very important. In one sense, it refers to the ability of a debtor to meet his obligations on time. Almost always, it means his ability to pay cash, when due, whatever his net worth position. That is, liquidity of a debtor is different from his solvency. The latter is only concerned with the question of the net worth of a debtor : whether it is positive or not.

It is possible that a debtor may have positive net worth, but not all his assets may be perfectly (or even highly) liquid. This brings us to the second sense in which the term liquidity is used. In this sense, liquidity is the property of an asset. This property refers to the ease with which an asset can be converted into cash on demand (or short notice) without loss of value. In short, the liquidity of an asset refers to the degree of its encashability. In this sense, money is prefectly liquid. Time deposits of banks and short-term marketable assets are highly liquid. Corporate bonds, though liquid, are much less so. Hence there arises a need for encashing imperfectly liquid assets before payments due can be made. And such needs can frequently arise for individual units on account of unforeseen developments.

The financial system provides a mechanism whereby particular kinds of non-money financial assets (such as bills, bonds, equities. *etc.*) can be converted into cash. The system does this through stock markets where marketable financial assets are bought and sold openly (see Section 3.8.2).

The existence of stock markets (and other financial mechanisms to be discussed later in the book) allows creditors to make longer-term loans even when their matching liabilities are of shorter maturity. For, in time of need, they can turn to the market for meeting their needs for cash through sale of some of their non-cash assets. Of course, they run the risk of making capital losses through such sales. But, it is better than being not in a position to meet their obligations to pay cash to their creditors, or letting the opportunity of making higher profits by making longer-term advances/investments slip by. The efficiency and success of a financial institution depends, among other things, on how well it can combine the twin considerations of liquidity and profitability.

Term-wise credit is usually divided into three broad classes : *(i)* short-term credit, (ii) medium-term credit, and (iii) long-term credit. Short-term credit is usually for a year or less. (In agriculture, it goes even upto 18 months.) Medium-term credit is for more than a year, but less than ten years. Long-term credit, then, is for ten years or more.

In actual practice, however, borrowers may and do use short-term credit for financing durable investments and long-term credit for meeting working-capital needs. For, short-term credit and long-term credit are not water-tight compartments. They all are liquid funds that can be used in any manner except that it is not prudent to finance long-term investments by short-term credit. But, there may be some delay in the receipt of long-term funds. In the meantime, short-term funds may be used for long-term investments. Then, continuous renewals of short-term credit converts it into virtual long-term funds, though the borrower does run the risk of non-renewal of short-term credit.

2.5.5 The Cost of Credit

The cost of credit is another dimension of credit. It varies over a wide range for different classes of borrowers and for credit from different sources. There are no hard and fast rules for classification of credit by cost. Following common usage, we may suggest only a broad three-fold classification: *(a)* cheap, *(b)* dear, and *(c)* usurious. Cheap, dear, and usurious are relative terms. Their numerical measures in rates per cent per year cannot be specified for all situations. Two complicating circumstances are specially noteworthy. One is the premium for any risk of default; the other is the expected rate of inflation. Quoted rates of interest are gross rates which include provision for both in addition to the pure rate of interest for the loan. And the provisions for the two aforesaid factors may vary greatly over time, space, and the circumstances governing borrowing and lending. Then an element of usury, small or large, may also be present, depending on the relative bargaining strength of the lender and the borrower.

Thus, several factors will have to be weighed before classifying a particular rate of interest as representing cheap, dear, or usurious cost of credit. But, such a judgment is essential in any design of credit policy. Quite often the monetary authorities attempt to achieve policy goals by influencing the cost of credit through policy tools at their disposal. So, we read about a deliberate cheap money or dear money policy. More about it later in the book.

NOTES

1. The figures in Table 2.1 have been rounded off liberally, as we are interested in only broad orders of magnitudes and the relative importance of several financial assets in the total. The values of assets 1 to 3 have been taken from the R.B.I, Report on Currency and Finance 1990-91, Vol II, statement 28 and of assets 4 and 5 from statements 105 and 95, respectively. The estimates for asset 6 have been taken from the R.B.I. : Annual Report, 1991-92, Appendix Table V.2 (P.200). The values of assets 7 and 8 are guess estimates based on the data for the previous five years (1985-90) from the RBI : Annual Report, 1990-91, Table 9.2 (P.90).

CHAPTER 3

Financial Markets

3.1 Introduction

A financial system operates through financial markets and institutions. Financial markets deal in financial assets and instruments of various kinds such as currency, deposits, cheques, bills, and bonds, etc. In this chapter we describe briefly the main types of financial markets operating in India.

Analytically, financial markets are very much like markets for goods and services. As such, they have their own demand, supply, quantities, prices, *etc.* More important, the whole financial system is a loose assemblage of credit markets and institutions of various kinds, which differ from each other in various says—in organization, functions, size of individual units on the supply side, geographical coverage, methods of working, cost of credit, type of credit, *etc.* Some parts of the credit system are more closely connected with each other than others. Within each part of the credit system or within each credit market, there is, in general, greater competition than between any two parts or two markets. Thus, credit markets should not be viewed as constituting one prefectly competitive system, dispensing one homogeneous good (credit) at one uniform price (the rate of interest), but a loose structure of markets dealing in credit of various kinds at widely varying prices and under a wide variety of organizations. Therefore, to understand well the Indian financial system, it is essential to know the main features of its individual parts.

3.2 The Structure of Financial Markets

The structure of financial markets can be studied from different angles, namely, functional, institutional, or sectoral. Accordingly, financial markets, institutions, and instruments can be classified in any one or more of these ways. The functional classification is based on the term of credit, whether the credit supplied is short-term or long-term. Accordingly, markets are called money markets or capital markets. The institutional classification tells us whether the financial institutions are organized on commercial or cooperative principles and whether they belong to the organized or unorganized sector. The sectoral classification identifies credit arrangements for various sectors of the economy: agriculture, manufacturing industry, trade and others.

Various classifications are not intended to be water-tight or mutually exclusive. Their aim is to give a broad idea of the scope of financial markets, their several dimensions and functions. Combining the first two bases of study, we give a single functional-cum-institutional classification in Figure 3.1.

Functionally, financial markets are broadly sub-divided under two heads: money markets and capital markets. The former are markets in short-term funds; the latter in long-term funds. We have interpreted the term money market more broadly to include within its folds also the notional money market of monetary theory. This market is co-terminous with the entire economy. The asset it deals in is money; the demanders are the holders of money (the public) and the suppliers are the government, the RBI and banks. Money itself is acquired in the normal process of selling goods, services, and assets in all markets, as money is the common medium of exchange (in all monetised transactions). There is no special or separate market for money like the ones we have for bills, bonds, or equity shares. In academic discussions of monetary theory and policy whenever the term money market is used, we mean the market for money as explained above. But in business parlance the term money market is almost always used in the sense of short-term credit market.

Structurally, the short-term credit market is divisible under two sectors: organized and unorganized. The organized market comprises the RBI and banks. It is called organized because its parts are systematically co-ordinated by the RBI. Non-bank financial institutions such as the LIC, the GIC and subsidiaries, the UTI also operate in this market, but only indirectly through banks and not directly. Quasi-government bodies and large companies may also make their short-term surplus funds available to the market through banks.

Besides commercial banks that dominate the organized money market, there are co-operative banks. They are a part of co-operative credit institutes that have a three-tier structure. At the top there are state co-operative banks (co-operation being a state subject). At the district level there are central co-operative banks. At local level there

Figure 3.1
Functional-cum-Institutional Classification of Financial Markets

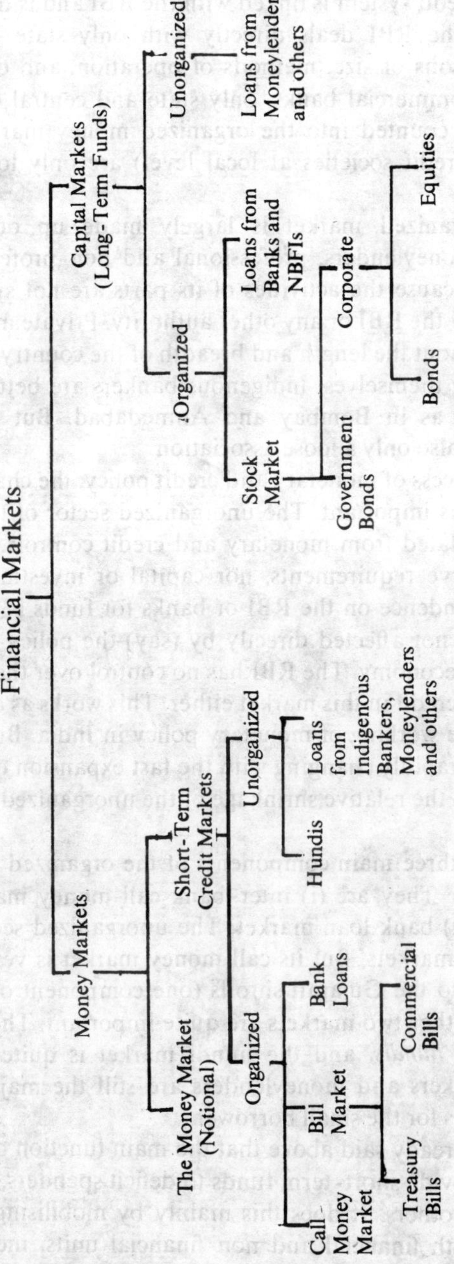

are primary credit societies and urban co-operative banks. The whole co-operative credit system is linked with the RBI and is dependent on it for funds. The RBI deals directly with only state co-operative banks. For reasons of size, methods of operation, and dealings with the RBI and commercial banks, only state and central co-operative banks need be counted into the organized money market; the rest (co-operative credit societies at local level) are only loosely linked with it.

The unorganized market is largely made up of indigenous bankers and moneylenders, professional and non-professional. It is unorganized because the activities of its parts are not systematically co-ordinated by the RBI or any other authority. Private moneylenders operate throughout the length and breadth of the country, but without any link among themselves. Indigenous bankers are better organized on local basis, as in Bombay and Ahmedabad. But this kind of organization is also only a loose association.

For the success of monetary and credit policy, the character of the money market is important. The unorganized sector of the market is practically insulated from monetary and credit controls. It is neither subject to reserve requirements, nor capital or investment requirements. Its dependence on the RBI or banks for funds is very limited. Therefore, it is not affected directly by (say) the policy of monetary restraint of the economy. The RBI has no control over the quality and composition of credit in this market either. This works as an important limitation to the working of monetary policy in India. But since 1947 the situation is rapidly changing with the fast expansion of banking in the country and the relative shrinkage of the unorganized sector of the money market.

There are three main components of the organized sector of the money markets. They are (i) inter-bank call money market (ii) bill market, and (iii) bank loan market. The unorganized sector also has its comparable markets. But its call money market is very small and restricted only to the Gujarati shroffs (one component of indigenous bankers). The other two markets are quite important. The indigenous bills are called *hundis*, and the hundi market is quite active. The indigenous bankers and moneylenders are still the major source of short-term loans for the small borrower.

We have already said above that the main function of the money market is to provide short-term funds to deficit spenders, whether the government or others. It does this mainly by mobilising short-term surpluses of both financial and non-financial units, including state governments, local governments, and quasi-government bodies.

Banks do it by 'selling' deposits of various kinds, participation certificates, and bills discounted. Then, there are treasury bills sold 'on tap' by the RBI. The RBI itself serves as the lender of last resort to the market. Funds have also to be moved between regions and from one place to another according to demand. An efficient and well-developed system does it fast and at low cost. Also, it does not allow regional or sectoral scarcities of funds to emerge. The surpluses in some centres or sectors get immediately transferred to others in short supply. Thereby an even supply of funds and liquidity is maintained throughout the economy. For this, banks and other constituents of money market must have an inter-connected network of branches and offices, rapid communication and remittance-of-funds system, and well-trained staff.

The real economy may also have a seasonal pattern, giving rise to seasonal ups and downs in the demand for funds. In the Indian economy this kind of seasonality mainly arises from the seasonal character of agriculture and some agrobased industries (such as sugar) and their large weight in the overall economy. Thus, traditionally, the Indian money market has been facing two seasons : busy season from October to April and slack season from May to September. During the busy season the main (Kharif) crops are harvested and marketed and sugarcane is crushed. So, the demand for bank credit to traders and sugar manufacturers goes up. During the slack season this demand for funds goes down. The RBI has been following a pro-seasonal monetary policy so that any special strigency of funds does not arise during the busy season which may hurt legitimate economic activity. For some time past, with increased double cropping of cultivated land, hefty increases in the output of wheat (a major rabi crop) and autumn rice, growth of perennial industries, and a higher proportion of bank credit going to manufacturing industries, the previous seasonal ups and downs in the demand for funds have largely lost their importance. This trend is likely to gain in strength over time.

The capital market deals in medium-term and long-term funds. The importance of such funds for carrying out investment in fixed capital has already been pointed out in Section 2.3. Like money market, the capital market also is divisible into two sectors : organized and unorganized. The organized sector comprises the stock market, the RBI, banks, development banks (such as the Industrial Development Bank of India), LIC, GIC and subsidiaries, and the UTI. The unorganized sector is mainly made up of indigenous bankers and money-lenders; chit funds, nidhis and similar other financial institutions; investment companies, finance companies and hirepurchase companies; and company deposits. The role of the unorganized sector in the capital market is of very limited importance.

In the following sections we explain briefly the organization and functions of important specialised financial markets.

3.3 Call Money Market

This is the most active and sensitive part of the organized money market. It is centred mainly at Bombay, Calcutta, and Madras, the market at Bombay being the most important. It deals in one-day loans (called call loans or call money) which may or may not be renewed the next day. The participants are mostly banks. Therefore, it is also called inter-bank call money market. The borrowing side is limited exclusively to banks, who are temporarily short of funds. On the lending side, too, there are mostly banks with temporary excess of cash. As special cases, a few other financial institutions like the LIC and the UTI are also allowed to place on call their short-term funds and earn interest on them. All others have to keep their funds in term deposits of minimum 15 days with banks in order to earn interest. For, banks are prohibited from paying interest on deposits made for less than 15 days. Such deposits are treated as current account deposits. In the past, companies (financial or non-financial) as well as quasi-government bodies and individuals with large short-term surpluses were allowed to place such funds on call with banks. Such money from companies and individuals, known as 'house money', used to be an important source of call money for banks. Finance brokers used to act as intermediaries between borrowing banks and lending houses. All this has changed now. From march 1978 banks have been prohibited from paying brokerage for arranging call loans for them.

Among banks, the State Bank of India (SBI), because of its formidable liquid position, is always on the lenders' side of the market. It acts as the 'lender of intermediate resort', whereas the RBI as the country's central bank is the 'lender of last resort'. The call advances by the SBI are made against government securities, whereas call loans by all others are made without security (against only deposit receipts of the borrowing banks). Since call loans are made on a 'clean' basis, the lending banks have to be highly cautious in adjudging the ability of borrowing banks to repay at call. Therefore, as borrowers, smaller banks are always at a disadvantage as compared to larger banks.

The call money market operates through brokers who keep in constant touch with banks in the city and bring the borrowing and lending banks together. The main function of the market is to redistribute the pool of day-to-day surplus funds of banks among other banks in temporary deficit of cash. The business of banking is such that the cash position of banks keeps on changing from hour to hour. As a result of a day's clearing their closing cash position may be vastly different from their opening cash position. Some may end the day with large amount of surplus cash and some with deficit, though banks as a whole may be holding the desired amount of cash. Moreover, to-day's surplus-cash banks may turn into tomorrow's deficit-in-cash banks. Therefore, there must be an institutional arrangement for making the surpluses of some banks available to others in temporary deficit for smooth and efficient functioning of the banking system. The call money market provides just this sort of arrangement. It helps banks economise their cash and yet improve their liquidity by providing them with the facility to borrow on call basis. It also signals such banks as are constantly on only one side (whether borrowing or lending) of the market to put their house in order. For, either they are overstretching themselves in making loans and investments or are not doing enough to buy earning assets.

The call money market is a highly competitive and sensitive market. It registers very quickly the pressures of demand and supply for funds operating in the money market. Thus it acts as possibly the best available indicator of the liquidity position of the organized money market. In adjusting its day-to-day monetary policy, the RBI, therefore, takes due notice of it. The market experiences some regular seasonal changes. It is normally tighter during the busy season (October-April) than during the slack season (May-September). It is much tighter during the peak of the busy season (April) before the final dates of quarterly tax payments by firms, and on the eve of the floatation of government loans.

By its nature the call money rate (of interest) is highly volatile. The pressures of excess demand push it up easily and of excess supply pull it down easily. Thus, the highest call money rate of interest in 1990-91 was 70 per cent, 85 per cent in 1991-92 and 85 per cent in 1995-96. But, each year, it got down to manageable levels.

3.4 Treasury Bill Market

The treasury bill market is the market that deals in treasury bills.

These bills are short-term (91-day) liability of the Government of India. In theory, tney are issued to meet temporary needs for funds of the government, arising from temporary excess of expenditure over receipts. In practice, they have become a permanent source of funds, because the amount of treasury bills outstanding has been continually on the increase. Every year more new bills are sold than get retired. Then, almost every year a part of treasuty bills held by the RBI are funded, that is, are converted into long-term bonds.

Treasury bills are of two kinds : *ad hoc* and regular (or ordinary). *Ad hoc* means 'for the particular end or case at hand'. Thus *ad hoc* treasury bills are issued for providing investment outlets to state governments, semi-government departments and foreign central banks for their temporary surpluses. They are not sold to the general public (or banks) and are not marketable. However, their holders, when in need of cash, can get them rediscounted with the RBI, that is, sell them back to the RBI. The treasury bills sold directly to the RBI for its keep by the government are also *ad hocs.* The treasury bills sold to the public or banks are regular or ordinary treasury bills. They are freely marketable. Their buyers are almost entirely commercial banks.

All treasury bills, *ad hoc* or ordinary, are sold by the RBI on behalf of the central government. Until July 12, 1965 they used to be sold by tender at weekly auctions. From that date they are made available 'on tap' throughout the week at a rate of discount fixed by the RBI. This change was made to make ready supply of bills available to all investors at all times for investment of their temporary surpluses and also to mop up larger amounts of such surpluses for the government. The latter, of course, has been eager to borrow all the funds offered to it.

Bills (of all types) are bought and sold on 'discounted basis'. That is the amount of interest due on it is paid in the form of discount in the price charged for the bill. This price is thus lower than its face (par) value by the amount of interest due on the bill. Technically speaking, the price is simply the discounted (or present) value of the bill and the rate of discount implied (or used) is the treasury bill rate. When the RBI buys back bills, it is said to rediscount them, that is, discount them all over again for their remaining lives. Discounting a bill means purchasing it at its discounted value.

The treasury bill market in India, as compared to such markets in the U.S.A. and the U.K., is highly undeveloped. There are no dealers in them outside the RBI who may be willing to buy and sell any amount of such bills at market. The RBI is the sole dealer in them. In the U.S.A. and the U.K. treasury bills are the most important money market instrument. They are a very popular form of holding short-term surpluses by financial institutions, other corporations and firms, because they are free from any risk of default, are highly liquid, and yield a reasonable rate of return. For the government, they are a very important form of raising funds. For the central bank, they are the chief instrument of open market operations. This is not so in India. The RBI itself is the chief holder of treasury bills. All other holders such as commercial banks, state governments, and semi-government bodies hold them in very small amounts. Non-bank financial institutions, corporate and non-corporate firms with short-term surpluses do not invest their surpluses in treasury bills. All this is because treasury bill (discount) rate in India had been kept pegged at the very low level of 4.6 per cent per annum since July 1974. Business firms with cash credit facility (see Section 5.5) with banks deposit their short-term surpluses in their cash credit accounts to reduce their cash credit outstanding and thereby save interest cost at the prevailing (currently 17.5% per annum) rate of interest. There is also a reasonably active *inter corporate* funds market (see Chakravarty Committee Report, 1985, para 12.66), whereby corporate units with seasonal funds lend them to other companies at a competitive rate of interest.

The very low treasury bill rate had, no doubt, kept the interest cost of treasury bill debt to the government very low. But this has been gained at a huge cost to the economy. First, the low rate has been maintained by converting the RBI into a passive or captive holder of these bills, as the RBI had to purchase whatever *ad hocs* were sold to it by the government and also rediscount whatever amount of these bills were presented to its rediscounting window by banks and others. This had led to large-scale 'monetisation of government debt' (that is conversion of such debt into Reserve Bank money), which, among other things, has been the main source of the excessive expansion of money supply and so also of inflation in the economy. Also, due to the low treasury bill rate, the government has been continuously tempted to use the short-term financial instrument of treasury bills as a long-term source of funds to it, as already pointed out in the beginning of this section. The low rate has also kept the treasury bill market undeveloped by not attracting non-RBI short-term surplus funds in it.

It had, therefore, been felt for quite some time that the treasury bill rate should be unfrozen from its artificially low level and made into a competitively attractive and flexible rate (keeping in view its special advantages over other short-term financial instruments) such that it would act as a pace setter for other rates in the money market, enable banks (and others) to adjust to changes in their short-term liquidity through the purchase and sale of treasury bills, and allow the RBI to exercise control over money market operations. The treasury bills are a short-term instrument and should be used as such to meet only the temporary needs of the government. They should not be used as a cheap source of long-term funds and cannot be so used without taking recourse to the RBI in a big way, as has been happening for several years now.

Ultimately, sale of 91-day treasury bills was introduced by the RBI in January 1993. In addition, 364-day bills were also sold by auction, which was started on April 28, 1992 on a fortnightly basis. The market response was very good. Depending on the market conditions, the sale of bills has been fluctuating from time to time. For example, a gross amount of Rs. 12,450 crore was raised in 1994-95 through the auctions of 91-day treasury bills. The implicit rate of interest on them ranged from 9.87 per cent per year to 11.94 per cent per year.

In the post -1982 period, the accumulated treasury bills were funded into 4.6 per cent rate of interest per annum special securities and all of them have been held by the RBI. These securities have no specific date for redumption. At the end of March 1994, the outstanding amount of these special securities was Rs. 71,000 crore. Besides, the outstanding amount of *ad hocs* stood at Rs. 21,480 crore.

It should be remembered that *ad hocs* represent automatic monetisation of the GOIs budget deficit. Therefore, an agreement was made between the GOI and the RBI on September 9, 1994. It has the following clauses:

(*a*) that at the end of financial year 1994-95, the net issue of *ad-hoc* treasury bills should not exceed Rs. 6,000 crore;

(*b*) that the issue of *ad-hoc* treasury bills should not exceed Rs. 9,000 crore for more than 10 continuous working days at any time during the financial year 1994-95. Otherwise, the RBI will automatically reduce the excess by auctioning the treasury bills or floatation of GOI's dated securities;

(*c*) similar ceilings for the net issues of treasury bills will be applicable for 1995-96 and 1996-97;

(*d*) that from 1997-98, the system of *ad-hoc* treasury bills will be totally discontinued.

3.5 Commercial Bill Market

Like treasury bills, commercial bills also have a market of their own. The latter bills are issued by firms engaged in business. Generally, they are of three-month maturity. They are like postdated cheques drawn by sellers of goods on the buyers of goods for value received. An examples of typical bill of exchange is given below :

Delhi, 18 May, 1979

Mr. Mohan Lal,

Three months after date please pay to the undersigned or order the sum of Rupees fifty thousand for value received.

Signed : Bhagat Ram

In the above example, Bhagat Ram is the drawer of the bill and Mohan Lal is the drawee. The former has sold the latter goods worth Rs. 50,000—on three-month credit. The seller may, however, need cash now. So he draws a bill and sends it to the buyer for acceptance. The latter, in acknowledgement of his responsibility to make payment on the due date, writes 'accepted' on the bill, or arranges to get the bill accepted on his behalf by his bank. The bank charges acceptance commission and assumes responsibility of making the payment if the drawee defaults. Once the bill has been so accepted, it becomes a marketable instrument. On receipt, the drawer can now sell it in the market for cash. Again, a bank normally comes into the picture. The drawer goes to his bank and gets the bill discounted. This simply means that he sells it for cash to the bank, which pays him the face value of the bill, less collection charges and interest on the amount for the remaining life of the bill. The rate of interest charged is known as the *discount rate* on bills. At the time of selling the bill, the seller (drawer) endorses the bill in favour of the buying bank. This makes him liable to meet the bill at maturity should the drawee (or his 'accepting' bank) fail to do so. Thus, the buying bank is protected against the risk of default. If need be, this bank can later sell the bill to some other bank or get it rediscounted with the RBI.

Thus, bills are a very important device for providing short-term finance to trade and industry. They have a fixed term to maturity called *usance*. This usance is reasonably short for banks to invest their funds in them and reasonably long for the buyers of goods (drawees of bills) to recover the cost of goods from their resale or processing and sale. The latter consideration makes bills self-liquidating. This reduces considerably the risk of default on bills. Moreover, bills are marketable paper, that is, they can be resold any number of times in the money market. They also carry competitive rate of interest. For all these reasons, banks have a preference for investment in such bills. In the past, several monetary economists were of the view that banks should invest only in bills. This view is known as the '*real bills doctrine*' in the literature. But most economists have regarded it as an extreme view. One good asset should not monopolise the show. Also, during periods of business recession or credit squeeze the expected sales or receipts may not materialise and drawees may find it difficult to honour their bills. Thus, the self-liquidating character of bills is a fair-weather friend.

The commercial bills are of *various kinds*. The bases of distinction among them are many. One distinction is that between modern bills of exchange and indigenous bills. What we have explained above are modern bills. Indigenous bills are called *hundis* (see Chapter 10). Another distinction is that between inland bills and foreign (trade) bills. As the name indicates, the former are used to finance inland trade, the latter to finance foreign trade. It follows that import bills are used to finance imports and export bills to finance exports. A third kind of distinction is that between trade bills and finance bills. The former are also called documentary bills as they carry with them papers pertaining to genuine trade transactions. As such, they are also known as genuine (trade) bills. Finance bills, on the other hand, are 'clean' bills. They do not carry any documents of sale of goods with them, as they do not arise out of any genuine trade transaction. They are only 'accommodation bills' drawn and accepted as a device for short-term credit. A large proportion of indigenous bills (hundis) are finance bills. Yet another distinction is that between drawers' bills and drawees' bills. The same bill may be of either kind. It all depends on who presents the bill to a bank for discounting: drawer or drawee. If the former, then the bill is a drawer's bill; if the latter, then the bill is a drawee's bill. Generally, the rate of interest charged by banks on the latter kind of bills is higher than that charged on the former kind of bills. This is presumably because when a drawee comes to a bank for getting the bill discounted, it shows that he does not have enough credit-worthiness in the eyes of the bill's drawer.

A distinction is also made between demand (or sight) bills and time (or usance) bills. The former are payable on demand or presentation, the latter after a definite time period (of say 30, 60, or 90 days) stipulated in the bill. There is a corresponding distinction between purchase and discounting of bills. Discounting pertains to usance bills, purchase to demand or sight bills. Though the demand bills do not allow any credit to the buyer of goods, there is a time lag between the despatch of goods and their receipt by the (outstation) buyer. The latter will pay only on receipt of goods. For the period goods are in transit or have not been taken delivery of by the buyer, the seller will be out of funds. Therefore, he may sell the bill to his banker and get cash.

Purchase of demand documentary bills is freely undertaken by bankers on behalf of their customers, subject to a maximum limit granted in each case. Normally, for banks, purchase of bills is an easier operation than the discount of bills, because in the case of demand bills, the banker will have possession of documents of title to goods (such as railway receipt or lorry receipt endorsed in the name of the bank) until payment of bills, whereas in the case of usance bills, possession of goods is transferred to the buyer against his acceptance. But even in the case of demand bills, banks can be cheated when for example, documentary bills are spurious or unscruplous lorry operators deliver the goods to the buyer without the lorry receipt.

Earlier we had said that in order to make a bill freely marketable, it must be accepted by a bank or some other institution or house of good standing. Normally, the bill should have two good signatures:

one that of the drawee and the other that of the accepting bank. This kind of bank's business is called *'acceptance business'* and the credit implied in it as 'acceptance credit.' Since acceptance of bills on behalf of one's constituents involves risk of default by drawees, a bank accepts bills only for those of its customers in whose credit-worthiness it has confidence and only for the amount it considers safe. This requires a bank to have full credit information on such constituents. In the UK there are specialised firms, known as 'acceptance houses', who do this kind of acceptance business for commission. In India we do not have such acceptance houses. In the UK the bill discounting business is also handled by specialised firms, known as 'discount houses'. In India this work also is handled by banks. The bill business here has not developed so much as to call for specialised institutions to handle it.

The following factors have been mainly responsible for impeding the growth of a bill market in India:

(i) the prevalence of cash credit system (see Section 5.5) as the main form of bank lending, and
(ii) the reluctance of the larger buyer in the public and private sectors to accept the payment discipline involved in the bill market.

In addition, the lack of uniformity in drawing bills in different parts of the country; the practice of sales on credit without any specified time limit, usually undertaken to promote sales; and high stamp duty on usance (time bills) have also hampered the growth of bill finance.

Keeping in view the usefulness of bills as instruments of credit to both business and banks, their self-liquidating character, and easier regulation of banks' bill finance by the RBI, the latter has been making efforts to encourage the use of bills and develop a bill market in the country. It has had only limited success so far. Its main strategy has been to induce banks to encourage their borrowers to resort more and more to bill finance. From time to time individual banks fall short of cash. They meet their needs for cash partly from the call money market, partly by selling treasury bills to the RBI, and partly by borrowing from it against government securities. The RBI has offered to make its refinance available to banks against eligible commercial bills as well. This has widened the scope for banks' borrowing from the RBI and acted as a spur for the growth of bill finance in the country. The main features of two specific bill market schemes of the RBI are given below.

3.6 The New Bill Market Scheme

The old bill market scheme of the RBI introduced in January 1952 was a miserable failure. Therefore, the RBI introduced a new bill market scheme in November 1970 with the object of developing a genuine bill market in India. It has been modified since then from time to time. We do not go into all the details of the new scheme. Only two main features of it are specially noteworthy:

(*i*) The bills covered under the scheme must be genuine trade bills, i.e. bills which evidence sale and/or despatch of goods;

(*ii*) The RBI rediscounts these bills. That is why it is also (and more appropriately) called 'Bills Rediscounting Scheme'.

In both the above respects the new scheme is an improvement over the old scheme which covered even improvised usance bills and did not provide for the rediscounting of even genuine trade bills by the RBI. The bills were used only as security against advances to banks. Under the new scheme also the eligible bills should have maximum usance of 90 days left at the time of rediscount. Banks can get bills rediscounted with not only the RBI but also the LIC, GIC and subsidiaries, UTI, and ICICI, but not with private persons.

The advantages of a genuine bill market to the banking system and others are summed up below.

1. Normally, bills are self-liquidating and the date of repayment of a bank's advances by way of the discounting/rediscounting of bills is definite. In contrast, cash-credit is not self-liquidating;

2. Bills offer greater liquidity to their holders as they can be shifted to others in the market in case of need for cash;

3. A well-developed bill market helps greatly in evening out liquidity throughout the financial system, as those with short-term surplus funds of whatever duration can invest them in bills of desired maturities and can always hope to unload their holdings of bills to others in the market whenever they need cash. Thus, the short-term surpluses of some become available through the market to meet the short-run deficits of others. Thus, the former do not suffer from the surfeit of liquidity (or cash) and the latter with the lack of it. In the absence of an active bill market banks in need of cash have to depend either on the call money market or on the RBI's loan window;

4. The commercial bill rate is much higher than the treasury bill rate. Therefore, commercial banks and other financial institutions

with short-run surpluses to invest find bills attractive not only for their liquidity but also for their return;

5. To the borrower, the cost of bill finance is somewhat lower than that of cash credit, because the bills carry the additional security in the form of acceptor's signature, are time-bound, and can be sold in the market;

6. Extensive use of bills as an instrument of short-term commercial credit and rediscounting of bills by the RBI makes the monetary system highly elastic. Whenever the economy is in need of more cash, banks can get a part of the bills in their portfolios rediscounted with the RBI and thereby increase the supply of money. The process comes in handy to meet the enhanced needs of busy-season finance. The seasonal expansion-contraction of money supply also becomes automatic and obviates the need for policy actions by the RBI. In the absence of such an automatic mechanism, the RBI has had to intervene actively in the money market to meet the busy-season needs for funds of the economy. We have, however, to remember that this kind of flexibility is not an unmixed blessing as it can contribute to excessive expansions of money supply, as has actually happened several times since 1973–74.

A full-scale evaluation of the working of the scheme cannot be given here. But two aspects of its *actual working* need to be pointed here.

1. The scheme has been used by banks and their borrowers to beat the credit-restriction measures of the RBI. During 1973–5 as the RBI tried to tighten bank credit in the economy as an anti-inflationary measure but left the bills rediscounting facility unrestricted, banks increasingly utilised this facility to gain Reserve Bank credit and pass it on to their borrowers. Thus, whereas the average value of commercial bills rediscounted with the RBI was only about Rs.7 crores in 1972–3, it shot up to Rs.75 crores in the next year and to Rs.193 crores in 1974–5. Consequently, the RBI was forced to put certain restrictions on its bill rediscounting facility and later place it wholly on discretionary basis. Thus, the misuse of the facility in the form of excessive borrowing under it from the RBI has to be constantly guarded against.

2. Though over the years during the 1970s the volume of commercial borrowings from banks under the head 'bills purchased and discounted' (i.e. bill finance) has increased significantly from the average value of Rs. 975 crores on the last Friday of March 1971 to about Rs. 5,000 crores on the Last Friday of March 1986, a genuine bill

market has yet to grow in the country. Several reasons are responsible for this outcome. The key reason is customer preference for cash credit and dislike for bill finance, since the latter requires honouring bills when they fall due for payment and allow little discretion to borrowers in the end-use of credit. The banks also willingly fall in line, especially with big borrowers, and still allow conversion of their loans and advances into usance bills. The rediscount market is open only to banks and to selected financial institutions, and not to all the dealers of bills.

3.7 The Stock Market

The stock market deals in long-term securities, both private and government. It is the most important component of the capital market. The latter deals in long-term funds of all kinds, whether raised through open-market securities or through negotiated loans not resulting in market paper. Open-market securities are securities (or market paper) that are bought and sold openly in the market (like marketable goods) and can change hands any number of times. The negotiated loans have to be negotiated directly (or through a broker) between the borrower and the lender. They appear only in the account books of the lenders and the borrowers' promissory notes which are not salable in the market.

The scope and structure of the stock or securities market are shown in Figure 3.2.

Figure 3.2
The Structure of Securities Market

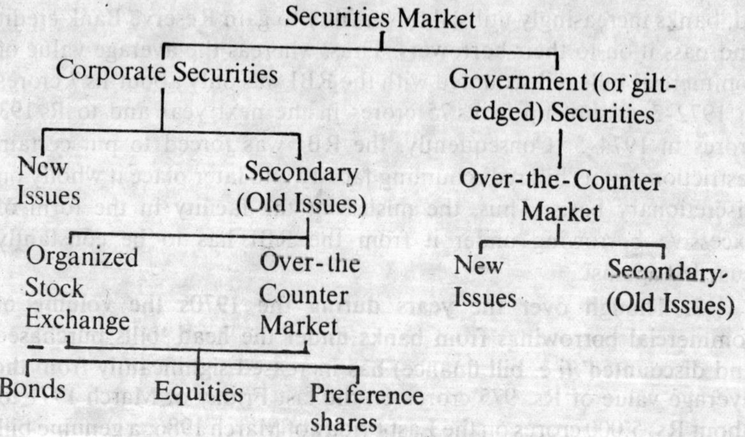

The stock market comprises several distinct markets in securities. The most important distinction is that between the market for corporate securities and the market for government securities. We shall study them separately in the next two sections. Corporate securities are instruments for raising long-term corporate capital from the public. The stock market organization provides separate arrangements for the new issues of securities and for buying and selling of old securities. The former market is known as the 'new issues market' and the latter market as the 'secondary market'. Both kinds of markets are essential for servicing corporate borrowers and investors.

3.7.1 The New Issues Market

The essential function of the new issues market is to arrange for the raising of new capital by corporate enterprises, whether new or old. This involves attracting new investible resources into the corporate sector and their allocation among alternative uses and users. Both ways the role is very important. How fast the corporate industrial sector grows depends very much on the inflow of resources into it, apart from its own internal savings. Equally important is the movement of sufficient venture capital into new fields of manufacturing crucial to the balanced growth of industries in the economy and in new regions for promoting balanced regional development.

The new issues may take the form of equity shares, preference shares or debentures. The firms raising funds may be new companies or existing companies planning expansion. The new companies need not always be entirely new enterprises. They may be private firms already in business, but 'going public' to expand their capital bases. 'Going public' means becoming public limited companies to be entitled to raise funds from the general public in the open market.

For inducing the public to invest their savings in new issues, the services of a network of specialised institutions (underwriters and stock-brokers) is required. The more highly developed and efficient this network, the greater will be the inflow of savings into organized industry. Till the establishment of the Industrial Credit and Investment Corporation of India (ICICI) in 1955, this kind of underwriting was sorely lacking in India. Instead, a special institutional arrangement, known as the managing agency system had grown. Now it has become a thing of the past.

The new institutional arrangements for new corporate issues in place of the discredited managing agency system started taking shape with the setting up of the ICICI in 1955. Soon after (1956) the LIC joined hands. The new system has already attained adulthood under the leadership of the Industrial Development Bank of India (IDBI). Apart from the ICICI and the LIC other important participants in the new issues market are the major term-lending institutions such as the UTI, the IFCI, commercial banks, General

Insurance Corporation (GIC) and its subsidiaries, stock brokers, and investment trusts (see Chapter 9). Foreign institutional funds from the World Bank and its affiliates, International Development Association (IDA) and International Finance Corporation, are also channeled through the all-India term-lending institutions (IDBI, ICICI, and IFCI).

Managing successful floatation of new issues involves three distinct services: (*i*) origination, (*ii*) underwriting, and (*iii*) distribution of new issues. The *origination* requires careful investigation of the viability and prospects of new projects. This involves technical evaluation of a proposal from the technical-manufacturing angle, the availability of technical know-how, land, power, water and essential inputs, location, the competence of the management, the study of market demand for the product (s), domestic and foreign, over time, financial estimates of projected costs and returns, the adequacy and structure of financial arrangements (promotors' equity, equity from the public, debt-equity ratio, short-term funds, liquidity ratios, foreign exchange requirement and availability), gestation lags, etc., and communication of any deficiencies in the project proposal to the promoters for remedial measures. All this requires well-trained and competent staff. A careful scrutiny and approval of a new issue proposal by well-established financial institutions known for their competence and integrity improves substantially its acceptability by the investing public and other financial institutions. This is specially true of issues of totally new enterprises.

Underwriting means guaranteeing purchase of a stipulated amount of a new issue at a fixed price. The purchase may be for sale to the public or for one's own portfolio or for both the purposes. If the expected sale to the public does not materialise, the underwriter absorbs the unsold stock in its own portfolio. The underwriter assumes this risk for commission, known as underwriter's commission. The company bringing out the new issue agrees to bear this extra cost of raising funds, because thereby it is assured of funds and the task of sale of stock to the public or others is passed on entirely to underwriters. Mostly, underwriting is done by a group of underwriters, one or more of whom may act as group leaders. The group (or consortium) underwriting distributes risks of underwriting among several underwriters and enhances substantially the capacity of the system to underwrite big issues.

Distribution means sale of stock to the public. The term-lending institutions, the LIC, the UTI and several other financial institutions usually underwrite new issues as direct investments for their own portfolios. For them, there is no problem of sale of stock to the public. But, under the law, a part of the new public issue must be offered to the general public. This is placed with stockbrokers who have a system of inviting subscriptions to new issues from the public. In normal times it is their distributive capacity which determines the extent of the public participation in new issues. During periods of stock market boom the demand for new issues from the public also goes up. New issues of well-known houses and issues underwritten by strong institutions generally have a good public response. It is the placing of the issues of small companies that continues to be the Achilles' heels of the new issues market. For loosening the grip of monopoly houses on the industrial economy of the country, it is necessary that new entrepreneurs are encouraged. For this, special efforts need be stepped up further for promoting small issues.

Broadly speaking, there are three main *ways of floating* new issues : *(i)* by the issue of a prospectus to the public, *(ii)* by private placement and *(iii)* by the rights issue to the existing shareholders. What we have described above is the first method. The issue of a public prospectus giving details about the company, issue, and the underwriters is the last act in the drama and is an open invitation to the public to subscribe to the issue. Private placement means that the issue is not offered to the general public for subscription but is placed privately with a few big financiers. This saves the company the expenses of public placement. It is also faster. Rights issue means issue of rights (invitations) to the existing shareholders of an old corporation to subscribe to a part or whole of the new issue in a fixed proportion to their shareholding. Such an issue is always offered at a certain discount from the going market price of the already-trading shares of the company. The discount is in the nature of a bonus to the shareholders. Obviously, a rights issue is open only to an existing public limited corporation, not to a new one. Old corporations also increase their capitalisation (paid-up capital) by declaring bonus to their shareholders, which means issue of new shares to them in a fixed ratio to their shareholdings without charging any price from them. This is a way of converting a part of accumulated reserves into company's paid-up capital.

3.7.2. The Secondary Market in Old Issues

This market deals in existing securities. Its main function is to provide liquidity to such securities. Liquidity of an asset means its easy convertibility into cash at short notice and with minimal loss of capital value. This liquidity is provided by providing a continuous market for securities, that is, a market where a security can be bought or sold at any time during business hours at small transaction cost and at comparatively small variations from the last quoted price. This, of course, is true of only 'active' securities for which there are always buyers and sellers in the market. 'Activeness' is a property of individual securities, not of the market.

The function of providing liquidity to old stocks is important both for attracting new finance and in other ways. It encourages prospective investors to invest in securities, old or new, because they know that any time they want to get out of them into cash, they can go to the market and sell them off. In the absence of any organized securities market, this will not be easily feasible. So, the investing public will keep away from securities. Then, the secondary market provides an opportunity to all concerned to invest in securities and when they like. This opens a way for continuous inflow of funds into the market. This is specially important for such investors who do not want to risk their funds by investing in new ventures, but are perfectly willing to invest in the securities of on-going concerns. On the other end, there are venturesome investors who invest in new issues in the hope of making capital gains later when the new concerns have established themselves well. In a sense, they season new issues and sell them off when the market acceptability of these issues has improved. With their funds released from sale of their old holdings, they can move into other new issues coming into the market. Thus, investment into new issues is facilitated greatly by the operations of the secondary market.

The new investment is influenced in another way too by what is happening in the secondary market. The latter acts as an important indicator of the investment climate in the economy. When stock prices of existing securities are rising and the volume of trading activity in the secondary market goes up, new issues also tend to increase as the new issues market (underwriters, stockbrokers, and investors) is (are) better prepared and more willing to accept new issues. This is also a good time for companies to come forward with new issues. When the secondary market is in doldrums, the new issues market also languishes. The underwriters are reluctant to underwrite and stockbrokers reluctant to assume the responsibility of selling new issues to the public. Then, firms are also advised to postpone their new issues for better times.

There are two segments of the secondary market: (a) organized stock exchange, *(b)* over-the-counter market. The latter deals in such securities as are not 'listed' on an organized stock exchange. These are securities of small companies and have only a limited market. Their prices are determined through direct negotiation between stock brokers and not through open bidding as is the case with 'listed' securities on a stock exchange. The main action of the stock market is concentrated on these exchanges. We explain briefly their organization and functioning.

Stock Exchanges. A stock exchange is an organization for orderly buying and selling of 'listed' (approved) existing securities. The organization includes an association of persons or firms to regulate and supervise all transactions, rules, regulations and standard practices to govern all market transactions, authorised stock brokers, and an exchange floor or hall where stock brokers or their authorised agents meet during fixed business hours to buy and sell securities. At present in India there are 11 recognised stock exchanges in various parts of the country. The one at Bombay is the leading stock exchange. It leads other exchanges in terms of the number of securities listed there, the importance of companies whose stocks are traded there, the average volume of daily business, and its capacity to absorb big buy and sell orders.

Listed securities are securities that appear on the approved list of a stock exchange. Approval depends on several considerations, such as the size of the issue, whether it is widely held by the public or closely held in a few hands, timely production of annual accounts, etc. Only listed securities are traded on the floor of the exchange. Therefore, listing improves marketability of a stock.

An organized stock exchange is an 'auction' type market, where prices of traded stocks are settled by open bids and offers on the floor of the exchange. Therefore, it is said that these prices are formed competitively. To the extent that is so and to the extent buyers and sellers are well-informed and while bidding prices they take into consideration all the relevant factors, present and prospective, concerning not only the particular enterprise and the industry, but also the general economic and political conditions, the stock prices will be good measures of the true real worth of enterprises. In the process, better-run profit-making enterprises will appreciate in real value as compared to others. In a private-ownership economy (or sector) this helps and guides greatly the allocation of new resources.

In actual practice, nearly all the statements of the previous paragraph need to be qualified. Competition is not perfect in the stock market. This market is no leveller of the high and low. Big investors carry more weight and can influence the market their way. Already, the weight of big financial institutions, such as the LIC, the UTI, the GIC and subsidiaries has come to be felt. This need not always be to the disadvantage of the small investor. Problems arise only when there is artificial manipulation of the market or when the firm holding of good stocks by institutions (and promoters) reduces too much the floating supply of such stocks in the market. Then, a slight increase in the demand for such stocks shoots their prices up. Also, small investors are not that well-informed. Nor do they have the requisite ability to analyse and interpret the myriad forces that impinge on stock prices. Therefore, without the leadership of financial institutions, the prices formed by their transaction need not be good indicators of the true values of stocks. They are easily swayed by 'animal spirits'. The result is frequent ups and downs of stock prices. There is also an excess dose of speculation present in the market, especially during periods of market booms. Then, in a planned mixed economy, allocation of resources cannot be left to the operations of free market forces. A more purposive and socially informed allocation is needed. This is one of the justifications of the public sector and the Capital Issues (Control) Act that operated in the country.

8 The Gilt-edged Market

The gilt-edged market is the market in government securities or the securities guaranteed (as to both principal and interest) by the government. The former include securities of the Government of India and of the state governments; the latter are securities issued by local authorities (like city corporations, municipalities, and port trusts) and autonomous government undertakings like development banks, state electricity boards, etc. The term gilt-edged means 'of the best quality'. It has come to be reserved for government securities as they do not suffer from the risk of default. Besides, government securities are highly liquid, as they can be easily sold in the market at their going market price. The open market operations of the RBI are also conducted in government securities (see Section 19.4).

Government securities have become a very important component of capital market in several countries. In India they have gained steadily in importance since 1954-55 as the pressure for raising funds to finance public sector projects under five year plans built up. The total amount outstanding of the *internal government debt* in the form of market loans, special bonds and treasury bills was about Rs. 2,75,000 crore at the end of March 1995.

In addition, there was direct mobilisation of household financial savings through post office deposits, 'small savings schemes' and public provident funds run by the post offices, government provident funds and 'compulsory deposits' from the public.

The gilt-edged market may be divided in two parts: the treasury bill market and the government bond market. We have already studied the former in Section 3.4; the organization of the latter is explained below. On the borrower side, the RBI manages entirely the public debt operations of the central as well as state governments. As such, it is responsible for all the new issues of loans. This will be explained further in Section 4.3. There is also a large secondary market in old issues of government loans. It is heavily concentrated in Bombay with supporting markets in Calcutta, Madras, and Delhi. This market largely works through a few large stockbrokers who keep in constant touch with the RBI and other prospective buyers and sellers. Sometime financial institutions negotiate directly with the RBI. But this is not very common. The RBI keeps the market informed through recognized brokers about its buying and selling prices for various loans outstanding. It keeps on ready sale securities of various maturities to meet the market demand for them. In all this, the RBI's position is that of a monopolist. There are only brokers or investors in the market and no dealers or jobbers (other than the RBI) who would make a market in government loans by standing ready to buy and sell any amount of government securities on their own account.

A new development has taken place when the RBI announced in November 1995, the appointment of *primary dealers* in government securities to strengthen the securities market infrastructure and bring about an improvement in secondary market trading, liquidity and turnover and induce wider holding of government securities amongst a wider investor base.

On the demand side, the gilt-edged market is dominated by financial institutions. Apart from the RBI, the major holders are commercial banks, insurance companies, provident funds, and trust funds. These financial intermediaries mobilise savings of the public and through their investment in government securities transfer these savings to the government. They constitute what is called the *'captive market'* for government securities, as they are required statutorily to hold certain minimum proportions of their total liabilities (assets) in government securities (see Section 19.6 and Chapter 9). Therefore as the total liabilities of these institutions grow, the captive demand for government securities also grows. Besides these financial institutions, local authorities, semi-government bodies, and nonresidents also invest some amounts in government securities. The demand for these securities from non-financial companies and individuals is negligible.

Since 1992, several important changes have come about in the gilt-edged market. We have already said about the auction sale of treasury bills of 91 days and 364 days which has resulted in a substantial rise in the short-term rate of interest. In addition, in the market for dated government securities, the following three developments are worth noting:

(*a*) with the gradual reduction in the SLR requirement for banks and some other FIs, the captive demand for government securities has gone down;

(*b*) the rate of interest on these securities is market-determined, has gone up, on average, and has been changing with changes in market conditions; and

(*c*) there is a tendency towards shortening of the term to maturity of securities. Most of them now are for a period of 10 years, on average.

CHAPTER 4

The Reserve Bank of India

4.1. Introduction

A central bank is the apex institution of a country's monetary system. Since the monetary system (which includes commercial banks) is the dominant part of the financial system of a country, in any case in a developing country, a central bank is also the apex institution of its financial system. As such, it plays a leading role in organizing, running, supervising, regulating, and developing the monetary-financial system. In as much as the continued good health and development of a modern money- and credit-using economy depend crucially on an efficient financial system, the role of a well-run central bank is very important. The design and conduct of the monetary and credit policy are its special responsibility.

The present chapter is devoted to a discussion of the functions and performance of the country's central bank, the Reserve Bank of India (RBI). Questions of monetary and credit policy will be discussed in Part Three.

The RBI was established on April 1, 1935 under the Reserve Bank of India Act, 1934. Initially it was constituted as a private shareholders' bank with a fully paid-up share capital of Rs. 5 crores. It was nationalised on January 1, 1949. The executive head of the Bank is called the governor, who is assisted by deputy governors and other executive officers in the administration of the Bank. For general direction, the Bank has a central board of directors, supplemented by four local boards at Delhi, Calcutta, Madras, and Bombay for four regional areas : northern, eastern, southern, and western, respectively. The head office of the Bank is at Bombay.

The RBI performs all the major functions of a central bank. They are discussed individually in the next six sections.

4.2 RBI as Currency Authority

The RBI is the sole authority for the issue of currency in India other than one-rupee notes and coins and small coins which are issued by the Government of India. The bulk of the currency (about 93 per cent of it) is in the form of Reserve Bank notes, which are currently issued in the denominations of rupees two, five, ten, twenty, fifty, one hundred. and 500. Earlier, notes of higher denominations of rupees one thousand, five thousand, and ten thousand were also issued. But they were demonetized to discourage black-market operations through them.

The issue of notes by the RBI is kept separate from the rest of its banking operations. For this, the RBI is organized under two separate deparments, the Issue Department and the Banking Department, the former being solely responsible for the issue of notes. All the currency issued by the RBI (*i.e.*, its Issue Department) is its monetary liability. Under the law, it must be backed by assets of equal value (held in the Issue Department). These assets consist of gold coin and bullion, foreign securities, rupee coins, and Government of India rupee securities. Whenever the Issue Department acquires any of these assets, it does so by issuing its currency. The conditions governing the composition of these assets determine largely the nature of the 'currency standard' prevailing in the country. For example, for the period 1935–56, India had 'proportional reserve system' under which the RBI was required to hold against notes issued at least 40 per cent assets in its Issue Department in the form of gold (coin or bullion) and sterling (later foreign) securities, and only the balance in the form of rupee securities, with the further provision that gold (coin or bullion) at any time was not less than worth Rs. 40 crores. In October 1956 this system was replaced by a 'minimum of foreign reserves system', which required the RBI to hold as assets in its Issue Department only a minimum of Rs. 515 crores worth of foreign reserves (Rs. 115 crores of gold and Rs. 400 crores of foreign securities) and all the rest in rupee securities, whatever the amount of its currency outstanding. Even this was diluted further a year after. Since then the only binding requirement has been to hold at least Rs. 115 crores worth of gold as backing against the currency issued the rest of the backing being in the form of rupee securities.

This has placed India on 'managed paper currency standard'. At the end of March 1995, the amount of Reserve Bank currency outstanding was about Rs. 1,00,000 crore. In comparison, the minimum gold-reserve requirement of Rs. 115 crores, fixed for all times, is truly paltry.[2] It does not put any constraint on the future expansion of currency, all of which can be fully supported by rupee securities. This is, then, simply a method of '*monetising*' a part of the public debt—the debt of the Government of India. The public debt itself is a non-monetary liability, *i.e.*, it is not money. But when a part of the public debt is placed with the RBI, it serves as the basis for the issue of Reserve Bank currency, which is money. Hence, this is monetisation of public debt with the RBI.

Historically, the Central Government could borrow any amount of money from the RBI through the issue of *ad-hoc* treasury bills to it. The RBI, in turn, used to finance its credit to the government by the issue of its currency and hold the treasury bills in its Issue Department. (The same still holds true for the government securities acquired by the RBI.). As already explained in Section 3.4 above, to check the automatic monetisation of the government's budget deficit, an agreement was made between the GOI and the RBI in September 1994. This has put serious restrictions on the government's *ad hoc* borrowings from the RBI.

The issue of currency into circulation and its withdrawal from circulation (i.e., expansion and contraction of currency respectively) take place through the Banking Department of the RBI. The mechanics is best explained with the help of an example. When the Central Government incurs a deficit in its budget and borrows from the RBI by selling treasury bills to the Banks' Banking Department, the latter pays cash by either drawing down its stock of currency and/or by getting currency from the Issue Department against equivalent transfer of eligible assets. The government by spending new currency puts it into circulation.

Though the one-rupee notes and coins and small coins are issued by the Central Government, their distribution to the public is the sole responsibility of the RBI. For conversion of notes and coins of various denominations for the public and banks, the RBI maintains currency chests and small-coin depots as distribution centres throughout the country. Such facilities are made available at all offices of the RBI and a large number of other centres in the country, mainly by agency arrangements with the State Bank of India and its associate banks, most other nationalised banks, and government treasuries and sub-treasuries.

4.3 RBI as Banker to Government

The RBI acts as banker to the government—the Central as well as state governments. As such, it transacts all banking business of the government, which involves the receipt and payment of money on behalf of the government and carrying out of its exchange, remittance and other banking operations. In return, the governments keep their cash balances on current account deposit with the RBI.

As government's banker, the RBI provides short-term credit to the government to meet any shortfalls in its receipts over its disbursements. It also provides short-term credit to state governments as ways and means advances. But, some state governments do resort to over-drafts at times for short periods. The RBI has not been able to stop this practice.

As government's banker, the RBI is also charged with the responsibility of managing the public (i.e., the government) debt. In discharge of this responsibility, the RBI manages all new issues of government loans, services the public debt outstanding, and nurses the market for government securities. The last function is very important for the success of government's borrowing programme from the public (including banks), which has itself become increasingly important for mobilising resources for financing public-sector projects.

To this end the RBI and the government have taken several measures which will be only briefly mentioned here. The most important of these measures is the statutory requirement for investment in government securities. Under this requirement, various financial institutions like commercial banks, the LIC, GIC and subsidiaries, and provident funds are required by law to invest designated minimum proportions of their total assets/liabilities in government securities (and other 'approved securities'). This provision concerning banks is administered by the RBI and will be studied more fully in section 19.6 under the 'Statutory Liquidity Ratio' (SLR) as a monetary-credit control measure of the RBI.

The RBI's other (secondary) responsibilities in this field are to ensure smooth functioning of the market, to see that government securities of various maturities are available to potential buyers in adequate amounts, that the maturity-structure of interest rates on these securities does not get

out of line due to excess supply of some maturities and deficient supply of others, that the government bond market is not subject to sudden and large fluctuations, that the liquidity of investments in government securities is reasonably maintained, and that the new issues of government loans are well received in the market.

As manager of the new loans of the Central and State governments, the RBI advises these governments on the quantum, timing, and terms of such loans and co-ordinates their borrowing programmes. To ensure success of new loan operations, it 'grooms' or prepares the market for receiving new loans by acquiring securities nearing maturity. On the one hand, this puts cash in the hands of investors (mostly financial institutions) which they can use to subscribe to new loan floatations; on the other hand, this helps lengthen the average maturity of the government debt outstanding. Normally, the Bank itself buys large amounts of new loans and later sells ***on tap*** **a large variety of new and old issues to cater to the diverse demands of investors.** Overall, the Bank has done a good job of its function of government debt management.

As the country's central bank, the RBI also acts as adviser to the government on all banking and financial matters, including matters concerning international finance, the financing pattern of five year plans, the mobilisation of resources and banking legislation, among other things.

4.4. **RBI as Bankers' Bank and Supervisor**

As bankers' bank, the RBI holds a part of the cash reserves of banks, lends them funds for short periods, and provides them with centralised clearing and cheap and quick remittance facilities. In the early stages of the development of central banking, banks used to keep some of their cash reserves voluntarily with a leading bank which gradually took over the role of a central bank. The obvious advantage to individual banks was that of the facility of centralised inter-bank clearing it automatically provided. Reserve-holding banks could settle their daily mutual clearings by drawing upon or crediting to their individual accounts with one bank, the central bank. Thus, the mere entries in the books of the central bank can settle claims against each other among banks without the actual transfer of cash. The pooling of cash reserves of banks with one bank as the central bank also led to a great economy of cash reserves for the banking system as a whole, becasue individual banks could borrow from the central pool of reserves with the central bank whenever they fell short of cash.

The conditions are substantially different in India. The RBI as the country's central bank is authorised statutorily to require scheduled commercial bank to deposit with it a stipulated ratio (lying between 3 per cent and 15 per cent) of their net total liabilities. This ratio is called Cash Reserve Ratio (CRR) (see Section 19.3). These reserves of banks with the RBI are held neither voluntarily nor are available to them for meeting inter-bank clearing drains except temporarily over the reserve period, that is, the period over which the daily average of the required cash reserves is calculated. Till March 29, 1985, this reserve period used to be a week. From that date the length of this period has been doubled to a fortnight. The true rationale of the statutory reserve requirement now is that by varying it within limits the RBI can use it as a tool of monetary and credit control (see section 19.5). To meet any clearing drains, banks must hold extra reserves over and above their statutory reserves or raise cash in other ways. The pool of bank reserves with the RBI, however, does serve as the common fund out of which the RBI can and does make advances to banks in temporary need of funds. Normally, banks are supposed to meet their shortfalls of cash from sources other than the RBI and go to it only as a matter of last resort, because the RBI as the central bank is supposed to function as only 'the lender of last resort' (see Section 19.4).

Under the Reserve Bank of India Act, 1934 and the Banking Regulation Act, 1949 (as amended from time to time), the RBI enjoys extensive powers of supervision, regulation, and control over commercial and co-operative banks. The Bank's regulatory functions relating to banks cover their establishment (i.e. licensing), branch expansion, liquidity of their assets, management and methods of working, amalgamation, reconstruction and liquidation. The control by the Bank is exercised through periodic inspection of banks and follow-up action and by calling for returns and other information from them. The objective of such supervision and control is to ensure the development of a sound banking system in the country.

4.5 Controller of Money Supply and Credit

A very important founction of RBI as the central bank is to control the total supply of money and bank credit in the best interest of the national economy. In the context of planned economic development, managed paper curency system, and strong inflationary tendency of the economy, the task has assumed added importance and gravity. The RBI has to satisfy diverse and competing claims on it and the rest of the banking system for credit in a manner that promotes maximum output and employment with price stability, a high rate of economic growth with distributional justice, and reasonable balance in the country's balance of payments. To perform its allotted function well, the RBI uses several control instruments at its disposal such as open-market operations, changes in statutory reserve requirements for banks, lending policy towards banks, control over interest- rate structure of banks, statutory liquidity ratio of banks, etc. The whole question of monetary and credit control is so important that the entire Part Three of the book will be devoted to its discussion.

4.6 Exchange Management and Control

The RBI acts as the custodian of the country's foreign exchange reserves, manages exchange control and acts as the agent of the government in respect of India's membership of the IMF. Exchange control was first imposed in India in Septembr 1939 at the outbreak of World War II and has been continued since. Under it, control was imposed on both the receipts and payments of foreign exchange. The foreign exchange regulations under the law required that all foreign exchange receipts, whether on account of export earnings, investment earnings, or capital receipts, whether on private account or on government account, must be sold to the RBI either directly or through authorized dealers (mostly major commercial banks). This resulted in centralisation of country's foreign exchange reserves with the RBI and facilitated planned utilization of these reserves, because all payments in foreign exchange were also controlled by the authorities. The exchange control was so operated as to restrict the demand for foreign exchange within the limits of the available supplies of it. Foreign exchange was rationed among competing demands for it according to the government policy. All this became essential in the context of actual or potential shortage of foreign exchange, which had been an important constraint on India's efforts at planned economic development, most of the time.

Faced with acute foreign exchange crisis, the new government at the Centre (constituted in June 1991), took several successive steps to meet the problem :

(i) The Rupee was devalued by 18% against the US Dollar and other hard currencies in two steps in quick succession in early July 1991 to correct substantially the over valuation of the Rupee and thereby to make Indian exports more competitive in world markets and to make imports into India costlier than before.

(ii) The new trade policy of July 1991 introduced a system of EXIM scrip, under which exporters earned freely tradeable import entitlements equal to 30 per cent (or 40 per cent in some cases) of the value of their exports. The scrips commanded premium when sold. This system was soon discarded in favour of a system of partial (60:40) convertibility of the Indian Rupee into foreign exchange.

(iii) Finally, in the budget for 1993-94, the Rupee was made fully convertible on trade account. That is, the system of a single unified exchange rate of the Rupee was introduced in place of the previous dual rates system. This single rate is determined entirely by the forces of demand and supply and not officially. This, of course, does not mean that one can go to a bank and buy any amount of foreign exchange one likes against rupees. The entire gamut of foreign exchange restrictions remain, placing a strict limit on the overall demand for foreign exchange. The RBI continues to act as the ultimate guardian of the foreign exchange value of the rupee and as such intervene, that is, buy and sell rupees in the foreign exchange market at its discretion. Even now, it is only the authorised dealers in foreign exchange (mostly banks) who can buy and sell foreign exchange and maintain only a minimum ''position'' that is unmatched by buy and sell orders. Thus, large speculators in foreign exchange have not been allowed in the market;

(iv) Receipts and payments on capital account continue to be subject to controls; and

(v) All transactions are conducted within the framework of exchange control regulations which are being liberalised progressively.

4.7 Monetary Data and Other Publications

The RBI acts as the source of all monetary and banking data, which are so essential for the formulation and critical evaluation of economic policies. Among other things, the RBI collects, collates, and publishes these data regularly in its weekly Statements, in the *Reserve Bank of India Bulletin* (monthly), in its anual *Report on Currency and Finance*, and other periodic publications. Besides, these publications and other reports carry much useful information, reviews, comments, and analysis of contemporary policy actions and other developments in the field of money and finance.

4.8 RBI's Promotional Role[2]

In addition to performing the traditional functions of a central bank discussed so far, the RBI, after India's independence in 1947, has been playing an active role in two main directions : (a) in building up and strengthening the country's financial infrastructure, filling up major institutional gaps through the setting up of new financial institutions and reorganizing the existing ones in the context of changing development and other policy needs of the economy and (b) in devising new measures for influencing the allocation of credit in socially-desired directions. In the discharge of its promotional role, the RBI has several accomplishments to its credit and is continuously engaged in the performance of several non-traditional tasks. In this section, only a few of them will be briefly discussed, while others either only listed or briefly summed up, as they have been discussed elsowhere in the book. In the latter cases, appropriate references have been readily provided.

4.8.1 Promotion of Commercial Banking

Under the Banking Regulation Act, 1949, vast powers of supervision and control of commercial banks have been vested in the RBI. The latter has tried to use these powers (a) to strengthen the commercial banking structure in the country through compulsory liquidation of weak banks or their amalgamation into stronger banks and through improvement in the operational standards of banks by regular inspection and general surveillance, (b) to extend banking facilities throughout the country, especially in small towns and rural areas so as to improve the geographical coverage of banks, and (c) to extend the functional coverage of banks so as to improve the sectoral distribution of bank credit in favour of the priority sectors such as agriculture, small-scale industries, etc. (see Section 6.3.) and make more of it available to small borrowers (see Section 4.8.8.). The RBI has also arranged for the education and training of different categories of banking personnel.

To inspire greater public confidence in bank deposits and thereby spread banking habit in the country, particularly among the people of small means, insurance of deposits with commercial banks was introduced in January 1962 and a *Deposit Insurance Corporation*[4] was set up for the purpose as a subsidiary of the RBI. In later years the scheme of deposit insurance has been gradually extended to eligible co-operative banks and regional rural banks as well. The amount of deposit eligible for insurance cover in respect of each depositor in each bank has also been revised upward from time to time. On July 1, 1990 it was fixed at Rs. 30,000. At the end of June 1995, 70% of total assessable deposits (of Rs. 4,09,000 crores) of commercial and co-operative banks were insured.

4.8.2 **Promotion of Co-operative Banking.** See Section 7.7.

4.8.3 **Promotion of Bill Market.** See Sections 3.6 and 3.7.

4.8.4 **Credit to Priority Sectors.** See Section 6.3.

4.8.5 **Promotion of Rural (Agricultural) Credit**

The provision of adequate amounts of institutional credit for agricultural and other rural activities was recognized as one of the special responsibilities of the RBI even at the time of its birth and appropriate provisions were made to this effect in the Reserve Bank of India Act, 1934, a separate Agricultural Credit Department of the Bank constituted, and the development of co-operative credit movement (which from its inception in 1904 has remained a rural or agricultural movement) made the Bank's special charge. Much was not done in this sphere till about the mid 50s, when, on the recommendation of the All-India Rural Credit Survey Committee (1954), the (then) Imperial Bank of India and other state-associated banks were nationalised and converted into the State Bank of India and associate banks. This group was made responsible for a vigorous programme of branch expansion in rural areas with a view to provide rural credit as well as mobilise rural savings. This strategy got a further fillip with the nationalisation of 14 other major commercial banks in July 1969 (Section 6.2.1.). Other important developments in this field have been the operations of the Agricultural Refinance and Development Corporation (a wholly-owned subsidiary of the RBI, 1963-82); strengthening of the co-operative credit organisation and provision of increasing amount of RBI's refinance to it on concessional terms (Section 7.7); setting up of regional rural banks (Section 5.3), and channeling of increasing amounts of commercial bank credit to agriculture as a priority sector (*see* Section 6.3). With the setting up of the National Bank for Agriculture and Rural Development in July 1982 to oversee the entire rural credit system and the take over of the ARDC by it, the direct role and responsibility of the RBI in this sphere have been substantially reduced (*see* Section 8.6).

As a result of the measures listed above and increasing emphasis on the provision of institutional finance for agriculture, the picture of such finance has been undergoing rapid changes in favour of agriculture, especially after the nationalisation of 14 major commercial banks in July 1969. The latest position is summed up in Table 4.1. (See also Section 6.3). We may note for comparison that at the end of March 1995 total gross scheduled commercial bank credit outstanding was Rs. 1,93,000 crores, about 39% of which had gone to industry.

Table 4.1

Institutional Finance for Agriculture

(at the end of March 1994)

Loans Outstanding

(Rs. in crores)

	Source of Finance	*Direct Finance*	*Indirect Finance*	*Total*
1.	Co-operatives	14,400	2,600	17,000
2.	Scheduled commercial banks	19,100	2,100	21,200
3.	Regional rural banks	2,000	—	2,000
4.	State governments	—	—	—
5.	Rural Electrification Corporation	—	5,700	5,700
6.	Total	35,500	19,400	45,900

SOURCE: RBI, Report on Currency and Finance, 1994-95 Vol. I, Tables V-12 and V-13.

4.8.6. Promotion of Industrial Finance

While with some change in the credit policy of commercial banks, the short-term credit needs of large-scale industries could be taken care of relatively easily, the need for special measures was specially acute in two spheres: (*a*) the provision of long-term development finance and (*b*) bank credit for small-scale industries. In both the spheres on the active advice and participation of the RBI special measures have been successfully taken. For providing long-and medium-term finance as well as underwriting of new issues, specialised financial institutions in the form of industrial development banks such as the IDBI, IFCI, ICICI, SIDBI, SFCs and SIDCs have been established in the public sector and the ICICI in the private sector (see Chapter 8). The RBI subscribed to the share capital of public sector development banks. It provides them loans from its *National Industrial Credit (Long-Term Operations) Fund* to which the RBI makes annual contributions from its profits. Started in July 1968 with an initial contribution of only Rs. 10 crore, the Fund had grown to Rs. 5,678 crore on June 30, 1995 and the loans and advances from it stood at Rs. 5,460 crore.

For the small-scale industries, finance is made available by SIDBI, SFCs, and SIDCs (see Chapter 8) and more importantly by commercial banks which are the most important source of credit to them. The recognition of small-scale industries as a 'priority sector' has made all the difference. At the end of June 1995, credit outstanding to these industries from public sector banks stood at Rs. 26,800 crore which was about 40% of the total priority sector advances (excluding export credit). Additionally, this finance is provided on concessional terms. One important measure in the promotion of credit to small-scale industries has been the Credit Guarantee Scheme for such industries instituted in 1960 and operated by the RBI on behalf of the Government of India (see Section 4.8.9).

4.8.7 Promotion of Export Finance[3]

(i) Various steps have been taken to provide export credit at internationally competitive rates of interest. For example, a scheme was made operative in October 1993 for rediscounting export bills abroad at rates linked to international interest rates. Under another scheme of November 1993, exporters are given pre-shipment credit in major foreign currencies for financing imports. The RBI provides export credit refinance limits to banks. On March end 1995, they were Rs. 9,400 crore. Export credit refinance limits for post-shipment credit was about Rs. 6,700 crore during 1994-95. Moreover, the rate of interest on export credit has been decontrolled.

The percentage outstanding export credit to net bank credit was 9.3 per cent as on March end 1995. But, the percentage of export credit refinance limits of banks to their outstanding export credit eligible for such refinance was 48 per cent.

(ii) *Export-Import Bank.* The government has set up in January 1981 an *Export-Import Bank*, which has taken over the functions of the international financing wing of the IDBI and which acts as the apex institution relating to financing of foreign trade (see Section 8.5).

4.8.8 Credit to Weaker Sections

Providing adequate, cheaper, and timely credit to weaker sections is the hardest nut to crack for the policy-makers. The inherent difficulty of the task will be analysed in Chapter 16 and Section 20.6. The two measures in this respect taken by the RBI are: (*a*) the establishment of the Credit Guarantee Corporation of India in 1971 (merged into the Deposit Insurance Corporation in July 1978) and (*b*) the adoption of the Differential Rate of Interest (DRI) Scheme in 1972. The two measures are discussed successively in the next two subsections. (See also relevant parts of Section 6.3.2).

4.8.9 Credit Guarantees

One of the important tasks assigned to the RBI has been to channelise increasing proportion of bank credit in favour of designated priority sectors and small borrowers. Among other things, one major reason for reluctance of banks to provide credit to such priority borrowers has been 'excessive' degree of credit risk involved in lending to them. Traditional theory would suggest that the free working of market forces will determine appropriate market rate of interest including risk premium for each category of borrowers and that at such rates of interest all borrowers, priority or otherwise, will get as much credit as they would be willing to have. But the market for institutional credit in actual life does not function in this way. The lending rate of interest is officially determined. In such event, high-risk borrowers are simply rationed out and not given credit at higher rates of interest (see Section 16.4).

An alternative way out is provided by institutional measures that cover the risk of lending agencies. The risk coverage is organized by applying the principle of insurance of pooling individual risks, so that the statistical law of large numbers reduces substantially the credit risk per unit of credit. This kind of risk coverage has been attempted mainly in the form of credit guarantees. Three separate credit guarantee schemes are now in operation. Their main common feature is to provide guarantees to banks against risk of default of credit extended to designated borrowers eligible for the guarantee cover, the guarantee cover varying form 66.66% to 100% of the credit under defualt. The three schemes are explained briefly below.

(i) *Credit Guarantee Scheme for Small Scale Industries.* To encourage institutional lending to small-scale industries, the Government of India, in consultation with the RBI, introduced a Credit Guarantee Scheme in July 1960 for the guarantee of advances granted by banks and other credit institutions to these industries. The task of administering the Scheme was entrusted to the RBI as the agent of the Central Government. The scope and provisions of the Scheme have been liberalised from time to time. It extends to all types of credit facilities allowed to small-scale industrial units. The guarantee facilities are available at a small charge to approved credit institutions, including commercial and co-operative banks, regional rural banks, and state financial corporations. Besides, the RBI and the IDBI offer preferential refinance facilities to scheduled commercial banks in respect of short-term lending to small-scale industries covered by the guarantee scheme.

(*ii*) *Credit Guarantee Corporation of India.* The Credit Guarantee Scheme for small-scale industries did not solve the problem of meagre availability of institutional credit to weaker sections of small transport operators, traders, artisans, self-employed persons, small business enterprises, farmers and agriculturists, etc. Such small borrowers are much less acceptable credit risks to banks than small-scale industries. Therefore, the RBI, realizing the need for encouraging greater flow of bank credit to small borrowers, established in January 1971 the Credit Guarantee Corporation of India (CGCI) to provide guarantee cover to approved banks in respect of loans and advances to small borrowers. In July 1978 this Corporation was merged with the Deposit Insurance Corporation which has been renamed as Deposit Insurance and Credit Guarantee Corporation.

(*iii*) *Export Credit and Guarantee Corporation (ECGC).* This Corporation, established by the Government of India in 1964, is under the administrative control of the government, and not of the RBI. We are studying it in this chapter, as a part of its business is that of issuing credit guarantees. The guarantees are offered to banks and other financial institutions against risk involved in providing export credit, whether in respect of pre-shipment or post-shipment of goods. The guarantees have been designed to encourage banks to give liberal credit and other facilities for exports. Besides, the ECGC provides insurance covers to exporters against the risk of not receiving payments in respect of export of goods and services.

4.8.10 Differential Rate of Interest (DRI) Scheme

The Scheme has been in operation since 1972. But its progress has been very slow. At the end of June 1995, the advances outstanding under the Scheme from all public sector banks stood at about Rs. 700 crore, constituting 0.33% of their total advances as against the target of 1%. The advances covered about 23 lakh accounts. About 60% of these advances had gone to members of scheduled castes/scheduled tribes. They showed a very high percentage of over-dues to demand. Such schemes can provide only marginal help to the needy. Much more important are package measures that combine credit facilities with the provision of information, training, inputs, and marketing.

Due to the well-publicised securities-bank scam, 1992 has turned out to be a very trying year for the RBI. The Scam has exposed RBI's poor supervision of banks, and its own public debt office, responsible for recording transactions in Government of India securities worth thousands of crore rupees per day. Several accusing fingers have been raised against the RBI's demonstrated incompetence, shallow vigilance and the like.

NOTES

1. See Section 20.3 for further developments.
2. Also see Appendix H.
3. Also see Section 6.3.2 (5) for export credit.

CHAPTER 5

Commercial Banks—I

Commercial banks are the single most important source of institutional credit in India. In the present chapter we study their functions and major items of their liabilities and assets. Other aspects of commercial banking will be taken up in the next chapter. Co-operative banks will be discussed in Chapter 7 and development banks in Chapter 8.

5.1 **What is a Bank?**

A bank is an institution that accepts deposits of money from the public withdrawable by cheque and used for lending. Thus, there are two essential functions which make a financial institution a bank: (1) acceptance of chequable deposits (of money) from the public and (2) lending. The former is its unique or most distinctive function. Three things about deposits are noteworthy: *(i)* they are deposits of money and not of goods or non-money financial assets; *(ii)* deposits are accepted from the public at large and not merely from its shareholders or members; *(iii)* the deposits are repayable on demand and withdrawable by cheque, *i.e.,* the deposits are demand deposits as defined in Section 1.4 above. The second essential function relates to the use of deposits. They are used for lending to others, and not for financing its own business of any kind (say manufacturing or trade). In fact, as bank (under the Banking Regulation Act, 1949) is not allowed to carry on any such business (other than that of banking). The word lending is used here broadly to include both direct lending to borrowers and indirect lending through investment in open-market securities.

The above discussion implies that neither of the functions alone is sufficient to earn an institution the status of a bank (in the modern sense of the term). Thus, acceptance of chequable deposits from the public is only a necessary, but not a sufficient, function of a bank. It must also lend to others. For this reason, Post Office savings banks are not banks in the accepted sense of a bank, even though some of them accept chequable deposists. The reason they are not banks in the ordinary sense of the term (and are called savings banks) is that they do not perform the other essential function of a bank—that of lending to others. The Post Office savings banks are run as departmental agencies of the Central Government, and all the funds deposited with them are in fact lent to the Government, their owner.

Similarly, lending alone does not make a financial institution a bank. In fact, leaving out Post Office savings banks, all other financial institutions do the work of lending to others. But only those of them are banks that also accept chequable deposits them. All others are non-bank financial institutions. The examples are the LIC, UTI, the IDBI, etc. We shall study about them in later chapters.

Banks are said to be department stores of financial services as they render a wide variety of such services to their customers. The range of these services differs from bank to bank, depending mainly on the size and type of banks. So far we have highlighted only two of them, because, in combination, they are the necessary services which a bank as a bank must perform. They are also the two most important functions of a bank. We sum up briefly below the main services which banks in India generally perform. This should help appreciate the role which banks play in the economic life of the country.

The main banking services are :

1. Acceptance of money on deposit from the public. As explained already in Section 1.4, broadly speaking, these deposits are of three main types, viz., current, savings and fixed, which can be reclassified under two main heads of demand and time deposits. For attracting small savings into deposits, banks have introduced several special deposit schemes tailored for various types of depositors and some linked with insurance and other benefits. But the bulk of their deposits continue to be held in the traditional forms of deposits;

2. Grant of credit to *all* sectors of the economy, and not merely to trade and commerce as the designation *commercial* banks might suggest.[1] This is done in various forms such as loans and advances, discounting of bills, and investment in open-market securities, both government and private. These several forms will be discussed in the next chapter.

3. Collection of cheques, drafts, bills, hundis, and other instruments (inland and foreign) for their depositors;

4. Issue of performance and financial guarantees;

5. Provision of remittance facilities by issue of drafts, mail transfers, and telegraphic transfers;

6. Provision of facilities of safe custody of deeds and securities and safe deposit vaults;

7. Purchase and sale of securities for their constituents;

8. Provision of special investment services as underwriters and bankers for new issues of securities to the public. In selected cases, banks also arrange for the private placement of securities;

9. Acting as executors and trustees;

10. Rendering of agency services of various kinds such as that of sale of national savings certificates, units of the UTI, purchase and sale of foreign exchange, acceptance of income-tax payments, etc.;

11. Miscellaneous services such as the issue of travellers cheques, gift cheques, provision of tax assistance and investment advice, etc.

5.2 Classification of Commercial Banks

Commercial banks in India are largely Indian (both public sector and private sector), with a few foreign banks. The Indian banks are those which have been incorporated in India and so have their head offices in India. Foreign banks, on the other hand, have been incorporated in foreign countries and have their head offices outside India. The bulk of Indian banking business is in the hands of Indian banks. But foreign banks also occupy a place of importance in the Indian banking industry, especially in the financing of foreign trade and in the field of merchant banking (i.e. underwriting and promotion of new capital issues). Large Indian banks also have their branches abroad. So their total business comprises business in India and business abroad.

The public-sector banks constitute the dominant part of commercial banking in India. The government entered the field with the nationalisation of the (then) Imperial Bank of India in 1955 and its conversion into the State Bank of India from 1 July 1955. In addition to itself, this bank has seven other State Banks as its subsidiaries. Together they constitute a very large group of eight banks and dominate commercial banking in India. In July 1969, fourteen other large banks and in April 1980 six more banks were nationalised giving a total of 28 such banks in the public sector. Together they control more than 90 per cent of total bank deposits.

5.3 The Regional Rural Banks

The regional rural banks are the newest form of banks that have been set up in the country on the sponsorship of individual nationalised commercial banks. At the end of March 1994, they numbered 196, with about 14,500 branches covering 408 districts.

These banks have been set up with the express objective of developing the rural economy by providing credit and other facilities for agriculture and other productive activities of all kinds in rural areas. The main emphasis is supposed to be on the provision of such facilities to small and marginal farmers, agricultural labourers, rural artisans, and other small entrepreneurs working in rural areas. Other special features of these banks are: (i) the area of operation of each rural bank has been limited to a specified region comprising one or more districts in any state; (*ii*) the lending rates of these banks cannot be higher than the prevailing lending rates of co-operative credit societies in any particular state; and (*iii*) the salary structure of the employees of these banks has been fixed in consonance with the salary structure of the employees of the state government and local authorities of comparable level and status in the bank's area of operation.

The paid-up capital of each rural bank is Rs. 25 lakhs, 50 per cent of which has been contributed by the Central Government, 15 per cent by the state government concerned and 35 per cent by the sponsoring public-sector commercial banks, which are also responsible for the actual setting up of RRBs. Thus, the latter are also public sector banks.

At the end of April 1995, their total deposits (mostly savings and fixed) were of about Rs. 8,800 crore and advances outstanding (more than 90% of them to weaker sections) were of about Rs. 5,260 crore. Their lending operations suffer from the problem of very high percentage of overdues.

They are helped by higher-level agencies in various ways. The sponsoring banks lend them funds and advise and train their senior staff; the NABARD gives them short-term and medium term loans, the RBI has kept the CRR for them at 3% and SLR at 25% of their total net liabilities, whereas for other commercial banks the respective minimum required ratios have been varied over time (see ch. 19).

The RRB are a step in the right direction—a step towards the proper implementation of multi-agency approach to credit in rural areas. But right from the beginning their viability has been posing a serious problem. To become (and stay) viable and play the important role of small man's credit institutes assigned to them, these banks will have to exert hard to build up efficient credit delivery and supervision system so as to reduce their high overdues and not let them (overdues) grow too much and establish an adequate liason system with various development and marketing agencies at the local level.

5.4 Liabilities and Assets of Banks

Banks as financial intermediaries deal mainly in financial assets. This fact shows up well in their balance sheets—in statements of their liabilities and assets at a point of time. A consolidated statement of the liabilities and assets of all (202) reporting scheduled commercial banks for the year-end 1987 is given in Table 5.1. These are the latest available data. They are inclusive of inter-bank credits and debits as well as of foreign business of

Table 5.1
Liabilities and Assets of Scheduled Commercial Banks (Main Items) at end of March 1995

	(*Rs. crores*)
A. Liabilities	
1. Paid-up capital and Reserves[1]	
2. Deposits:	3,87,000
(*i*) Time	3,10,000
(*ii*) Demand	77,000
3. Borrowings	7,600
4. Other liabilities	32,400
Total Liabilities	4,27,000
B. Assets	
1. Cash in hand and with RBI	63,000
2. Money at call and short notice	3,000
3. Investments	1,49,000
4. Loans, advances, and bills discounted and purchased	2,12,000
Total assets	4,27,000

SOURCE: RBI, *Report on Currency and Finance,* 1994-95, Vol. II, Statement 56. (Figures rounded off liberally.)

Indian banks. The table shows (*a*) that banks raise the bulk of their funds by selling deposits—their dominant liability, and (*b*) that they hold their assets largely in the form of (*i*) loans and advances and bills discounted and purchased, together constituting bank credit, (*ii*) investment, and (*iii*) cash. A brief explanation of the main items of liabilities and assets is offered below.

5.4.1 Liabilities of Banks

1. *Capital and Reserves*[1]. Together they constitute owned funds of banks. Capital represents paid-up capital, *i.e.,* the amount of share capital actually contributed by owners (shareholders) of banks. Reserves are

retained earnings or undistributed profits of banks accumulated over their working lives. The law requires that such reserves are built up and that not all the earned profits are distributed among the shareholders. The banks also find it prudent to build up reserves to improve their capital position, so as to meet better unforeseen liabilities or unexpected losses. Reserves should be distinguished from 'provisions' made for redeeming known liabilities and affecting known reductions in the value of certain assets. Since, for various reasons, exact amounts of these liabilities and losses may not be known at the time of preparing the annual balance sheet, adequate 'provision' for them is essential, both under the law and for business prudence. Banks also maintain what are known as 'secret reserves' to further strengthen their capital position. As the name amply suggests, these reserves are kept secret from the public and not reported in the balance sheet. Profits are the unallocated surplus or the retained earnings of the year, which get added on to the reserves of the following year.

The owned funds constitute a small source of funds for banks, the principal source being deposits of the public. This is unlike an industrial undertaking for which the owners provide a much larger proportion of total funds used in business. Since banks risk other people's money in carrying on their business, they call for effective regulation by the authorities. The chief function of owned funds is to provide a cushion against losses suffered by a bank and thus some protection to its depositors and other creditors. Since 1962 the burden of protecting the deposits of individual depositors (upto a maximum of Rs. 30,000 of each deposit since July 1980) is borne by the Deposit Insurance and Credit Guarantee Corporation (see Section 4.8.9). The nationalisation of major commercial banks has further reduced the importance of owned funds in this direction.

2. *Deposits.* Deposits from the public are the principal source of funds with banks. We have already described above the various kinds of deposits banks 'sell' to the public (*see* Section 1.4). The growth of total deposits and deposits of various kinds along with factors determining such growth will be discussed in Section 6.2.7.

At the present level of financial development in India, banks are the premier financial institution. Deposit mobilisation by them remains the most important (though not the only) form of mobilisation of savings of the public. Therefore, to the extent the promotion and mobilisation of savings is a necessary prerequisite for stepping up the rate of economic growth, mobilisation by banks *in real terms* must be given its due weight.

3. *Borrowings.* Banks as a whole borrow from the RBI, the IDBI, the NABARD, and from the non-bank financial institutions (the LIC, the UTI, the GIC and its subsidiaries, and the ICICI) that are permitted to lend by the RBI in the inter-bank call money market (see Section 3.3). Individual banks

borrow from each other as well through the call money market and otherwise. The borrowing facilities from the RBI will be discussed in Section 19.6 and from the IDBI and the NABARD in Chapter 8.

4. *Other Liabilities.* They are miscellaneous items of various descriptions such as bills payable, etc.

Then there are *participation certificates*, a new form of issuing banks' liability (not shown in Table 5.1) about which we study in the next sub-section.

5.4.2 **Participation Certificates** (PCs).

The PCs are a new form of credit instrument whereby banks can raise funds from other banks and other RBI-approved financial institutions such as the LIC, the UTI, the GIC and subsidiaries, and the ICICI. Formally, a PC is a deed of transfer through which a bank, sells or transfers to a third party (transferee) a part or all of a loan made by it to its client (borrower). It is called a participation certificate because through it the PC holder participates in a bank loan, and so also in the interest, the security of the loan, and any risk of default on a proportionate basis. The actual management of the loan stay with the bank. For its services of loan-making, follow-up, and recovery of the loan, the bank charges a fee.

The PC Scheme is supervised by the RBI. It was started on an experimental basis in July 1970. For seven years, it was extended from year-to-year. It was made permanent in July 1977 and all scheduled commercial banks were permitted to sell PCs. The RBI fixes the maximum rate of interest at which PCs can be issued to non-banks, which has been kept at 10% per year since 1978-79. The PCs to non-banks have a fixed term to maturity of 30, 60, 90 or 180 days. The RBI has not permitted maturity of less than 30 days and more than 180 days of such PCs. However, there are no restrictions on the period of the PCs issued to other commercial banks or on the rate of interest paid on them.

The PCs are an important device for (*a*) making maximum use of funds within the commercial banking system for making loans and advances, especially to large borrowers, and (*b*) attracting short-term funds of approved non-bank financial institutions (NBFIs) into the market for bank credit. The RBI does not publish data giving out how much PC finance is inter-bank and how much of it is contributed by NBFIs.

The significance of each of the two roles of PCs is explained briefly. The participation arrangements among banks lead to fuller utilisation of loanable funds of the banking system as a whole, as they make possible the use of surplus funds of some banks to finance partly the loan portfolio of other banks. This evens out liquidity within the banking system. For all the banks, it is a helpful development, because surplus banks get commercially profitable outlets for their surplus funds and deficit banks are not forced to the RBI's loan window and yet meet the credit demands of their borrowers.

All this sounds very good. But, truly speaking, participation arrangements work mainly to the benefit of big borrowers and to the detriment of small borrowers. The participation arrangement is basically a variant of *consortium banking* under which a few banks get together (form a consortium) to finance a big loan on participation basis. This makes the financing of big loans easier. Instead of a big borrower going to several banks and raising funds from them individually, under participation arrangement, a single bank makes the loan and raises funds from other approved sources to finance the loan. The loss to small borrowers from such arrangements is neither direct nor apparent. It is indirect. It occurs because surplus banks are now able to channel their surplus funds into big loans made by other banks. In the absence of this facility they would have taken pains to develop their own loan portfolio and tried to reach new and small borrowers, who suffer maximum from credit rationing. This particular implication of inter-bank PCs has not received the RBI's attention it deserves.

The NBFIs permitted to buy PCs from banks are all term-financing institutions. They have no arrangements of their own to make short-term advances. The PCs permit them to enter the market of short-term bank credit at attractive rates of interest and without worrying about actual loan-making and management. Theoretically, the approved term-financing institutions invest only their short-term surpluses in PCs. But, in practice, the PCs have also led to the diversion of long-term funds into them on a continuing basis through renewal of maturing PCs. How important is this diversion is hard to say. Nevertheless, it must be asked at this stage: how far is it advisable to allow the diversion of long-term funds for short-term credit on a regular basis? Is it the case that there is an excess supply of long-term investment funds in the economy as a whole or is it the case that only the large-scale industrial sector is suffering from the surfeit of such funds?

The availability of short-term funds from the said NBFIs can create problems of monetary/credit control for the RBI, since during a period of inflation a part of speculative inventory build-up can be financed by these funds through the agency of banks. The experience of 1977–79 confirmed it as the PCs outstanding had increased from Rs. 233 crores at the end of May 1977 to Rs. 646 crores two years after. The RBI has not found such large and rapidly growing use of extra-banking resources through the banking industry consistent with credit planning and control. Therefore, during 1979 it brought the PCs also under the purview of the SLR (Statutory Liquidity Ratio) and CRR (Cash Reserve Requirement). Formerly, the PCs were treated as only 'contingent liabilities' of the issuing banks, and so did not attract the SLR or the CRR imposed on banks by the RBI. Under the new rules of the RBI *(a)* the PCs are now treated as deposits of the issuing banks; *(b)* as such, they are subject to the SLR/CRR requirements as in the case of other deposit liabilities. Further, the amount of PCs issued is not to be excluded from the figure of their total advances by the issuing banks, as was the practice earlier. This now gives a truer picture of their advances to various parties and also of their credit deposit ratios. The banks purchasing the PCs now do *not* include them in their advances, but show them under 'advances to banks', *i.e.* due from banks. Subsequently (in March 1980) the RBI also advised banks to bring about a significant and lasting reduction in their recourse to PCs. As a result of these control measures, the PCs now have lost some importance as a source of funds to banks.

5.4.3 Assets of Banks

Banks, like other business firms, are profit-making institutions, though public-sector banks are also guided by broader social directives from the RBI. To earn a profit, a bank must place its funds in earning assets, mainly loans and advances and investments. While lending or investing, a bank must look at the net rate of return obtained and the associated risks of holding such earning assets. Furthermore, since a large part of its liabilities are payable in cash on demand, a bank must also consider the liquidity of its earning assets, that is, how easily it can convert its earning assets into cash at short notice and without loss. Thus, the twin considerations of profitability and liquidity guide a bank in the selection of its asset portfolio. A bank tries to achieve the twin objectives by choosing a diversified and balanced asset portfolio in the light of institutional facilities available to it for converting its earning assets into cash at short notice and without loss and for short-term borrowing. In addition, it has also to observe various statutory requirements regarding cash reserves, liquid assets, and loans and advances. We describe below various classes of assets banks hold. They will also describe the uses of bank funds. They are discussed in the decreasing order of liquidity and increasing order of profitability.

1. *Cash.* Cash, defined broadly, includes cash in hand and balances with other banks including the RBI. Banks hold balances with the RBI as they are required statutorily to do so under the cash reserve requirement (see Section 4.4). Such balances are called statutory or required reserves. Besides, banks hold voluntarily extra cash to meet the day-to-day drawals of it by their depositors.

Cash as defined above is not the same thing as cash reserves of banks. The latter includes only cash in hand with banks and their balances with the RBI only. The balances with other banks in whatever account are not counted as cash reserves. The latter concept (of cash reserves) is useful for money-supply analysis and monetary policy, where we need to separate the monetary liabilities of the authorities from the monetary liabilities of banks. Inter-bank balances are not a part of the monetary liabilities of the monetary authority, whereas cash reserves are. These balances are only the liabilities of banks to each other. So, they are not included in cash reserves.

2. *Money at Call at Short Notice.* It is money lent to other banks, stock brokers, and other financial institutions for a very short period varying from 1 to 14 days. Banks place their surplus cash in such loans to earn some interest without straining much their liquidity. If cash position continues to be comfortable, call loans may be renewed day after day.

3. *Investments.* They are investments in securities usually classified under three heads of *(a)* government securities, *(b)* other approved securities and *(c)* other securities. Government securities are securities of both the central and state government including treasury bills, treasury deposit certificates, and postal obligations such as national plan certificates, national savings certificates, etc. Other approved securities are securities approved under the provisions of the Banking Regulation Act, 1949. They include securities of state-associated bodies such as electricity boards, housing boards, etc., debentures of LDBs, units of the UTI, shares of RRBs, etc.

A large part of the investment in government and other approved securities is required statutorily under the SLR requirement of the RBI (see Section 19.8). Any excess investment in these securities is held because banks can borrow from the RBI or others against these securities as collateral or sell them in the market to meet their need for cash. Thus, they are held by banks because they are more liquid than loans and advances even though the return from them is lower than from loans and advances.

4. *Loans, Advances and Bills Discounted or Purchased.* They are the principal component of bank assets and the main source of income of banks. Collectively, they represent total 'bank credit' (to the commercial sector. We have already studied about bills in Section 3.5. Nothing more need be added here. bank advances in India are usually made in the form of cash credit and overdrafts. Loans may be demand loans or term loans. They may be repayable in single or many instalments. We explain briefly these *various forms of extending bank credit.*

(a) Cash Credit. In India cash credit is the main form of bank credit. Under cash credit arrangements, an acceptable borrower is first sanctioned a *credit limit* upto which he may borrow from the bank. But the actual utilization of the credit limit is governed by the borrower's '*withdrawing power*'. The sanction of the credit limit is based on the overall creditworthiness of the borrower as assessed by the bank. The 'withdrawing power', on the other hand, is determined by the value of the borrower's current assets, adjusted for margin requirements as applicable to these assets. The current assets comprise mainly stocks of goods (raw materials, semi-manufactured and finished goods) and receivables or bills due from others. A borrower is required to submit a 'stock statement' of these assets every month to the bank. This statement is supposed to act partly as evidence of the on-going production/trade activity of the borrower and partly to act as a legal document with the bank, which may be used in case of default of bank advances. To cover further against the risk of default, banks impose 'margin requirements' on borrowers, that is, they require borrowers to finance a part of their current assets (offered as primary security to banks) from their owned funds of other sources. (In addition, banks ask for second surety for whatever credit is granted.) The advances made by banks cover only the rest (on average, the maximum of about 75 per cent) of the value of the primary security. The margin requirements vary from good to good, time to time, and with the credit standing of the borrower. The RBI uses variations in these requirements as an instrument of credit control. In case of acute shortage of particular commodities, bank financing against the inventories of such commodities can be curtailed by raising the margin requirements for such commodities. Keeping in view the importance of the cash credit system in banking in India, a separate section (5.5) will be devoted in full to its evaluation.

(b) Overdrafts. An overdraft, as the name suggests, is an advance given by allowing a customer to overdraw his current account upto an agreed limit. The overdraft facility is allowed on only current accounts. The security for an overdraft account may be personal,

shares, debentures, government securities, life insurance policies, or fixed deposits. An overdraft account is operated in the same way as a current account. The overdraft credit is different from cash credit in two respects of security and duration. Usually, for cash credit, the security offered is current assets of business, such as inventories of raw materials, goods in process or finished goods, and receivables. In the case of overdraft, the security is generally in the form of financial assets held by the borrower. Then, generally, the overdraft is a temporary facility, whereas the cash credit account is a longer-run facility. Also, the rate of interest on overdraft credit is somewhat lower than on cash credit because of the difference in risk and servicing cost involved. In all other respects, overdraft credit is like cash credit. In the case of overdrafts, too, interest is charged only on credit actually utilised, not on the overdraft limit granted.

(c) Demand Loans. A demand loan is one that can be recalled on demand. It has no stated maturity. Such loans are mostly taken by security brokers and others whose credit needs fluctuate from day to day. The salient feature of a loan is that the entire amount of the loan sanctioned is paid to the borrower in one lump sum by crediting the whole amount to a separate loan account. Thus, the whole amount becomes immediately chargeable to interest, whatever the amount the borrower actually withdraws from the (loan) account. This makes loan credit costlier to the borrower than (say) cash credit. Therefore, businessmen in need of supplementing their working capital prefer to borrow on cash credit basis. On the other hand, banks prefer demand loans, because they are repayable on demand, involve lower administrative costs, and earn interest on the full amount sanctioned and paid. The security against demand loans may also be personal, financial assets, or goods.

(d) Term Loans. A term loan is a loan with a fixed maturity period of more than one year. Generally this period is not longer than ten years. Term loans provide medium-or long-term funds to the borrowers. Most such loans are secured loans. Like demand loans, the whole amount of a term loan sanctioned is paid in one lump sum by crediting it to a separate loan account of the borrower. Thus, the entire amount becomes chargeable to interest. The repayment is made as scheduled, either in one instalment at the maturity of the loan or in a few instalments after a certain agreed period. For making big term loans (of say, Rs. one crore or more) to big borrowers, banks have started using the consortium method of financing in a few cases. Under this method, a few banks get together to make the loan on

participation basis. This obviates the dependence on multiple banking under which a borrower borrows from more than one bank to meet his credit needs. Consortium banking can make for better credit planning. Term loans as a form of bank credit are gaining rapidly in importance.

5.5. **Evaluation of the Cash Credit System**

The cash credit system of extending bank credit has been a subject of much debate. The current efforts at its reform will be discussed in the next section. In this section we study its pros and cons from the point of view of borrowers, banks, and credit planning. From the borrowers' point of view the cash credit system has certain highly desirable features, given below.

(1) Within the agreed limit and subject to the 'withdrawing power' the borrower is free to draw upon his credit account any number of times according to his needs and convenience. He is also free to repay into the account as frequently as he likes. All this makes cash credit highly flexible.

(2) Interest is payable only on the net amount of credit actually utilised and not on the limit granted.

(3) The securities furnished by the customer can be varied according to the amount withdrawn. He is also free to replace one kind of security by another of equal value.

(4) Though legally cash credit is a short-term advance repayable on demand and secured by current assets, in practice, it acts as a continuous borrowing account the level of which is renewed from time to time depending on the performance of the unit.

From the point of view of banks and credit planning, the cash credit system suffers from serious drawbacks given below.

(1) A bank has no control over the actual level of its cash credit advances. All that it controls is the total amount of cash credit limits. The actual utilitsation of these limits is decided by the borrowers.

(2) Under the cash credit system the task of cash management is passed on by the borrower to the bank. The borrower can credit his surplus cash from day to day to his cash credit account, thus reduce the outstanding balance in the account, and save on his interest cost to the bank. Looked at in another way, the borrower thereby nationally earns interest on whatever short-run surplus funds he generates and at the same rate as the lending rate of banks—a rate of return not easily available to him elsewhere in the economy. On the other hand, the bank has to find ways and means of promptly utilising these surplus

funds so as not to suffer a loss of interest income.

In the opposite situation, too, the flexibility of the cash credit system generates uncertainties for individual banks. Normally, a bank 'oversells' its credit, that is, grants more credit limits than it can honour, because it knows from experience that not all the limits get actually utilised. But, at times, there can be sudden spurts in their utilisation. Then, a bank has to go out scurrying for funds in the money market.

(3) The cash credit system militates against restrictive credit policies of the RBI. The system of credit limits has an in-built bias towards providing surplus or unutilised borrowing power to bank borrowers. Normally, this surplus borrowing (or drawing) power is quite substantial and is known to rise with credit limit. This surplus borrowing power gets drawn upon in a period of credit squeeze imposed by the RBI, unless the banks also follow suit immediately and cut down already sanctioned limits. Normally, however, banks find it difficult to do so in the face of customer resistance, despite the RBI's advice to this effect. First, the advice itself comes much too late, mostly after much damage has already been done and inflationary forces have taken hold of the situation. Second, the banks themselves are oftentimes reluctant to curtail their credit as this would eat into their interest income and annoy established borrowers who can legitimately argue that at higher prices their needs for nominal credit for holding even the old real amounts of inventories have gone up. In fact, the borrowers get mostly anxious to hold larger real amounts of inventories partly to gain from the expected price rise or to ensure at least for some time against the expected increase in the costs of their raw materials or their possible shortages.

(4) The cash credit system, as it operates, makes it difficult for banks to have any effective control over the end-use of credit. So long as a borrower maintains a certain level of inventories and other current assets and the account is fairly active (indicating that the current assets offered to the bank as primary security against the cash credit are not dead assets), the borrower is under no obligation to repay any part of the bank loan. He can use the advance as almost a permanent source of finance and can use it in whatever manner he likes, whether for speculative purposes, or for investment in the stock market, for acquiring controlling interests in new concerns or for purchasing fixed assets. Thus, the cash credit becomes a method of monetising a large part of bankable current assets.

(5) The cash credit system allows enough opportunity for a dishonest borrower to swindle a bank, because even with the best of intentions no bank can devise a fully fool-proof system of evaluation, inspection, and supervision of primary securities, without being unduly obstructive in day-to-day running of the business of its clients, and also increasing its own costs of loan-making and supervision.

(6) The cash credit system tends to favour big and established borrowers to the disadvantage of small and new borrowers. The former tend to pre-empt too large a part of the lending capacity of banks, leaving too little for the latter. In periods of credit squeeze, too, the latter suffer the impact of this squeeze relatively more than the former.

(7) The cash credit system leaves enough room for multiple finance, which results when a firm borrows simultaneously from several banks. If it were to route its entire business through one bank, the banker would be in a better position to exercise control over its borrowings. To escape such control or scrutiny or raise more funds, a customer may borrow from more than one bank. The practice is reported to be widely prevalent among large borrowers. Consortium banking with one bank acting as the leader, can greatly minimise the abuse resulting from multiple banking.

5.6 A New Simplified Loan System

This system was introduced in April 1995. For large borrowers (with assessed maximum permissible bank finance of Rs. 20 crore and above), the cash credit component was initially restricted to 75 per cent with a minimum loan component of 25 per cent for short-term working capital purposes, including commercial paper and bills. Since September 1995, the cash credit component has been reduced to 60 per cent and the loan component raised to 40 per cent. The ceiling on term loans has also been raised to Rs. 1,000 crore for projects involving expansion/modernisation of power generation capacities.

NOTES

1. Important developments have taken place concerning capitalisation of public sector banks after 1992-93. For example, under the new policy, in October 1993, the SBI raised over Rs. 3,200 crore by public issues of equity shares (with 10 per cent voting rights) and bonds. Thereby, the RBI shareholding has been reduced from 99 per cent to 66 per cent.

Similarly, other nationalised banks have also been allowed to assess the capital market for debt and equity.

Among other changes, it may be noted that 9 new private banks have already started functioning.

CHAPTER 6

Commercial Banks—II

6.1 Development of Commercial Banking Before Independence (1947)

Modern commercial banking made its beginning in India with the setting up of the first Presidency Bank, the Bank of Bengal, in Calcutta in 1806. Two other Presidency Banks were set up in Bombay and Madras in 1840 and 1843 respectively. They were private shareholders' banks, though the East India Company also contributed to the share capital of each of them. The bulk of the share capital had come from private shareholders, mostly Europeans. These banks were given monopoly of government banking. After 1823, they were also given the right of note issue. This right was, however, taken over by the government in 1862. They were amalgamated into the Imperial Bank of India in 1921, which was nationalised into the State Bank of India in 1955.

The Indian joint-stock banks have had a history of checkered growth from their inception till about the middle of the twentieth century. There were long periods of slow growth interspersed with short periods of rapid growth of bank formation, followed by banking crises which saw the failure of banks in large numbers. For example, during the period 1913-36, 480 banks failed and another 620 banks failed over a shorter period of 1937–48. Thus recurrent bank failures was the main feature of the growth of banking in India over this period. This was not peculiar to India as it was also the experience of most other countries in the early stage of banking development.

The victims of bank failures, most of the time, were small banks, which sprang up like mushrooms during periods of high economic activity and died soon thereafter. Several causes were responsible for these periodic failures. The main among them were insufficient paid-up capital and reserves and poor liquidity of assets, combination of trading with banking, reckless and injudicious lending (unrestricted loans to director and concerns in which they were interested and long-term loans of short-term deposits), speculative investments, incompetent and dishonest management, absence of a central bank to supervise, guide, and help other banks, and of suitable banking laws to regulate banking. The periodic failures of banks hampered greatly the growth of commercial banking in the country by hurting the public confidence in it.

Yet the period before the first World War did see the establishment of some banks which have grown into some of the large banks of today. We have already spoken of the three Presidency Banks of Calcutta, Bombay and Madras, which were later amalgamated into the Imperial Bank of India. The Allahabad Bank and the Punjab National bank were established in 1865 and 1894 respectively. Under the stimulus of the Swadeshi Movement some other large banks of to-day that got established between 1906 and 1913 are the Bank of India, the Central Bank of India, the Bank of Baroda, the Canara Bank, the Indian Bank, and the Bank of Mysore.

The major banking events of the inter-war period (1918–39), were the amalgamation of the three Presidency Banks into the Imperial Bank of India in 1921 and the establishment of the Reserve Bank of India in 1935 as the central bank of the country. The establishment of the Imperial Bank of India, with its large network of branches all over India, strong capital base, and conservative management, according to the principles of commercial banking, lent stature and strength to commercial banking in India. The setting up of the RBI filled a big gap in India's banking structure and met one of the necessary conditions for a healthy growth of banking in the country.

The progress of banking during the Second World War and its immediate aftermath was again characterised by over-rapid expansion and large-scale failure of banks. When India became independent in 1947, it inherited an extremely weak banking structure, with 640 banks of which only 96 were scheduled banks and the rest small non-scheduled banks. The banking facilities were heavily concentrated in metropolitan centres, cities, and port towns, with a very high proportion of total advances going to trade.

6.2. Major Developments in Commercial Banking after Independence

Several important developments have taken place in commercial banking, transforming it drastically, after India became a free country in 1947. They are discussed briefly in this section. Their quantitative measures since 1951 are summed up in Table 6.1. The significance of these measures will be commented upon in appropriate sub-sections in the sequel. The changes in the sectoral allocation of commercial bank credit deserve fuller discussion and so will be taken up in the next full section. (On the allocation of bank credit, see also Chapter 16.)

Table 6.1
Commercial Banks in India, 1951-94
End of year

		1951	1961	1969	1994
	(1)	(2)	(3)	(4)	(5)
1.	Number of Scheduled Banks (Reporting)	566	292	85	309*
2.	Number of Offices of banks in India	4,150	5,000	9,000	62,1000
3.	Population per office (in thousands)	87	88	60	14
4.	Total Deposits in India (Rs. crores at current prices)	908	2,0116	5,1735	3,87,000
	Time Deposits (% to total)	33	060	656	80
5.	Number of Employees (in thousands)	N.A.	115	220	1,000

N.A. = Not Available

* Includes 196 Regional Rural Banks

SOURCES : RBI, *Report on Currency and Finance,* 1994-95 Vol. II, Statement 56.

6.2.1 Nationalisation of Banks

The role of the public sector in commercial banking has been greatly enhanced through progressive nationalisation of banks. The first to be nationalised was the RBI, the country's central bank, from 1 January 1949. Then came the take over of the (then) Imperial Bank of India and its conversion into the State Bank of India in July 1955, the conversion of eight major state-associated banks into subsidiary banks of the SBI in 1959, merger of two such banks into one from the beginning of 1963, thus reducing the number of the associate banks to seven, nationalisation of 14 other major Indian scheduled banks in July 1969 and of 6 more in April 1980. The regional rural banks (see Section 5.3) from their inception are being set up in the public sector. As a result, the public-sector banks occupy a position of dominance in commercial banking in India. Among the public-sector banks, the SBI group of banks is the largest chain of commercial banks in the country, controlling more than a quarter of total bank deposits.

Two main tasks were set before the public-sector banks, namely, (*a*) mobilisation of deposits through a massive programme of branch expansion, especially in unbanked rural and semi-urban areas, and (*b*) diversification of bank credit to ensure flow of financial assistance to the neglected sectors and sections of the economy in an increasing measure. The progress made by the banking system in these (and some other directions) will be discussed later in the chapter.

6.2.2 **Regulation of Banks by the RBI**

The RBI has come to play an increasingly important role in the regulation, control, and development of banking in all its aspects. This has been made possible by the Banking Regulation Act (formerly called the Banking Companies Act), 1949 and its several amendments from time to time. Under the Act, the RBI has been vested with extensive powers of supervision and control over banks. These powers cover all important aspects of banking from the licensing of banks to their liquidation. The RBI has made good use of these powers and several of the features discussed below are, to a large extent, the result of the systematic exercise of these powers.

6.2.3 **Liquidation and Amalgamation of Banks**

The number of commercial banks has gone down considerably from 566 at the end of 1951 to 271 (including 188 RRBs) at the end of 1990 (see Table 6.1, row 1). This is a result of a deliberate policy of the RBI of systematic weeding out of substandard non-viable banks through delicensing and amalgamations and liquidations.

During World War II there had been a mushroom growth of small and ill-managed banks. They were a source of great weakness to the whole banking system. Their frequent failures were possibly the most important reason for the slow spread of banking habits among the public. Therefore, the strengthening of the banking system required a vigorous implementation of the aforesaid policy. This has not been an unmixed blessing. Whereas with the weeding out of the non-viable units, bank failures have now become a thing of the past—a great achievement, no doubt—the progressive replacement of small banks by large banks has denied the small borrower the special attention he used to get more easily from a small local bank. Moreover, a small local bank used to enjoy the advantage of adapting its working to the special conditions prevailing in the small area of its operation, which the branch of a big national bank managed under an all-India policy does not have.

6.2.4 **Branch Expansion**

The geographical coverage of banking facilities has improved markedly, especially after the nationalisation of 14 major banks in July 1969. Till 1956 the RBI was very cautious in giving licences for new branches. Its major effort was devoted to the consolidation and strengthening of the banking system (as explained under Section 6.2.3 above), and not to expansion. Consequently till 1954 there was a continuous decline in the total number of banking offices, mainly due to the amalgamation of smaller banks with larger banks and closure of the offices of non-scheduled and smaller banks. 1956-61 was a period of slow expansion of banking offices, the number of banking offices increasing from 4,067 to only 5,012. From July 1962 the RBI followed a systematic programme of branch expansion, encouraging banks to open their offices in semi-urban, rural, and other unbanked areas. Under the programme, upto December 1970, the number of banking offices more than doubled from about 5,000 to about 11,000. The nationalisation of 14 major banks in July 1969 imparted a new sense of urgency and major impetus to branch expansion in unbanked, especially rural and semi-urban, areas expeditiously. One of the major objectives of bank nationalisation has been this kind of expansion of banking facilities in the country. For, the private-sector banks all along had hesitated opening bank offices in small centres, as they did not expect such offices to be remunerative for several years. Therefore, it was thought that the state must come forward in a big way (through the ownership of banks) to open up the countryside to banking and meet the initial costs involved in the interest of larger social goals of saving promotion and mobilisation and making available institutional credit and remittance facilities, even in rural areas, for the growth of agriculture and rural industries. Ever since their nationalisation, the SBI group of banks has played an important role in this direction. Since October 1975 the effort has been supplemented by setting up Regional Rural Banks (see Section 5.3).

Since nationalization of banks, the number of bank offices has multiplied rapidly—from 8,300 in July 1969 to more than 62,000 at end June 1995. This has improved substantially the availability of banking facilities in the country. Whereas in 1969 there was only one bank to serve 65,000 population; by the end of 1995, there were five banks for the same number of persons.

The picture becomes much more impressive when we look at the striking increase in the number of bank-offices in rural areas—from a mere 1860 in July 1969 to more than 47,000 in June 1995. Taking rural and semi-urban centres together, the number of bank-offices increased from about 4,200 in July 1969 to more than 47,000 in June 1994, whereas the number of bank-offices in urban and metropolitan and port towns increased from 3,100 in July 1969 to 8,300 in June 1994.

Also, in recent years, there was greater emphasis on extending banking facilities in deficit districts and in unbanked areas. With the provision of adequate banking infrastructure throughout the country, particularly in rural areas, the RBI has given up its old branch licensing policy and given greater freedom to banks to rationalise their existing branch network in non-rural area.

6.2.5 **Lead Bank Scheme : The New Strategy of Banking and Area Development**

The branch expansion programme of banks in the post-nationalisation phase was supposed to be interwoven with the Lead Bank Scheme of the RBI, adopted in December 1969. The Scheme was recommended by a Study Group (known as the Gadgil Group) of the National Credit Council. The Group was of the view that because of the diversity of conditions all over the country, an *area approach* was essential for appropriate credit arrangements on the basis of local conditions. Accordingly, it suggested making major scheduled banks responsible for providing integrated and all-round banking facilities under their leadership in all the districts of the country in a well-planned and phased manner. It was hoped that through the instrumentality of credit, these banks would act as catalysts of local development.

Under the Scheme, as adopted, all the 398 districts in the country have been distributed among major scheduled banks (in the public sector). They were supposed to play the lead role in the expansion of banking facilities and to act as consortium leaders for co-ordinating the activities of co-operative, commercial banking and other financial institutions in their respective districts. Each lead bank is expected to survey the district, identify unbanked centres, and set up branches in a phased manner. It is also expected to identify and study local problems, evolve an integrated credit plan for the supply of inputs and processing, storage and marketing facilities and other services, which may be locally needed and provide for participation among financing and development agencies operating in the district.

6.2.6 **Deposit Growth**

Total bank deposits in nominal terms (i.e. at current prices) have grown rapidly after 1961, more so after 1969 (see Table 6.1., row 4).

What is the growth of bank deposits in real terms due to ? What is the relative importance of different factors ? How reliable is the estimated contribution of each factor ? The questions can be answered with the help of monetary theory and econometric analysis of the data. But we are not prepared to undertake such a study. We only note heuristicaly that the growth of bank deposits in real terms is due to the growth of real income, the spread of banking facilities, the spread of banking habits, strengthening of the banking system, and the increase in the rate of interest on bank deposits.

6.2.7 **Changes in the Composition of Deposits**

The relative proportions of demand and time deposits have undergone significant changes (see row 4 of Table 6.1). Over the period covered, the share of time deposits in total deposits has shot up from 33% to 82%. The rise in this ratio has been relatively more spectacular over the last 20 years. The recorded shift in the composition of deposits is due to several factors, such as changes in the composition of bank depositors in favour of households in place of firms, spread of banking facilities in the country, liberalisation of withdrawal conditions in respect of savings deposits, increases in the rates of interest paid on fixed and savings accounts, ban on the payment of interest on current deposits after 1961, and change in the division of savings deposits between demand and time deposits favouring the latter since 1978.

6.2.8 Bank Staff, Productivity and Profits

With the expansion of banking offices and banking operations, the number of bank employees has increased several-fold from 79,000 in 1958 to 10 lakh in 1990. The productivity of their services and the quality of customer service is said to have gone down. This is a genuine cause for concern for the public as well as authorities. It has affected adversely, among other things, the profitability of banks per rupee of their total earnings. The decline in this profitability (in the short-run) can also be attributed partly to rapid branch expansion.

6.3 Sectoral Allocation of Commercial Bank Credit

No other aspect of credit policy has attracted more attention in public discussion, pressure-group operations, and with the authorities than that of the sectoral allocation of commercial bank credit. The policy has undergone several changes from time to time over the past 40 years (1951–1991). The full period may be conveniently subdivided into two sub-periods for purposes of our study : (*a*) Pre-Nationalisation (of Banks) Period : 1951-68 and (*b*) Post-Nationalisation Period : after July 1969. Two kinds of sectoral classification have been popular. One is by main sector of economic activity and generally involves four-fold sectoral classification of the economy, *viz.* (*i*) agriculture, (*ii*) industry, (*iii*) trade, and (*iv*) others. Whenever necessary, each sector can be further sub-divided into smaller sub-sectors, such as large and medium-scale industry and small scale industry. The other kind of classification divides the economy into only two broad categories : (*a*) priority sectors and (*b*) non-priority sectors. This kind of classification was adopted for policy purposes for the first time in 1968. The highlights of the sectoral allocation of commercial bank credit over the two sub-periods and the two schemes of sectoral classification are discussed in the sub-section below.

6.3.1 Pre-Nationalisation Period (1951-68)

The highlights of this period are summed up below.

1. *Dramatic Increase in the Share of Industry and Decline in that of Trade and Others.* The share of industry in scheduled commercial banks' credit rose rapidly over the period. From 34 per cent in 1951 it rose to 51 per cent in 1961 and to 67.5 per cent in 1968, thereby doubling itself in a span of 17 years. There was a corresponding decline in the share of trade from 36 per cent to 19 per cent and that of the miscellaneous category from 28 per cent to 11 per cent. Within the

industrial sector, the bulk (about 80 per cent) of bank credit went to the corporate sector and only a small fraction to the small-scale industry. Of the incremental bank credit to the industrial sector, the main beneficiaries were newer industries such as engineering, iron and steel, and chemicals.

The factors responsible for the aforesaid shift in the advances pattern operated on both the demand and supply sides of bank credit. On the one hand, the state policy, under the framework of a mixed economy and five-year plans initiated in 1951, sought the industrial development of the country largely through the promotion of large industries in the corporate sector. To that end, it entailed several supportive measures, which offered new profit opportunities to large industry and encouraged greatly its demand for bank credit. On the other hand, large industry and established business houses, because of their ownership or control of big commercial banks, could claim easily an increasing proportion of the incremental bank credit and banks themselves were prefectly happy to fall in line. This is explained further under the next point.

2. *Heavy Concentration of Bank Credit*. Another feature of the pattern of bank advances to industry is its highly skewed distribution in favour of large borrowers. According to one source[3], the size distribution of borrowal accounts of commercial banks (in mid-sixties) showed that 70% of total industrial advances went to only 1% of the total number of borrowal accounts, each with credit outstanding of over Rs. 5 lakhs, whereas 12% of the accounts with outstanding of less than Rs. 10,000 each received barely 4% of the total. A similar concentration was observed in the case of guarantees (in respect of deferred payments) issued by banks. The number of borrowal accounts itself had stayed nearly stagnant during the sixties till 1968, increasing from 10.78 lakhs in April 1961 to only 11.27 lakhs in March 1968[4].

What factors were responsible for such heavy concentration of bank credit for industry in favour of a few large borrowers ? A theoretical explanation will be offered in Chapter 16. It will explain how and why the security-oriented credit in search of safety against risk of default tends to favour large borrowers in general. This will be so even when banks are free from effective control by big borrowers. This will be all the more so if banks are owned and controlled by big borrowers. And this was the situation before the nationalisation of 14 major banks in July 1969, at least so as far as the ownership was concerned. A few facts are worth noting[5]. The commercial banks in India had a very low capital base. The ratio of paid-up capital to deposits was too low and was going down over time. The low capital base facilitated concentration of 'controlling' of bank shares in a few hands and gave them command over the deployment of rapidly growing deposits. This represented concentration of enormous economic power. Understandably, therefore, all proposals from the RBI for the strengthening of the capital base of banks by new issues of share capital (which would have led to some dilution of ownership and control) met with stiff opposition from the chambers of commerce and the Indian Banks' Association.

Another institutional mechanism used for exercising control over the credit policy of banks has been the interlocking of directorship. An official survey of directorships of 20 leading banks, conducted in 1963, had "brought out that 188 persons who had been serving on the Boards of these 20 banks, had 1,452 directorships of other companies also. The total number of companies (excluding non-profit making organizations) under these directors were 1,100"[6]. 'It was further revealed that through common directors, banks were connected with insurance companies, finance companies, investment trusts, manufacturing and trading companies and non-profit organizations.

Yet another institutional device used by large industrial borrowers for appropriating the bulk of bank credit going to industry was by cornering industrial licences and on their bases obtaining long-term financial assistance and underwriting (of new issues) facility from development banks (see Chapter 8) and other term-lending institutions (see Chapter 9). These arrangements are usually treated as good indicators of the soundness of projects for which commercial banks willingly provided working capital. The rediscounting and refinance facilities offered to banks by the IDBI for industrial loans of various kinds and at concessional rates of interest further encouraged commercial banks to advance industrial credit liberally.

3. *Low Share of Agriculture.* Throughout the period (1951–68), agriculture continued to command a very low proportion (a little more than 2%) of total commercial bank credit, firstly because commercial banks were reluctant to provide such credit and so were not geared

to that end and secondly because, as a matter of deliberate policy (of functional specialisation), the needs of agricultural credit were supposed to be met by the co-operative credit system. But from about the mid-sixties, the latter was finding it increasingly difficult to meet the credit requirements of both large farmers adopting new technology under the HYVP (High-Yield-Variety Programme) and the weaker sections. Against the background of severe shortage of foodgrains production in the country and the consequent need for promoting the HYVP and to support also the weaker sections on political considerations, pressures came to be exerted on the RBI to provide adequate refinance to the co-operative credit system. Since the RBI as the central banking authority considered it inadvisable to stretch its help beyond a reasonable limit and since there were inherent organizational and structural limitations on the co-operative banking system in raising its own resources, a multi-agency approach for the provision of agricultural credit with commercial banks as the other source of credit came to be initiated. To start with, the SBI was assigned the role of providing credit to agricultural marketing and processing societies. As these societies were dominated primarily by big cultivators and traders with semi-urban and urban contacts and as agriculture became more paying under the new technology, the demand for more of agricultural credit from commercial banks became stronger over time. Things started changing in this direction soon after the nationalisation of 14 major banks in July 1969.

4. *Miscellaneous Category*. In March 1951 about 28% of total commercial bank credit went to such parties as non-bank financial companies, including indigenous bankers (12.7%), private persons in the form of personal loans (6.8%) and others. With the steep rise in credit to industry, the share of this residual category had declined to about 11%.

6.3.2. **Post-Nationalisation Period**

The key feature of the post-nationalisation period in the field of allocation of credit has been growing functional diversification with increasing emphasis on credit to 'priority sectors' and emergence of 'food credit' (that is, credit for the procurement of foodgrains) as an important item. These twin developments have led to reallocation of sectoral credit from what it was in the pre-nationalisation period. The new developments are discussed below.

1. *Priority Sectors.* The concept of priority sectors for the allocation of commercial bank credit took definite shape during the brief period of the Social Control of Banks (1968). Initially, at the recommendation of the National Credit Council, three sectors, namely, agriculture, small industries, and exports, were officially recognized as priority sectors. Later, a few more categories came to be added to the list, namely, road and water transport operators, professional and self-employed persons, retail trade and small business, and education. Exports came to be treated separately in their own right. Targets of priority sector credit for public sector banks were set and revised from time to time as a matter of government policy. The targets were set in terms of percentages of bank credit outstanding. For example, it was put as 40% to be attained by March 1985. In most cases, the targets were exceeded. Sub-targets were also set. For example, it was said that at least 15% of total credit must go to agriculture by way of direct finance and that at least 25% of priority-sector advances (or 10% of total credit) must go to the weaker sections.

The data on the priority sector credit outstanding are presented in Table 6.2.

Credit to agriculture and other priority sectors is discussed below.

Credit given to agriculture is of two types : (*a*) direct finance and (*b*) indirect finance. More than 80% of it is direct finance and the rest in indirect finance. The former comprises the following:

(*i*) Short-term loans (including crop loans) given for the purchase of production inputs such as seeds, fertilizers, pesticides and to meet the cost of cultivation. These loans are generally repayable within a period of 12 months and in certain cases within 15 to 18 months. The repayment schedule is related to the harvesting and marketing of particular crops;

(*ii*) Medium/long-term loans granted for the development of agriculture, such as development of small irrigation (tube wells and other wells), purchase of tractors and other agricultural implements and machinery, improvement of land. The period of repayment of these loans is generally 3 to 10 years. It may be longer where refinance is available from the NABARD and such refinance is quite substantial (see Section 8.6). More than half of direct finance is in the form

Table 6.2

Public Sector Banks—Advances to Priority Sectors (Rs. crore): December 1994

Note: (a) Column (3) shows percentage of Column (2) to total Priority Sector Advances;

(b) Column (4) shows percentage of column (2) to Net Bank Credit.

Sector (1)	*Amount (in Rs. Crore)* (2)	*Percentage* (3)	*Percentage* (4)
I. Agriculture	22,200	38.7	14.5
II. Small Scale Industries	23,350	40.7	14.2
III. Other Priority Sectors	11,800	20.6	8.7
Total	57,350	100.0	37.4

SOURCE: RBI, *Report on Currency and Finance*, 1994-95, Vol. II, Statement 75.

of term loans, also called investment or development finance. Such finance, no doubt, is very helpful for asset formation in (and development of) agriculture. But we must also recognize that its main beneficiaries have been and are likely to be relatively large farmers (with more than 10-acre holdings), whereas small farmers have fared better with short-term loans; and

(*iii*) loans for allied agricultural activities such as dairying, poultry farming, piggeries, pisciculture, etc.

Indirect finance to agriculture is finance given to agencies or individuals engaged in the marketing of agricultural commodities, supply of production inputs and other services for agriculture, like credit for financing the distribution of fertilisers, pesticides, and other inputs, loans to State Electricity Boards for financing their programmes of tube-well energization, loans to primary agricultural credit societies, investment in debentures issued by land development banks, etc. Since nationalisation, advances to agriculture have recorded a substantial increase and so have the advances outstanding to it. At the end of June 1995, the latter had stood at Rs. 22,200 crores (see Table 6.2).

Yet 60% of the assisted families could not cross the poverty line. So, under the 7th plan, in addition to covering 10 million families as new beneficiaries, supplementary assistance was given to 'deserving' 10 million families that had been assisted during the 6th plan period.

2. *Fall in the Share of Bank Credit to Large and Medium Industry and Rise in that of the Small-Scale Industry.* There has been a persistent decline in the share of bank credit from scheduled commercial banks to industry as a whole and to large and medium industry in particular. This share of industry decreased from 67.5% in March 1968 to 48.8% in March 1986. The share of large and medium industry declined from 60.6% in March 1968 to 34.7% and that of small industry rose from 6.9 (in March 1968) to 14.1% in March 1986. Some part of the measured changes in relative shares as between March 1968 and later dates might have arisen due to changes in the classification of data—a purely measurement (or statistical) phenomenon. However, a major part of the measured changes is genuine and the shifts in the sectoral allocation of credit are mainly the result of policy changes. With the increased diversification in industry, the structure of industry-wise allocation of bank credit has also undergone changes: the relative shares of textiles, engineering and sugar have declined and those of newer industry groups have improved.

3. *Rise in the Share of Food Advances.* With rising trend in the domestic output of foodgrains, market surpluses of food, public distribution of foodgrains, public procurement of food, and the size of buffer stocks of food, a rising share of bank credit has taken the form of food advances. For example, in March 1968, the amount outstanding of food advances of Rs. 109 crore constituted only 3.5% of total advances of scheduled commercial banks; by March 1995, these advances had increased to Rs. 12,300 crore, constituting about 6.2% of total advances. In order to encourage banks to meet this new and growing demand, the RBI not only issued appropriate guidelines to banks, but also offered them its refinance facilities against increases in such advances. Over time as the food advances grew, the RBI has been tightening the conditions of refinance from time to time and made the commercial banks to finance larger amounts of such

advances from their internal resources.

4. *Bank Credit to Public Sector Units*[7]. Apart from providing funds to the Central and State governments through investment in government bonds and bills, and investments in market bonds issued by State Electricity Boards, Port Trusts, and other quasi-government bodies. Commercial banks also make loans and advances to public sector units. These units include the Food Corporation of India and similar state government units.

The main factors responsible for the increasing share of the public sector units in bank credit are : (*a*) the increasing relative importance of such units in the non-financial sector of the economy. With the expansion of economic activities of such units, it is legitimate for such units to claim their share, along with others in bank credit ; (*b*) low profitability, on average, of public sector units, so that they generate less of internal funds for financing their growth and depend relatively more on borrowed funds ; and (*c*) privileged position of public sector units—both the government and the RBI advise and expect preferential treatment of public sector units from banks, especially public-sector banks.

The consequence of the above development has been relative decline in the share in bank credit of both large and medium industry and wholesale trade in the private corporate sector. The latter has, therefore, been exerting pressure for more bank credit. The resolution has come about mostly in the form of excessive annual increases in total bank credit, so that, at least in nominal terms, the absolute incremental demands for bank credit from several powerful pressure groups can be satisfied. The RBI has also permitted, and at times actively co-operated with banks in, such excessive increases in bank credit.

5. *Export Credit*. In view of the paramount need to promote exports to earn sufficient foreign exchange to be able to meet the country's large and growing foreign exchange obligations, the government, in recent years, has adopted several fiscal and credit policy measures. To induce banks to increase their credit for exports, the RBI has been providing increasingly liberal refinance to them for such credit and at low concessional rate of interest. The refinance rule for increase in export credit has also been revised upward from time to time. In 1994-95, the export credit of banks was more than Rs. 25,400 crore or 12.8 per cent of the net bank credit.

6.4 *Financial Diversification by Banks*

The commercial banks have made significant strides in their diversification activities through their subsidiaries into new areas like merchant banking, mutual funds, housing finance, hire purchase/equipment leasing and factoring services.

NOTES

1. They are the State Banks of Bikaner and Jaipur, of Hyderabad, of Indore, of Mysore, of Patiala, of Saurashtra, and of Travancore.

2. The deposits with rural branches of banks are not exactly the same thing as the deposits held by the rural population, as some of the rural rich hold some of their deposits in bank branches in semi-urban and urban areas.

3. See Ghosh (1979), pp. 124-125.

4. See Ghosh (1979), pp. 124-5.

5. See Ghosh (1979), pp. 125-30 for details.

6. See Ghosh (1979), pp. 129-30.

7. Also see section 19.6 and 20.3 for investments of banks in government and other 'approved securities' under the SLR.

CHAPTER 7

Co-operative Banks

7.1 Introduction [1]

An important segment of the organized sector of the Indian banking system is represented by a group of financial institutions collectively called co-operative banks. They are so called because they have been organized under the provisions of the co-operative societies law of the states. Under the law, the co-operative societies may be organized for credit or for other (non-credit) purposes. In this book we shall be concerned with only credit societies.

The co-operative banking system is much smaller than the commercial banking system. At the end of March 1994 the net total credit outstanding of commercial banks (with the commercial sector) was Rs. 1,64,000 crore. In comparison, the net credit outstanding of the co-operative banking system was about Rs. 17,000 crore or 10% of the commercial bank credit outstanding. However, this comparison is not a true indicator of the relative importance of the co-operative banking system, which arises, on the one hand, from the sector of the economy it serves and, on the other hand, from the structural features of the co-operative banking system in relation to the requirements of rural finance. The major beneficiary of co-operative banking is the agricultural sector in particular and the rural sector in general. Till about the nationalisation of 14 major commercial banks in July 1969, these (commercial) banks hardly provided any credit for agriculture and other rural economic activities, and rural finance was pretty much left to moneylenders and other private sources, supplemented marginally by institutional finance from co-operatives and the government. Of the latter two, co-operatives were much the more important. Thus till 1969 co-operative credit societies were practically the only institutional source of rural (agricultural) credit. Since then the government has adopted a 'multi-agency approach' under which both co-operative banks and commercial banks, supplemented by 'regional rural banks' (see Section 5.3) are being developed and encouraged to serve the rural sector.

Under the new policy, too, the prime role in the provision of rural finance is supposed to be played by the co-operative credit system. The main reasons for this continued policy emphasis are summed up below: *(i)* despite several organizational weaknesses, village level primary co-operative credit societies are best suited to the socio-economic conditions of Indian villages *(ii)* the existence of a vast network of such societies (called primary agricultural credit societies —PACS) throughout the length and breadth of the country which has been built over the past more than 80 years and which cannot be either duplicated or surpassed easily, and *(iii)* intimate knowledge of the local conditions and problems which the co-operative institutions at various levels have built up with them.

The true importance of the co-operative credit system lies in its geographical coverage—in providing credit outlets, spread over the entire country, located in villages, and easily accessible to units they are supposed to serve—and in the structure of higher financing agencies in the form of central co-operative banks (CCBs) and state co-operative banks (SCBs) and land development banks for providing long-term credit for agriculture. For any effective credit delivery system for rural areas, some such structure is essential and the co-operatives provide that structure. That is why every committee or commission that has examined the working and role of co-operative banking system in India (and they have been many in number) has held the common view that 'cooperation remains the best hope of rural India' even though it has not been very successful so far. Therefore, all effort needs to be made to strengthen and improve the co-operative credit structure. The present chapter will be devoted to a study of this structure and its main constituents.

As the RBI's decennial surveys of rural debts and investment show, the co-operative credit societies have already become a force to reckon with, their weaknesses notwithstanding. Of the total debt outstanding of cultivator households, in 1951, only 3.7% was owed to co-operative societies; ten years later the relative share of co-operatives had grown to 11.4%, and in 1971, this share had increased further to 22.0% and in 1981-82 to 28.6%.

The financial assistance extended by the co-operative banking system to the ultimate beneficiaries outstanding at the end of March 1993 was Rs. 14,650 crore, of which loans and advances to the primary agricultural credit societies were of Rs. 10,250 crore and to land development banks of Rs. 4,400 crore.

7.2 The Structure of Co-operative Banks

A variety of co-operative credit institutions are operating in the economy. They are categorised under two main heads: agricultural and non-agricultural. Agricultural credit segment is by far the dominant part of the entire co-operative credit structure. In the field of agricultural credit there are separate institutions to meet the needs for short and medium-term credit and for long-term credit. For the former, the co-operative credit structure is three-tier and federal. At the apex is the State Co-operative Bank (SCB) in each state (co-operation being a state subject in India); at the intermediate (district) level there are Central Co-operative Bank (CCBs); and at the village level there are primary agricultural credit societies (PACS). Long-term agricultural credit is provided by land development banks, which will be discussed separately in Section 8.7. Other constituents are discussed in this Chapter.

One key feature of the co-operative credit structure is best explained at the outset. It is the pyramidical shape of the three-tier structure. A large number of primary credit societies at the local level provide a very broad base to it; at the intermediate (district) level are CCBs, and at the apex (state level) are SCBs. The SCBs and the CCBs are also called higher or central financing agencies (for primary societies).

The three-tier structure is interconnected through a two-way flow of funds–one (larger) flow going downward from the higher financing agencies to the lower lending agencies and the other (smaller) flow moving in the opposite direction from lower credit agencies to the higher agencies.

The rationale of the two-way flow of funds is discussed below. The larger of the two flows is in the downward direction—from a SCB to the CCBs under its jurisdiction and from the latter to the primary credit societies, which then lend to their borrowing members. A SCB does not lend directly to primary societies in areas where a CCB exists and CCB lends only to primary societies and not to their members or other individuals (except in a few cases). This is in the interest of functional specialisation, manageability, and cost effectiveness. This is also the rationale of the three-tier organizational structure. The basic need for higher financing agencies arises, because the PACS (the predominant part of the primary credit societies responsible for distributing credit to rural borrowers) are not able to raise enough funds by way of deposits from the public. About 60% of their working capital comes at loans from the CCBs, who, in turn, borrow about one-third of their working capital from higher financing agencies.

The SCBs themselves, apart from raising funds by way of owned funds (share capital and reserves) and deposits from co-operative societies and individuals and others, borrow a good deal from outside sources—mainly the RBI and NABARD. This is one (direct) way in which the RBI/NABARD make their credit available to the cooperative banking system. In addition, the NABARD provides long-term loans to state governments for contributions to the share capital of co-operative credit institutions. It is mainly through such borrowing facilities, among other things, that the co-operative banking system is linked with the rest of the financial system in the country.

The RBI/NABARD do not and possibly cannot lend to primary credit societies whose number of 87,000 is forbiddingly large. They do not even lend directly to CCBs whose number at 350 is not too large, or not to even better run and relatively large top (say) 100 CCBs. The basic reason is the adherence to the discipline of the three-tier structure, which is hierarchical. For the same reason, the state governments also provide funds to the co-operative credit system (as contributions to the share capital) only through the SCBs; the CCBs are not allowed to lend to each other, but keep their surplus funds with their SCB: and similarly, primary credit societies are not allowed to inter-lend among themselves, but keep their surplus funds with their respective CCB. This whole arrangement suggests that the problem of providing institutional credit to the rural sector is not merely one of earmarking at the top a certain amount of total credit for this sector, but much more importantly of having an appropriate organizational structure for supervising, managing, and executing the distribution of credit to millions of borrowers in small villages all over the country.

The reverse internal flow of funds is from the primary credit societies to CCBs and from them to SCBs. This is affected way of contributions to the share capital (and, therefore, also to reserves on pro rata basis) of higher financing agencies—of SCBs by the CCBs and of the latter by the primary societies—and by way of deposits. The loans given by the higher financing agencies to their affiliates is linked with the share capital holdings by these affiliates of the lending agency. Thus, normally, a primary credit society can borrow from a CCB almost upto 10 times its contribution to the share capital of the CCB. A similar condition governs the borrowing limits of CCBs from their SCB. This kind of linking between the share capital contribution and the borrowing limit is partly to restrict borrowing by the lower level institutions, partly to raise funds for the higher financing agencies that lend only to affiliated banks and societies and not to individuals, and partly to create stakes of the lower level institutions in the health and vitality of those above them.

Besides, lower-level institutions are required to keep all their surplus funds on deposit with those a step above them and not inter-lend among themselves. This also represents a reverse flow of funds in the upward direction within the co-operative banking system. This is to ensure better allocation of funds within each district and each state. Such inter-bank deposits within the co-operative banking system are a large proportion (almost 40%) of its total deposits.

A phenomenon worth noting is the net reverse flow of funds from the co-operative banking system to the government (state governments). It is generally thought that the government is the net lender of funds. This is not correct; instead, the government is the net debtor to the co-operative banking system. First, a large part (about 50%) of the government's financial assistance in the form of its contribution to the share capital of societies is advanced by the NABARD. Second, the co-operative banking system (including LDBs) provides funds to the government by way of investment in its securities. For SCBs and CCBs, such investment is required by the RBI under its 'Statutory Liquidity Ratio' requirement (see the next section). Since total investment outstanding in government securities by the co-operative banks is generally greater than the total financial contribution outstanding of the government to the system, there is net withdrawal of funds by the government from the system. If account is taken of the NABARD's tied credit to the government for assistance to the co-operative banking system, the government's withdrawal from the latter rises further.

We now discuss the individual constituents of the short-term co-operative banking system. SCBs are discussed briefly. Major attention is devoted to PACS, the co-operative credit agencies that deal directly with the rural population.

7.3 State Co-operative Banks

State Co-operative Banks (SCBs) constitute the apex of the three-tier co-operative credit structure, organized at the level of individual states. At the end of June 1985, there were 28 SCBs, 14 of which were scheduled banks. The SCBs occupy key position in the co-operative credit structure, as (*i*) it is only through them that the RBI provides credit to co-operatives, (*ii*) they operate as 'balancing centres' for CCBs, making surplus funds of some CCBs available to other CCBs, as CCBs are not allowed to borrow and lend among themselves, and (*iii*) they raise funds on their own to make them available to the CCBs and through them or directly to primary societies in such districts where CCBs are not in operation. Besides financing the affiliated banks and societies, the SCBs exercise control and supervision over their operations and provide leadership and guidance to the co-operative movement in their respective states.

At the end of March 1995, the SCBs had owned funds of Rs. 800 crore and aggregates of Rs. 3,850 crore of deposits and inter-bank deposits of Rs. 7,300 crore. Besides, they had borrowed Rs. 2,870 crore from NABARD and state governments. They had extended credit (in the form of loans, cash credit and bills purchased and discounted) whose outstanding amount was Rs. 5,300 crore. Their total advances to central co-operative banks and primary credit societies stood at about Rs. 8,000 crore.

SOURCE: RBI, *Report on Currency and Finance*, 1994-95, Vol. II, Statement 68.

The share capital is raised mainly from member co-operative societies, including CCBs, and practically the rest from the state government concerned. The deposits also are held largely by co-operative societies who contribute roughly 80% of them.

The SCBs also are subject to the CRR and SLR requirements of the RBI, but only at their minimum levels of 3% and 25% respectively of their total net liabilities.

The SCBs lend almost entirely to co-operative societies—CCBs and primary societies—mostly as short-term loans (mainly) for seasonal agricultural operations. About half of the medium-term credit is simply short-term credit converted into medium-term loans to facilitate repayment by borrowing societies; the rest is for various agricultural and non-agricultural purposes such as purchase of pump-sets, sinking or repair of wells, etc. In 1994-95 the loans issued were about Rs. 13,000 crore.

7.4 Central Co-operative Banks

The Central Co-operative Banks (CCBs) constitute the intermediate rung in the three-tier co-operative credit structure of which a SCB is the apex and primary credit societies in a state are the base. At the end of June 1989, there were 350 CCBs, with more than 15,000 offices. Their main function is to lend money to affiliated primary societies. Their total working capital of about Rs. 15,000 crore was derived mainly from deposits (54%), borrowings and other liabilities (34%) and owned funds (12%). The share capital is raised largely from affiliated cooperative societies and the rest (about 30%) from state governments. The societies contribute to the share capital, as their borrowings are linked to their share-holdings (mostly in the ratio of 10:1). As deposit-holders, individuals and others lead the co-operative societies by nearly a margin of 2:1. Rs. 2,300 crore of borrowings had come from the RBI/NABARD and SCBs. Besides, the RBI/NABARD give long-term loans to state governments to enable them to contribute to the share capital of CCBs.

The loans and advances of CCBs are almost entirely to co-operative societies. About 75% of these loans are short-term and the rest medium term, and mostly for agricultural purposes. The bulk of medium-term loans are conversion/rephasement/rescheduled loans.

The overdues to demand ratio at 37% was very high. The reasons for such high overdues ratio are best summed up to thus: "Apart from natural calamities such as floods, drought, etc., affecting the repaying capacity of borrowers, the poor recovery performance (of CCBs) can be attributed to the inadequate or inefficient supervision exercised by the banks, the poor quality of the management of societies and banks, absence of linking of credit with marketing, reluctance to coercive measures, or where resorted to, the inability of the machinery to promptly execute the decrees" (RBI, *Review of The Co-operative Movement in India*, 1974-76, pp. 88-89). In great many cases the last-mentioned factor is itself the result of protection/support provided by political bosses to defaulters.

7.5 **Primary Agricultural Credit Societies** (PACS)

PACS occupy a predominant position in the co-operative credit structure and form its base. A PACS is organized at the grass roots level of a village or a group of small villages. It is this basic unit which deals directly with the rural (agricultural) borrowers, gives them loans and collects repayments of loans given. It serves as the final link between the ultimate borrowers on the one hand and the higher financing agencies, namely the SCBS, and the RBI/NABARD on the other hand. As such, the health and strength of the co-operative credit movement depends crucially upon the health and strength of these societies. But, despite much official effort and support, and numerical expansion of the PACS in membership, working capital, loans given and other activities, their health and working leave much to be desired.

At the end of June 1989 there were 87,000 PACS. These societies covered about 90% of 5.8 lakh villages. Their membership of 9 crores covered about 65% of the total estimated population of about 14 crores of rural households. More than half of the members of PACS are persons of small means—small farmers, agricultural labourers and rural artisans and about 25% of them belong to scheduled castes and tribes. All these are very strong features of the co-operative credit organization, as it alone provides the vast network of institutional credit agencies throughout the length and breadth of the country of subcontinental size, covering the large bulk of Indian villages. And yet the organisation is not fulfilling its role adequately due to several weaknesses about which we shall study in Subsection 7.5.5.

The working capital of the PACS is derived mainly from borrowings from the CCBs and in smaller proportions from owned funds and deposits. That the PACS have failed to attract deposits is not so much a reflection of low savings habits of the rural population as a reflection of the availability of better assets to rural savers in terms of both rate of return and riskiness. The richer farmers either invest their savings directly in physical assets or lend them directly as agriculturist moneylenders to others in the village or hold them in deposits with banks or post offices. Only the residual savings of those households come to the PACS who want to borrow later from these societies or who want to wield influence in the actual working of the societies. To attract more deposits, these societies must be in a position to pay higher interest rates on their deposits than offered by other institutions and must inspire greater confidence regarding safety of deposits with them. For this, the societies must be managed efficiently as well as honestly.

High net borrowings from CCBs show that PACS act mainly as distributional channels for funds mobilised elsewhere. Even this role is not played well by them, as they suffer from a very high ratio (of more than 40%) of overdues to loans outstanding/demand.

Only the members of a PACS are entitled to borrow from it. Most loans are for agricultural purposes and are short-term. Medium-term loans for such purposes as sinking or repair of wells, purchase of machinery (mostly pump sets for irrigation) and cattle are also given. But consumption loans, given mostly to landless labourers, artisans and marginal farmers, are negligible. The share of loans given going to weaker sections is usually about 40% of loans. The amount of loans and advances outstanding at the end of June 1989 was about Rs. 6,000 crores.

A varying number of PACS also undertake non-credit activities such as handling the supply of farm requisites, distribution of consumer goods among their members, constructing godowns, marketing of agricultural produce and the processing of it.

7.5.5 Deficiencies and Remedies

Any number of committees and study groups have enquired into the working of the co-operative banking system and found uniformally the PACS the weakest link in the structure. Despite all the effort that has gone into strengthening these societies into strong and viable units, the position continues to be highly unsatisfactory so that not all earn profits or have full-time paid secretaries/managing directors. While there is not complete unanimity about the test of viability, the two indicators of it used in the previous sentence are not without merit.

The major deficiencies of the PACS and their credit and the steps necessary to remove them are discussed briefly below.

1. *Organizational Weakness.* At the primary level, the co-

operative credit structure has twofold weakness: *(a)* inadequate coverage and *(b)* weak units. Though geographically, active PACS cover about 90% of 5.8 villages, there are parts of the country, especially in the north-east, where this coverage is very low. Further, the rural population covered as members is only only 50% of all the rural households. This inadequacy of coverage itself is attributable to the financial and organizational weakness of individual PACS. In a sense, they are caught in a vicious circle: they are weak because of inadequate membership and they do not attract enough membership because they are weak. This vicious circle must be broken through policy measures of reorganization of PACS. We shall study about them a little later.

A distinction needs to be made between nominal coverage as given by mere membership and 'effective coverage' (in the RBI's terminology) as given by the proportion of borrowing members in the total membership. On the latter criterion only in the four states of Punjab, Haryana, West Bengal and Tamil Nadu is the effective coverage of 50 per cent or more. Such coverage is much lower in U.P. and Bihar. Better criteria than the one of 'effective coverage' (used by the RBI) would be *(i)* borrowing members as a proportion of the rural households *(ii)* the average amount of loan issued per borrowing member, and *(iii)* the proportion of loans going to the weaker sections. On these criteria, though a single composite index cannot be easily constructed, the states of Maharashtra, Gujarat, Punjab, Haryana and Tamil Nadu are found to fare better than other states.

Why is the borrowing membership low in the PACS? In the judgment of the Banking Commission (1972, p. 155) which still holds good, in most cases, one or more of the following reasons are responsible for the low borrowing membership: *(i)* defaults of members in loan repayment and inability of societies to raise resources, *(ii)* inability of the members to provide the prescribed security, *(iii)* lack of up-to-date land records or inalienable rights to land or inability to produce sureties, *(iv)* ineligibility of certain purposes for loans, *(v)* inadequacy of credit limits prescribed, and *(vi)* onerous conditions prescribed such as share capital contribution at 10 or 20 per cent of loans outstanding and compulsory thrift deposits.

The PACS are passing through a long phase of *re-organization* which was formally started in early 1960's, following the recommendation of the Committee on Co-operative Credit (1960). But its progress to date has been very slow. Currently the reorganization work is running along the following lines: *(a)* the PACS are being reorganized so that every reorganized PACS covers a gross cropped area of 2000 hectares within a radius of 10 kms.; *(b)* Non-viable units are either amalgamated with reorganized societies or liquidated. But compulsory amalgamation/liquidation is not easy, as it often meets with stiff resistance from local beneficiaries and functionaries and the state governments have hesitated using compulsion in the matter; and *(c)* the setting up of new types of societies called Farmers Service Societies (FSS) and Large-Sized Multi-Purpose Societies (LAMPS) for tribal and hill areas. The FSS, that are being organized since August 1975, are intended to cater particularly to the credit needs of the weaker sections and provide integrated credit supplies, services and technical guidance to the farmers at one contact point. In the organization of these societies preference is being given to districts covered by special development programmes, such as 'Small Farmers Development Agency (SFDA), Command Area Development Programme' (CADP), 'Drought Prone Areas Programme' (DPAP), etc. LAMPS are being organized in tribal and hill areas somewhat on the lines of FSS for providing all types of credit, viz., short-term, medium and long-term including that for meeting the social needs, agricultural and consumers' requisites, technical guidance in the intensification and modernisation of agriculture and arranging for the marketing of agricultural and minor forest produce. Both FSS and LAMPS are linked for financial accommodation either to a central co-operative bank or a commercial bank. Their progress is understandably slow becasue of the difficulties in meeting certain essential prerequisites to the success of the new programme, viz, liquidation or amalgamation of other existing non-viable societies in the areas of FSS and LAMPS so as to provide the new units an exclusive area of operation, as also the provision of managerial and technical staff for them.

Since June 1970 the commercial banks have also been associated by the RBI in the rehabilitation of weak PACS. Under the RBI's scheme, commercial banks take over societies for giving them short-and medium-term loans. Both the number of societies and the amounts involved so far are small.

2. *Inadequate Resources.* The resources of the PACS are much too inadequate in relation to the short-and medium-term credit needs of the rural economy. The bulk of even these inadequate funds came from higher financing agencies and not through owned funds of societies or deposit mobilisation by them. The resource-mobilisation capacity of the PACS will improve substantially, if through reorganiza-

tion and related measures, they are converted into strong and viable units. Then, they should be able to attract both more deposits and more loans from higher financing agencies.

3. *Overdues.* Large overdues (of more than 40 per cent of demand and of credit outstanding) have become a big problem for the PACS. They check the circulation of loanable funds, reduce the borrowing as well as lending power of societies, and give them the bad image of the societies of defaulting debtors. The RBI data for various years show that the percentage of overdues is much lower for tenant cultivators and agricultural labourers and much higher for landowners; among landowners, the percentage of overdues was relatively lower for smaller farmers (upto 2 hectares each) and higher for larger farmers. This suggests that a large part of the overdues might be wilful and that bigger landowners take undue advantage of their relatively stronger position in villages in both appropriating cheaper co-operative credit and not paying back their loans in time. In years of poor crops due to bad weather conditions, some overdues in the areas of heavy crop failures are understandable. But year after year upward of 40 per cent of loans outstanding being overdue cannot be so justified. And this is after some unknown portion of loans issued during a year are simply renewals of loans overdue. The overdues position is not uniform across the states. It has been particularly bad in Bihar, Assam, and Madhya Pradesh.

According to the Banking Commission (1972, pp. 191–2), in most states, overdues are due to *(a)* indifferent management or mismanagement of societies; *(b)* unsound lending policies leading to overfinancing, or financing unrelated to actual needs, diversion of loans for other purposes; *(c)* vested interests and group politics in societies and wilful defaults; *(d)* lack of adequate supervision over the use of loans by the borrowers and poor recovery effort; *(e)* lack of adequate control of banks (CCBs) over the primary societies; *(f)* lack of appropriate link between credit and marketing institutions; *(g)* failure to take prompt action against wilful defaulters; and *(h)* uncertain agricultural prices. These factors still hold good.

4. *Inadequate and Restricted Credit.* Co-operative credit is inadequate in several senses. First, the PACS provide credit to only a small proportion of the total rural population. Second, the societies do not provide full credit even for all productive agricultural activities. The credit given is confined mainly to crop finance (seasonal agricultural operations) and medium-term loans for identifiable purposes such as digging of wells, installation of pump sets, etc. Most of the

societies do not provide credit for other productive activities undertaken by the agriculturists. Even for approved productive activities, the credit given is usually not adequate to meet in full the need for credit. In most cases, non-agricultural credit needs even for productive purposes are not met at all Consumption loans are generally not given.

What is required is to improve the effective coverage of societies by providing credit to increasing proportion of rural households, especially of weaker sections, to widen the range of eligible purposes for which credit is given, and then to meet an approved borrower's entire credit needs. To realize this objective in practice, the societies must be made organizationally as well as financially strong along the lines already suggested above.

5. *Other Linked Inputs, Extension Service, and Marketing.* The provision of adequate and timely credit is only one of the necessary conditions for improving the productivity of farmers and others in villages. Additional facilities in the form of the supply of inputs (like better seeds, fertilisers, pesticides, etc.), extension and marketing service must also be provided to small and marginal farmers to enable them to make good use of the credit given to them. Already a step in this direction has been taken in the form of Farmers Service Societies (FSS) for small and marginal farmers. But what is required is not proliferation of new (forms of) societies, as of revitalizing weaker societies into stronger units, most possibly by reorganizing them into larger-sized multi-purpose co-operatives.

7.6 Primary Co-operative Banks (PCBs)

A large number and variety of primary non-agricultural credit societies have also been organized. Of these, PCBs are the most important. At the end of March 1995, they were more than 1,400 in number. Of them, more than 1,200 were 'urban co-operative banks', the rest were 'salary earners' societies'. The development of the PCBs is looked after by the RBI, as they operate only in urban and semi-urban areas and so are not a charge on the NABARD.

The working capital of these banks is drawn largely from public deposits (from members and non-members) and to a relatively smaller extent from owned funds and borrowings. Both the RBI and the IDBI offered them concessional refinance facility on a selected basis. These banks provide housing finance and loans and advances for various other purposes such as petty trade and industry. Their total deposits were about Rs. 20,000 crore, with loans outstanding of Rs. 15,000 crore and owned funds of about Rs. 3,200 crore.

These banks are doing useful work in mobilising deposits and financing small borrowers. They deserve to be encouraged in all possible ways, as there is both need and potential for them in both the spheres of deposit mobilisation and the provision of credit to small borrowers through them. Large national banks have a tendency to prefer large to small borrowers. Small urban banks, with the area of operation of any bank restricted to a town or a part of a major city, on the other hand, have an opposite bias in favour of small borrowers and small individual loans. Therefore, for credit to small borrowers, special efforts should be made to encourage them.

7.7 The RBI/NABARD and Co-operative Banking System

Though the co-operative credit movement was made a special responsibility of the RBI right from the latter's birth in 1935, much was not accomplished in this sphere till about the mid-1950s. The real turning point in the Bank's role in the movement came only after the Bank's All-India Rural Credit Survey Committee submitted its monumental report in 1954. The Survey Committee had found that while the co-operative societies and government provided only 3% each of the loans raised by the cultivator, the private credit agencies (the moneylender and the trader) lent more than 70% of what the cultivator borrowed. The moneylender charged very high rates of interest and did not concern himself with the purpose of the loan. The Survey Committee summed up the position of agricultural credit thus : It fell short of the right quantity, was not of the right type, did not serve the right purpose and often failed to go to the right people. It also said that 'co-operation had failed but co-operation must succeed'. For this success, the Survey Committee recommended an 'integrated scheme of rural credit', of which the main features were:

(i) state partnership in co-operative credit institutions through contribution to their share capital;

(ii) full co-ordination between credit and other economic activities especially marketing and processing; and

(iii) administration through adequately trained and efficient personnel, responsive to the needs of the rural population.

The RBI was assigned a crucial role in the scheme of integrated credit and in the building up of the co-operative credit organization. The consequent steps taken by the RBI in pursuance of the recommendations of the Survey Committee and later committees like the Committee on Copoeprative Credit (1960) transformed the Bank's role from that of a conventional central banker to that of an active agency that takes all necessary measures for enabling the co-operative system to provide a growingly larger share of rural credit. The adoption of special programmes for increasing agricultural production and the spread of green revolution based largely on intensive use of fertilisers, water, better seeds, and machine power have enhanced the RBI's responsibilities further. The RBI had also started offering greater financial assistance to co-operatives for credit facilities to small farmers and other weaker sections and for minimising disparities in the flow of credit to various regions.

With the setting up of the National Bank for Agriculture and Rural Development (NABARD) in July 1982 (see Section 8.6), the RBI's functions relating to the co-operative movement have been taken over by the NABARD. Now, the RBI's role is primarily restricted to the provision of finance to the NABARD through its contributions to the two national rural credit funds (see Section 8.6), already transferred to the NABARD, and additional loans and advances to the latter. Besides, the RBI still offers loans and advances to SCBs.

The NABARD measures are basically a continuation of the RBI measures. They are studied below under two main heads: *(A)* provision of finance and *(B)* building up of the co-operative credit structure.

(A) **Provision of Finance.** All the NABARD finance is provided to the co-operative sector through the SCBs. The bulk (almost 90%) of it goes to finance agriculture. The finance is of all the three types, viz., short-term, medium-term, and long-term.

(i) Short-term Agricultural Finance. This is given primarily for seasonal agricultural operations which is interpreted to include mixed farming activities, *i.e.,* animal husbandry and allied activities jointly undertaken with agricultural operations.

(ii) Medium-term Agricultural Finance. The NABARD provides medium-term loans to SCBs for periods of 3 to 5 years. These loans are provided for *(a)* agricultural purposes (purchase of agricultural machinery, sinking and repair of wells and tube wells, etc.), animal husbandry, poultry farming and for purchase of shares of co-operative sugar factories and other processing societies by agriculturists, and *(b)* conversion of short-term agricultural loans into medium-term loans whenever such conversion becomes necessary on account of wide-spread crop failure as a result of drought, floods or other natural calamities. All medium-term loans are fully guaranteed as to the repayment of the principal and the payment of interest by the state government concerned.

(*iii*) *Long-term Agricultural Credit.* Long-term credit for agriculture is provided mainly through investment in the debentures of SLDBs (see Section 8.7). In addition, the National Bank makes long-term loans to state governments for contribution to the share capital of co-operative credit institutions, most of which goes to strengthen co-operative credit for agriculture.

The financial accommodation of all kinds indicated above is provided at concessional rates of interest which vary between the Bank Rate and upto 3% below the Bank Rate.

(*iv*) *Non-agricultural finance.* The NABARD also provides *short-term finance* for (*i*) the production and marketing activities of selected cottage and small-scale industries (mostly handloom weavers' co-operative societies) and (*ii*) the purchase and distribution of fertilisers. The loans are generally provided through SCBs against guarantees of the state governments. However, all such finance has constituted a small proportion (5 to 7 per cent) of the total Reserve Bank short-term finance to co-operatives: the bulk of it goes to agricultural co-operatives.

During 1994-95, the total amount of financial assistance sanctioned by NABARD was about Rs. 5,300 crore. Of this, about Rs. 4,800 crore were short-term credit and Rs. 500 crore were medium-term credit. The outstanding amount of financial assistance was about Rs. 3,700 crore.

(B) **Building up of the Co-operative Credit Structure.** From around 1951 the RBI made efforts to (*a*) strengthen the co-operative credit structure at all the three levels and (*b*) reorient the operational policies of co-operative banks in more purposive directions. Under the former, the RBI had taken steps to get SCBs established in such states that did not have them and strengthen them where they were weak. The RBI had also tried for the rehabilitation of weak CCBs by prescribing action to recover overdues, strengthen the bad debts reserves and improve the quality of the administrative and supervisory staff. Similarly, the Bank played an active role in the reorganization of primary societies. The Bank had also made arrangements for the training of personnel of co-operative departments and institutions and undertaken periodical inspection of SCBs, CCBs, and SLDBs to promote healthy and sound growth of co-operative banking in the country. All these functions are now being performed by the NABARD.

CHAPTER 8

Development Banks

8.1 What are Development Banks ?

An outstanding financial development of the post-independence period has been the rapid growth of development banks in the country. These banks are specialised financial institutions which perform the twin functions of providing medium and long-term finance to private entrepreneurs and of performing various promotional roles conducive to economic development. As the name clearly suggests, they aredevelopment-oriented banks. As banks, they provide finance. But they are unlike ordinary commercial banks in three ways. First, they do not seek or accept deposits from the public as ordinary banks do. Second, they specialise in providing medium-and long-term finance, whereas commercial banks have specialised in the provision of short-term finance. Third and most important, they are not mere purveyors of long-term finance like any ordinary term-lending institution. As development banks (with emphasis on the word 'development') their chief distinguishing role is the promotion of economic development by way of promoting investment and enterprise (the two most scarce inputs in LDCs) in their chosen (or allotted) spheres, whether manufacturing, agriculture, or some other. This promotional role may take a variety of forms, like provision of risk capital, underwriting of new issues, arranging for foreign (exchange) loans, identification of investment projects, preparation and evaluation of project reports, provision of technical advice, market information about both domestic and export markets, and management services. How much of these services a development bank is in a position to render depends upon the technical expertise it has been able to build up, the competence of its staff and their experience. The Indian development banks have as yet not developed so much as to be able to provide a whole gamut of development services. But their contribution in the channelling of finance has been sizeable and large-scale industry in the private sector has been the main beneficiary.

The financial assistance to industry is given in the following four main forms: *(i)* term loans and advances, *(ii)* subscription to shares and debentures, *(iii)* underwriting of new issues, and *(iv)* guarantees for term loans and deferred payments. The first two forms place funds directly in the hands of companies as subscriptions to shares and debentures are subscriptions to new issues. The last two forms facilitate the raising of funds from other sources. We have already explained in Section 3.8.1 the meaning and importance of underwriting of new issues. For attracting risk capital into the industry, such underwriting of shares by development banks is at least as important as the direct subscription to these shares. Guarantees from development banks assure creditors (banks and others) that their credit to industry whether in the form of loans or deferred payments is secure. For development banks, it only involves 'contingent liabilities,' that is liabilities which become payable only when the underlying agreements are not fulfilled. Therefore, such liabilities do not lock up funds of development banks, but are instrumental in attracting funds from other sources.

The development banks in India are a post-independence phenomenon (except the land development banks). Their structure is indicated in Figure 8.1. Some of them are for promoting industrial development; some for the development of agriculture; and one for foreign trade. Some are all-India institutions; others are state or lower level institutions. At present, at the all-India level, there are five industrial development banks, one agricultural development bank and one export-import bank. The development banks for the industry are the Industrial Development Bank of India (IDBI), the Industrial Finance Corporation of India (IFCI), the Industrial Credit and Investment Corporation of India (ICICI), and the Industrial Reconstruction Corporation of India (IRCI) for large industries and the Naitonal Small Industries Development Bank of India (SIDBI) for small-scale industries. For agriculture, it is the National Bank for Agriculture and Rural Development (NABARD). The National Industrial Development Corporation (NIDC), which was set up by the Government of India in 1954 for the promotion and development of industries, had also provided some finance till 1963. But since then it has been acting as only a consulting agency. The state level industrial development banks are the State

Financial Corporations (SFCs), the State Industrial Development Corporation (SIDCs) and the State Industrial Investment Corporations (SIICs). For promoting agricultural development, there are mainly district-level banks, called land development banks. The present chapter is devoted to a discussion of these several development banks, (Most of the data in the chapter have been taken from RBI; Report on Currency and Finance, 1990-91, Vols. I and II.)

Figure 8.1

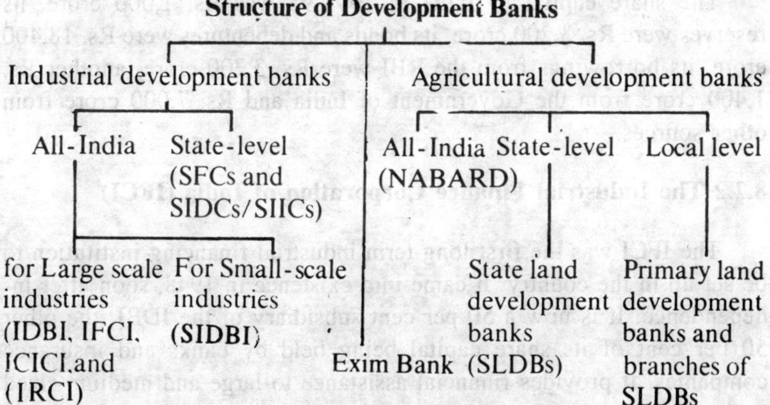

8.2 **Industrial Development Banks for Large Industries** (All-India)

In this section we study very briefly particular features of individual industrial banks for large-scale industries. The common features of their functioning with critical assessment will be taken up separately in the next section.

8.2.1 **The Industrial Development Bank of India** (IDBI)

It is the apex institution in the field of industrial development banking in the country. Set up as a wholly-owned subsidiary of the RBI in July 1964, it was made an autonomous institution in February 1976. Another industrial development bank, the IFCI, and an important all-India investment trust, the UTI, are its subsidiaries. As a development bank, the IDBI provides term finance and other development services to industry along with other development banks. It also provides export credit (term finance and guarantees) in participation with commercial banks.[3] As apex bank, it co-ordinates the activities of other development banks (and term-financing institutions) in the field. Again, as apex bank, it performs yet another important function—that of providing refinance to eligible banks and term-financing institutions, such the IFCI and SFCs, against the term-financing of these institutions to industry. The said refinance is provided in three ways: (*i*) by subscription to the shares and bonds of term-financing institutions, (*ii*) by refinancing term loans to industry and export trade, and (*iii*) by rediscounting the usance bills arising out of sales of indigenously produced machinery on deferred payment basis.

The share capital of IDBI in 1994-95 was Rs. 1,000 crore, its reserves were Rs. 3,200 crore, its bonds and debentures were Rs. 18,400 crore, its borrowings from the RBI were Rs. 3,300 crore, another Rs. 1,400 crore from the Government of India and Rs. 7,000 crore from other sources.

8.2.2 The Industrial Finance Corporation of India (IFCI)

The IFCI was the first long-term industrial financing institution to be set up in the country. It came into existence in 1948, soon after independence. It is now a 50 per cent subsidiary of the IDBI, the other 50 per cent of its share capital being held by banks and insurance companies. It provides financial assistance to large and medium-sized limited companies in both the private and public sectors and to co-operative societies. Though it is empowered to provide assistance in all forms, namely, loans (in rupees and foreign currencies), underwriting, subscriptions to share and debenture issues, and guarantee of deferred payments and loans, it has been essentially a lending agency, mostly of rupee resources. During the first 10-15 years of its operations, it had lent predominantly to sugar (mostly co-operative factories) and textile industries. In later years it has lent increasingly to other industries as well. As a development bank, it has been rather conservative, acting mostly as a lending agency and a highly reluctant underwriter of new issues. In recent years it has started taking interest (along with other development banks) in such promotional activities as the organization of techno-economic surveys and setting up of technical consultancy organizations. In the past, its lendings have suffered from too high rates of defaults of interest and principal.

8.2.3 The Industrial Credit and Investment Corporation of India (ICICI)

The ICICI was set up in 1955 as a private-sector development bank. All its share capital was contributed by banks, insurance companies, and foreign institutions, including the World Bank. Right from its inception, the World Bank has played a key role in its organization, functioning (development of project-appraisal techniques and operating procedures) and raising of foreign currency funds. The ICICI has played a leading role in two key areas, namely, (*i*) the development of underwriting facilities in the country and (*ii*) the provision of foreign currency loans. Now the IDBI acts as the leader in the former field. The ICICI has concentrated its assistance over a few growth industries, like metal and metal products, chemicals and machinery manufactures. The beneficiaries are large units only. Because it has been very choosy in the selection of units to be assisted, its default ratio has been very low.

8.2.4 The Industrial Reconstruction Bank of India (IRBI).

The IRBI was set up in April 1971 with the objective of reviving and revitalising sick industrial units in public or private sectors. Apart from providing finance, it attempts to achieve its objective through such measures of reconstruction as restructuring of management, provision of technical and managerial guidance, securing assistance of other financial institutions and government agencies. So far its area of activity has remained limited mainly to West Bengal. Its share capital has been subscribed by the IDBI, IFCI, ICICI, LIC and nationalised banks. Keeping in view the enormous problem of growing industrial sickness in the country, the financial resource of the IRBI are rather limited. Dealings with only sick units have also loaded the IRBI with increasing amounts of bad and doubtful debts.

Cumulatively, at end-March 1995, sanctions and disbursements amounted to about Rs. 2,760 crore and about 1,870 crore, respectively. Most of the loans go to the private sector and most (70 per cent) are term-loans—going to large and medium sick units. The toal resources at the disposal of the IRBI were about Rs. 1,300 crore.

8.3 All-India Industrial Development Banks—Main Features with Evaluation

It will be tedious, highly space-intensive, and less revealing if we study various features of the organization and working of individual development banks in detail. Also these banks belong to one broad class of financial institutions already identified as industrial development banks for large industries. Therefore, we take a consolidated view of all of them put together and study the main features of their operations. The figures given below have been rounded off liberally and are intended to give only rough orders of magnitudes involved. Most of the time, amounts outstanding are those at the end of March or June 1995.

1. *Total Finance.* At the end of March 1991, the total financial resources (liabilities or assets) had amounted to about Rs. 70,000 crore.

For 1994-95, the total new financial assistance sanctioned and disbursed by these banks was about Rs. 41,000 crore and Rs. 20,000 crore. In comparison, during 1994-95, all non-governmental companies had raised through new issues total capital of Rs. 26,400 crore only.

In the above picture, the IDBI as the apex bank, occupies dominant position, followed by the ICICI and the IFCI. In comparison, the IRBI is very small. In the total financial resources of about Rs. 70,000 crore in their hands at the end of March 1995, about Rs. 38,000 crore were with the IDBI, about Rs. 19,600 crore with the ICICI and about Rs. 11,200 crore with the IFCI. (The resources with the IRCI were only Rs. 1,300 crore).

In the total financial assistance sactioned by the three large development banks of Rs. 41,000 crore during 1994-95, the share of IDBI was Rs. 20,000 crore, that of ICICI Rs. 15,000 crore and of IFCI Rs. 6,000 crore. The respective disbursement were Rs. 11,000 crore, Rs. 7,000 crore and Rs. 3,000 crore. The outstanding total financial assistance as at March-end 1995 was Rs. 33,000 crore from the IDBI, Rs. 31,000 crore from the ICICI and Rs. 15,000 crore from the IFCI

2. *Sources of Finance.* The key point to note here is the difference in the sources of finance of development banks on the one hand and other financial institutions such as banks, insurance companies, and the UTI on the other hand. The latter class of institutions raise funds by mobilising savings of the public through their sale of deposits, insurance policies and units. But the financial resources of development banks in India have been raised, not directly from the public, but, in the main, from the Government of India, the RBI, other financial institutions, and foreign sources (mainly the World Bank and its affiliates, the International Finance Corporation, IFC and International

Development Association, IDA).

The forms in which this is done are two : (*i*) subscriptions to their share capital and debentures and (*ii*) borrowings from the RBI/IDBI. For example, the entire share capital of (Rs. 1,000 crore) of the IDBI has been provided by the Government of India. The former, in turn has subscribed to the share capital of the IFCI, which is its 50 per cent subsidiary, and the IRBI. The remaining share capital of the last two institutions is in the hands of the LIC and nationalised banks. The share capital of ICICI is owned by banks, insurance companies and foreign financial institutions. The total share capital amounted to only about Rs. 550 crore and reserves were another Rs. 730 crore.

The two most important sources of finance for development banks are bonds/debentures and borrowings from the RBI. At the end of March 1991 they had contributed something like Rs. 17,000 and Rs. 3,700 crore, respectively. Bonds are marketable securities. Therefore, one may possibly infer that their proceeds are collections from the public. But this is not correct. The key feature of the bond issues of IDBI and the IFCI is that they are guaranteed by the Government of India, as to both principal and interest. For all practical purposes, this makes these bonds equivalent to Government of India Bonds. The ICICI bonds, though not guaranteed by the government, are treated as 'trustee securities' for purposes of investment by financial institutions. This and the status of ICICI make them comparable with government bonds. Consequently, the rate of interest on the development bank bonds is also (roughly) the same as that on the Government of India bonds of comparable maturity. The RBI co-ordinates these bond issues with the issues of government bonds. For illustration, we may only note that it has created a Development Assistance Fund out of which loans are made to the IDBI. The line of credit from the International Development Association (IDA, a soft-loan affiliate of the World Bank) is also used to make loans to the development banks. The total foreign loans outstanding at the end of the March 1995 were of the order of Rs. 7,400 crore.

Most of the Reserve Bank credit is extended through the IDBI. This credit is made available from the National Industrial Credit (Long-Term Operations) Fund of the RBI which was created along with the setting up of the IDBI in July 1964 with the objective of providing loan funds to the IDBI. The RBI has been contributing to this Fund every year from its profits. At the end of June 1995, this Fund stood at about Rs. 5,675 crore and other sources of finance were like this : foreign currency loans : Rs. 4,200 crores, out of which loans of Rs. 2,600 crores had been raised by the ICICI and the rest by the IFCI. The funds derived from other sources were about Rs. 6,600 crores.

This shows that the development banks are financial intermediaries mainly for the allocation of term finance. They do nothing to raise funds directly from the public as do banks, insurance companies, and the UTI.

This kind of arrangement has provided large industry with cheap, organized, assured, large and growing amount of term finance. No wonder this sector of industry has become over-dependent on development banks for term finance. Loans, as preferred form of finance, have encouraged very high debt-equity ratios and low rate of interest on loans has encouraged high capital-intensity in industry.

3. *Allocation of Funds.* As financial intermediaries, the main function of development banks is as allocators of funds (and not as mobilisers of savings from the public). Therefore, their degree of success must be judged on the quality of their performance of this role. Two questions are important here: (*i*) the form of financial assistance, equity, debentures, or loan capital and (*ii*) to whom finance is provided. On both counts, the development banks have not worked to the satisfaction of social objectives, which have themselves been never clearly specified.

Consider first the form of financial assistance. The bulk of this assistance has been provided in the form of debt capital, predominantly in term loans. This form of loan financing has, no doubt, assured the development banks a steady return on their funds, without involving them into difficult managerial problems equity participation would entail. But, this (apparent) security has been bought at a high price. First, it has distorted the capital structure of the borrowing industrial enterprises in favour of loan capital. Their debt-equity ratios in most cases have assumed values which are considered too high by generally-accepted standards even in industrially-developed countries. In the casc of new enterprises, this is specially serious, because right from inception, their financial health is wcak. The burden of fixed interest payments is much too heavy on them. Consequently, the default rate is also high, as we have already noted in the case of the IFCI finance. This is one source of growing industrial sickness in the country. Second, the government loses potential corporation tax, because, for tax purposes, interest is treated as a cost item in arriving at corporate profits. All income earned by the IDBI, including interest income, is tax-free, so that in its case interest does not get taxed even when it is received by the IDBI. This encourages the IDBI to resort excessively to debt financing, rather than equity financing of enterprises. In the case of other development banks, interest income earned by them is, no doubt, taxable. But the government would presumably gain more tax revenue if the financing was more in the form of equity capital than in the form of debt capital. For, the income from equity capital would be taxed in the hands of industrial companies as profits and then again when a part of it is distributed as dividends. Other important consequences are the socially adverse distribution of asset ownership in the corporate sector, slow development and spread of industrial entrepreneurship in the economy, and tardy growth of the developmental role of development banks. We shall discuss them under point (5) below.

The bulk of debt capital is provided in the form of term loans. Debentures are marketable security, whereas loans are not. Companies prefer the latter to the former, because though the interest cost on both the kinds is usually the same, the servicing cost of raising term loans is much lower than the cost of a debenture issue. Much more importantly, default on loans is easier than on debentures. Defaults on loans can be directly negotiated with the lending agencies and payments rescheduled without much difficulty.

The danger of foreclosure on collaterals is also minimal to defaulting parties, because the development banks, as a matter of policy, resort to this step only sparingly. Also, defaults generally are not made public. In the case of debentures, all these facilities will be absent, especially if they are openly traded in the market and not closely held by a few lending agencies. The defaulting companies would lose a lot of market goodwill, and it would be very difficult for them to raise new funds in the market. The prices of their equities would also suffer. Loan capital protects companies against this kind of healthy market discipline. It tends to breed and has actually bred soft or weak companies, which fall on the sick list at the first opportunity. Given the relatively small equity base and very much smaller proportion of promoters' equity, the total atmosphere of corruption and false manipulations, it is easy enough for unscrupulous persons to show losses in the companies under their control and let the lending agencies bear the burden, without suffering any loss of their own investments and profits. Such a climate is fast spreading in the industry. The irony is that the soft lending policy adopted by the development banks has made no mean contribution to it.

As a by-product of the lending policy of the development banks, the corporate bond market has not developed much in the country. In the first instance, very small amounts of corporate bonds or debentures are issued. And whatever are issued are generally bought and held closely by the financial institutions themselves. There is very little active trading in them. Thus, their prices (or yield rates on them) are not formed by the forces of demand and supply in the market. Consequently, companies do not get differentiated in terms of their borrowing power and all are able to borrow at the same rate of interest. Little wonder that there is so little concern on the part of so many corporate borrowers to manage their affairs more efficiently. Our observations would, of course, apply only to large-sized corporate borrowers and neither to small public limited companies nor to private limited companies or co-operative societies.

Who are the beneficiaries of the financial assistance provided by the development banks ? What is the size-distribution of enterprises and projects assisted ? Are they new enterprises or expansion and diversification projects of existing concerns ? Are the new enterprises promoted by new entrepreneurs/technocrats or by existing business houses ? Are the latter big monopoly houses ? Do the beneficiaries fall in the category of MRTP (Monopolistic Restriction of Trade Practices) companies ? Are the assisted companies healthy or sick ? What is their export performance? What is the industry-wise distribution of financial assistance ? What is the geographical distribution of this assistance ? How far have backward areas been helped ? The list of questions can be lengthened further. This indicates that the allocation of financial assistance has many dimensions. In this book, satisfactory answers to all these questions cannot be provided or even attempted. For such answers, a full-scale independent study will be required. The purpose of posing the questions was to make the readers aware of the several aspects of the allocational role of the development banks.

Yet, a few very brief answers must be given. As a matter of government policy, the development banks under study have been designed to serve large industries. Both the IDBI and the ICICI cater to the needs of relatively larger enterprises. A part of the assistance provided by the IFCI goes to medium enterprises also. (The smaller enterprises are supposed to be assisted by the SFCs). The beneficiaries are a mixed bag of new and old enterprises, (a few of the new enterprises have been promoted by technocrats too), healthy as well as sick, those run by monopoly houses as well as others, and some falling in the category of backward areas. The distribution of assistance over industries is getting diversified over time. In the absence of clear-cut guidelines and well-developed criteria of evaluation, it is difficult to pass a summary judgment or accord marks.

4. *Cost of Funds and other Terms and Conditions.* Apart from providing large blocks of funds to large companies (a very important help in itself), the development banks render them assistance in other forms, too. The normal rate of interest of 14 per cent per year (since March 1981), at which development banks make loans is on the low side in a capital-scarce country like India. It is much lower than what would be determined by the capital market, if the large companies were to raise the same amounts of funds in the open market. Then, the IDBI provides concessional finance for specified purposes, such as, for units in specified backward areas. The IDBI provides refinance to banks and others at concessional rates with the stipulation that their primary lender's rate does not exceed appropriate ceilings.

All these concessions put together, coupled with the easy availability of term finance amount to pampering of private large-scale industry by public financial institutions, constitute excessive subsidisation of this sector, and have bred soft industrial enterprise with low overall efficiency. The low cost of funds (in relation to the true social cost of capital in the capital-scarce economy of India) has encouraged the adoption of highly capital-intensive technology and thus contributed to the problem of growing unemployment in the country.

5. *Building Up of a Technical-Managerial-Consultancy Service Complex.* As development banks, the promotional and consultancy service role of the banks is no less important than the provision of term finance, especially for new entrepreneurs. In this context three things are worthy of note. First, trained personnel are needed in good number for the servicing of their financing activities, *viz.*, for project appraisal, requiring evaluation of the technical and managerial feasibility and financial projections of the projects submitted for assistance, project supervision and follow-up activities, careful scrutiny of periodic progress reports, and competent persons to serve as nominee-directors on the boards of directors of assisted companies. With the growth in total business and its increasing diversity, increasing amount of trained human input is required. The shortfalls in quantity and quality in this field cannot be ruled out.

Second, to map the industrial potential in the country, the

development banks have conducted Industrial Potential Surveys of all the backward states and union territories. Much more remains to be done at district levels. Much is not known about the follow-up action. This will necessarily take its own time.

Third, Technical Service Organizations (TCOs) have been organized for the promotion of industrial activities. Their stated objectives are a package of services under one roof to entrepreneurs, in particular to the small and medium entrepreneurs, from the stage of project identification to successful implementation. These services are said to include preparation of feasibility studies and project reports covering technical, market, commercial, financial and economic aspects of a project, and various kinds of services to existing entrepreneurs facing problems and planning expansion or diversification. A successful working of the TCOs will require adequate professional staff which they at present lack.

All told, there is urgent need for developing further and fast the human factor (including consultancy services) needed for a balanced and equitable industrial growth of the country—a task which the development banks have paid much less attention to as compared to the provision of term finance.

8.4 State-Level Industrial Development Banks

At the state-level, too, there is a combination of financing agencies and industrial development banks, mainly for the development of medium and small-scale industries in respective states, with some emphasis on the industrial development of their backward regions. They are State Financial Corporations (SFCs) which are primarily financing agencies. Besides, most individual states have either a State Industrial Development Corporation (SIDC) or a State Industrial Investment Corporation (SIIC). In 1994-95, there were 18 SFCs and 26 SIDCs/SIICs. We study the two kinds of institutions separately.

8.4.1 The SFCs

The SFCs came to be organized in individual states after the enabling Central Act to this effect came into force in August 1952. They are state-level organizations for the provision of term finance to medium and small scale industries. The share capital has been contributed by the state governments, the RBI (transferred to the IDBI after its separation from the RBI in February 1976), the IDBI, scheduled banks, insurance companies, and others. The control of SFCs is shared by the state governments and the IDBI. At the end of March 1995, the total paid-up capital and reserves of all the SFCs stood at about Rs. 1,200 crores. The two most important items of liabilities were bonds and debentures and borrowings from the IDBI. The IDBI, which is the main source of loans, provides funds mainly in the form of refinance. It also administers the International Development Association (IDA) credit to them in the form of foreign currency loans. The SFCs also borrow from the SIDBI and IDBI.

The SFCs are authorised to provide financial assistance in all the four major forms, namely loans and advances, subscription to shares and debentures, underwriting of new issues, and guarantee of loans from third parties and deferred payments. As in the case of all-India development banks, the bulk of the SFC finance (about 90 per cent) is made available in the form of loans and advances. They have not yet developed much other forms of financial assistance.

The SFCs are playing an increasingly important role in the development of medium and small industries. A major part of their credit goes to small-scale industries. Upto March 1995, cumulative sanctions and disbursements of financial assistance had aggregated about Rs 19,000 crore and Rs. 15,000 crore, respectively. Liberal assistance is given to technician entrepreneurs and to industrial units in specified backward areas. The latter are given finance on concessional terms. Industry-wise assistance is getting more diversified.

The operations of the SFCs suffer from a very high ratio of overdues/defaults, excessive concentration of loan finance, weak promotional role, and delays in sanctioning and disbursing assistance. The calibre of their personnel is relatively poor and needs to be upgraded through training and proper recruitment. The removal of these and other operational and organisational deficiencies is essential for making the SFCs play their assigned roles better.

8.4.2 The SIDCs/SIICs

The SIDCs/SIICs came on the scene much after the SFCs. Whereas the SFCs are under the dual control of the state governments and IDBI (earlier, the RBI), the SIDCs/SIICs have been set up entirely by state governments. Besides providing finance, these institutions perform a variety of promotional functions, such as arranging for land, power, roads, licences for industrial units, sponsoring the establishment of such units, especially in backward areas, etc. They score over other development banks in that about one-third of their total finance is provided in the form of underwriting/direct subscription assistance and only about two-thirds of it in the form of term loans. Since inception upto March 1995 the total amount of assistance sanctioned and disbursed by them was about Rs. 9,800 crores and Rs. 7,000 crores, respectively. A significant part of this assistance goes to units in the joint sector and the public sector and only the rest to the units in the private sector. The funds are raised from the usual sources, *viz,* share capital and reserves, borrowings from the IDBI, the state governments and banks, and bonds and debentures. These institutions also suffer from the problems of defaults, inadequate and inexperienced staff, and organizational deficiencies.

8.5 **Export-Import (or Exim) Bank of India**

This bank was established on January 1, 1982. It has taken over the export-finance function of the IDBI and acts as the apex institution relating to the financing of foreign trade. Its main functions are to provide financial assistance to exporters and importers, act as the principal financial institution for coordinating the work of other institutions engaged in the field of financing international trade, and undertake limited development and merchant banking activities in relation to export-oriented industries. It provides financial assistance by way of direct loans and advances for the purpose of export or import, refinance of loans and advances, granted by banks or other notified financial institutions for purposes of export or import, rediscounting of finance export bills for banks, provision of overseas investment finance and lines of credit for Indian companies and the guaranteeing of obligations, jointly with banks, on behalf of project exporters in the fields of construction, turnkey, supply and consultancy. The total financial assistance provided by the bank and outstanding at the end of March 1995 was about Rs. 2,600 crores. The loans sanctioned and disbursed during the year 1994-95 were about Rs. 2,900 crore and Rs. 1,560 crore, respectively, with outstandings of Rs. 3,300 crore.

8.6 **National Bank for Agricultural and Rural Development** (NABARD)

This apex National Bank was established in July 1982 to oversee and develop the entire rural credit system including agricultural credit. Consequently, the major functions of the Agricultural Credit Department of the RBI and the entire undertaking of the ARDC (Agricultural Refinance and Development Corporation), were taken over by it; the assets and liabilities of the RBI relating to the National Agricultural Credit (Long Term Operations) Fund and the National Agricultural Credit (Stabilisation) Fund were transferred to it; also it took over from the RBI the refinance, development and statutory inspection of co-operative banks and RRBs (regional rural banks—see Section 5.3). (The RBI, however, continues to retain its essential control over these banks. The primary urban co-operative banks are also its charge.)

The NABARD provides rural credit by way of refinance and loans and advances to SCBs (State Cooperative Banks), LDBs (Land Development Banks), RRBs and other approved financial institutions for financing production, marketing and investment activities relating to agriculture, rural development, small-scale industries, industries in tiny and decentralised sector, cottage and village industries, handicrafts and other crafts and other allied economic activities in rural areas (see Section 7.7).

The NABARD's share capital of Rs. 330 crore was contributed equally by the Central Government and the RBI and its reserves were Rs. 1,230 crore, giving owned funds of Rs. 1,560 crore as at March end 1995. Its other sources of funds are mainly (*a*) borrowings from the Central Government, the RBI and the market and (*b*) its two national rural credit funds. Thus, at the end of March 1995, of the total funds of about Rs. 18,000 crore at its disposal, the borrowings from various sources were about Rs. 3,500 crore and it had a general line of credit open to it from the RBI of Rs. 4,000 crore. The two national funds are National Credit (Long Term Operations) Fund and National Rural Credit (Stabilisation) Fund. At the end of June 1995, the two Funds had accumulated Rs. 8,000 crore and Rs. 800 crore respectively.

At the end of March 1995, total loans and advances outstanding of NABARD were about Rs. 18,000 crore, of which medium-term and long-term refinance was more than Rs. 10,000 crore and short-term general line of credit was of more than Rs. 4,000 crore. In addition, the cumulative number of schemes sanctioned was about 1,17,000, total financial assistance (refinance) sanctioned was about Rs. 39,000 crore and disbursements were about Rs. 25,000 crore. Purposewise, the largest part of refinance assistance has gone for schemes of minor irrigation, farm mechanisation, storage and market yards and dairy development, etc.

As said above, the NABARD provides long-term refinance for its approved schemes by way of loans and advances to commercial banks, SLDBs, SCBs and subscriptions to debentures of SLDBs. *In the year 1994-95*, the total refinance committed had amounted to Rs. 3,800 crore and disbursements to about Rs. 3,000 crore. The bulk of the latter amount had gone to SLDBs and scheduled commercial banks. The total number of schemes covered were 7,500. The refinance by the NABARD under the IRDP was only Rs. 620 crore.

8.7 Land Development Banks

For the supply of long and medium-term credit to agriculture, specialised institutions in the form of land development banks have been organized in the country effectively since 1929. Though they are registered as co-operative societies, they are limited liability organizations. They have a two-tier structure. At the top (state) level are 19 state (or central) land development banks (SLDBs). At the local level are branches of SLDBs and primary land development banks. The SLDBs give loans to their members for productive investment. The period of the loan varies from 15 to 30 years. At the end of March 1993 the LDB loans outstanding were of Rs. 4,400 crores.

The SLBDs raise their resources from share capital and reserves, deposits, loans and advances, and debentures. The bulk of the funds come from debentures. They are guaranteed (both as to capital and interest) by the state government concerned. Such guarantees have improved the marketability of these debentures. The debentures are mostly subscribed to by the NABARD, the LIC, commercial banks, and the central and state governments. As pointed out in the previous section, they also get refinance from the NABARD for its several schemes.

The working of the LDBs suffers from several defects common to the co-operative credit movement in India (see Section 7.5.1). Among them mention may be made of the problem of overdues, inadequate and incompetent staff incapable of doing project appraisal, monitoring, and evaluation, corruption, and excessive dependence on outside sources of funds.

NOTES

1. In 1994-95 and 1995-96, the IFCI and the IDBI have been made into public limited companies and allowed to raise equity capital in the market with the proviso that the GOI retains at least 51 per cent of share capital. Besides, the authorised capital of IDBI was increased from Rs. 1,000 crore to Rs. 2,000 crore, which can be raised further upto Rs. 5,000 crore.

CHAPTER 9

Non-Bank Financial Intermediaries

9.1 Introduction

Non-Bank Financial Intermediaries (NBFIs) is a heterogeneous group of financial institutions other than commercial and co-operative banks. They include a wide variety of financial institutions, which raise funds from the public, directly or indirectly, to lend them to ultimate spenders. The development banks (such as the IDBI, IFCI, ICICI, SFCs, land develpment banks, etc.) about which we studied in the previous chapter fall in this category. They specialise in making term loans to their borrowers. Three other all-India big term-lending institutions are the LIC, the GIC and its subsidiaries, and the UTI. Of these, only the UTI is a pure NBFI, the others raise funds as premia from the sale of insurance. Then, there are provident funds and post offices that mobilise public savings in a big way for onward transmission to ultimate spenders. A large number of these institutions are public-sector undertakings. Besides them, there is a large number of small NBFI, such as investment companies, loan (or finance) companies, hire-purchase finance companies and the equipment leasing companies which are private sector companies, with only a few exceptions. We shall study briefly about each of them (except the development banks already discussed in the previous chapter) in this chapter. Then, there are also specialised finance corporations for providing finance for only one specific economic activity. The important examples are Rural Electrification Corporation, Housing and Urban Development Corporation (HUDCO), Housing Development Finance Corporation (HDFC) and Film Finance Corporation. We shall not discuss them in this book, as they are not of a general character but, as their names indicate, are restricted to the financing of only one designated type of economic activity and/or do not mobilise funds from the general public.

In the USA and the UK the NBFIs have made phenomenal progress after the First World War. They compete vigorously with banks for the public's savings and as sources of finance to deficit spenders. In India their progress is more recent and that, too, with a lot of initiative from the government and the RBI. They fill important gaps in the financial structure of India's economy and have come to play an important role in the industrial as well as agricultural development of the economy. There is still vast scope as well as need for growth of the existing NBFIs and improvement in their organization and working and for promoting new types of NBFIs, especially those that specialise in the provision of mortgage finance for residential houses, like the building societies in the UK or the savings and loan associations in the USA which, unlike the HUDCO and the HDFC, mobilise directly the savings of the public for housing finance.

In Section 2.3 we have already discussed in general terms the nature and role of financial intermediaries, including the NBFIs. It will be useful for readers to read it again.

9.2 The Life Insurance Corporation of India (LIC)

The LIC was established in 1956 by nationalising all the life insurance companies operating in India. Since then in the field of life insurance the LIC has near-monopoly, as the amount of life insurance business through postal insurance and state insurance is relatively much smaller. Life insurance is a very important form of long-term contractual savings. It both promotes savings and results in their institutionalisation or mobilisation. The income-tax concession provides further incentive to higher-income persons to save through life insurance policies. The total volume of insurance business has also been growing in the country with the spread of insurance consciousness in the country. It can grow at a faster speed, if the organizational and operational efficiency of the LIC can be improved (and there is a lot of scope for it), new kinds of insurance covers introduced, its services extended to smaller places, the message of life insurance made more popular, and the general price level is kept stable, so that the insuring public does not get cheated of a large chunk of the real value of its long-term savings through inflation.

The importance of the LIC as a capital-market or a term-financing institution is very high. The annual net accrual of investible funds from life business (after meeting all kinds of payments liabilities to policyholders) and net income from its vast investment are quite large. Equally, its size of the investment portfolio outstanding is also very large. At the end of March 1995 this was about Rs. 53,500 crore.

The LIC is a heavy investor of funds in government's dated market securities. In 1994-95, it had invested more than Rs. 44,000 crore in them. Besides, it had sanctioned and disbursed financial assistance to the corporate sector amounting to Rs. 1,790 crore and 1,340 crore, respectively. Like banks, the LIC also is a captive investor in government bonds. Under the law, the LIC is required to invest at least 50% of its accruals in the form of premium income in government and other approved securities, subject to a minimum of 25% in central government securities. Besides, it has to invest in debentures of co-operative land development banks, and give loans to approved authorities (like state governments and electricity boards) for such social schemes as housing, water supply, electricity, etc. These investments and loans should add upto at least 87.5% of the premium income. Only the remaining 12.5 per cent can be made available directly to the private sector. We must, however, reckon with the indirect finance, too. For example, a part of the funds raised by the government flow back to the private sector as direct loans and indirectly through the development banks studied in the previous chapter. The loans for housing and investments in the share capital and bonds of other financial institutions, especially land development banks go, in the main, to the private sector. Therefore, the contribution of life funds to the private sector is much more than what is indicated by the figures of its direct assistance to the sector.

The LIC funds are made available directly to the private sector through investment in shares and debentures and loans. The largest amount is invested in equity shares, followed by preference shares and then debentures. The LIC has played a leading role (along with the ICICI) in developing the underwriting (of new issues) business. Now other financial institutions led by the IDBI have also become very important. Underwriting of new issues by the LIC is usually done with the objective of purchasing the issue for its own portfolio and not for sale to the public. The bulk of the LIC's purchases of industrial securities is, however, made in the second-hand market, and not the new issues market for the simple reason that there are not enough good new issues forthcoming in the market to meet the demand for such issues from the financial institutions and the investing public.

The LIC is a very powerful factor in the securities market in India. It was the single largest shareholder in the market. (The UTI is now in this position.) Its shareholding extends to a majority of large and medium-sized non-financial companies and is significant in size. In a great many individual companies its equity shareholding is sizeable, going upto 30 per cent. Thus, the ownership interests of the LIC alone in industrial equity show the hold the public sector financial institutions have come to acquire in the private corporate sector. Add to this the share-holding of other public financial institutions and their convertibility rights. The total would make the public financial institutions the single largest group of owners of a large number of private-sector companies. However, these ownership rights (actual and potential) have been exercised to a very limited extent so far.

As would be expected, the LIC's investments in large companies are large. This is because the shares of such companies are normally more profitable to hold commercially and are relatively easier to acquire, too. The floating market supply of shares of good small companies is generally small.

The LIC acts as a kind of downward stabiliser for the share market, as the continuous inflow of fresh funds with it enables it to buy even when the market is weak. Since it is a long-term investor rather than a speculator, it is happy to buy good scrips when their prices are low and therefore benefit from their price appreciation when the market improves. But, for the same reason, it does not usually sell shares from its holdings even when the market has overshot. This is partly due to the continuous pressure for investing new funds and partly due to the disincentive of the capital gains tax. The result is that on the upward movement the stock market is not mellowed by the presence or the investment policy of the LIC. In this context it should also be noted that this kind of investment policy of the LIC (as also of the UTI and the GIC and its subsidiaries) does not facilitiate or promote wider participation by the public in equity investment by acting as 'seasoning' houses for shares, releasing them for the general public when it is willing to hold them and buying back a part of them on the market downturn at lower prices. This way price fluctuations on the stock market will be smaller, the public confidence and participation in the stock market will improve, and the public financial institutions will gain, if they do not count out the tax they pay the government on the capital gains they make in the process.

9.3 General Insurance Companies

The general insurance companies sell insurance against specified risks, such as of loss from fire and accident, to property of various kinds (motor vehicles, marine cargo and hull, goods, machinery, buildings, etc) and also against risk of personal accident and sickness. The policies do not include any savings feature. The purchaser of general insurance simply buys a service and not any financial asset. The general insurance companies are thus not financial intermediaries in the full sense. However, they do acumulate pools of funds from premium and investment income for meeting claims under their policies. Thus, they do manage portfolios of assets like other financial insitutions.

The general insurance industry in India was nationalised with effect from January 1, 1973. At the time of nationalisation, more than 100 small companies and only a few large companies were operating in the field. With the nationalisation, one holding company by the name of the General Insurance Corporation of India (GIC) was set up. All the existing companies were merged and reorganized into four subsidiaries of the GIC, which now carry out the business of general insurance. After nationalisation, the GIC and its subsidiaries have made good progress and they, too, have become important sources of funds to both the government and the private sector. They are required by law to invest at least 35% of their fresh accruals of investible funds in government and other approved securities, with a minimum of 25% in central government securities. The companies are large investors in corporate securities, mostly debentures, and participate in the underwriting of new issues and in giving term loans to industry. In 1994–95, they had sanctioned total financial assistance (to industry) of about Rs. 700 crore and disbursed about Rs. 400 crore of it.

9.4. The Unit Trust of India (UTI) and Other Mutual Funds

Mutual funds are a very important form of NBFIs for promoting as well as mobilising financial savings. They also act as important investment institutes, especially for the corporate sector. The term mutual fund is commonly used for such NBFIs in USA and Canada and is now increasingly used in India, too, whereas similar financial institutions are called 'unit trusts' in the U.K. It is just a matter of historical accident that when the first mutual fund of this kind was set up in India in 1964, it was named as the *Unit Trust of India.* In recent years (since 1988), such institutes have invariably carried the generic title of a mutual fund in their names. Mutual funds are fast becoming an important medium for mobilizing savings of the community, particularly of the middle-class and small investors, as they (supposedly) provide benefits of portfolio management of stock-market securities to their share-holders. A mutual fund does it by minimising risk and raising its rate of return through portfolio diversification, having an appropriate mix of securities, watching expertly market developments all the time and turning over the portfolio to benefit to the maximum from the ever-changing market scene. Other things being the same, the gains to the shareholders of a mutual fund generally depend upon the quality of its portfolio selection and management.

In the mutual-funds industry in India, the UTI occupies top-most and dominating position. Established in 1964, it is a 50 per cent subsidiary of the IDBI (formerly of the RBI). The rest of the share capital has been subscribed by the LIC, the SBI, other scheduled commercial banks, the IFCI and the ICICI. The tax concessions accorded by the Government of India to the UTI and its unit-holders for about first 25 years of its operations have played an important role, among other things, in popularising the UTI among the saver-investors and providing it a firm footing in the market.

The UTI is free in the investment of its funds. It is not constrained statutorily like the LIC and banks to invest specified minimum proportions of their funds in government and other approved securities. Thus, at the end of March 1995, of the total investible funds of Rs. 63,000 crore with the UTI, about 80 per cent of them were invested in corporate equity and debentures, term loans and special deposits, etc. Its investment in government securities at end-June 1995 was about Rs. 10,000 crore.

In recent years, 21 other mutual funds (besides the UTI) have also come up in the market. 11 of them are in the private sector and 10 are in the public sector. The latter have been set up mainly by the merchant banking subsidiaries of some public sector banks, *viz.*, the S.B.I., Canara Bank, Punjab National Bank and Bank of India and also by the LIC of India and by the GIC of India. The UTI, the SBI and Canara Bank have also established offshore funds to raise foreign exchange resources.

9.5 **Provident / Pension Funds**

The Provident/pension funds represent the most important form of long-term contractual saving of the household sector. The annual contribution to them is currently running at double the rate of annual contribution to life insurance, another major form of long-term contractual saving. In the financial year 1994-95, about Rs. 1,11,000 crore had accumulated in the P.F. and other accounts with the GOI. The resources mobilised by the funds during the same year were Rs. 20,600 crore.

The provident funds are practically a post-independence phenomenon. Under the law, provident funds have been made compulsory in the organized sector of industry, coal mining, plantations, and services (such as government, banking, insurance, teaching). Separate provident fund legislation exists for coal mining, industries, and Assam tea plantations. With the growth of the organized sector of the economy and in wage employment, savings mobilisation through provident funds will grow further. The wage employees are encouraged to join provident fund schemes and make contributions to them, because thereby alone they earn employers' matching contribution to the fund. Then, for income-tax purposes, deductions are allowed for provident fund contributions. Provisions also exist in all cases for borrowing against one's provident fund accumulation. The provident fund collections are made through deduction at source. This makes for convenience, regularity, and certainty of collection. The provident funds are required to invest at least 30% of their accruals in government and other approved securities, with a minimum of 15% in central government securities. The balance is mostly held in fixed deposits with banks.

9.6 **Post Offices**

Post offices serve as the vehicle for mobilising small savings of the public for the government. Their large number and wide geographical distribution throughout the country help in this mobilisation at very low additional cost. Small savings are mobilised under different schemes of small savings launched by the central government. The small savings instruments broadly comprise 'deposits' and 'certificates'.

Small savings constitute an important source of capital receipts for the government. In 1990-91 they had yielded almost Rs. 18,000 crore in gross terms. At the end of March 1991, total small savings stood at about Rs. 53,000 crore.

The rate of interest offered on some of the small savings instruments is higher than the rates on other comparable instruments like bank deposits. Furthermore, investments in 'small savings' carry many fiscal incentives (tax concessions), which go to raise the effective rate of interest to investors falling in high-income taxable categories. Attractive effective interest rates have helped greatly the mobilisation of savings under the 'small savings' schemes.

9.7 **Other 'Non-Bank Financial Companies'** (NBFCs)

A wide variety of non-bank companies (NBCs) accept deposits from the public. The RBI divides them broadly into two categories: (*a*) financial companies and (*b*) non-financial companies. Only the former (*i.e.* NBFCs) can be called NBFIs as they raise funds from the public and also lend to it, whereas non-financial companies are basically companies engaged in manufacturing or trade and accept deposits from the public for their own use. The RBI collects annually data from all companies reporting deposits, whether public limited or private limited, government or non-government. The latest RBI survey gives data for March 31, 1988 (*RBI Bulletin,* July 1991). On this date, there were about 10,300 such reporting companies, of which 7,600 were financial companies and the rest were non-financial companies. The total amount of deposits (mostly in the form of fixed deposits) outstanding were about Rs. 24,000 crore, of which about 70% were with the non-financial NBCs and the rest were with NBFCs. Thus, the average amount of deposits per NBFC was only about Rs. one crore, indicating very small size of such companies.

Collectively, these deposits of NBFCs formed only 6.3% of total deposits with scheduled commercial banks at about Rs. 1,18,000 crore as on March 31, 1988. This indicates the NBFCs do not pose much competition to commercial banks and do not also pose any serious problem for monetary and credit policies of the RBI. However, they do call for much stricter regulation of their activities and proper inspection of their books of account so as to safeguard better the deposits of the public and curtail their several alleged malpractices.

Their finance also is highly costly as compared to bank finance. However, they do serve the needs of the small savers and the borrowers. That is why they are showing a respectable rate of growth of more than 15% per year in their operations.

We discuss below individually several NBFCs operating in India. The data given are all drawn from the *RBI Bulletin* (July 1991, pp. 543-74).

9.7.1 **Investment Companies**

The investment companies are pure financial intermediaries that specialise in the mobilisation of public savings for investment in corporate securities. Unlike commercial banks and insurance companies, they do not render any other service than that of financial intermediation. Their special service comprises entirely of professional management of a large and diversified portfolio of corporate securities. The gain to their investors, therefore, rests purely on the quality of this service.

The invention of the joint stock company paved the way for large-scale industrial enterprises in the private sector. Through corporate securities as financial assets long-term savings of the public can be mobilised for financing corporate activities. To the investing public, equity shares offer an opportunity whereby it can participate in the profits of companies without taking part in their management. But investment in corporate securities, especially ordinary shares, is both risky and tricky. There can be wide fluctuations in stock prices for any number of reasons, converting expected profits into large capital losses. It is neither feasible nor worthwhile for small investors to keep track of the developments likely to affect the prices of stocks they are holding and take corrective action in time. The pooling of risks through portfolio diversification is also not fully open to a small investor on account of the small size of his investment portfolio. Hence there arose a need for the services of financial intermediaries specialising in investment in corporate securities in a diversified manner and under professional management. The public, then, could entrust their savings to these intermediaries and reap the gains of investment in corporate securities under professional management at a small management fee. What these intermediaries do essentially is to transmute primary securities they buy, which are individually risky, into secondary or indirect securities of their own which are much less risky. By buying shares of these intermediaries, the investor essentially buys a prorata share in the diversified securities' portfolio of the intermediary.

In response to the above need, two main types of investment companies have grown in the industrially-advanced west. They are (*a*) closed-end investment companies and (*b*) open-end investment companies. Following convention, we shall call the former only investment companies. The latter are called 'unit trusts' in the UK and 'mutual funds' in the USA and Canada. Closed-end investment companies are so called, because at any time such a company has a fixed amount of share capital. That is, its share capital end is closed. On the other hand, an open-end investment company always stands ready to sell and redeem its shares at prices based on the current value of their assets. Its capital end is always kept open.

Investment companies are not important mobilisers of public savings in India. Most of them are very small. At the end of March 1988, there were 4,000 reporting investment companies (of which 800 companies were public limited and the rest were private limited), with Rs. 425 crores of net owned fund and Rs. 730 crores of deposits, borrowings and other receipts. Private limited companies are set up to manage the investment of a few private persons. Public limited companies sell equity and debt to the public in the same way as industrial companies do. They distribute the income which they earn on their investments by way of dividends. Their securities trade in the stock market in the same way as do other corporate securities. The market prices of their securities may or may not equal the current value of their assets. There are only a few genuine public limited investment companies or trusts with diversified securities' portfolio and they are small. Most are controlled by large business or industrial groups and their investments are concentrated in the companies of the industrial groups to which they belong. Almost all prominent industrial groups have their own investment companies. The major objective of these companies is to control, manage, and assist companies within their particular groups. They do not provide the public the advantage of diversified portfolio holding. Hence they have not been able to attract much public savings. In the changed institutional set up with a variety of public financial institutions to meet the credit needs of both large and small companies, there does not seem much of a case or scope for investment companies in India.

9.7.2 Loan Companies

Another type of NBFIs are loan companies (also called finance companies) found all over the country. (In addition, there is a large number of individual and partnership firms that are engaged in loan business, but are not covered by the RBI survey). At the end of March 1988, there were 1550 reporting loan companies (of which 800 companies were public limited), with total liabilities of about Rs. 7,100 crores. About 60% of this amount was raised in the form of borrowings, other receipts and deposits, and the rest represented their net owned funds. Loan or finance companies are able to attract fixed deposits from the public (especially small savers) mainly by offering high rates of interest, coupled with various kinds of prize, gift, insurance, and other schemes. The services of agents (mostly part-time) are also used to solicit deposits. A part of the funds are kept in fixed deposits with banks and the rest are used to make loans and advances to wholesale traders, retailers, small scale industries, and self-employed persons. The borrowers are persons who cannot get any or adequate credit from commercial banks. The loans of finance companies are generally unsecured. The effective rate of interest charged on loans is very high—anywhere from 36 to 48 per cent per year. Yet their business is increasing because there is a large number of borrowers with unsatisfied demand for credit who have nowhere else to turn to for credit. The business of finance companies is not regulated by the authorities. The really effective solution lies in banks offering effective competition to these companies in their lending business.

9.7.3 Hire-Purchase Finance Companies

Hire-purchase means purchase on an instalment plan. The credit involved in the instalment plan is provided by financial institutions. Hire-purchase facilities are needed mostly by small buyers of equipment, whether engaged in farming, fishing, or manufacturing, small transport operators for purchase of vehicles (new or old) and their spare parts, and households for purchase of consumer durables, such as bicycles, cars, electric-fans, sewing machines, refrigerators, TV sets, etc. In all these cases, purchase of durable goods is involved. Small buyers may find it difficult to buy them cash. Durable goods give a flow of income or service over a number of years over which the purchasers may like to make payment. Therefore, they are encouraged to buy them if instalment credit on reasonable terms is available. Under appropriate arrangements, goods themselves can serve as security till the loan has been fully repaid. Invariably, the goods are hypothecated to the lender. For encouraging small entrepreneurs to set up shop and existing small producers (farmers and others) to use modern tools and implements, hire-purchase credit can play an important role.

In India the facilities for the provision of hire-purchase credit are limited and undeveloped. Three major types of financial institutions operate in this field : commercial banks, SFCs and the National Small Industries Corporation (NSIC), and hire-purchase finance companies. The bulk of the hire-purchase credit goes to the road transport industry for the purchase of vehicles (new and old) and their spare parts.

At the end of March 1988, there were 630 reporting hire-purchase finance companies with Rs. 1,000 crores of total capital, of which Rs. 200 crores were net owned funds and the rest were fixed deposits, borrowings and other receipts. In addition to companies, there is a large number of individuals and partnership firms operating in the field. Such institutions are better developed and organized in the southern region than in other areas. Most of them suffer from the problem of shortage of resources. Their orgnizational structure is weak. Their credit is very costly. Therefore, there is a clear need to institutionalise hire-purchase credit, to encourage the formation of strong and viable units, to introduce compulsory licencing of all hire-purchase finance units, and to regulate their operations, including the rates of interest charged by them. May be the commercial banks should enter the field in a bigger way by organizing a few subsidiary hire-purchase finance companies.

9.7.4 **Chit Funds**

The chit funds are of many variations. They are essentially savings institutions. The members of a chit fund make regular periodical subscriptions to the fund. The periodic collection is given to some member of the fund, selected in a previously-agreed manner. Each member is assured of his turn before anyother gets it the second time. A major part of the total chit fund business is done in Kerala and Tamil Nadu. At the End of March 1988, 1160 chit companies, with deposits and other receipts of Rs. 800 crores, had reported to the RBI. Timberg and Aiyar (1980) had estimated an anual turnover of Rs. 250-300 crores of credit through chit funds for late 1970s. The credit involved is totally unregulated.

9.7.5 **Nidhis**

The nidhis are peculiar to South India, particularly Tamil Nadu. They act as mutual benefit funds and so deal only with their members. They are popular mainly among middle-class families in urban centres. The major source of their funds is deposits from the members. They make advances to their members usually for such purposes as house construction or repairs, etc. The loans are mostly secured. The rates of interest charged are reasonable. Nidhis are highly localised, single office institutions that offer low-cost financial intermediation services to their members. The deposits mobilised by them are not large.

9.7.6 **Equipment Leasing Finance Companies**

The past few years have witnessed a very rapid growth of such companies. At the end of March 1988, there were only 76 reporting leasing companies with Rs. 666 crore of capital. Most of these companies are small private limited companies. But, in recent years, big business houses have also entered the field and set up their own subsidiary leasing and hire-purchase firms to finance, among other things, the sale of their products and thereby boost their sales. Perceiving a vast potential for lease business, the commercial banks have been permitted (since August 1984) to invest in the shares of leasing companies or to set up their own subsidiaries for transacting equipment leasing business. The SBI (and also the ICICI) have already set up such subsidiaries.

Leasing is a form of rental system. So, the main function of leasing companies is to lease out equipment on rent to industrial companies. The rental covers accelerated depreciation of machines, interest on initial capital value (computed at higher than its own average borrowing rate) and service charges. Several companies combine lease business with hire-purchase business. Apart from net owned funds, the leasing companies raise funds in the form of deposits from the public and their shareholders and borrowings from other companies, banks and other financial institutions. They are allowed to borrow upto 10 times their net owned funds.

The chief gains to the lessee from equipment leasing it arise from the following: (*i*) it does not have to arrange for capital funds to invest in equipment and yet carry out its plans for expansion or modernisation. In a tight credit situation, the funds so released can be used profitably elsewhere; and (*ii*) full tax write-off can be claimed on the high lease rentals paid.

9.7.7 **Housing Finances Companies**[1]

As the name indicates, such companies provide housing finance. As yet, they have not made much progress in India. At the end of March 1992, there were 18 such reporting companies, with borrowings of Rs. 1,620 crore from the National Housing Bank in the year 1994-95.

NOTES

1. Sec also Appendix H.2 for National Housing Bank.

CHAPTER 10

Unregulated Credit Markets

10.1 Introduction

A myriad of private credit agencies other than those discussed in previous chapters operate in the country. Unlike banks their forms of organization and methods of working are not standardised. Instead, there is great diversity in their organizations, methods, functional areas of operation, sources of funds, effective rates of interest charged on their loans, etc. Their common characteristic is that they are not regulated by any authority. The credit markets in which they operate are 'unorganized' or segmented and not integrated with each other. They are not linked with the organized sector of the credit market either, represented by banks and term-lending institutuions. The rates of interest charged by them differ over a wide range. Reliable and complete information is not available about their operations, because there is no official or unofficial central agency to whom unregulated financiers report their operations. This represents a big gap in our knowledge about the finance industry in India and hampers credit policy formulation.

The study and knowledge of unregulated credit markets is important because they meet a large part of the working capital needs of several segments of the Indian economy such as wholesale trade (e.g in cloth, foodgrains, jute, etc.), several manufacturing industries (e.g., powerlooms and handlooms, pharmaceuticals, biri-making, etc.), export trade, retail trade, film production, construction, restaurants, etc. Speaking roughly, upto 30 per cent of total credit used in the urban economy is said to be provided by these markets. In rural areas, moneylenders are still the largest single source of credit for agriculture and village artisans.

Unregulated credit agencies play a role which is both competitive with and complementary to that of banks. They compete with banks by attracting loanable funds from surplus units, a sizeable part of which would have otherwise flowed to banks. Gujarati and Marwari indigenous bankers also compete with banks in their lending operations and remittance facilities. But, in most cases, the loan operations of unregulated credit agencies are complementary to those of banks, because they provide credit generally for such uses and to such users as cannot be accommodated by banks. Therein also lies the rub. The allocation of unregulated credit does not conform to social priorities. In parts at least, it often runs counter to the credit control objectives and measures of the monetary authority. This reduces the overall effectiveness of credit planning and selective credit controls of the RBI. How much damage is done to the objective of socially-ordered allocation of credit will depend obviously on the size of unregulated credit relative to that of regulated credit and the degree of distortion in the allocation of the former. A broad judgment can be made only after we know what the unregulated credit markets are, how they function, etc.

The subject-matter of this chapter is vast. Incomplete information makes the picture at several places hazy and intriguing. We shall describe briefly various forms of unregulated credit agencies and their key features, evaluate them, and bring out their implications for credit planning in the country.

10.2 Types of Unregulated Credit Agencies

Organizationally as well as functionally, various agencies constituting the unregulated or unorganized sector of the Indian credit market may be grouped under the following five broad categories:

1. unregulated NBFIs,
2. indigenous bankers,
3. finance brokers,
4. moneylenders, and
5. other lenders.

The unregulated NBFIs, namely finance companies, hire-purchase finance companies, chit funds, and nidhis, have already been discussed in the previous chapter along with other NBFIs. In this chapter we study only the other unregulated credit agencies. Before doing so, we explain briefly the key indigenous instrument of credit, the hundi, in the next section.

10.3 The Hundi

The hundi is the indigenous bill of exchange (see Section 3.5), generally written in one of the vernacular languages. It is of various forms. But a distinction between what are called *darshani* hundis and *muddati* hundis is perhaps the most important. *Darshani* hundis are like sight bills. They are paid immediately on presentation, sight or demand. There are generally three parties to a *darshani* hundi, viz., a drawing shroff, a paying shroff, and a payee. A shroff is an indigenous banker. The paying shroff is usually another branch of the firm of a drawing shroff in another place or another shroff with whom the drawing shroff has a reciprocal accommodation arrangement. The *darshani* hundi is used for remitting funds through indigenous banking channels from one place to another and for financing inland trade. They are cheap means of transmitting funds, as the commission charged on hundis is smaller than on bank drafts. They can be encashed at any time of day or night. They are typically negotiated several times before ultimate encashment and thus serve as a medium of exchange (or money) till encashed.

The *muddati* hundi is like a usance (time) bill (see Section 3.5). It becomes payable after a stipulated period from the date of the hundi or after sight. The usance of these hundis is normally 30, 60, 90, or 120 days, the 90-day usance being the most popular. The *muddati* hundi is used to finance inland trade and to raise money. In the first case it is like a trade bill or a post-dated cheque drawn by the purchaser of goods in favour of the seller of goods (drawee). In the second case it is like a finance bill issued to raise unsecured loan. Most *muddati* hundis are finance bills.

The rate at which indigenous bankers discount hundis is called the 'bazar bill rate'. It is not uniform in all markets, but differs among markets (e.g. of Bombay, Calcutta and Madras) and even among bankers in the same city.

10.4 Indigenous Bankers

Indigenous bankers are private firms or individuals who operate as banks and as such both receive deposits and give loans. Like banks, they are also financial intermediaries. They should be distinguished from professional moneylenders whose primary business is not banking but moneylending. A pure moneylender lends his own funds, but an indigenous banker raises a part of his loanable funds from the public in deposits or other forms. A moneylender conducts his transactions in cash, while a large part of the transactions of an indigenous banker are based on dealings in short term credit instruments like hundis and commercial bills.

The system of indigenous banking in India dates back to ancient times. Until the middle of the nineteenth century the indigenous financial agencies constituted the bulk of the Indian financial system. They provided credit not only to traders and producers but also to the governments of the day. The advent of the British had an adverse impact on their business. The European bankers began to enjoy state patronage and prestige. The foreign (exchange) banks took over the financing of external trade. In metropolitan areas and important commercial centres the setting up of modern commercial banks took away more and more the business of indigenous financial agencies, who were gradually pushed to the financing of internal trade. With the growth of commercial and co-operative banking geographically as well as functionally, especially since the mid 1950s, the area of operations of these agencies has contracted further. Still there are thousands of family firms, especially in the western and southern parts of India, who continue to operate as traditional-style bankers. Many of these firms have continued in this business for several hundred years. Indigenous bankers are, by and large, urban-based. Their business, besides being hereditary, is confined to a few castes and communities.

The size of the indigenous banking class and the volume of their credit operations are not known with certainty. The Banking Commission (1972, Chapter 18) had estimated their number to be in the neighbourhood of 2,000 to 2,500. Timberg and Aiyar (1980) have placed this number at a minimum of 20,000 leaving out Central India and Eastern India outside Calcutta. They have further estimated that in late 1970s the total credit extended by these bankers was in the neighbourhood of Rs. 1,500 crores, which was equal to 10 per cent of the total commercial bank credit in the year 1977–8.

Indigenous bankers do not constitute one homogeneous category. The Banking Commission (1972) had grouped them under four main sub-groups : Gujarati shroffs, Shikarpuri or Multani shroffs, Chettiars of the South, and Marwari Kayas of Assam. Timberg and Aiyar (1980) do not cover Assam and so leave out Marwari Kayas. But they have found that Rastogi bankers numbering about 500 are also an important sub-group serving craftsmen and traders in the Oudh area of U.P. and providing about Rs. 100 crores of credit.

The Gujarati shroffs are active in the industrial and trading centres of Gujarat, Bomaby, and Calcutta, joined by the Marwari shroffs in Bombay and Calcutta. The Shikarpuris operate mainly in the metropolitan areas of Bombay and Madras and elsewhere in the South where the Chettiars are also active. The Marwaris operate also in the tea gardens of Assam and other parts of North-East India. Thus, the major concentration of indigenous bankers is in the West and South. According to Timberg and Aiyar (1980), the Chettiar bankers, numbering about 2,500, extended credit of about Rs. 380 crores (in late 1970s) at rates ranging between 18 and 30 per cent per annum. They have further estimated that about 40,000 Chettiar pawnbrokers extended credit (of an incredibly large amount) of Rs. 1,250 crores.

Of the four main types of indigenous bankers, the Gujarati shroffs are the most important. In recent years Shikarpuri shroffs have lost more and more their old character of indigenous bankers and taken on the role of 'commercial financiers', who mainly lend out of their owned funds. We study only about these two types. This will also throw light on the main functions performed by other types of indigenous bankers as bankers, once we remember that none of them performs all these functions, and that there are differences in the methods of operation of various types of indigenous bankers.

Gujarati Shroffs. The Gujarati shroffs are of two types : *(a)* pure bankers and (b) bankers and commission agents. Timberg and Aiyar (1980) have estimated their total number to be about 5,000 of whom about 1500 are pure bankers. The comparable estimates of the Banking Commission were only 350 and 150 respectively. The pure bankers are limited only to Gujarat itself, with heavy concentration in Ahmedabad. The more numerous Gujarati and Marwari firms in Bombay and Calcutta combine banking with commission agency or trade in cloth, grains, and other commodities and their banking operations are more or less ancillary to their trade.

The Gujarati shroffs, especially pure bankers, perform most of the major functions of a commercial bank. They accept deposits, make loans, and provide means of remittance and collection of money. They accept both current and fixed deposits and pay interest even on current deposits at a rate of 7.5 per cent in Gujarat and 6 per cent in Bombay. On longer-term deposits they pay upto 12 per cent per year. These deposits represent anywhere from 30 to 90 per cent of their total funds. Some bankers also offer chequing facility to their current-account depositors. But the cheques have only a limited local circulation and are not accepted by commercial banks. They advance money on call and for short periods on personal credit or on security. For most part, this is done by issue of *darshani* hundis drawn on their firms or other shroffs at other centres and by discounting *muddati* hundis and commercial paper of various kinds, out-of-station current cheques and post-dated cheques, etc. For Bombay alone, Timberg and Aiyar (1980) have estimated an annual hundi turnover of Rs. 1500 crores with Gujaratis and of Rs. 500 crores with Marwaris. The Gujarati shroffs arrange for the remittance of funds by issuing *darshani* hundis and also undertake the collection of hundis for their clients. Some big shroffs have branches in mofussil centres. For example, one Gujarati shroff had 93 branches. Besides these branches, shroffs have arrangements of mutual accommodation for acceptance and payment of hundis at various places both within and outside the state boundaries. This arrangement enables these shroffs to conduct commission agency work and exchange operations, raise and lend funds in the most profitable manner, and direct surplus funds to those places where they are needed.

The working capital of Gujarati shroffs comes from their own funds, deposits from the public, and inter-firm borrowings. Deposits (estimated at about Rs. 800 crores by Timberg and Aiyar) represent about half of their total funds. They hardly borrow from commercial banks to finance their banking operations. The Gujarati shroffs have developed their own call-money market, analogous to the inter-bank call-money market, in which short-term surplus funds are lent and borrowed. This call market and the associated inter-firm borrowings are a very distinctive feature of the operations of Gujarati shroffs.

Shikarpuri or Multani Shroffs. Next to Gujarati shroffs, they are the most important sub-group of indigenous financiers. The Banking Commission (1972) had estimated their number at about 400. But Timberg and Aiyar (1980) put this number at 1200, of which about one half are members of local Shikarpuri Bankers' Associations and the other half are non-members. Their capital resources are variously estimated at between Rs. 300 crores and 600 crores. These bankers operate mostly in Bombay and South India.

Functionally, what distinguishes Shikarpuri financiers from Gujarati shroffs is their major reliance on their owned funds and borrowings from commercial banks rather than deposits from the public as the source of their funds. Since 1970 banks have reduced drastically their refinance to Shikarpuris and the latter have come to rely largely on their own funds. As a result the Shikarpuri business has not grown with the economy, the character of Shikarpuris has changed from that of bankers to that of 'commercial financiers', and the cost of their credit to their borrowers has almost doubled.

The Shikarpuris traditionally used to lend mainly by discounting 'Multani hundis', which are 90-day term notes. In the past they used to borrow from commercial banks by getting these hundis rediscounted. With the decline of rediscount facilities with banks, they have moved more and more towards lending against demand promissory notes (endorsed for a term) and giving instalment credit. In the smaller centres in the South 90 per cent of Shikarpuri advances are done on the basis of demand notes. On overall basis, 45 per cent of Shikarpuri advances in the South are in the form of instalment credit. The instalment notes are commonly supported by post-dated cheques, one for each instalment payment. The main borrowers of Shikarpuris are traders and small manufacturers. Other (less important) borrowers are transport operators and small exporters. These borrowers are often in urgent need of clean (or unsecured) loans for marginal short-term requirements of their business. The Shikarpuri banker tries to meet this kind of demand. The clientele is varied and not limited to a few communities as in the case of Gujaratis. The Shikarpuri finance is much more costly than that provided by the Gujarati shroffs. The Shikarpuris have developed a system of sharing risks among themselves. If a borrower's requirements are large, a broker will arrange to break it up into smaller notes taken by several Shikarpuri shroffs thereby reducing the risk of any single banker. Shikarpuri-type financiers are found in every major market.

10.5 Indigenous bankers—An Evaluation and Suggestion for Reform

The indigenous bankers have survived successfully the stiff competition for business offered by commercial banks. Factors favourable to them are in operation on both the demand side and the supply side. They are summed up below. The first three factors relate to the demand side, the last one to the supply side.

1. In the urban areas, particularly in the metropolitan cities of Bombay, Madras and Calcutta, the services of indigenous bankers are widely used by small traders and small manufacturers, because commercial bank lending to this segment of borrowers is inadequate in relation to their needs;

2. A part of the credit provided by the indigenous bankers is in the form of clean advances which small borrowers badly need; commercial banks do not offer them such risk finance;

3. The services offered by indigenous bankers are prompt, flexible, informal and personalised, which their borrowers value

very much. The latter are saved the bother of completing commercial bank formalities of submitting various statements relating to their operations and sources of investment, making several trips to bank offices, etc;

4. The indigenous bankers enjoy a certain cost advantage over commercial banks. Their operating costs are lower. So are their establishment costs. Their information costs are also lower, because they know their borrowers well, who are invariably local parties, and have been old traditional customers in both banking and trade. Consequently, their default experience is not bad. Then, unlike banks, indigenous bankers are not required to keep cash reserves with the RBI or invest heavily in low-interest government securities, which also is cost-economising for their credit operations.

Shortcomings of the Indigenous Banking System

1. The main charge against indigenous bankers is that rate of interest charged by them on their credit is very high as compared to the lending rates of banks. The usual rates of interest range between 18 and 36 per cent per annum against the average lending rate of 15 per cent of banks. A part of the extra high lending rates can be justified as the allowance for extra risk which the indigenous bankers undertake in making clean advances and the reward for other services they render to their borrowers. But, it is hard to justify all the excess on rational economic grounds. A large part of the excess must be attributed to the indigence of the small borrower and the non-availability of adequate institutional finance to him. The indigenous banker takes advantage of the weak borrowing position of small borrowers and is able to charge him an excessively high rate of interest.

The effective rate of interest is higher than the quoted rate of interest, because of several factors, such as the inclusion of other charges like brokerage and charity in interest payments, the practice of advance deduction of interest, etc.

2. Indigenous banking is almost totally unsupervised and unregulated. The unregulated lending operations by indigenous bankers weaken the credit control of the RBI. The indigenous bankers care much less than banks about the end-use of credit, that is, whether the credit given by them is used for productive or for speculative purposes. In certain situations of high speculative activity in certain commodities in short supply, this can undo a part of the selected credit control measures adopted by the RBI.

3. The indigenous credit market, besides being local, is highly segmented. Unlike the organized market for bank credit, funds in it do not move easily from one place to another or from one segment of a market to another within the same city. This is less true of Gujarati bankers than of others. But this is more a difference of degree than of kind. As a consequence, credit does not flow to the most eligible use and user. The rates of interest also differ systematically among various segments of the market. Thus, the lending rates of Shikarpuris are double or even higher than the lending rates of Gujaratis and Marwaris. This may be attributed to differences in perceived (not actual) risks of default in lending to the special clientele of the two sets of bankers. Basically this is due to differences in the net worth and income positions of the two sets of borrowers. Rates of interest in the south are higher and credit supply tighter than in the West or the North.

Suggestions for Reform

It is widely held that the indigenous banking system should be reformed and made an adjunct of the organized banking system rather than replaced totally by commercial banks. Despite the sharp growth of the latter and emphasis on larger bank credit to the weaker sections of the community, the banks have not been able to meet adequately the credit needs of the small borrower, owing mainly to the relatively high cost of servicing small loans, high risk, and the high demand pressures for bank credit from the large organized sector of industry and trade. In the circumstances, the indigenous bankers, with their prompt and flexible credit and informal methods of operation, have also been able to flourish by making credit available to the small productive sector not fully catered to by commercial banks. In the foreseeable future, too, the same conditions are likely to persist, despite the high cost of indigenous banker's credit. So, the indigenous bankers have still a role to play. The best course would be to reform the indigenous system and rid it of its defects. This will require institutionalising the lending and borrowing operations of the indigenous bankers. How best to do it ?

Two lines of reform are possible. One is the direct link of indigenous bankers with the RBI; the other is the indirect control of the business of indigenous bankers by the RBI mediated through commercial banks.

In the past (once in 1937 and then 1941) the RBI had drawn up schemes for the direct linking of indigenous bankers with it. But the schemes could not be put through because the chief condition of such direct linking was not acceptable to indigenous bankers. The RBI had rightly insisted that the bankers must segregate their banking business from their non-banking business if they want to enjoy the privilege of rediscount facilities of eligible paper with the RBI and its remittance facilities. The indigenous bankers have not been willing to separate their banking and non-banking businesses, because, in their view, the facilities being offered by the RBI are not worth the cost involved in the required separation of the two kinds of business. After independence the major effort of the RBI has been to strengthen and expand the modern banking system without any attempt to bring into its folds the indigenous bankers.

The Banking Commission (1972) examined the whole question afresh in the new context of substantially enlarged commercial and co-operative banking system. In its view its was 'neither necessary nor practicable to have a direct link' between the RBI and the indigenous bankers. The direct link was considered inpracticable because refinancing of indigenous bankers by the RBI would involve considerable labour disproportionate to the amounts of expected refinance, as the hundis are for small amounts and the day-to-day turnover in them would be large. Regulation in the form of detailed supervision and inspection of indigenous bankers was also not considered practicable as it would involve building up a large and costly inspection machinery.

The Commission, therefore, came out in favour of the indirect control of the RBI over the business of indigenous bankers through the medium of commercial banks. This would necessitate that the latter offer steady and uninterrupted accommodation to the former through the discounting of hunds. At present this assistance is highly irregular. The SBI had stopped completely the discounting of hundis from March 1965. The flow of credit from other commercial banks is not regular, assured or automatic. The Commission has recommended that the flow of funds from banks to the indigenous sector should be made regular.

The Commission has also recommended that banks should offer their discounting facilities only to such indigenous bankers as do not engage themselves in trading activities, have minimum prescribed capital, maintain accounts in the usual recognized manner and get them audited annually and submit annually to the RBI summary statements of the volume and nature of their business. While granting limits to indigenous bankers, commercial banks should undertake systematic evaluation of the financial statements of such bankers. The

RBI should lay down guidelines for commercial banks for their dealings with indigenous bankers. These guidelines could pertain to the type of hundis to be selected, the overall quantum of limits to be sanctioned, the maximum amount per banker, and some formula for sanctioning individual limits. The RBI should also indicate periodically the spread between the rate of interest charged by the indigenous banker from their borrowers and the rate of interest banks charge these bankers. The commercial banks should see that no indigenous banker availing himself of bank credit facilities charges interest rates higher than those based on the spread. No action has so far been taken on the recommendations of the Commission or on some other lines.

10.6 Finance Brokers

Finance brokers are found in all major urban markets. They are specially active in cloth markets in Bombay, Kanpur, Delhi, Amritsar, and other cities, in jute market in Calcutta, in grain markets and in other commodity markets. Some are full-time brokers, others work part time. As the name shows, finance brokers work as brokers or middlemen between lenders and borrowers. The lenders may be commercial financiers such as Shikarpuri bankers or non-commercial lenders with surplus funds. Unlike Gujarati shroffs, Shikarpuris typically lend through brokers who have personal knowledge about the creditworthiness of prospective borrowers they recommend. Brokers also keep a close watch over the state of business activity and major expenditures of their borrowing clientele, because their own standing in the market as brokers depends on how well their clientele honour their loan commitments. Non-commercial lenders are not full-time professional lenders. They are individuals such as rich professionals, widows and pensioners, as well as firms with surplus funds to lend or invest.

The borrowers may be commercial financiers themselves and non-financial firms, including limited companies. Since during the previous decade the amount of bank refinance to Shikarpuris has declined drastically, these financiers have come to use increasingly the services of brokers not only for finding them good borrowers but also getting them good lenders. The brokers used by Shikarpuris often receive as high as 2 per cent commission. Similarly, non- financial firms also use the services of brokers for arranging loans for them.

There are big and small brokers. There are brokers who work in the inter-corporate call money market in Bombay and Calcutta,

/here call loans for a day or so are arranged among corporate firms. The deals involve big sums with a minimum of Rs. five lakhs. The brokerage fee is usually $\frac{1}{2}$ per cent of the loan amount and the current rate of interest is 8.5-to10 per cent per year. Most often these big brokers are stockbrokers. They also broker company deposits. Some of the other finance brokers may also do big business. For example, Timberg and Aiyar (1980, p. 285) have cited the case of a broker who gathered funds from 350 different sources in amounts from Rs. 10,000 to Rs. 100,000 and re-lent them to 37 large-sized public limited companies. The smaller set of brokers arranging intramarket and intermarket credit for proprietory firms and partnerships represent considerable range. At one end there are brokers who handle more than Rs. one crore a year for 100–150 clients in minimum amounts of Rs. 50,000. At the other end are brokers who carry back and forth as little as Rs. 5,000 to Rs. 25,000 at a time between borrowers and lenders. A typical small broker has 15–25 clients and deals in minimum loan transactions of Rs. 5,000 or so.

Brokers also syndicate loans among Shikarpuri bankers, that is arrange to break up a large loan into smaller notes and sell them to a group of bankers. In large cities, Gujarati shroffs also use brokers, but the brokers' role is not as crucial for them as it is for Shikarpuris. The Rastogi bankers in U.P. also have begun using brokers in their effort to enter into new fields of borrowers.

10.7 Moneylenders

The moneylenders are a heterogeneous lot. They include professional moneylenders, rural and urban, whose main source of income is moneylending, itinerant moneylenders, like pathans, kabulis, and qistwalas, and non-professional moneylenders who combine moneylending with other activities. The latter include large farmers, merchants, traders, *arhatias* (commission agents), the ubiquitous village bania, goldsmith, jobbers and sardars of labourers in urban areas, etc. They are known by different names, such as sahukar, mahajan, seth or bania. They are individual enterprises or family partnerships. Their methods of operation differ almost from moneylender to moneylender. Each moneylender generally operates in a small local market. The key features of moneylenders as source of credit are summed up briefly below.

1. Moneylenders' funds are mostly owned funds. Generally, they do not borrow from each other, or banks, or other financial

institutions. They may receive small amounts of temporary deposits from clients, relatives, and friends. But such deposits are a very small proportion of the total money-lenders' capital.

2. The borrowers from moneylenders are mostly economically weaker sections of the community—small and marginal farmers, agricultural labour and village artisans in rural areas, factory and mine workers, peons, menials, and other low-paid workers and small traders. Richer farmers in need of funds are able to borrow from co-operative credit societies and other institutional agencies. They may also be borrowing for short periods from *arhatias* (commission agents). But the bulk of moneylenders' finance goes to meet the needs for credit of small borrowers. It is the latter to whom the doors of institutional credit are still practically closed. Most of the remaining features of moneylenders' credit derive from this simple fact of the borrowers being weak, indigent, and nowhere else to go to for credit.

3. The moneylenders' credit has been known to be highly exploitative. The exploitation has taken various forms, such as usurious rates of interest going upto 100 per cent or more per annum, frequent compounding of interest, false manipulation of loan records in numerous ways, extra impositions in the form of *begar* (free labour in moneylenders' fields and homes), the requirement to sell produce to the moneylender at local prices which would be invariably lower than the prices in mandis. Historically, moneylending has also been the chief instrument through which the ownership of land has passed from debtor-cultivators to others, non-agriculturists or agriculturists. With legal restrictions on the transfer of land to non-agriculturists, the chief gainers of such land transfers have been the agriculturist money lenders. Thus, moneylenders' credit has contributed, in no small measure, to the increasing pauperisation in rural India.

4. The moneylenders' credit is unregulated. Loans are made for productive purposes as well as for consumption. Consumption loans taken for ceremonial purposes usually sit as dead-weight burden on the backs of borrowers. The burden increases rapidly over time as small borrowers are rarely in a capacity to repay loans taken at high compound rates of interest. This results in the aforesaid loss of property of borrowers at cheap prices.

5. The moneylenders' credit may be secured or unsecured. The security has been land, cattle, crops, ornaments, and other material objects. Unsecured loans are advanced purely on the promise to pay, supported by entries in the account books and/or by signature or thumb impression on blank papers. For recoveries of loans and

interest, all kinds of strong-arm methods or threats may be used. Only in exceptional cases, the matter is taken to the courts of law. Since the borrowers are local persons, they do not find an easy escape from the moneylenders who usually wield much more economic, social, and political influence in their localities.

6. The moneylenders' credit has the saving grace of being prompt, informal, and flexible. On regular and timely payment of interest, the loans are easily renewed, because the moneylenders are mainly interested in their interest income if they are assured that the capital sums of their loans are safe. But to the borrowers, all this is small compensation for all the ills that go with this type of credit.

It is generally agreed that, in the absence of adequate institutional sources of credit for the most needy and hence the most vulnerable sections of the population, moneylenders' credit has to be accepted as a necessary evil. In the past several legislative measures have been passed in the form of restrictions on the alienation of land, control on the rates of interest charged, restriction on the maximum amount of interest of a loan so that the total does not exceed double the initial amount of the loan, the requirement for taking out of licences for doing the business of moneylending and the requirement for the licenced moneylenders to maintain proper books of account and to give the borrowers regular statements of accounts. But most of these legal provisions have remained unenforced, because, given the methods of operation of the moneylenders and the nature of demand for their credit, these provisions are not easily enforceable. What is required is to develop the institutional sources of credit. The main emphasis should be on the quantity of credit made available and not on the concessional rates of interest. Keeping in view the high cost of servicing small loans and small borrowers and the problem of recovery of loans and associated overdues, financial institutions should not be asked to carry the extra burden of providing loans at concessional rates of interest. This is sure to discourage them from providing whatever credit they otherwise would. This has also been the experience so far. What the small borrowers need is adequate institutional credit. If it is given to them at the organized market rates of interest, it is highly concessional to them as compared to the moneylenders' credit. So, they would not grudge paying the market cost of loans. Just make the loans available to them and give them other help required to improve their repaying capacity.

Poverty is both the cause and the effect of their continued indebtedness to usurious moneylenders. It is the cause because, being poor, they have to go in for debt even for consumption purposes and borrow from sources which are highly exploitative. It is the effect because they are continuously fleeced for loans once taken. It is an irony that the weakest are the most exploited. The moneylenders can play a useful social role without fangs only in a climate of healthy competition from alternative sources of credit. It is their monopoly of credit for the poor that lies at the root of all the ills of their credit.

10.8 **Other Lenders — The Informal Loan Market**

A good deal of borrowing and lending takes place among private parties, which cannot be placed in any of the financial-market categories discussed so far. For want of a better term we call such borrowings and lendings as 'informal' loan transactions and the market in them as 'informal' loan market.[1] The borrowing and lendings in the informal loan market are analogous to (but not quite the same as) company deposits collected by public limited companies from the public through open advertisements in newspapers. This method of inviting public deposits is not open to unincorporated firms. The financial intermediation provided by finance brokers in this sphere has already been discussed in Section 6 above. In addition, the informal method of direct personal contact is also made much use of to attract funds.

The borrowing firms are able to attract funds from relatives, friends, and others who know directly or indirectly the proprietors of borrowing firms and have reasonable faith in the honesty and solvency of such firms, so that they feel reasonably assured against risk of default. In addition, the borrowers offer higher rates of interest than are paid to their depositors by banks, other financial institutions, and non-financial companies (on company deposits). Then, they accept willingly loans of black money' and also offer to keep such loan transactions including interest payments unaccounted for tax purposes. Thereby the lenders escape both income tax and wealth tax on moneys involved. This boosts up further effective gross (equal to net) of tax rates of return from the above-mentioned private placements of funds. The borrowing firms stand to gain from such borrowings, because they pay only the rate of interest which is currently prevailing in the informal market, are saved from the discipline of institutional credit, can use privately-borrowed funds to meet the margin requirements for bank advances, and can finance black-money transactions. Thus, black money supports the informal private borrowing and lending as it can be lent in only such informal ways. Since black money is an important adjunct of the so-called parallel economy, it also leads to its further multiplication and growth. Thus, a vicious spiral of black money, parallel economy, and black money flourishes in the country.

In the informal loan market, borrowers are mostly business firms of all sizes (including even corporate firms) and the lenders are mostly businessmen themselves who have either spare funds to lend or keep on deposit with firms they do business with, professionals, rich farmers, members of the salaried class, and pensioners. The lenders are not professional moneylenders, but only holders of liquid wealth, white or black, who try to maximise returns on their loanable funds. The informal market operates mostly through the market forces of demand and supply which determine the going average rate of interest in the market. This rate, therefore, is much more flexible than the administered rates of the organized markets. As such, it responds more fully and quickly to such influences as inflationary expectations.

No estimates are available on the total amount of credit outstanding in the informal loan market or on the net inflow of new funds into the market. But the general impression is that both the amounts are quite large. This market, obviously, is not subject to any regulation by the monetary authority. Nor is the credit allocation in it according to any credit plan or social priorities. What determines this allocation are the brute market forces of demand and supply, of expected private profitability from the use of borrowed funds, supported by standing in the market or creditworthiness as rated by potential lenders, and the costs/returns on loans.

10.9 Unregulated Credit and Black Money

It is important to recognize that unregulated credit markets operate in both 'white money' and 'black money' and that 'black money' flows freely in these markets. The source of 'black money' is 'black income', which is income not declared to income-tax authorities. A part of this black income is spent on consumption and another part saved. The former gives rise to 'black consumption expenditure', the latter to 'black savings'. The accumulation of such savings results in 'black wealth', which also includes wealth which has not been declared for wealth tax or other property taxes due on it. Black wealth is held partly in the form of cash and partly in the form of non-cash assets. Strictly speaking, it is only the former which is 'black money'. More popularly, however, no distinction is made between 'black money' proper, 'black income', and 'black wealth'. The resulting looseness in usage gives the false impression as though the entire black wealth is held in the form of black money or that demonetisation of high-denomination currency notes can solve at least the problem of the stock of black wealth existing in the country. Since black money is only a part of black wealth, the above is not true.

Enough is not known about the size and the *modi operandi* of the markets in black money. It is however commonly held that black money represents a substantial proportion of owned funds invested in businesses of all kinds and residential houses, that black money is also a fairly large proportion of unregulated credit, and that black money in both forms is growing at a rapid rate. This has created further difficulties in the path of credit planning.

The unregulated credit markets both carry out transactions in black money and provide means of converting black money into white money at a price. Such conversion is done through fictitious book entries, discounting of fictitious hundis, and in a variety of other ways. These operations are helped by chartered accountants, income-tax lawyers, and finance brokers. The whole system runs quite smoothly with relatively low default rate. The rates of commission, discount, and interest for black money transactions are pretty standard in each local sub-market, though they do vary from place to place and adjust reasonably fast to pressures of demand and supply in each sub-market. Because of the easy supply of black money relative to the demand for it in the market, the rates of interest on black-money credit are known to be lower than on white-money credit. For example, direct lending of black money is usually done at rates of 12–15 per cent per year in Bombay (24 per cent in Madras), whereas the corresponding white-money rates are 18–24 per cent.

Black-money credit is specially important in highly risky businesses of film production, smuggling and other illegal activities, speculation in commodity and bullion markets, real estate, hotels and restaurants, etc. For example, of the estimated Rs. 750 crores involved in film finance, about Rs. 500 crores are estimated to be black money. About 500 brokers in Bombay are said to be involved in arranging film finance at rates of interest ranging from 36 to 60 per cent and occasionally running as high as 120 per cent. (Timberg and Aiyar, 1980).

10.10 Unregulated Credit Markets and Credit Policy

The unregulated credit markets create serious problems of credit control for the monetary authority, both at the aggregate level and at the level of credit allocation. The existence of these markets means that a part of the total loanable funds of the economy get leaked into these markets. The bigger the leakage, the larger the portion of the total that falls outside the direct control sphere of the authorities. This does not mean that thereby the credit control policy of the RBI is rendered totally nugatory, because if the credit conditions are tightened in the organized segment of the credit market, the impact is felt in the unregulated markets as well. This happens in two ways. One, a part of the unsatisfied demand gets diverted to the unregulated markets. Two, a part of the supply of funds fed from the organized market disappears. Thus, tightness is extended to the unregulated market as well. As a consequence, rates of interest in these markets are pushed up and borrowings get curtailed. How well and how fast this mechanism works is hard to say in the absence of well-documented empirical evidence. Also, how much of a nuisance for credit policy the unregulated credit markets actually are, will depend upon the relative size of these markets vis-a-vis that of the organized market. On this score also nothing definite is known.

The problem is much more serious when it comes to the operation and success of selective credit controls (see Section 19.10), because requests for bank credit that get rejected under the imposition of selective credit controls by the RBI can be at least partly accommodated in the unregulated credit markets, albeit at much higher rates of interest. The higher cost of credit does act as a disincentive against speculative hoarding of essential commodities in short supply. But the escape route provided by the unregulated credit markets to speculators and hoarders does blunt the cutting edge of the selective credit control measures. Also the allocation of credit in the unregulated credit markets is not according to any social design and cannot be made a part and parcel of any overall credit allocation plan for the economy as a whole.

NOTES

1. Our use of the word 'informal' is deliberately much narrower than that of some World Bank economists who have used the term informal credit markets in a much broader sense to stand for what we have called unregulated credit markets in this chapter.

2. White money is also used to finance transactions in parallel economy—another term for 'black markets' or markets in which such goods are transacted whose production and/or sale violate some law or government regulation.

Part Two : Theory

Variations in the stock of money influence income, output, prices, and other correlates of economic activity. But the influence is neither direct nor one-sided. Monetary factors not only influence other (non-monetary) macro variables, they are also influenced by the latter. To understand the working of monetary forces and their interaction with the rest of the economic system, we need the guidance of theory. The function of theory is to provide a conceptual framework in which to analyse this interaction.

The relevant theory for monetary analysis is the macroeconomic theory. This theory analyses the working of the economy at the aggregate level. Monetary theory is a branch of macroeconomic theory. In a macroeconomic framework, this theory analyses the role of monetary forces. It also studies the internal working of the monetary sector itself, which, in the narrow sense, is concerned with the theory of the demand for money and of the supply of it and, in the broad sense, with the analysis of all financial factors and markets.

The subject of macroeconomic theory and monetary theory is vast and complex. In an introductory textbook we have to be simple and selective. The selected material is presented in this Part under seven chapters (11–17). The discussion opens with a study of the demand for money (chapter 11), so essential for understanding the role of money in the economic sphere and also in the money market. The question of the relation between money and prices is older than the science of economics itself. The classical (or neoclassical) theory of this relation, popularly called the quantity theory of money, is discussed in Chapter 12. The theories of inflation are studied separately in Chapter 14.

Keynes' influence looms large on both macro theory and monetary theory. With him, monetary theory, instead of being a theory of the price level, became a theory of rate of interest, output, and employment. Thus, his monetary theory is inextricably wound with his macro theory. We study it and Hicks' reformulation of it (his IS-LM model) in Chapter 13.

Chapter 15 is devoted to a study of the theory of money supply. Till the beginning of this chapter it is implicitly assumed that the stock of money is a policy variable, determined by the monetary authority. In actual life changes in the stock of money are brought about by the actions of the authorities, the public, and banks. The theory of money supply attempts to provide a conceptual framework for the study of all these forces (and their interaction) that bring about changes in the stock of money.

A close correlate of money supply is the total stock of bank credit. The theory of its determination at the aggregate level and of its allocation among individual borrowers are discussed in Chapter 16. The next chapter (17) closes the discussion of this Part with a study of the loanable-funds theory of *the* rate of interest and of the factors responsible for interest-rate differentials in actual life.

CHAPTER 11

The Demand for Money

11.1 Introduction

To be able to analyse the effects of changes in the stock of money, it is essential to study the equilibrium of the money market. Money is an asset of the holding public. As such, it must have a demand for it and a supply of it, and so also a market for it. The demand for it comes from the general public (excluding the producers of money). The supply of it comes from its producers, the government and the banking system, whose liability money is. The money market, then, is simply the market comprising these demanders and suppliers of money.[1]

The theory of money supply will be discussed in Chapter 15. Till then we shall assume the supply of money to be autonomously given by the monetary authority. The equilibrium of the money market and this market's interaction with other markets of the economy will be taken up in the next chapter. Before going into these issues, the demand for money, which is the keystone of the arch of monetary theory, needs to be carefully understood. This will be attempted in the present chapter.

Money is a stock variable. The stock of it refers to its quantity at a point of time. As an asset, the demand for it is the public's demand to hold money, whatever the motive for holding it and whatever the length of the time period for which it is held. Holding cash in one's pocket for spending it is as much a part of the demand for money as burying currency notes in a pot under ground. The several motives for holding money will be studied later in the chapter.

Monetary analysis is aggregative analysis. Therefore the demand for money relevant to this analysis is also the aggregate demand for money of the public as a whole. It is the sum of all the money demanded by individual members of the public, whether households or firms.

The theory of the demand for money is mainly concerned with answering the question : what are the determinants of the public's demand for money and why ? A related question is : why does the public demand money ? Several explanations have been offered in reply. The present chapter will survey them briefly. Each explanation has its own implications for explaining further the economic effects of money supply changes. The latter explanations will be studied in the next two chapters. The theory of the demand for money has been widely tested empirically. As a consequence, much empirical evidence has accumulated around it. The main findings will be presented in a simple manner in the last section of the present chapter.

11.2 Nominal versus Real Cash Balances

At the outset it is important to introduce the distinction between nominal and real cash balances. Cash balances is another term for money. Nominal cash balances are money of the current purchasing power of a unit of money (say, a rupee). Real cash balances are money of some base-year purchasing power. A nominal rupee is nominally always a rupee. But its purchasing power in terms of real goods and services can vary from time to time with changes in the general price level. Then, it is said that the real value (purchasing power) of a (nominal) rupee has been changing over time. For making real-value comparisons, first a reference point or a base year is chosen. Suppose we choose 1961–62 as our base year with the wholesale price index number = 100. A rupee in this year had a certain amount of purchasing power at the prices prevailing during the year. Suppose the average value of this index number for the year 1979–80 was 400. Then, the purchasing power or value of a nominal rupee at the 1979–80 prices was only one-fourth of what it was at the 1961–62 prices. That is, one rupee in 1979–80 could buy only as much goods and services as only 25 paise could buy in 1961–62. The intervening fourfold rise in prices has reduced the real value of a rupee from that of a rupee to that of a quarter of a rupee. If some other year (say, 1938–39) with a lower price level than that of 1961–62 were chosen, the real value of a nominal rupee in 1979–80 would turn out to be lower still in comparison with its real value in the new base year.

Thus, technically, real cash balances are given by nominal cash balances deflated by the price level. That is if M and P are used to denote nominal money and the price level (index number) respectively, then the real cash balances will be given by M/P. The latter will be measured in terms of the purchasing power of money in the year which serves as the base year for the price index number measuring P.

Whenever changes in P take place, the distinction between nominal and real cash balances (and for that matter, between any nominal quantity and its real value) becomes relevant. For the analysis of the demand for money therefore, we have to decide whether what the public wants to hold is some nominal quantity of money or some real quantity of it. This is one way of bringing P as one of the determinants of the nominal demand for money. The importance of the distinction between nominal and real money will become clear when we study the quantity theory of money in the next chapter.

11.3 The Neoclassical Theory

There are two main streams of monetary theory: the neoclassical and the Keynesian. Concerned with the demand for money, we first discuss the neoclassical theory in this section.

The early neoclassical theory of the demand for money was put forward by the Cambridge economists Marshall and Pigou. In the *Cambridge approach,* the following demand for money function was hypothesised :

$$M^d = K Y, \quad (11.1)$$

where M^d = amount of money demanded,
Y .ıoney value of national income and
K is a constant.

Since, by definition, Y = Py, where P is the general price level and y is real national income, equation (11.1) can be written alternatively in its equivalent form as

$$M^d = K P y \quad (11.1a)$$

K is called the Cambridge K. It gives us the demand for money per rupee of 'income per unit time'. since, from equation (11.1), $K = M^d/Y$. Alternatively speaking, K shows what proportion of money income the public likes to hold in the form of money. Money income Y is flow per unit of time, say, per year. M^d is a stock at a point of time. That is, it does not have any time dimension as per day, per month or per year. Therefore, K has the dimension of time. To illustrate, suppose M^d is Rs. 1,000 crores and money income is Rs. 4,000 crores *per year.* Then, for equation (11.1) to hold exactly, K will have the value of $\frac{1}{4}$ *year.* The economic meaning of it is simple, but important. It is that, on average, the public *likes to hold* money that is equal to one-fourth of its annual income.

This point may be explained further. Suppose we talk in terms of monthly income in place of annual income. In the above example, the average monthly income would be Rs. 333.33 crores. But the amount of money demanded, being a stock variable, will be independent of the length of time period chosen. So, it would stay at Rs. 1,000 crores. Relating this to monthly income would give us the value of 3 *months* for K, which is the same thing as $\frac{1}{4}$ *year.* Thus, K can be stated in equivalent time units of year, months, weeks or days. In the present example, we can as well say that K has the value of 3 months or 13 weeks, each of which is equal to $\frac{1}{4}$ year. Henceforth we shall follow the convention of measuring Y per year and so K in terms of a year.

Before proceeding further, we may illustrate equation (11.1) diagrammatically as in figure (11.1). M^d is shown to be a linear function of Y. It goes through the origin. The tangent of the angle which it makes with the horizontal axis $= M^d/Y = K$.

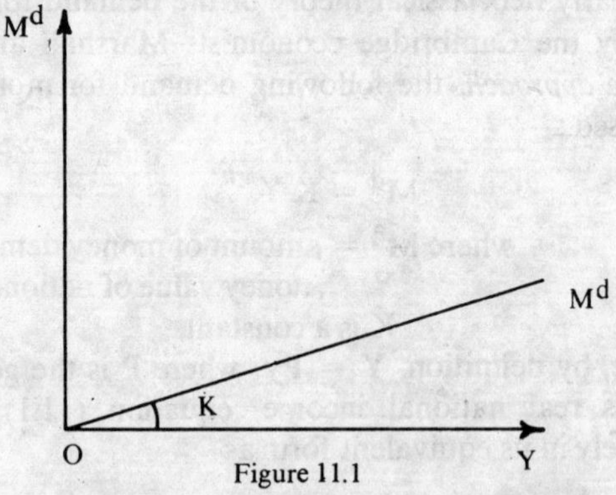

Figure 11.1

The Cambridge Demand for Money Function

The key feature of the Cambridge equation is that it makes the demand for money a function of money income, and only of it. The rationale of the dependence of M^d on Y is important. In the original formulation, the money value of transactions carried through money had appeared in place of Y. If we denote such transactions by T and their average price by P_T, their total money value can be denoted by P_TT. Then it was thought that money was demanded as a medium of exchange and as such the demand for it would depend upon the money value of transactions of all kinds to be carried through money (P_TT). How much money to hold per rupee of transactions is a choice variable of the money-holding public, and not a technical requirement. It will dpend upon the convenience yield from holding money to the public, the public's income and wealth position, and also the rate of interest. But, *as a first approximation*, these other factors were assumed to remain constant, in any case so over any short period. They were supposed to determine the level of K at any time. The important question of variations in K caused by variations in any of these factors was largely ignored. We shall have more to say on this point later.

What is the interpretation of the demand for money relation in terms of Y ? Why the shift from P_TT to Y ? There are empirical as well as theoretical reasons. Empirically, data are available on Y, not on P_TT. Theoretically with the publication of Keynes' *General Theory* (1936), the problem of income determination came to occupy the centre of the stage of monetary theory. It became more and more fashionable to state behavioural relations in terms of income. Most important, Y can offer better behavioural explanation of M^d than P_TT. The latter betrays some kind of a mechanical relation between it and M^d, as though P_TT represents the total amount of *work to be done* by money as a medium of exchange. This tends to make M^d a technical requirement, and not a behavioural function. A similar charge cannot be easily levelled against Y.

It can be counter-argued that, in the Y-approach, real income y is being used as a proxy for T, because the data on T are not easily available. This might be correct. But it is not necessary to depend upon this interpretation. Instead, it can be asserted that y is a proxy for real wealth, and that the demand for real money as an asset is a function of real wealth. However, this is going too far, because this interpretation was not put forward by the Cambridge economists. What can be claimed for them, at best, is that they had hypothesised that at each level of y there is a determinate amount of real money which the public wants to hold.

The last statement is embodied implicitly in equation (11.1a). To make it explicit, we divide both sides of the equation by P to get

$$(M/P)^d = K.y. \tag{11.2}$$

The above equation gives us the demand function for real money. It makes M^d/P a function *only* of y. It does not admit of other influences on M^d/P in its specification. As said earlier, the Cambridge economists did recognize that other variables, such as the rate of interest, might influence the value of K and thereby M^d/P. But these influences were not systematically incorporated in their analysis. It was left to Keynes, another Cambridge economist, to highlight the influence of the rate of interest on the demand for money and change the course of monetary theory.

A third feature of equation (11.1) is its proportional form. It says that M^d is a proportional function of Y, K being the factor of proportionality. Similarly, equation (11.1a) also has proportional form, making M^d a proportional function of both P and y. This has two important implications : *(i)* that the income elasticity of demand for money is unity and *(ii)* that the price elasticity of demand for money also is unity. The second property is generally alternatively stated by saying that M^d is homogeneous of degree 1 in P, so that any change in P will lead to an equal proportionate change in M^d.

Both the implications are testable hypotheses. The income elasticity of demand for money can well be different from unity. There is no theoretical or empirical necessity for it to be equal to unity. There is also no theoretical or empirical necessity for the homogeneity assumption to hold. A change in P may induce change in M^d which is different from equiproportionate.

These criticisms, it needs be recognized, are against the specific mathematical form of the Cambridge demand function for money. They do not strike at the root of the M^d Y relation, the key hypothesis of this function. Empirically, in several countries, it has been found to be a very sturdy relation.

Equation (11.1) is the simplest demand function for money. It has played a very important role in the development of neoclassical monetary theory, particularly the quantity theory of money. We shall discuss this role in the next chapter.

11.4 Keynes' Theory

What is known as the Keynesian theory of the demand for money was first formulated by Keynes in his well-known book, *The General Theory of Employment, Interest and Money* (1936). It has been developed further by other economists of Keynesian persuasion. We shall study Keynes' theory in this section and post-Keynesian developments in the next section.

In understanding Keynes' theory two questions need to be separated. One is why is money demanded ? The other is what are the key determinants of the demand for money ? Both the questions are interrelated.

11.4.1 Why is Money Demanded ?

The question to be asked in full is why is money demanded when money does not earn its holders any income whereas there are competing non-money financial assets in the economy which yield some income to their holders? One general answer can be that money yields its holders convenience yield of non-pecuniary nature. This yield is rooted in the peculiar characteristic of money as the only generally acceptable means of payment, and so its perfect liquidity. More concretely, Keynes said that money was demanded due to three main motives: *(1)* the transactions motive, *(2)* the precautionary motive and *(3)* the speculative motive. Ever since this threefold classification of motives has become standard stock-in-trade of monetary economists. Later efforts to add other motives such as the finance motive by Keynes (1937) and Robertson (1938) and the diversification motive by Gurley and Shaw (1960) have not been successful.

The three motives and corresponding demands for money are explained briefly first, to be followed by somewhat extended discussion of the individual components of the demand for money. The transactions motive gives rise to the transactions demand for money which refers to the demand for cash of the public for making current transactions of all kinds. This is inextricably bound with the use of money as the medium of exchange in a money-exchange economy. The precautionary motive induces the public to hold money to provide for contingencies requiring sudden expenditure and for unforeseen opportunities of advantageous purchase. This motive (demand) is a product of uncertainties of all kinds. The speculative motive giving rise to the speculative demand for money is the most important contribution Keynes made to the theory of the demand for money. It explains why the public may hold surplus cash (over and above that demanded due to the other two motives) in the face of interest-earning bonds (and other financial assets). The reason is that the holders of such speculative balances may anticipate such fall in future bond prices as will make the loss of foregone interest earnings look relatively smaller. So they wait with cash for bond prices to fall, avoid expected capital losses, and switch into bonds when the anticipated fall in bond prices has been realized. The speculative demand for money is sometimes also called the asset demand for money—not a happy term, because, money being an asset, the entire demand for it is an asset demand.

Related to the above is the distinction between active and idle balances made in the Keynesian literature. The active balances are defined as balances used as means of payments in national income-generating transactions. The rest are called idle balances. The distinction is useful to explain how changes in the income velocity of money come about and how the same quantity of money can support higher or lower levels of money expenditure when idle balances are converted into active balances or *vice versa.*

11.4.2 The Determinants of the Demand for Money

Keynes made the demand for money a function of two variables, namely income (Y)[4] and the rate of interest (r). Being a Cambridge economist, Keynes retained the influence of the Cambridge approach to the demand for money under which M^d is hypothesised to be a function of Y. But he argued that this explained only the transactions and the precautionary demand for money,[5] and not the entire demand for money. The truly novel and revolutionary element of Keynes' theory of the demand for money is the component of *the speculative demand for money.* Through it Keynes made (a part of) the demand for money a declining function of the rate of interest, the latter a purely monetary phenomenon and the sole carrier of monetary influences in the economy. Thus the speculative demand for money constitutes the main pillar of Keynes' revolution in monetary theory and Keynes' attack on the quantity theory of money. This is explained below.

The speculative demand for money arises from the speculative motive for holding money. The latter arises from the variability of interest rates in the market and uncertainty about them. For simplicity, Keynes assumed that perpetual bonds are the only non-money financial asset in the economy, which compete with money in the asset portfolio of the public. Money does not earn its holders aby interest income, but its capital value in terms of itself is always fixed. Bonds, on the other hand, yield interest income to their holders. But this income can be more than wiped out if bond prices fall in future. It can be shown algebraically that the price of a (perpetual) bond is given by the reciprocal of the market rate of interest times the coupon rate of interest. Suppose the coupon rate (i.e. interest payable on a bond) is Re 1 per year and the market rate of interest is 4 per cent per year. Then the market price of the bond will be Rs. 1/.04×1 = Rs. 25. If the market rate of interest rises to 5 per cent per year, the market price of the bond will fall to Rs. 1/.05×1 = Rs. 20. Thus, bond price is seen as an inverse function of the rate of interest.

Economic units hold a part of their wealth in the form of financial assets. In the two-asset model of Keynes, these assets are money and (perpetual) bonds. Bond prices keep on changing from time to time. Therefore, they are subject to capital gains or losses. Thus, to a bond-holder the return from bond-holding per unit period (say a year) per Re. is the rate of interest $\pm$ capital gain or loss per year. At the time of making investment in bonds, the market rate of interest will be a given datum to an individual, but the future rate of interest or bond price, and so the expected rate of capital gain or loss will have to be anticipated. Hence the element of speculation in the bond market and, as shown below, also in the money market.

The speculators are of two kinds : bulls and bears. Bulls are those who expect the bond prices to rise in the future. Bears expect these prices to fall. In Keynes' model, these expectations are assumed to be held with certainty. Bulls, then, are assumed to invest all their idle cash into bonds. Bears instead will move out of bonds into cash if their expected capital losses on bonds exceed interest income from bond-holding. Thereby they minimise their losses. Thus, the speculative demand for money arises only from bears. It is the demand for bearish hoards. These bears build up their cash balances to move into bonds when either bond prices have fallen as expected or when they come to expect that bond prices will rise in future.

The above model implies an all-or-nothing behaviour on the part of individual assetholders. Either they are entirely into bonds (bulls) or entirely into cash (bears). That is, their portfolios are pure and not diversified. This result of Keynes has been revised by Tobin (1958), as explained later in this section. To move to the aggregate speculative demand for money, Keynes assumed that different assetholders have different interest-rate expectations. Thus, at a certain very high rate of interest (and very low price of bonds), all may be bulls. Then, the speculative demand for money will be equal to zero. But at a lower rate of interest (higher bond price) some bulls will become bears and positive demand for speculative balances will emerge. At a still lower rate of interest (and still higher bond price), some more bulls will become bears and the speculative demand for money will be higher still. Thus, Keynes derived a downward-sloping aggregate speculative demand curve for money with respect to the bond rate of interest, as shown in Figure 11.2.

Keynes also suggested the possibility of the existence of what is called the *liquidity trap*. This refers to a situation when at a certain very low rate of interest the (speculative) demand for money becomes

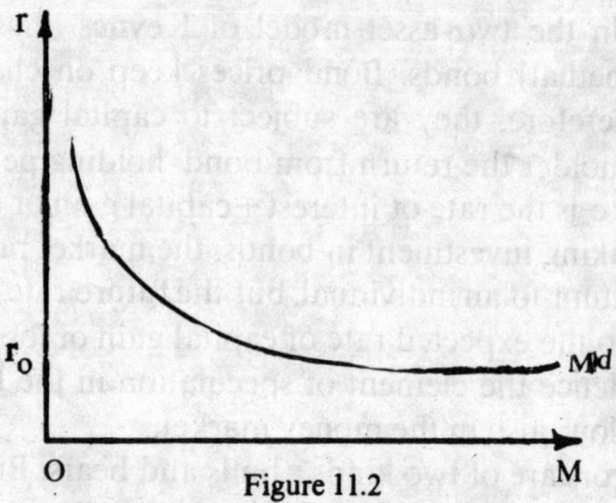

Figure 11.2

Keynes' Speculative Demand for Money

perfectly elastic. This will come about when at that rate all the assetholders turn bears, so that none is willing to hold bonds and everyone wants to move into cash. In Figure 11.2, such a situation occurs at the rate of interest r_o. Then, no amount of expansion of money supply can lower the rate of interest further. The public is willing to hold the entire extra amount of money at r_o. The extra liquidity created by the monetary authority gets trapped in the asset portfolios of the public without lowering r. The r_o serves as the minimum r below which it cannot be lowered.

Another element in Keynes' theory of the speculative demand for money is the concept of the 'normal' rate of interest. Keynes postulated that at any moment there was a certain r which the assetholders regard as 'normal', as the r which will tend to prevail in the market under 'normal conditions'. This 'normal' r acts as the benchmark with repect to which any actual r is judged as high or low. Differences of r expectations among asset holders then can be interpreted as differences about the level of the 'normal' r. The amount of money demanded for speculative purposes depends on the current level of r relative to this 'normal' r as seen by various individuals. If the latter changes, the quantity of money demanded at any particular r will also change. Since 'normal' r, or people's expectation about it, cannot be taken as a time constant, Keynes' argument implies that the relation between the demand for money and r will not be stable over time. This is an important result which has not been fully appreciated even by Keynes' followers. It can be seen to damage Keynes' own theory of the interest rate determination, but more so the quantity theory of money and the effectiveness of monetary policy. These implications will be taken up in the next two chapters.

Keynes' micro theory of the speculative demand for money has been called into question by *Tobin* (1958). It was noted above that for an individual Keynes' explanation leads to a pure asset portfolio of either money or bonds. This is contrary to experience. In actual life mixed asset portfolios are the rule. Tobin's alternative formulation yields such portfolios even at individual level. For this, unlike Keynes, he assumes that an individual does not hold his interest-rate expectations with certainty. Then liquidity preference is analysed as behaviour towards risk under uncertainty. Acting on uncertain interest-rate expectations means assuming some risk of capital loss. The degree of risk increases with every increase in the proportion of bonds in the asset portfolio. Normally, asset holders are risk averters, so that they will require a higher compensation (rate of interest) for undertaking higher risk. Thus, at a higher r more bonds and less money will be held in the portfolio and at a lower r less bonds and more money will be preferred. The result is a diversified asset portfolio and a downward sloping asset demand curve for money with respect to r even at the micro level. On suitable assumptions, the aggregate asset demand for money is also shown as a declining function of r.

Keynes' theory of the speculative demand for money has also been criticised on the ground that it treats all non-money financial assets (NMFAs) as bonds. Such treatment is an unwarranted simplification, because a large number of such assets are unlike bonds in that their capital values are nominally fixed and do not vary (inversely) with r. In India, the examples of such NMFAs are fixed deposits with commercial banks, post offices, and public limited companies, national savings certificates, UTI units, etc. Substitution between them and money does not entail Keynes' speculative motive, because they are not subject to variation in their nominal capital values. In their case, their rates of return influence M^d as simple opportunity-cost variables without any element of speculation.

Gurley and Shaw (1960) also do not favour keeping the M^d function confined to a simple two-asset world. In their analysis of the effects of financial growth, exhibited by security differentiation and the growth of secondary securities, they have stressed the growing competition or asset substitution which money has to face from the NMFAs in the asset portfolios of wealth-holders. According to them, other things being the same, this ever-growing asset substitution has led to downward displacements of the demand for money, has made this demand less stable, and made monetary policy less effective than before. Much systematic empirical work has not been done on these hypotheses. Most empirical studies on the demand for money have tended to ignore them. What little empirical work has been done for the USA (Fiege, 1964) does not lend definite support to the Gurley and Shaw hypotheses.

After a fairly long detour, we come back to Keynes' theory of the demand for money. This is summed up in the following equation:

$$M^d = L_1(Y) + L_2(r). \qquad (11.3)$$

It is an additive demand function with two separate components. $L_1(Y)$ represents the transactions and precautionary demand for money. Keynes made both an increasing function of the level of money income. In the Cambridge tradition, he tended to assume that $L_1(Y)$ had proportional form of the kind represented in Figure 11.1. The second component $L_2(r)$ represents the speculative demand for money, which, as shown above, Keynes argued to be a declining function of r. As shown in Figure 11.2, this relation was not assumed to be linear.

Keynes' additive form of the demand function for money of equation (11.3) has been discarded by Keynesians and other economists. It has been argued that money is one asset, not two, three, or many. The motives to hold it may be of any number. The same unit of money can serve all these motives. So the demand for it cannot be compartmenalised into separate components independent of each other. Also, as argued in Baumol-Tobin theory in the next section, the transactions demand for money also is interest elastic. The same can be argued for the precautionary demand for money too. The explanation of the speculative demand for money shows that this kind of demand will be an increasing function of total assets or wealth. If income is taken as a proxy for wealth, the speculative demand also becomes a function of both income and the rate of interest. These arguments have led to the following revised form of the Keynesian demand function for money:

$$M^d = L(Y, r), \qquad (11.4)$$

where it is hypothesised that M^d is an increasing function of Y and a declining function of r.

The replacement of the simple M^d function of equation (11.1) by that of equation (11.4) has been the single most important revolutionary development in the field of monetary theory. It has also been the cause of many battles between the neoclassical economists and the Keynesians. It has necessitated integration of value theory with monetary theory or of the real sector with the monetary sector, of which Hicks' IS–LM model (see Section 13.9) is a well-known example. This makes the simple quantity theory of money model suspect by making the income-velocity of money responsive to changes in the rate of interest. The latter changes can come about by any number of factors originating in the money market or the commodity market. All these points will be explained at appropriate places in the next two chapters. Our main purpose in adding this paragraph to the text is to emphasise once again the importance of the demand function for money in monetary theory.

11.5 The Transactions Demand for Money

In the previous section the transactions demand for money was only introduced and not discussed. We discuss it in the present section. Two explanations of this demand are available. One is the popular textbook explanation; the other is based on the application of inventory theory to the transactions demand for money. They are discussed below.

11.5.1 The Popular Textbook Explanation

The popular textbook explanation of the transactions demand for money is a mechanical, not a behavioural, explanation. First this demand is explained for an individual household on the following assumptions : *(i)* that it receives a given money income at regular intervals, say weekly or monthly implying fixed income period, and *(ii)* that the time-pattern of its expenditure is also given, the usual assumption being that all the income received at the beginning of the period is spent regularly at a steady rate over this period till the entire money income is exhausted at the end of the income period. Then, at any point of time, the amount of unspent money balance is the amount of money held for transactions purposes. This amount is equal to the amount of money income received at the beginning of the income period, zero at the end of this period and steadily declines as one moves from the beginning of the period to its end. Further, the income-expenditure pattern and the resulting money-holding pattern for all income periods are assumed to be identical. The resulting money-holding profile is represented diagrammatically as in Figure

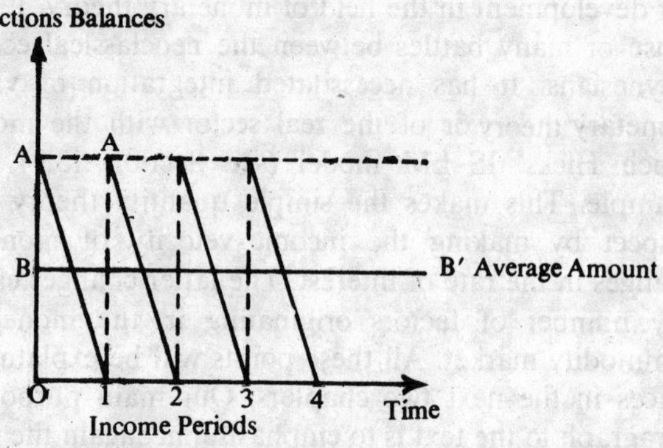

Figure 11.3
The Transactions Demand for Money

Consider period 0. Its time length is given by the horizontal distance 0–1. The vertical hight OA measures money income received per period. This also represents the maximum amount of transactions cash held at the beginning of the period. It has been assumed that this amount is spent away in equal amounts each day (hour) over the income period. The rest then is held as transactions balance Taking continuous approximation of the spending assumption, this transactions balance held at any point of time during the income period is shown by the downward sloping straight line A1. At the end of the income period this balance is reduced to zero. In continuous time this is also the beginning of the new income period 1 and the money income received as well as the transactions balance held jumps up to height of OA. This is shown by the height of the broken line 1A′. What had happened during the income period O is assumed to happen during the income period 1 and subsequent income periods as well. This is shown by the downward sloping solid parallel lines. This gives us the popular saw-tooth diagram of the Figure 11.3. Algebraically it can be shown that the average amount of transactions balance held over any income period will be one-half of the total amount held at the beginning of the period. Hence we get the horizontal line BB′, showing the average amount of transactions balances held. This explanation, then, is extended by analogy to the economy as a whole.

The above is a mechanical and highly contrived model. Even at the level of an individual wage-earner, the time-pattern of expenditure assumed is highly simplistic. In actual life all manners of time-patterns of expenditure are observed, which may be highly skewed and irregular, because it is highly wasteful of time and energy to go to market all the time to buy goods and services of even daily use. Some purchases are paid for only periodically as, for example, electricity and water bills, house rent, school and college fees, etc. Some purchases are made on credit and paid for later. The expenditure on consumer durables is lumpy and irregular. Thus even a wage earner has to decide actively how much transactions balance to hold at any time and how far to hold the inventory of goods instead.

At the aggregate level, the above simplistic model has to face further difficulties, because not all economic units get paid fixed incomes at regular intervals. The income receipts of non-wage households *(e.g.* of doctors, shopkeepers, rickshaw-pullers), may be daily, once or twice a year (as of farmers), or at irregular intervals. Then, business firms also hold transactions balances and their cash flows have all manners of time-pattern. Therefore, it is futile to follow the highly complex criss-cross of the *flows* of receipts and expenditures and their time patterns and then to derive the transactions demand for money as the amount of money *required* to carry out these transactions. This approach makes the transactions demand for money a *technical requirement* (see Hicks, 1967; Gupta, 1972a), and not a voluntary choice variable of the public, which it is. It either neglects the velocity of money or treats it implicitly as a constant, neither of which can be supported on theoretical or empirical grounds. For all these reasons, modern monetary theory does not give any credence to the above model, though at the textbook level it still continues to survive.

A satisfactory theory of the transactions demand for money cannot be constructed only on the non-synchronous character of receipts and expenditures. It has also to be explained why they are not synchronous in time and why money is held in the presence of interest-bearing and highly liquid short-term financial assets. The answer depends on the presence of transactions costs (such as brokerage fees) in moving in and out of non-money financial assets whereas money is the only generally acceptable means of payment. Then the problem is not merely of explaining why transactions balances are held but also of explaining what determines the optimal amount of such balances held by their holders. Besides the volume of expenditure and transactions costs, the rate of interest as the opportunity cost of holding even transactions balances also enters the picture. Big business firms with surplus transactions cash are known to invest it on short-term basis. The theory of it has been put forward by Baumol (1952) and Tobin (1956) in two separate articles. Both apply the theory of inventory holding to the transactions demand for money. Without going into formal mathematics, their basic argument and results are summed up below.

11.5.2 Baumol-Tobin Theory of the Transactions Demand for Money

It is assumed that an individual (household or firm) faces the following situation : *(a)* a given income received periodically, *(b)* cash purchases of equal amounts spread over time throughout the period, *(c)* option of holding transactions funds in the form of money or risk-free income-yielding bonds (or non-money financial assets) and *(d)* given cost in exchanging bonds for cash per transaction. Then, the problem of the transactions demand for money is posed as the problem of determining the optimal amount of cash the individual would hold. Alternatively, this can be seen as the problem of minimising the total cost of financing transactions. This cost has two components : *(a)* interest foregone on the average of cash balances held and *(b)* transactions cost of buying and encashing bonds, if a part (or whole) of transactions funds are first held in bonds and then converted into cash in instalments. Clearly, if too much cash is held the interest income foregone will be too high, though the transactions cost in the bond market will be low. Conversely, if too little cash is kept on hand and so bonds initially bought are sold more frequently, the opportunity cost of interest foregone will, no doubt, be low, but the transactions cost in the bond market will be too high. Therefore, the optimal amount of transactions balances will lie somewhere in between and can be uniquely determined mathematically. The analysis yields the following interesting results:

1. The optimum level of transactions cash increases with the total value of expenditures to be made during the period. But it is found to be a function of the square root of total expenditures, implying strong economies of scale in an individual's transactions demand for cash. This is the most important result of the Baumol-Tobin theory and goes against the neoclassical theory which hypothesises the transactions demand for money to be a proportional function of income (or expenditure); and

2. The optimum level of transactions cash varies inversely with the rate of interest.

It should be understood that, in practice, the above results concerning the management of transactions cash are likely to be important for only large firms and organizations and not for small economic units. This model, too, like the simple model studied earlier, assumes that the micro results for an individual cash holder will also be applicable with equal force at the aggregate level. This will not be so, once we allow for differences in the cash management behaviour of individual units, as we have admitted in the beginning of this paragraph. Then the distribution variable in the form of time-patterns of income receipts and planned expenditures across individual units will also be important.

11.6 Friedman's Theory

Friedman's theory of the demand for money (Friedman, 1956, 1968b) is partly Keynesian and partly non-Keynesian. It is non-Keynesian in that Friedman neglects completely Keynes' classification of the motives for holding money and the corresponding component demands for money. Instead, for identifying the key determinants of the demand for money, he classifies the holders of money as between *(a)* ultimate wealth-holders and *(b)* business enterprises. All the essentials of his theory have been set out in respect of the former, and comparatively much less about the latter. He emphasises the role of money as an asset and in this he generalises Keynes' analysis of the speculative demand for money by treating the total demand for money as part of capital or wealth theory, concerned with the composition of the balance sheet or portfolio of assets. Because of its peculiar property as the generally acceptable means of payments, money is assumed to yield a flow of services to its holder. It is also assumed implicitly that money, too, is subject to the general principle of the diminishing marginal rate of substitution: that other things being the same, the larger the money balances the lower the marginal service yield of these balances relative to the yield of other assets.

Demand by Ultimate Wealth-Holders

The ultimate wealth-holders are households. To them money appears as a durable consumer good. As such the standard theory of demand for consumer goods can be applied to the demand for money. Also, this demand will be a demand for a quantity of real (and not merely nominal) money as the wealth-holders are basically interested in a certain command over real goods and services through money and not in the nominal amount of it (money) *per se.* Using this approach, Friedman specifies the following as the key determinants of this demand for money.

1. *Total wealth.* This is the analogue of the budget constraint in the usual theory of consumer choice. It is the total that must be divided among various forms of assets. In practice, estimates of total wealth are rarely available, more so when total wealth is defined to include not merely non-human or physical wealth but also human wealth, that is, the present value of the expected flow of labour income. So income is generally used as a surrogate for wealth. Income, as we know, includes both property income and labour income. But to serve as a good proxy for wealth, a longer-term concept of income, like Friedman's concept of 'permanent income', should be used in place of current income. The emphasis on income as a surrogate for wealth, rather than as a measure of the 'work' to be done by money, has been claimed by Friedman as the basic conceptual difference between his formulation of the demand for money and the earlier formulations, both neoclassical and Keynesian, concerned with the transactions approach to the demand for money.

2. *The division of wealth between human and non-human forms.* Since total wealth is assumed to include human wealth and institutional constraints limit narrowly the conversion of human into non-human wealth or the reverse, Friedman hypothesises the fraction of total wealth that is in the form of non-human wealth to be an additional important variable. In particular, he hypothesises the demand for money to be a declining function of the aforesaid fraction, as it is much easier to sell or purchase non-human than human wealth.

3. *The expected rates of return on money and other assets.* This is the analogue of the prices of a commodity and its substitutes and complements in the theory of consumer demand. The nominal rate of return on money may be zero as on currency or positive as it is on savings deposits, a large part of which is counted as demand deposits, or even negative, if current-account deposits are subject to net service charges. The nominal rate of return on other assets consists of two parts: first, any currently paid yield or cost, such as interest on bonds, dividends on equities and storage costs on physical assets, and second, expected changes in their nominal prices. It is through the second part (of expected capital gains or losses) that Keynes had introduced his speculative demand for money. Keynes, however, had considered only bonds as the competing non-money asset. Or, more correctly speaking, he had treated bonds as representing all long-term financial assets. Thus interpreted, the really novel and important

feature of Friedman's formulation is the extension of the margin of substitution for money to stocks of (durable) goods.[6] Obviously, for them the expected rate of change of prices (adjusted for storage costs) gives the appropriate rate of return, and this becomes especially important under conditions of inflation or deflation.

Other variables. Besides the above, there may be other variables that affect the utility attached to the services of money relative to those rendered by other assets, and so should be included in the demand function for money. One such variable suggested by Friedman is 'the degree of economic stability expected to prevail in the future'. According to him, wealth-holders are likely to attach considerably more value to liquidity when they expect economic conditions to be unstable than when they expect them to be highly stable. However, it is difficult to express this variable quantitatively.

Friedman's theory of the demand function for money for an individual wealth-holder is summed up symbolically below:

$$\left(\frac{M}{P}\right)^d = f(y, w; r_m, r_b, r_e, \dot{p}^e; u), \tag{11.5}$$

where M, P, and y have the same meaning as in the foregoing except that they relate to a single wealth-holder; w is the fraction of wealth in non-human form (or, alternatively, the fraction of income derived from property); r_m is the *expected* rate of return on money; r_b is the rate of return on fixed-value securities, including *expected* changes in their prices; r_e is the expected rate of return on equities, including expected changes in their price; $\dot{p}^e$ is the *expected* rate of change of prices of goods and hence the expected rate of return on real assets (unadjusted for storage costs); and u is a symbol for whatever variables other than income that may affect the utility attached to the services of money.

Equation (11.5) can be regarded as giving the aggregate demand function for money, with, M, y, and w referring to aggregate magnitudes if we are willing to assume that the amount of money demanded depends merely on the aggregate or average value of y and w, and not their distribution among households (and firms). This assumption is commonly made in deriving almost all macro relations from their micro counterparts.

11.7 Empirical Evidence

Any of the demand functions for money discussed above (or their reformulations) is only as good as the empirical evidence makes it out to be. Consequently, much empirical work has gone into identifying it and estimating the best values of its parameters using econometric technique of multiple regression analysis for several individual countries such as the USA, the UK, Canada, and also India. Several surveys of the work done have also appeared in print.[7] We summarise below the highlights of the main results.

1. The demand for money has been found to be a highly stable function of a few specifiable variables;

2. Real income has been found as the major determinant of the (real) demand for money. For the USA, the UK and Canada, real wealth or longer-run average income (Friedman's 'permanent income') has been found to perform better than measured (current) income as a scale variable. For want of reliable data, similar evidence is not available for India;

3. For India, the best estimate of the income-elasticity of the demand for money is unity;

4. For India, in most cases, the rate of interest has not been found to be a statistically significant explanatory variable. In contrast, for the USA, the empirical evidence clearly shows the demand for money tp be a decreasing function of the rate of interest;

5. For several countries that have suffered rapid inflation, there is overwhelming evidence to show that the demand for money responds negatively to the expected rate of inflation as the opportunity cost for holding cash balances. For India, too, a study by Trivedi (1980) shows that the demand for money in India is a declining function of the expected rate of inflation; and

6. For India, changes in the distribution of income as between the agricultural sector and the rest of the economy, represented by variations in the ratio of agricultural income (at current prices) to net national income (at current prices) have been found to affect negatively the demand for money.

NOTES

1. It will be useful to note that the money market of monetary theory is a purely theoretical construct devised by economists to analyse monetary phenomena. In actual life there is no separate market where ready cash might be bought and sold. Instead, money being general purchasing power trades on one side of all the other markets. What is called money market in actual life,truly speaking, is a market in short-term credit.

2. We have already seen above how this property of the demand for money equation (11.1 a) can be used to convert it into the real demand for money equation (11.2).

3. This motive can be interpreted broadly to include also the *finance motive* which refers to the tendency of firms to accumulate cash to finance investment expenditures in the near future. Funds that will be required to be spent after some time, if reasonably sizable, can always be invested in highly liquid short-term non-money financial assets.

4. In Keynes' theory the distinction between nominal income (Y) and real income (y) loses its relevance, because Keynes assumed his *numeraire* (*i.e.* unit of measurement), the money wage rate, to be a short-run constant. Most Keynesians use P as the deflator instead and assume P to be a short-run constant.

5. Note the clubbing together of the two components of the demand for money.

6. More generally, Friedman's theory of the demand for money extends the *range* of substitution (of money) to all non-money assets and durable consumers' as well as producers' goods. Interpreted thus, it encompasses the later contributions of Gurley and Shaw and of the 'portfolio-balance approach' to the demand for money, summarised towards the end of Section 11.4. The aforesaid generalisation has very important implications for the theory of the 'transmission mechanism' which explains how changes in money supply influence the levels of economic activity, and for the debate between the Keynesians and the monetarists, discussed in Section 12.7.

7. See Vasudevan (1977) and Gupta (1979, pp. 27–29 and Appendix A) for India and Laidler (1977, Chapter 7) for other countries.

CHAPTER 12

Money and Prices

12.1 Introduction

Variations in the quantity of money have important influence on the course of prices, money income, real income, rate of interest and other economic variables. The major task of traditional monetary theory has been to analyse this influence in a coherent manner. There are two main approaches to this task: One, the Quantity Theory of Money (called QTM hereafter) approach, the other, the Keynesian approach. This chapter is devoted entirely to the former; the next chapter to the latter.

The QTM has had several incarnations. We shall not offer a doctrinal history of them. Only the key features of several formulations will be discussed. Broadly speaking, a distinction may be made between the crude version and the sophisticated version. The former says that changes in the quantity of money lead to proportionate changes in the price level in the same direction. This is always the result of strict interpretation of a QTM equation of any form, discussed below. But their authors invariably knew better and never insisted on the strict proportionality thesis. The sophisticated version attributed to Milton Friedman claims "that substantial changes in prices or nominal income are almost invariably the result of changes in the nominal supply of money" (Friedman 1968, p. 39).

Two formulations of the QTM that have gained maximum currency are : Irving Fisher's transactions version (1911) and the Cambridge Cash-Balances version, attributed to Pigou (1917) and Marshall (1923). Each of these formulations and their various forms and interpretations will be discussed in some detail in this chapter. In the last section an overall appraisal of the QTM, including Friedman's key position on the QTM, is given. Some related aspects are discussed in Appendix B.

12.2 Fisher's Transactions Approach to the QTM

Fisher's quantity theory is best explained with the help of his famous equation of exchange.

$$M V_T = P_T T, \tag{12.1}$$

where the subscript T is added to V and P to emphasise that they relate to total transactions. Each side of the equation gives the money value of total transactions during a period. Let us see how. First consider the right-hand side of the equation. In the case of a single (say ith) transaction, with its price p_i and quantity t_i, its money value will be given by $p_i . t_i$. When money value of all such transactions, whether of goods, services, or assets, etc. are added up, we get $\sum_i p_i t_i$. Taking P_T as a suitably chosen average of all prices P_i and T as a suitably chosen aggregate of all quantities transacted t_i, we have

$$P_T T = \sum_i P_i t_i. \tag{12.2}$$

Now consider the left-hand side of equation (12.1). In it M is the total quantity of money in the economy and V_T is its transactions velocity, that is, the average number of times a unit of money changes hands to effectuate transactions during the period chosen. Then, MV_T will also give the money value of total transactions during the same period. Since *ex post* both MV_T and $P_T T$ measure the same total (money value of transactions during a period), the two must be equal to each other. Hence equation (12.1). That is why it is also called equation pf exchange.

Thus interpreted, equation (12.1) is an identity. Since *ex post* it must always be true, it is also a truism. Why is it then called a theory — a theory which says that a change in the quantity of money will lead to an equiproportionate change in P in the same direction ? Before discussing the answer of the QTM, a general point may be made. Equation (12.1) is one equation in four unknowns (or variables). Therefore, it can be used to solve for the value of only one of them in terms of the other three. That is, given the values of any three variables, the value of the fourth one has to be such as to satisfy the equation (12.1). What the QTM does specifically is to assume that T and V_T are constants, or at least autonomous of changes in M, that changes in M are autonomous of the other three (P, V_T, and T), and that consequently, changes in M lead to equiproportionate changes in

P. Since it highlights the relation between M and P and makes changes in the former the (major) cause of changes in P, it becomes 'a quantity of money theory of P'. Popularly it is called the QTM. This is explained more fully below.

We begin with the assumptions of the QTM with respect to individual factors (T,M,V_T, and P_T) assembled in the equation.

Transactions (T). In the QTM it is assumed that the physical volume of transactions (T) is determined by the basic physical and operational characteristics of the system, such as the real resources available to the economy, the efficiency with which they are used, the degree of business integration of the economy (which determines the number of transactions involved in the production and sale of final goods). More important, "all quantity theorists, at least since Hume, have recognized that changes in the stock of money may have transitional effects on T. However, they have generally regarded the average level of T and long-run changes in T as largely independent of the quantity of money although not of the existence of a money economy" (Friedman, 1968, p. 41). In addition, it is assumed that changes in V_T and P_T do not influence T (except temporarily). Thus, the demand-side influence on T is neglected completely.

Money (M). It is assumed that the factors determining the stock of M depend critically on the monetary system and are largely independent of the forces determining T.

Velocity of Circulation (V_T). The QTM is often associated with the assumption of a constant V—that V is something of a natural constant. This is not fully correct. No doubt, the transactions approach emphasises payment practices, such as the frequency with which people are paid, the irregularity of receipts and payments, as its key determinant. But Fisher and earlier quantity theorists did explicitly recognize that velocity would also be affected by, among other things, the rate of interest and also the rate of change of prices. They recognized that both high rates of interest and rapidly rising prices would induce people to economise on money balances and so tend to raise velocity and that low rates of interest and falling prices would have the opposite effect. However, all this was not woven systematically into a complete macro model. It was also assumed that payment practices, though responsive to cost considerations, were rather slow to change. Therefore, it was thought to be a good first approximation to assume that V was almost a constant.

Prices (P_T). P_T refers to the average price of market transactions of all kinds, whether in currently-produced final goods or services or intermediates, or old goods, or transactions of a purely financial nature. In the QTM, P_T is treated as the dependent variable. Assuming T and V_T to remain unchanged, or rather autonomous of changes in M, it makes P_T alone as the factor that absorbs all changes in M. That is, equation (12.1) can be used to solve for the value of P_T which will make the two sides of this equation equal. This gives

$$P_T = \frac{MV_T}{T}. \tag{12.3}$$

In the rigid version of the QTM presented above, P_T is seen to be a proportional function of M (given V_T and T): a doubling of the quantity of M will lead to the doubling of P. Also, since changes in M are assumed to be autonomous of P_T, the former are made the cause of changes in the latter. This sums up the theoretical content of the QTM (transactions approach).

The above theory suffers, no doubt, from several shortcomings. We shall discuss them later in the chapter. Before doing so, let us get familiar with two more versions of it.

Another Version

Following Fisher, it is customary to subdivide the left-hand side of equation (12.1) into two categories of payments : those effected by the transfer of currency (including coins) and those effected by the transfer of demand deposits. (Recall the commonly-accepted definition of money as the sum of currency and demand deposits.) One reason for the emphasis on this kind of division was the belief that the velocities of circulation of the two kinds of money were different. The other reason was the ready availability of data on bank clearings and so on the turnover or velocity of bank deposits.

Redefining M as only currency and V_T as its velocity, M as the volume of demand deposits and V'_T for their velocity, equation (12.1) can be recast as

$$MV_T + M'V'_T = P_T T. \tag{12.4}$$

This is not important enough to be pursued further.

12.3 The Quantity Equation in Income Form

In equations (12.1) and (12.4) of the transactions approach to the QTM, the magnitudes designated as T and P_T are conceptually ambiguous and difficult to measure with available data. Therefore, with the development of social accounting and Keynes' theory of income in the 1930s and consequent emphasis on national income, an important change occurred in the specification of the quantity equation, too. A tendency developed to express this equation in terms of real income (y) rather than transactions (T). With this P_T got replaced by P, the average level of prices of final goods and services that make up the national income of a country. National income accounting gives reasonably satisfactory measures of both y and the associated implicit deflator, P. Appropriately enough, the transactions velocity V_T has given place to '*income velocity of money*' V, which defines the average number of times per period a unit of money is used in making *income* transactions (that is, payments for final goods and services) rather than all transactions. When all these changes are incorporated in equation (12.1), we get the quantity theory equation in income form:

$$MV = Py. \tag{12.5}$$

The above equation is both conceptually and empirically more satisfactory than equation (12.1). Its categories do not suffer from the twin problems of conceptual ambiguity and difficulty of statistical measurement surrounding the categories of equation (12.1). The new equation is also closer in conception to the Cambridge Cash-Balance equation and to the modern version of the QTM. This makes movement from one to the other easier and helps view the QTM as one unified approach to monetary theory.

We need not repeat the earlier discussion of the four key factors captured in the quantity equation. The main thrust of the approach remains unaltered. However, the change in the variables should be kept in mind. The posture of the modern QTM with respect to them and the modifications introduced will be discussed later in the chapter.

Like equation (12.1), equation (12.5) can be and has been interpreted both as an identity and as a genuine equation. *Ex post* it, too, is an identity, or something which is definitionally true. This can be shown very simply. By definition,

$$V \equiv \frac{Y}{M} \tag{12.6}$$

In fact, this is how actual V is measured. Multiplying both sides of (12.6) by M and recalling that $Y \equiv P.y$, we have equation (12.5) as an identity.

However, this is not the QTM proper, whatever its other faults. As a theory, its equation (12.5) is a P determining equation, given V, y, and M. More important, on the assumption that V is a constant and y is determined by the real-sector forces operating elsewhere in the system, autonomous changes in M lead to equiproportionate changes in P.

12.4 The Cambridge Cash-Balances Approach

An alternative formulation of the QTM has been provided by the Cambridge economists, Marshall and Pigou, in the form of their cash-balances equation:

$$M = KPy, O < K < 1, \tag{12.7}$$

where K is assumed to be a behavioural constant and other symbols are as defined already. The above equation is, in fact, the equilibrium condition for the money market, which makes the demand for money equal to its supply. In Section 11.3 we have already discussed the demand function for money of the Cambridge approach, reproduced below:

$$M^d = KPy, O < K < 1. \tag{12.8}$$

It is assumed that the supply of money is given exogenously by the monetary authority, so that

$$M^s = \bar{M}. \tag{12.9}$$

Then, in equilibrium, when the quantity of money demanded by the public is equal to the amount of money supplied by the monetary authority, we shall have equation (12.7).

On comparing equation (12.7) with equation (12.5), we can see that the former is only a transformation of the latter, with K being the reciprocal of V. So, (12.7) determines P in the same sense in which (12.5) determines P.

Formally, this is true, because, as already explained in Section 11.3, K gives the ratio of money income (flow) the public likes to hold in the form of money (stock) and is measured in time units. Therefore, its reciprocal will give turnover per time period. For example, if the public likes to hold money which is equal in value to its money income of 13 weeks (or $\frac{1}{4}$ year), so that K= $\frac{1}{4}$ year, V will have the value of 4 per year. Therefore, when both sides of equation (12.7) are divided by K and on its left-hand side 1/K is replaced by its equivalent V, we have Fisher's equation (12.5) in its income version.

But inspite of the formal equivalence between the two equations, there are very important *conceptual differences* between the two approaches lying behind them. In the words of Friedman, "The two approaches stress different aspects of money, make different definitions of money seem natural, and lead to emphasis being placed on different variables and analytical techniques" (Friedman, 1968b, p. 45).

The transactions approach emphasises the medium-of-exchange function of money. Therefore, it makes it natural to define money as whatever serves as the medium of exchange. On the other hand, the cash balances approach stresses equally the store-of-value function of money which enables separation of sale from purchase. Therefore, this approach is consistent with a broader definition of money preferred by Friedman which includes even time deposits of banks along with demand deposits and currency held by the public.

More important, in its explanation of the determinants of V, the transactions approach stresses the mechanical aspects of the payments process and practices, such as the frequency of wage and other factor payments, the use of trade (or book) credit, the degree of vertical integration of businesses, the speed with which funds can be remitted from one place to another, and so on. In contrast, the cash-balances approach is behavioural in nature: it is built around the demand function for money, however simple. Unlike Fisher's V, K is a behavioural ratio. As such, it can easily lead to stress being placed on the relative usefulness of money as an asset, on the costs and returns from holding money instead of other assets, the uncertainty of the future, etc.

As to analytical techniques, we have already seen in the opening paragraphs of this section how the cash-balances approach fits in easily with the general demand-supply analysis as applied to the money market. (This is developed further in the next section.) A similar interpretation of the transactions approach to the QTM is not available.[2] For all these reasons, modern QTM (see Section 2.7) is very much in the tradition of the Cambridge QTM (at least in its empirical applications), with, of course, several qualifications.

In modern discussions of the QTM, a clear distinction is made between (a) the QTM as a theory of Y (money income) and (b) the QTM as a theory of P, with much greater emphasis on the former than on the latter. It is as a theory of Y that the QTM has been pitted against Keynes' theory of income (see Friedman and Meiselman, 1964) and has generated much controversy between 'monetarists' and

Keynesians. For the QTM to serve as a theory of P, it must first serve as a theory of Y. Then alone, on additional assumptions, it can be made out as a theory of P. These two roles of the QTM are discussed in the next two sections. The explanation of QTM as a theory of Y in its simple Cambridge form is spelt out in detail, because this presents to a large extent the essentials of the transmission mechanism implied in the Cambridge QTM, though not explicitly stated anywhere.[3]

12.5 The QTM as a Theory of Money Income

The QTM comes out easily as a theory of money-income (Y) determination when we analyse the equilibrium of the money market with the help of the Cambridge cash-balances equation (12.7). To see this, we first recall that, by definition, Py = Y, so that equations (12.7) and (12.8) can be alternatively rewritten as

$$M = K.Y \tag{12.10}$$

and $$M^d = K.Y, \tag{12.11}$$

respectively. The distinction between these two similar-looking equations should always be kept in mind. Equation (12.11) gives the Cambridge demand function for money (see Section 11.3), whereas equation (12.10) is the equilibrium condition of the money market, when the supply of money is given exogenously as specified in equation (12.9).

These relations are represented diagrammatically in Figure 12.1.

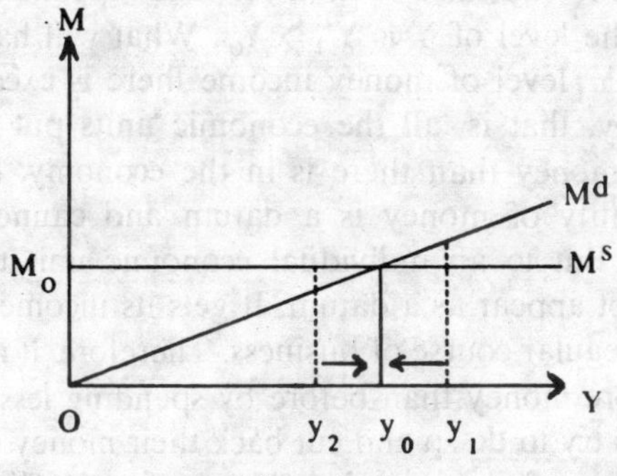

Figure 12.1

The Determination of Y—the QTM

In the above figure, the upward-sloping M^d line represents equation (12.11) (see Figure 11.1), showing that M^d is an increasing and proportional function of Y. Since M^s is assumed to be given exogenously by the monetary authority, the M^s line in the figure is shown to be perfectly inelastic to Y at the height of (say) Mc. The demand for money will be equal to the supply of money at only one level of Y, viz. Yo. Thus, given the M^d function and Mo, Yo is the equilibrium level of Y in the sense that it is only at Y_0 that the money market will be in equilibrium and equation (12.10) is satisfied. This makes Y purely a function of the quantity of money. Algebraically, using equation (12.10), we can solve for Y to get

$$Y = \frac{I}{K} . M$$

which, recalling that I/K = V, can also be written as

$$Y = V.M, \tag{12.12}$$

This says very simply that Y is determined by M. In what follows we shall have several occasions to refer to this equation and to compare the theory of it with the Keynesian theory of Y determination.

The explanation of the QTM as a theory of Y determination so far has been of a technical nature. It does not show explicitly why Y gets affected by M and how and why changes in Y bring about equilibrium in the money market. To answer these important questions, we undertake what is known as the stability analysis of the aforesaid equilibrium (of the money market) at Yo. The standard technique is to ask what would happen if, by a chance disturbance, Y # Yo or, for any reason, there is a discrepancy between actual and desired stock of money. This will also bring out the *adjustment mechanism* implicit in the simple QTM.[4] (See also Section 12.7 and Appendix C.)

Suppose the level of Y is $Y_1 > Y_0$. What will happen then ? In figure 12.1 at Y_1 level of money income there is excess demand for nominal money, that is, all the economic units put together desire to hold more money than there is in the economy. By assumption, the total quantity of money is a datum and cannot be increased endogenously. But to an individual economic unit the quantity of money does not appear as a datum. It gets its income in the form of money in the regular course of business. Therefore, if it so likes, it can try to hold more money than before by spending less. When several economic units try to do so and cut back their money expenditures in the commodity market (the only other market implicitly allowed in the simplified quantity theory model), aggregate money expenditures fall. As a consequence, Y also falls and the economy moves from Y_1 towards Y_0, as shown by the arrow in the figure. At a lower Y, the demand for money will also be lower. This process of adjustment continues till the entire excess demand for money is eliminated. When this happens, Y has settled back at Y_0 and the money market is once again in equilibrium.

The reverse happens at any $Y < Y_0$, say, Y_2 in Figure 12.1. Then there would be excess supply of money in the economy, that is, there is more nominal cash than households and firms like to hold at the prevailing level of Y. Individually, therefore, they try to get out of the extra cash they have by spending it in the commodity market on all kinds of services and goods, including consumer durables and capital goods. This does not reduce the total quantity of money in the economy, which is assumed to be exogenously fixed. But it does increase the level of money expenditure and so the level of money income. At a higher level of money income the excess supply of money is less than before. The above process continues till the entire excess supply of money is exhausted. Equilibrium is re-established at Yo level of money income when $M^d = Mo$.

Three points need to be specially noted about the above explanation :

(1) That, at the aggregate level, the public, by assumption, has no authority to change M^s to bring it into equilibrium with their aggregate M^d. But the efforts of the individual members of the public to adjust their individual cash balances to their desired values have the indirect effect of changing the flows of money expenditure and money income and, in turn, adjusting the aggregate demand for money to the given quantity of money;

(2) That the choice posited before the public is that between money and commodities, so that in the event of excess supply of money members of the public try to buy more commodities and in the event of excess demand for money they reduce their expenditure in the commodity market to build up their cash balances. In other words, the margin of substitution considered is that between money and commodities only. It is here that Keynes differed completely. Viewing money as an asset and as one component of wealth, he restricted the margin of direct substitution between money and bonds (as collective representative of all nonmoney financial assets) only. We shall study about the Keynesian theory in the next chapter;

(3) That it is only in equilibrium that equation (12.10) holds.

We can now explain the *equilibrium* effects of a change in the quantity of M, that is, effects of such a change when the money market has reattained equilibrium or, which is the same thing, when the public comes to hold willingly the increased amount of money.

Under Cambridge QTM, the effect of Δ M is, in the first instance and entirely, on the level of money expenditure or money income (Y). This can be easily derived from equation (12.12), which, taking first differences on both sides of the equation and holding V constant, gives

$$\Delta Y = V. \Delta M, \quad (12.13)$$

where Δ represents change in the variable immediately following it.

This is shown diagrammatically in Figure (12.2), itself based on figure (12.1)

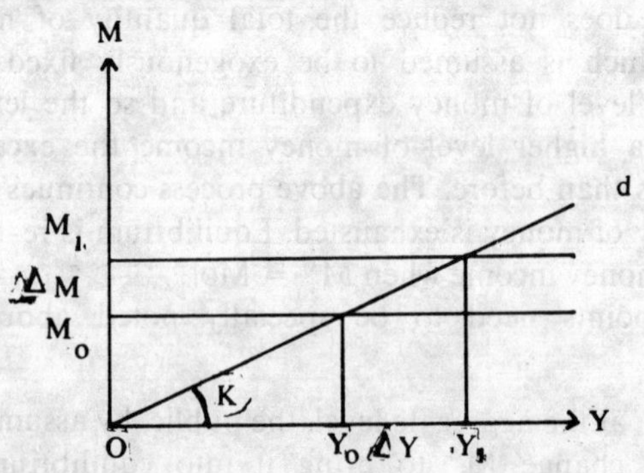

Figure 12.2
Effect of Δ M on Y

In Figure (12.2), with given M^d function and an initial stock of money at M_o, the equilibrium value of money income is Y_o. When the stock of money is increased[5] to $M_1$and equilibrium is reestablished in the money market, the equilibrium value of Y will be Y Thus, Δ Y results in response to Δ M. Knowing the slope of the M^d function to be equal to K, it can be seen that $\Delta Y = \frac{1}{K} \Delta M$. Since the reciprocal of K is the same thing as V, the *equilibrium* effect of Δ M on Y is that given by equation (12.13).

It is worth noting that it is in the form of equation (12.13) that Friedman and Meiselman (F and M hereafter) (1964) specified their test equation for the QTM against the test equation derived from Keynes' Income-Expenditure Theory:

$$\Delta Y = k. \Delta A, \quad (12.14)$$

where A = autonomous expenditure in the sense of Keynes and k is the Keynesian multiplier (see Section 13.5). The empirical results for the USA for the period 1897–1958 reported by F and M were interpreted by them to support the QTM more than the Keynesian theory as specified in its simplest form given in equation (12.14). Since then there have been several empirical studies pertaining to the USA and several other countries, replicating, extending, respecifying or examining the F and M study. For want of space, we cannot afford to go into a detailed discussion of all these results and their several aspects. The sole point in referring to them in this introductory book is to emphasise that QTM, correctly interpreted, is not a truism but a theory that yields a testable hypothesis about the behaviour of money income (Y).

12.6 The QTM as a Theory of P

Historically as well as more popularly, the QTM is known as a theory of P. To arrive at this version of the QTM, it must first hold as a theory of Y. But this is only a necessary and not a sufficient condition for the QTM as a theory of P. One additional condition must also be satisfied. It is that the value of real output must be given from elsewhere, that is, independently of the quantity of money (except that some minimum amount of money must exist in an economy for it to be a money-using economy). This is what the strict quantity theory generally assumes.

According to the neoclassical theory, the level of real output is determined by the real forces operating on the supply side in the economy, since it is believed that in a flex-price world there cannot be a deficiency of aggregate demand (Keynes' problem).[7] Real forces, in brief, are represented by factor inputs and technology. The latter is represented by a well-behaved aggregate production function which gives the maximum amounts of output that can be produced with alternative combinations of input under a given technology. To simplify, consider a two-factor world of labour and capital. In the short period, the stock of capital can be taken as historically given. The amount of labour services used (employment offered) is determined in the labour market by the interaction of the demand and supply of labour. The demand for labour is hypothesised as a decreasing function of the real wage rate only and the supply of labour as an increasing function of the real wage rate only. Thus, the interaction of the demand and supply of labour is made to determine uniquely both the equilibrium amount of labour per unit time and the real wage rate. Using this amount of labour in the aggregate production function with a given stock of capital gives the value of real output, say y_0. In the model, changes in M have no influence on y.

Armed with the above theory, we go back to equation (12.7). With $y = y_0$, it becomes

$$M = K P y_0 .$$

We can use this equation to solve for P :

$$\frac{1}{K} \cdot \frac{M}{y_0}. \quad (12.15)$$

This, then, is the P-determining equation of the QTM. With K as a behavioural constant and y_0 determined elsewhere (that is, independently of both M and P), P is seen to depend upon M only (see also Appendix A). Moreover, the relationship is proportional, so that a doubling of M will double P— the prediction given by the QTM of P. Such a strict quantity theory of P is not true of actual life even in the long run, not to say of short periods. Even the leading modern quantity theorist Professor Milton Friedman (1966) has admitted that the relation between M and P is quite loose and undependable, as several things relating the two can change from time to time. All this is discussed in the next section.

12.7 Modern QTM

Modern QTM refers to Friedman's reformulation or restatement of the earlier simple or crude QTM (or Friedman's QTM), first presented by him in his well-known article, "Quantity Theory of Money— A Restatement" (Friedman, 1956), repeated in Friedman (1968 b). The reformulation is a sophisticated attempt to rid the earlier crude version of the QTM of its shortcomings and overstatements or its main vulnerable aspects by underplaying the over-simple and crude 'quantity equation' and bringing instead a well-articulated theory of the demand function for money as the centre piece of the QTM. (More on this in the sequel.) Not all monetarists, however, agree to this shift in focus. But that is another matter.

As we have seen above, the QTM was usually stated in the form of an equation that looked like a tautology (as, e.g., in the case of Fisher's equation of exchange see Section 12.3). Even the Cambridge cash-balance equation (Section 12.4) was based on the crudest form of the demand function for money that did not point the possibility of any substitution between money and non-money assets and whose K, though a choice variable of the public, was nevertheless a constant. Thus, this equation also (despite its potential) failed to make the QTM a behavioural rather than a mechanical relation between M and Y and failed to provide systematically (on the basis of a well-articulated theory) for those factors that intervene the process whereby $\triangle$ M gets translated into $\triangle$ Y. Besides, the QTM needed rehabilitation against the devastating onslaughts of Keynes (1936) and his followers which had brought monetary policy into much disrepute.

Keynes' criticism was directed towards the stability of V (or K or the demand for money). He argued that *under conditions of unemployment equilibrium* V was highly unstable and would, for the most part, passively adapt to whatever changes independently occurred in money income or the stock of money. Hence, under such conditions, the QTM equation was largely useless for policy or prediction. In the limiting case of the 'liquidity trap', in fact, Y can change without a change in M and M can change without a change in Y (because of shifts between M_1 and M_2 corresponding to L_1 and L_2—see equation (11.3) and after).

Keynes' followers have argued further that, outside of the liquidity trap, changes in the quantity of money would affect only the interest rate on bonds and that changes in this rate in turn would have little further effect, because they argued that both consumption expenditures and investment expenditures were nearly completely insensitive to changes in interest rates. That being so, a change in M would merely be offset by an opposite and compensatory change in V, leaving P and Y almost completely unaffected. Tobin (1961) also asserted that only paper securities were substitutes for money, not real assets.

From all this, Friedman (1968 b, pp. 49-50) concluded that the issues raised for the QTM by the Keynesian analysis were empirical rather than theoretical. For example, is it a fact that the quantity of money demanded in a function primarily of current income and of the bond rate of interest? Is it a fact that the amount demanded is highly elastic with respect to this rate, especially when this rate is quite low? Is it a fact that expenditures are highly inelastic with respect to such a rate of interest? Or, is it a fact that velocity is a highly unstable and unpredictable magnitude that generally varies in a direction opposite to that of the quantity of money? Friedman's restatement of the QTM provides a firm analytical basis for such questions and his extensive empirical work and that of his camp-followers much empirical evidence in answer to these and related empirical questions.

With the above introduction in mind, we now proceed with substantive discussion of the key points of Friedman's modern QTM, discussed below.

1. *The QTM is a Theory of the Demand for Money.* In his restatement (1956, p. 4), Friedman has clearly stressed that "the quantity theory is in the first instance a theory of the *demand* for money." He has gone on to add that "it is not a theory of output, or of money

income, or of the price level," because "any statement about these variables requires combining the quantity theory with some specifications about the conditions of supply of money and perhaps about other variables as well."

2. *The Stability and Importance of the Demand Function for Money.* In the context of Keynes' criticism (studied above), Friedman has laid much stress on the stability of the demand for money function. As an empirical hypothesis he has claimed that this function is more stable than functions such as the consumption function that are offered as alternative key relations. By stability he means functional stability––that the functional relation between the quantity of money demanded and the variables that determine it is highly stable. This means that even the sharp rise in the velocity of circulation of money during hyperinflations is entirely consistent with a stable functional relation, as Cagan (1956) clearly demonstrated in his classic study, 'The Monetary Dynamics of Hyperinflation', where he could explain successfully this dynamic in terms of a highly stable demand for money as a function of only the expected rate of change of prices. This further means that the real quantity of money demanded per unit of output, or V, is not to be regarded as numerically constant over time. Further, functional stability also requires that the variables that it is empirically important to include in the function should be sharply limited and explicitly specified. For, to treat too many variables as empirically significant is to empty the hypothesis of its empirical content.

Modern QTM not only regards the demand function for money as stable, it also regards this funciton as playing a vital role in determining values (or time paths) of variables of great importance for the analysis of the economy as a whole, such as the level of Y and of prices. It is this consideration that leads the modern quantity theorist to put great emphasis on the demand for money than on, say, the demand for pins, even though the latter might be as stable as the former.

We have already studied Friedman's theory and specification of the demand function for money in Section 11.6 and highlights of the related empirical evidence in Section 11.7. We need not repeat the discussion except to note that Friedman's reformulation of the demand for money and so of the QTM has been strongly influenced by the Keynesian analysis of liquidity preference. So, it emphasizes the role of money as an asset and treats the demand for money as part of capital or wealth theory, concerned with the composition of the balance sheet or portfolio of assets, (More on this under the next point.) This marked a significant departure of Friedman's modern QTM from the earlier

QTM which has been based on money viewed as only a medium of exchange.

(3) *Monetary Transmission Mechanism.* The earlier statements of the QTM had practically neglected any discussion of the monetary transmission mechanism, that is, of the channels whereby monetary influences are transmitted to other sectors of the economy, particularly the commodity market. In simple words, they lacked any explanation of how changes in the quantity of money came to affect the commodity market. And it is this lack of the explanation of transmission mechanism which had rendered the earlier statements of the QTM mechanical. We had sketched above (Section 12.5) one plausible explanation of the transmission mechanism implicit in the Cambridge QTM. But its extreme assumptions and total neglect of portfolio choice should have struck the readers as near-caricature of reality and may be left them breathless. The Keynesian interest-rate mechanism (see Chapter 13) also suffers from being excessively narrow. Modern QTM has widened greatly the range of substitution between money and non-money assets, not restricting the latter to only financial assets, but including real physical goods as well.

In Friedman's words, "emphasis on the role of money as a component of wealth is important because of the variables to which it directs attention. It is important also for its implications about the process of adjustment to a difference between actual and desired stocks of money [that is, about the transmission mechanism]" (1968 b, p. 54). Since any such discrepancy is a disturbance in a balance sheet, "it can be corrected in either of two ways: by a rearrangement of assets and liabilities, through purchase, sale, borrowing and lending or by the use of current flows of income and expenditure to add to or subtract from some assets and liabilities. The Keynesian liquidity-preference analysis stressed the first and, in its most rigid form, one specific rearrangement: that between money and bonds. The earlier quantity theory stressed the second to the almost complete exclusion of the first. The reformulation [that is, modern QTM] enforces consideration of both" (Friedman, 1968 b, pp. 54-55). In our view, the relative importance of the two ways will differ from one economy to the other, depending on the level of financial development in an economy.

About the process of portfolio adjustment, Friedman has stressed its two features (see Friedman, 1968b, pp. 54-55); (i) that it is time consuming[8]— that whereas pure portfolio substitution may be relatively fast, the adjustment through flows is generally long drawn; (ii) that portfolio adjustment does not stay restricted to merely one asset of immediate impact (e.g. bonds of the Keynesian liquidity-preference theory), but tends to spread to other assets and liabilities in a balance sheet, as a change in one asset price spreads to changes in other asset prices in ever-widening ripples. In the process, relative prices of capital items and their services are also affected.

On another occasion Friedman has argued that the portfolio substitution process stimulates directly spending upon items not normally considered to be assets at all (see Friedman, 1972). He writes:

> "The major difference between us and the Keynesians is less in the nature of the process [of portfolio substitution] than in the *range of assets* considered [emphasis added]. The Keynesians tend to concentrate on a narrow range of marketable assets and recorded interest rates. We insist that a far wider range of assets and interest rates must be taken into account—such assets as durable and semi-durable consumer goods, structures and other real property. As a result, we regard the market rates stressed by the Keynesians as only a small part of the total spectrum of rates that are relevant . . . " He continues :
>
> "After all, it is most unusual to quote houses, automobiles, let alone furniture, household appliances, clothes and so on, in terms of the 'interest rate' implicit in their sales and rental prices. Hence the prices of these items continued to be regarded as an institutional datum, which forced the transmission process to go through an extremely narrow channel."

(4) *Independence of the Factors affecting Demand and Supply of Money.* Modern QTM holds that there are important factors affecting the supply of money (such as monetary policy of the authorities—see Chapter 15) that do not affect the demand for money. A stable demand function is useful precisely in order to trace out the effects of changes in supply, which means that it is useful only if supply is affected by at least some factors other than those regarded as affecting demand.

(5) *The Relation between M and Y.* The centre piece of Cambridge QTM is the relation between M and Y (see Section 12.5). To a degree, this is also implied in Fisher's equation of exchange. But as said under point (1) above, with Friedman QTM is not a theory of Y. The reason is that with the demand function for money (and so also V) of Friedman's specification (see equation (11.5)), even if we assume the supply of money to be autonomously given, the equilibrium equation of modern QTM will read as $Y = V(Y, w, rm, rb, re, \dot{p}e, u).M$. (12.16).

Obviously, this equation alone is not sufficient to determine Y. To convert the above equation into a complete model of Y determination, it will be "necessary to suppose either that the demand for money is highly inelastic with respect to the variables in V or that all these variables are to be taken as rigid and fixed" (Friedman, 1956, p. 15).

Making either of these assumptions reduces modern QTM virtually (or for all practical purposes) to simple Cambridge QTM, though under modern QTM, any of the variables in V can always he resurrected as needed—an option not open to Cambridge equation. Thus, the work of Friedman and Meiselman (1964) in which △ Y was explained by V. △ M appears puzzling if viewed in the light of Friedman's modern QTM. The only plausible answer to the puzzle seems to be provided by the title of their study (1964): "The Relative Stability of Monetary Velocity and Investment Multiplier in the United States". In this study, Friedman and Meiselman had only pitted V against the Keynesian multiplier as statistically more stable of the two, despite the observed variability of V due to the variance in its determinants, studied elsewhere (e.g., in Selden, 1956). In other words, Friedman holds that, as a matter of experience (not theory), though the relation between M and Y is not very close, that between △ M and △ Y is observed to be quite close under a wide variety of conditions.

(6) *Relation between M and P.* Most economists think that the QTM is essentially a theory of prices (P), but modern QTM rejects this view. As we have seen under point (5) above, equation (12.16) gives at most a theory of Y. But it tells us nothing about how much of any change in Y is reflected in real output and how much in prices. To infer this requires bringing in outside information, as, for example, that real output is at its feasible maximum (see Section 12.6). Only then, we can translate the change in Y into change in P. In practical applications it means that movements in P should be related with movements in the stock of money per unit of output rather than movements in M *per se.* In Friedman's words "inflation can be prevented if and only if the stock of money per unit of output can be kept from increasing appreciably." (Friedman, 1968 b, p. 62).

12.8 The QTM— An Appraisal

The QTM is one of the most venerable and well-known theories of Economics. It is also one of the simplest-looking. This simplicity is both its strength and weakness. It is its strength because it states the hypothesised relation between M and P (and between a change in M and the resulting change in P) most clearly and precisely, a statement which can be easily understood by the reader. It is its weakness because the relation hypothesised is too clear and too precise and in the economic field such precise relations are not observed. Therefore, they are bound to raise doubts. Also, in their attempt to arrive at the simple and clear relation between M and P, the early quantity theorists simplified too much—broad judgements about economic phenomena, which,at best, are true only to a first order to approximation, were assumed (for simplicity, no doubt) to hold true always.[9] This was bound to invite rejection of the QTM on various counts. The experience of the Great Depression of 1929–33 and the publication of Keynes's *General Theory* (1936) gave a severe blow to monetary theory built around the QTM. Interest in this theory was revived during the 1950s and thereafter mainly under the leadership of Milton Friedman who has given both a more sophisticated interpretation of the QTM than before and provided much empirical support to it. Several other economists have followed Friedman's lead, so that it is no longer unrespectable to lend qualified support to the theory. Yet there is no dearth of critics and of criticism of the QTM, some of which is either misplaced or based on misunderstanding ofthe theory. In this section we discuss briefly the main points of criticism as well as of defence of the QTM.

To conserve space, we shall not discuss separately the shortcomings of Fisher's version and of the Cambridge version of theQTM.The weaknesses of the former as compared to the latter have already been pointed out in Section 12.5. Therefore, in order to fix our object of appraisal, we choose the Cambridge Cash-Balances version of the QTM.[10] Modern QTM with serveral points of reformulation in theory but not so in empirical work is difficult to appraise without going into an extended debate around the large amount of empirical work which has been done and is being done on the subject. Most of the criticism will be discussed with reference to the QTM as a theory of Y. But by now the reader must have understood that this criticism is equally applicable to the QTM as a theory of P as well (see the previous section). Additional criticism of the QTM as a theory of P will appear in the end as the final point of criticism.

The major points of criticism of the QTM are discussed below.

1. *Constancy of V.* The most crucial assumption of the QTM is the constancy of V. In the Fisher version, V was interpreted as transactions velocity and taken to be determined by payments practices and other structural features of the economy influencing the use of money

as the medium of exchange. Since these factors were taken to be slow-moving, V was also assumed to be slow changing. More specifically, it was assumed to be independent of M or changes in M and also such endogenous variables as income, rate of interest, prices, etc. This has not been supported by empirical évidence which clearly shows that measured V (given by Y/M) is not a *short-run* constant. That being so, it is argued, the QTM cannot be accepted as a reliable theory for predicting short-run changes in Y.

That variations in V can do substantial damage to the QTM model can be easily explained. For this, recall the QTM equation (12.12):

$$Y = V.M. \tag{12.12}$$

If both M and V are allowed to vary, changes in Y will be given by the following equation:

$$\Delta Y = V.\Delta M + \Delta V.M + \Delta V.\ \Delta M, \tag{12.16}$$

derived from equation (12.12). The last term on the right-hand side of the above equation is the interaction (between ΔV and ΔM) term, which will go to zero as ΔV or ΔM goes to zero. If V is a constant (as assumed in the QTM), the last two terms on the right-hand side of equation (12.16) will disappear and we shall get back the QTM equation (12.13). In the presence of non-zero ΔV, the other two terms will have to be recokned with. Therefore, without knowing the value of ΔV we cannot say what ΔY will be consequent on ΔM.

To explain and predict the behaviour of V, we need some theory of V. This theory is provided by the theory of the demand for money (see Chapter 11), once it is assumed that actual V = *desired* V (V^d), because the latter is simply the reciprocal of M^d/Y, that is, of the demand for money per rupee of income. Therefore, anything that raises M^d per Re of Y will lower V^d and so V and conversely anything that lowers M^d (at the same Y) will raise V^d and so V. So, knowing the demand for money in an economy is of prime importance.

In Section 11.3 we have already seen that the simple demand function for money of the Cambridge Cash Balances theory directly yields constant V. Such a demand function for money may or may not obtain in an economy. Therefore, in theory at least, we must start with a more general demand function for money. We have already studied various important formulations of it in the previous chapter. To recall briefly, the demand for money in the Keynesian theory, besides being an increasing function of income, is made also a decreasing function of the rate of interest. This turned out to be a revolutionary development in monetary theory. It broke down the simplicity of the QTM, because, once an additional unknown in the form of the rate of interest (r) is introduced in the M^d function, the money-market equilibrium condition that makes $M^d = M^s$ cannot yield us the QTM equation (12.12). Instead, we get:

$$M^d\ (Y,r) = M, \qquad (12.17)$$

which is one equation in two unknowns and hence cannot be used for determining the equilibrium value of either Y or r. This makes Keynes' liquidity preference of the rate of interest equally invalid (see Section 13.3).

A resolution of the problems raised by equation (12.17) has been provided by Hicks (1937) through his IS—LM model (See Section 13.8). This resolution does further damage to the simple QTM. Since r is an endogenous variable (that is, a variable determined within the system) and is affected also by the real-sector forces (of, say, savings and investment), all the latter forces come to impinge on the determination of Y *via* r and M^d. Thereby even Y (nominal income) cannot be called a purely monetary phenomenon or we cannot say that changes in Y are determined only by changes in M or that ΔM affects only Y, as predicted by the QTM. It is this point of interaction between the monetary sector and the real sector in determining the equilibrium values of Y and r that was stressed by several monetary economists individually in their separate reviews of the monumental study, *A Monetary History of the United States,* 1867 - 1960 by Friedman and Schwartz (1963).

We have already studied Friedman's modern QTM in the previous section and also his view about QTM as a theory of Y—that if either the rates of interest did not vary or the sensitivity of the M^d function to observed changes in *r* was not significant, then the simple QTM of Y, in practical terms, was free from the Keynesian criticism. Since, in actual experience, rates of interest have varied a good deal, the whole debate boils down to the *r*-sensitivity of M^d. Friedman (1959) in his statistical study of the demand for money in the USA over the period 1869-1957 had found *r* to be statistically insignificant. Several other economists have found fault with Friedman's specifications and statistical methods and have produced their own estimates of the demand function for money for the USA which do show the demand for money to be r-sensitive. And the controversy continues.[11]

For India; we have already reported the state of empirical evidence on the demand for money, which does raise serious doubts about the statistical significance of the rate of interest for this demand (in India). In addition, it has also been found that the best estimate of the income-elasticity of demand for money is unity These two features of the demand for money in India lend special relevance to the simple QTM of Y for India (see Gupta 1979, Chapter 2). Yet the observed behaviour of V in India (Gupta 1979, Appendix B) indicates clearly that it has not been a time-constant. It has varied significantly from one year to the next, but mostly in a cyclical manner (of variable periodicity) and without any long-run tendency in the upward or downward direction. The significant feature is the flat trend in V, pointing towards long-run average constancy of V. This kind of empirical evidence suggests that the QTM model of Y can possibly be used fruitfully for only longer-term analysis of Y and not for short-term (year-to-year) analysis of Y (see Gupta 1979, Chapter 2). This is an important qualification or limitation of the QTM model of Y, which should be always borne in mind, while using this model for India.

2. *V's Independence of M.* The QTM (equation 12.12) assumes that V is independent of M. The assumption will come under strain if, as in Keynes' theory, r changes as M changes and V (or M^d) is r-responsive. This question of the responsiveness of V to changes in r has already been discussed under the previous point. An additional circumstance of V's dependence on changes in M has been pointed out by monetarists themselves (see Cagan, 1956). This arises under a situation of anticipated inflation. In Friedman's specification of the demand for money the expected rate of change of prices acts as an opportunity cost of holding money (see Section 11.6). Cagan (1956) in his classic study, *The Dynamics of Hyperinflation,* had found the expected rate of change of prices as the sole explanatory variable for the demand for money. The sequence which breaks V's independence of M then is the following : $\dot{M} \rightarrow \dot{P} \rightarrow \dot{p}^e \rightarrow V$, where the dotted variables are proportionate rates of change per unit time of respective variables M, P, and P^e and P^e stands for the expected P. This relation and the stability of P will be discussed in Appendix D. At this stage it may only be noted that the problem of any relation between V and $\dot{M}$ (not just M) becomes acute only when M is changing very fast.

3. *Exogeneity of M.* In all statements of the QTM it is assumed that M is exogenously given—that M is policy-determined. Modern theory of money supply shows clearly that the supply of money (M^s)

is an endogenous variable (see Chapter 15). This raises the possibility of changes in M^s occurring in response to 'autonomous' changes in P—changes in P that, for example, are occurring due to the operation of cost-push factors. The issue will be discussed in Section 14.9.

4. *Lack of Transmission Mechanism.* Quite often the QTM is stated only as a truism, which, of course, is true *expost.* Even when it is stated as a theory in *ex ante* terms, it is rarely supported by an explanation of the underlying transmission mechanism (or adjustment process) whereby ΔM comes to exert its influence on Y. We have tried to fill the gap in Section 12.5. The explanation is appropriate for only the crude QTM. Admittedly, this is only a part of the adjustment process, the other part provided by Keynes' monetary theory (see next chapter). Friedman as the leading quantity theorist of modern times admits both kinds of adjustment process (e.g., see Friedman, 1968 b, pp. 54-55, Section 12.7 and Appendix C).

5. *Equilibrium Equation.* If the QTM equation at worst is a truism, at best it is an equilibrium equation for the money market, that is , it will be true only when the money market is in equilibrium. This is true, but not a special failing of the QTM alone, since most results in economic theory are derived through equilibrium analysis. However, while applying these theories to practical situations, due allowance can be and should be made for possible lags in adjustment. Alternatively and more simply, we can say that the money-market equilibrium hypothesised in the QTM takes longer than a year (say, 5 years) to attain itself—that the QTM is a longer-term and not a short-term theory.

6. *Other Influences on Y.* The QTM gives a mono-variable explanation of changes in Y (or in money expenditure) in terms of autonomous changes in M (assuming real income y to be given by the real-sector forces). The Keynesian theory emphasises the role of autonomous expenditures and fiscal policy variables in the determination of Y. No doubt, Δ M and the Keynesian variables are not all that independent of each other as they are made out to be. But the two sets of variables are not identical either.

7. *Real Output determined by Real-Sector Forces only.* The QTM of P assumes explicitly that the real output (y) is determined by the real sector forces of factor supplies and technology on the supply side—that this supply creates its own demand (Say's Law). Keynes (1936) had revolted against this notion and emphasised the importance of aggregate demand in the determination of y in a world where the real and the monetary forces interact with each other. The point is

generally well taken now even by the so-called monetarists (Friedman and his followers). But as yet we do not have a trouble-free macro model which gives a simultaneous determination of P and y (see Gupta 1981, Branson, 1978, Chapter 7). However, the QTM does come into its own (with its other failings), once the object of analysis is the problem of inflation and the deficiency of aggregate demand can be assumed away. This problem will be pursued further in Chapter 14.

NOTES

1. For an explanation of real output (y) determination by real-sector forces alone in the neoclassical theory, see Section 12.6.

2. In Appendix A.1 it has been shown how the QTM equation (12.5) of the transactions approach can be interpreted as the equilibrium equation of the commodity market!

3. Based on Gupta (1971). For a comparable brief statement in terms of real *(not* nominal) income, see Laidler (1970). Such a real-income determination model is highly questionable as well as total misrepresentation of the neoclassical monetary theory which takes real income to be determined by the real-sector forces (see Section 12.6).

4. The question of adjustment or transmission mechanism is of great importance and has been raised time and again in the debate between the monetarists and their critics (the Keynesians). In subsequent discussion in the text, too, it will arise time and again. The more substantive part of the answer has been given in Friedman (1972), parts of which will be reproduced in Section 12.7 (under point 4). A formal answer is provided in the text above. A fuller discussion is given in Appendix C.

5. How additional M is generated is not discussed; it is simply assumed to be added exgenously to the existing stock (of M) by the monetary authority. Thereby all such effects as are generated in the very process of creating more M are neglected.

6. For an interpretation of V also as a multiplier, see Appendix A.2

7. The standard neoclassical defence of their proposition that 'in a flex-price world there cannot be a deficiency of aggregate demand' is provided by the theory of the real-balance effect. Without going into a full-scale discussion, this theory is discussed very briefly in Appendix B.

8. This argument is taken up fully with empirical evidence by Friedman (1961).

9. This is not true of all economists who supported the QTM. Some were careful in spelling out the circumstances under which the QTM relation will not hold strictly.

10. For whatever reasons, it is Fisher's Transactions Version of the QTM (long discarded outside India) that has been most popular with textbook writers in India. Consequently, several generations of Indian students have been brought up on this weakest statement of the QTM.

11. The debate between monetarists and Keynesians extends from theory to empirical methodology considered appropriate for isolating econometrically the independent effect of monetary policy upon the level of economic activity. Monetarists tend to emphasise the extreme complexity of the interaction among monetary variables, rates of return and aggregate expenditure. According to them, large simultaneous-equation econometric models, advocated by the new-Keynesians, cannot (and have not) captured successfully the variety of devious ways in which monetary variables influence other variables. Therefore, they prefer, in general, simpler reduced-form equations (or at most very simple simultaneous system of only a few key equations) to large structural systems.

CHAPTER 13

Money, Interest and Income

13.1 Introduction

This chapter is devoted to a discussion of the role of money in the Keynesian theory of income and employment. Till the appearance of Keynes' *General Theory of Employment, Interest and Money* (1936) monetary theory was mainly a theory of prices. With Keynes (1936) the whole character of monetary theory underwent a revolutionary change and it became primarily a theory of the rate of interest, income, output, and employment; prices came to occupy a back seat. These propositions will be discussed in this chapter. The discussion will be inextricably intertwined with Keynes' theory of income and employment. But since this is not a text-book in macroeconomic theory, we shall not go into a full-scale study of the Keynesian macro theory. Instead, we shall be highly selective and brief, with our main accent on Keynes' monetary theory, ideas, and policies, supplemented by Hicks' reformulation of Keynes' model in the form of His well-known IS–LM model. At appropriate places throughout the chapter they will be constrasted with their neoclassical counterparts derived from the quantity theory of money, discussed in the previous chapter.

One clarification about the meanings of terms used in this chapter (and elsewhere in this book) should be noted. We shall use the term 'Keynes' theory' for his theory as developed in his *General Theory* (1936) and the term 'Keynesian theory' more broadly to include this theory as well as modified or reformulated versions of it offered by Keynes' followers.

13.2 Keynes' Monetary Theory

J.M. Keynes was basically a monetary economist. Till the appearance of his *General Theory* (1936) most of his writings were on the subject of money. Even the theory of output and employment in his *General Theory* is that of a money-using economy in which money as an asset plays a crucial role in contrast with the neoclassical theory of output and employment, which was and still is a theory of a barter economy. Yet, most of the time, this aspect of Keynes' work is forgotten or deliberately neglected, because in his policy prescriptions he had downgraded monetary policy in comparison with fiscal policy. This was the outcome of his empirical judgement about the state of the money market and the economy of the times during which he wrote his *General Theory,* and not of any lack of belief in the importance of monetary forces in the working of a modern economy.

The key proposition of Keynes' monetary theory is that changes in the demand or supply of money (and both can change) operate on the level of economic activity not directly (as in the QTM) but indirectly through changes in the rate of interest and thereby through changes in real investment in the economy. This may be represented schematically thus:

$$M^s \xrightarrow{(1)} r \xrightarrow{(2)} I \xrightarrow{(3)} y \xrightarrow{(4)} N \xrightarrow{(5)} MP_L \xrightarrow{(6)} P,$$
$$\uparrow M^d \text{ (at } r\text{)} \qquad \uparrow W \text{ (at } P\text{)}$$

where M^s and M^d stand for the supply and demand for money respectively, r, I, Y, and N for the rate of interest, investment, income, and employment respectively, MP_L for the marginal product of labour, and P and W for the price level and the money wage rate respectively.[1]

The above scheme represents the main propositions of Keynes' monetary theory in the simplest and briefest possible manner. It also highlights the sequential nature of Keynes' analysis. The main propositions are numbered from (1) to (6). Briefly, they are

(1) that r is determined by the demand for and the supply of money;
(2) that r determines I via the investment-demand function;
(3) that I influences Y via the multiplier;
(4) that Y determines the level of employment via the aggregate production function;
(5) That given the aggregate production function and the stock of capital, N will give the value of MP_L; and
(6) that, given W, MP_L will determine P via the equilibrium condition $MP_L = W/P$.

Thus, the influence of M on P is seen to emerge at the end of a long sequence of relations and effects. According to Keynes, the relation between M and P is not as simple as the quantity theory of money (QTM) makes it out to be. The above six propositions are discussed in the following sections.

13.3 Keynes' Theory of the Rate of Interest

In Keynes' theory changes in the supply of money affect all other variables through changes in the rate of interest, and not directly as in the QTM. The rate of interest, according to Keynes, is a purely monetary phenomenon, a reward for parting with liquidity, which is determined in the money market by the demand and supply of money. This is in sharp contrast to the classical theory in which the rate of interest is made a real phenomenon, which is determined in the commodity market by savings and investment at a level which equates the two. It is also in contrast to the loanable-funds theory which is essentially a reformulation of the savings-investment theory of the rate of interest to take note of the phenomenon of hoarding or dis-hoarding and autonomous changes in the stock of money (see Section 17.2). To understand Keynes' theory, we go to his analysis of the money market.

We have already studied Keynes' theory of the demand for money or, which is the same thing, his theory of the liquidity preference of the public (Section 11.4). We simply recall his equation of the demand for money:

$$M^d = L(Y) + L_2(r). \tag{11.3}$$

Like other economists, Keynes also assumed the supply of money to be exogenously given by the monetary authority, so that

$$M = \bar{M}. \tag{13.1}$$

The money market will be in equilibrium when $M^d = M^s$, i.e..

$$L_1(Y) + L_2(r) = \bar{M}. \tag{13.2}$$

Implicitly assuming Y and so $L_1(Y)$ to be already known, he argued that the above equation would give the equilibrium value of r, the rate of interest. That is, for the money market to be in equilibrium, the value of r has to be such at which the public is willing to hold all the amount of money supplied by the monetary authority. There is a serious analytical flaw in this model which we shall discuss later. Before this, let us study Keynes' theory diagrammatically.

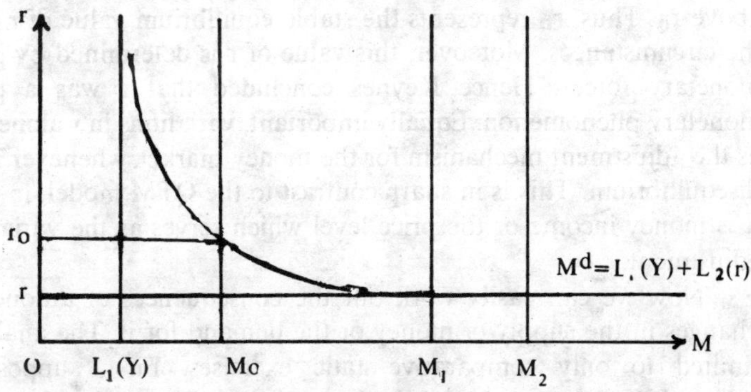

Figure 13.1
The Determination of the Rate of Interest—Keynes' Theory.

Consider Figure 13.1. In it the total demand for money is represented by the downward-sloping curve labelled $M^d = L_1(Y) + L_2(r)$. The first component of the demand for money, namely L_1 (Y), representing Keynes' transactions and precautionary demand for money, is assumed to be autonomous or r. Therefore, it is shown by the vertical line L_1 (Y). (How this amount is determined in Keynes' model was left unexplained and will be commented upon later in the chapter). L_2 (r) represents Keynes' speculative demand for money. It has not been shown separately in our figure, because the M^d curve itself becomes the L_2(r) curve when it is read with L_1 (Y) as the origin in place of O, which amounts to subtracting L_1(Y) horizontally from the M^d curve. The other three vertical lines represent alternative supplies of money at Mo. M_1, M_2, all of which are assumed to be given autonomously.

Given the M^d curve, when the supply of money is M_0, the money market will be in equilibrium only at one rate of interest r_0. At any other rate of interest, there will be disequilibrium in the money market and the working of market forces will push the rate of interest towards r_0 . For example, at a lower rate of interest (say) $\overline{r}$, there will be excess demand for money. In the two-asset world of Keynes' model, with money and bonds as two assets between which alone asset holders make their portfolio choices, this will mean excess supply of bonds in the market for bonds. (The bond market is not considered explicitly in Keynes; it is eliminated implicitly by using Walras' Law.) Therefore, the price of bonds will fall and the rate of interest go up. The process will continue till the rate of interest goes up to ro.The reverse will happen if a chance disturbance pushes the rate of interest above r_0. Thus, r_0 represents the stable equilibrium value of r under the circumstances. Moreover, this value of r is determined by purely monetary forces. Hence, Keynes concluded that r was a purely monetary phenomenon. Equally important, variations in r alone serve as the adjustment mechanism for the money market, whenever it is in disequilibrium. This is in sharp contrast to the QTM model, in which it is money income or the price level which serves as the variable of adjustment.

Now we can easily work out the consequences of autonomous changes in the supply of money or the demand for it. The analysis is limited to only comparative-static exercises. First, suppose the demand for money remains unchanged, but the supply of money is increased (autonomously) from M_0 to M_1. Then, the equilibrium value of r will fall from r_0 to $\bar{r}$. Any further increase in the supply of money, say to M_2, will not lower r, because at $\bar{r}$ it is caught in the liquidity trap (see Section 11.4.2). Thus $\bar{r}$ serves as the absolute minimum below which the rate of interest will not fall in a money-using economy. According to the 'liquidity-trap' hypothesis, there is some r low enough at which the public is willing to hold any amount of money instead of bonds.

There can also be autonomous shifts in the liquidity preference of the public due to any number of reasons, such as change in expectations or in uncertainty around them. Consequently, the M^d curve can shift up or down. Then, using Figure 13.1 and holding the supply of money unchanged (at, say, Mo), the resulting increase or decrease in r can be easily worked out, keeping in mind the liquidity trap at $\bar{r}$.

The implications of Keynes' theory for the effectiveness of monetary policy are briefly noted. Two things are important : one is the interest elasticity of the demand for money; the other is the initial position of economy. The said interest-elasticity varies from one point on the M^d curve to the other; it is assumed to be infinite at some very low value of r ($\bar{r}$ in Figure 13.1), which defines Keynes' liquidity trap. If the economy is caught up initially in this trap, no amount of increase in the supply of money by the monetary authority can lower r any further. Monetary policy operating through increases in the supply of money, then becomes totally ineffective in reducing r and thereby having any expansionary effect on I and Y. This happens because, according to the liquidity-trap hypothesis, the public is willing to hold all the extra quantities of money at the same r. This is an extreme situation, which as yet has not been empiricallly identified in any country. A less extreme situation obtains to the left of the liquidity trap. For some quantities of money, the interest elasticity of demand for them may be very high, though not infinite. This would imply that to attain a given reduction in r very large increase in the supply of money will be required or, which is the same thing, for a given increase in the quantity of money the reduction in r will be very small. Looked at either way, monetary policy does not have much effectiveness in lowering r, especially during depression. Presumably it was this incapacity of monetary policy to lower long-term r significantly that had made Keynes lose faith in monetary policy for fighting depression.[2] Thus, the interest-elasticity of the demand for money (neglected in the QTM) becomes the Key issues in the Keynesian monetary theory.

Modern quantity theorists like Friedman do not deny the theoretical case for the influence of r on M^d. But how important, this influence is or what is the value of the interest elasticity of the demand for money (infinite, high, or very low) is an empirical matter. Empirically, this elasticity has been found to be either quite low or statistically insignificant (see Section 11.7).

Now we evaluate critically special features of Keynes' theory of the rate of interest.

1. The money-market-equilibrium equation (13.2) which Keynes uses to determine r cannot be so used, because it is one equation in two unknowns r and Y. Only if the value of Y is already known, or known independently of r, can $L_1(Y)$ be treated as a known quantity as Keynes does, and equation (13.2) reduced to one equation in one unknown r. But this is not so in Keynes' model, where r affects the rate of investment (I) which in turn affects the equilibrium level of Y. (This will be discussed in a later section.) Thus, Y not only affects r through L_1 (Y) but is also affected by r through I; the two (r and Y) are interdependent or jointly-determined variables. In a later section discussing Hicks' IS-LM model we shall see how they can be jointly determined. Keynes' solution procedure, on the other hand, suffers from circularity of reasoning, because to determine r it assumes a given Y and to determine Y it assumes a given r and so a given I.

2. Through $L_1(Y)$ Keynes admits the influence of Y, a commodity-market variable, on the demand for money. This is very much in the tradition of the Cambridge cash-balances theory which Keynes had inherited from his early days (see Chapter 12). But Keynes' (unwarranted) assumption of a given Y for his analysis of the

money market ruled out completely any role for quantity-theory-type adjustment of *money income* in bringing about equilibrium in the money market. Consequently, the money-market-equilibrium condition that gave Cambridge cash-balances theory its theory of money income was converted by Keynes into a theory of r determination. The former result was achieved by neglecting totally any influence of r on M^d; the latter result was attained (by Keynes) by admitting the influence of Y on M^d, but by freezing Y at some predetermined value. Analytically, therefore, each of the two theories is a special case of a more general theory in which both r and Y are allowed to influence M^d as well as adjust to clear the money market. The Cambridge theory (or the QTM) suppresses the role of r and Keynes' theory the role of Y. Hicks' IS–LM model allows for both.

3. Keynes had assumed the money wage rate (W) to be a historically-given datum (and not a variable for his short-run model) and had used it (W) as the *numeraire* or the deflator for converting all nominal values into real values.[3] This made the distinction between nominal values and real values totally irrelevant for monetary analysis — an anti-QTM stance, because in the QTM changes in prices and through them changes in the real value of a given quantity of money play the most important role. This ruled out *by assumption* all adjustment in the money market that might come through changes in P (or W) even in the upward direction.

Once we get out of the framework of a static world into a real dynamic world, price expectations become important. In the present-day real world inflation has become a common experience. This generates *inflationary expectations,* that is, on the basis of actual experience of inflation, the public comes to expect a certain rate of inflation in the future as well (see Appendix D). Once the public comes to expect a certain rate of inflation, the market rate of interest will tend to rise over what this rate will be in the absence of inflationary expectations. This happens because in the presence of inflationary expectations both the supply curve and the demand curve for loans with respect to r will shift up. The upward shift in the upward-sloping supply curve of loans shows that lenders are willing to lend any real amount at only a higher r than before so that they can get compensated for the real loss they expect to suffer due to inflation. The upward shift in the downward-sloping demand curve for loans arises because borrowers would also be willing to pay higher r than before since they expect to recoup it from expected inflation. This kind of argument is widely accepted and the marked rise in the market rate of interest experienced in most countries including India over the past 10–15 years is usually attributed to inflationary expectations generated by actual inflation in these countries. This phenomenon has very damaging consequences for Keynes' theory of r, which says that monetary expansion can be used to lower r. But this will be true, at most, in a short run and for only moderate increases in the supply of money—more correctly, for increases in the supply of money which a growing economy can absorb at stable prices. Larger increases of M by causing inflation and inflationary expectations will tend to raise rather than lower r (see Friedman, 1968).

4. Keynes denied completely the influence of real factors, represented by real savings and investment (so much emphasised by both classical and neoclassical economists) in the determination of r. This is an extreme view which neo-Keynesians do not share. Now it is widely believed that both the real sector forces and money market forces determine r and real income, and the commonly-accepted model for their joint determination is Hicks' IS–LM model which we shall study in a later section.

5. A strong contender of Keynes' liquidity preference theory of the rate of interest is the neoclassical loanable funds theory of rate interest. The latter combines saving and investment with hoarding, dishoarding, and new injections of money for the demand and supply of the *flow* of loanable funds in the market. This theory will be discussed in Section 17.2.

13.4 Rate of Interest and Investment

The second proposition in Keynes' monetary theory is that the rate of interest influences the level of economic activity by first influencing the rate of real investment in the economy. The investment which Keynes talks of in the *General Theory* (1936) is investment in fixed capital or durable machines. Since this is only a small part of total private expenditure, it is important to note that Keynes makes only this small part possibly responsive to changes in r and that he leaves out the rest from such consideration by assumption. This view has been contested strongly by Friedman (1972) and others. We shall comment upon it a little later. First we explain briefly Keynes' explanation.

To study the influence of the rate of interest on I, Keynes first analysed the 'marginal efficiency of investment' (MEI).[4] The MEI is the *expected* rate of return from one more unit of investment. It is given by that rate of discount which makes the present value of the flow of *expected* income stream over the useful life of one more unit of investment (in, say, a machine) equal to the cost of investment in that machine[5]. This may be stated algebraically thus:

$$C_m = \sum_{i=1}^{n} \frac{Q_i^*}{(i+\rho)^i} \tag{13.3}$$

where C_m = the cost of a machine,

Q^* = the expected income from the machine (gross of depreciation),

ρ the rate of discount, and

n = the number of 'years' of useful life of the machine.

C_m and n are assumed to be given and Q^*s are assumed to be estimated by the investor. It is here that the factor of expectations enters the investment decision in a big way. When investors' expectations about the future are rosy, they estimate Q^* liberally and the expected ρ from any investment gains in value. The reverse happens when gloom and pessimism overtake investors. Given these expectations, C_m and n, equation (13.3) is solved for that value of ρ which makes its two sides equal. it is assumed that ρ will have a unique value. Then, this value is the value of the MEI from a unit of investment under consideration. While making fresh investment, the investor is assumed to make the most profitable use of his funds. So, the investment chosen will be the one which promises the highest ρ. From equation (13.3) it can be seen that ρ will be a declining function of C_m and an increasing function of Q^*.

Keynes argued that both C_m and Q^*s are affected by I—the former in the short period, the latter in the long period. In any short period, the supply price of machines was supposed to rise with increase in their production. Therefore, if I is stepped up leading to increased demand for machines, C_m will go up which will lower ρ. So it was concluded that the MEI would be a declining function of I. For this result, it was additionally assumed that Q^*s will stay unaffected, because the additional output of the new machines installed will be a rather small proportion of the total output. In a longer period, however, the new machines installed will have accumulated to a large enough proportion of the total fixed capital in place; consequently, the competition of output from new machines will reduce the values of Q^* s. In the long period, this may be a more important reason for the downward slope of the MEI function. The whole discussion is entirely heuristic and not firmly grounded in rigorous economic theory. The subject has not been improved upon since.

In the next step, the MEI function is converted into the investment demand (I^d) function by imposing the condition that, in equilibrium, I will be carried to the point where its MEI is equal to r, determined in the money market. Thus, at each r there will be a determinate I given by the MEI function and the latter becomes the I^d function, giving I^d as a declining function of r (see Figure 13.2).

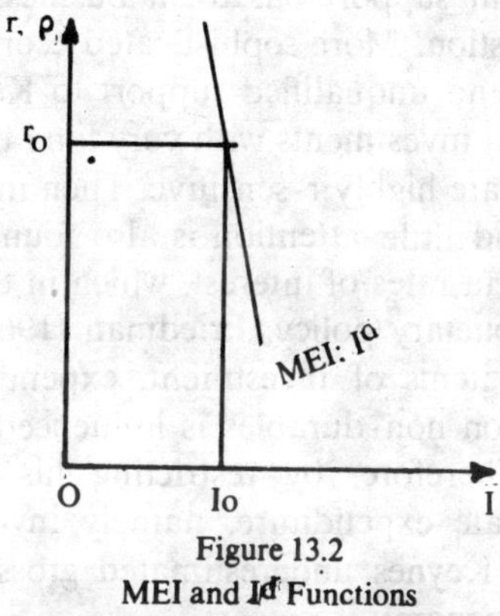

Figure 13.2
MEI and I^d Functions

In Figure 13.2 the downward-sloping MEI function shows MEI as a declining function of I or the equation

$$MEI = f(I), \frac{df}{dI} < O \qquad (13.4)$$

In this figure the same MEI line also represents Keynes' I^d function or the equation

$$\frac{dI^d}{dr} < O \qquad (13.5)$$

The passage from (13.4) to (13.5) via the equilibrium condition MEI = r should be carefully noted. Note must also be taken of the difference between the two equations (13.4) and (13.5): in the former I is the explanatory variable, in the latter the dependent variable.

In the second proposition of Keynes' monetary theory relating I to r, the responsiveness of I^d to changes in r (or the interest elasticity of I^d) is the important thing. If I^d is highly interest elastic, a given reduction in r will lead to a relatively large increase in I, which will have large expansionary effect on income. The interest elasticity of

I^d is an empirical question. In Keynes' empirical judgement, this elasticity is of rather low value. Most subsequent empirical studies have confirmed Keynes' suspicion. This, then, is an additional reason why Keynes thought monetary policy to be a rather ineffective tool to fight depressions with.

Several economists do not share Keynes' pessimism on this score either. The empirical support based on business questionaires has been called into question. More sophisticated econometric analysis of the data does not lend unqualified support to Keynes' hypothesis. It has been argued that investments with very long lives, such as houses and public utilities, are highly r-sensitive. Then inventory investment to which keynes paid little attention is also found to be sensitive to changes in short-term rates of interest, which in turn are much more manipulable by monetary policy. Friedman (1963) has argued that besided the above items of investment, expenditure on consumer durables and even on non-durables is influenced by changes in the rate of interest. Therefore, by restricting his gaze to only one component of private expenditure, namely investment in durable capital equipment, Keynes underestimated grossly the influence of changes in r in the economy.

13.5 **Investment and Income**

The third proposition of Keynes' monetary theory concerns the effect of autonomous changes in investment on the level of income. In Keynes' theory investment expenditure is supposed to be autonomous of income. As such, all changes in investment are also presumed to be autonomous of income. In the previous section we have seen that, given the downward-sloping MEI function and the expectations associated with it, Keynes had made I a declining function of r. Now, suppose that monetary policy is successful in reducing r which does increase I by some ΔI. What will happen then? The answer is provided by Keynes' theory of the multiplier. This is discussed very briefly below.

The theory of the multiplier is rooted in the circular flow of income, expenditure, and income and in the hypothesis that consumption expenditure is a stable function of current income. We discuss it in a closed-economy model, ignoring foreign trade completely. Keynes divided total domestic expenditure under three heads : consumption expenditure (C) by households, investment expenditure (I) by firms, and government expenditure (G). For simplicity, we ignore the government sector and its expenditure G as well as taxes collected by it. For C, Keynes hypothesised that

$$C = a + bY, \quad O < b < 1, \tag{13.6}$$

where by gives the marginal propensity to consume (MPC) or $\Delta C/\Delta Y$. It shows by how much consumption increases if income increases by a small amount. The MPC is assumed to be positive but less than 1. We have already seen in the previous section how I is determined. Given r and the MEI (or the I^d) function, there will be a determinate I. Suppose the money market determines r at r_o and the equilibrium I at $r_o = I_o$ (see Figure 13.2). Hence, for the commodity market, we can write

$$I = I_o. \tag{13.7}$$

Then total expenditure (E) is given by

$$E = C + I = a + bY + I_o. \tag{13.8}$$

E also gives aggregate demand for real output. Keynes in his *General Theory* (1936) was spelling out a model of a developed economy suffering from unemployment accompanied by unutilised capacity. He had assumed that the supply of output will be perfectly adaptive to demand, that the prevailing unemployment of resources was due to deficiency of aggregate demand, that consequently increase in demand will lead to increase in output and real income by equal amount, so long as the point of full employment was not reached.

For commodity market to be in equilibrium, it is necessary that

$$E = Y. \tag{13.9}$$

Using (13.8) in the above equation, we have

$$a + bY + I_o = Y. \tag{13.10}$$

The above is one equation in one unknown Y. So, we can solve it for Y to have

$$Y = \frac{a + I_o}{1 - b}. \tag{13.11}$$

Putting k = 1/1-b, we may rewrite the above equation as

$$Y = k \cdot (a + I_o). \tag{13.12}$$

k is called the 'keynesian multiplier' and $a + I_o$ is the multiplicand.

The value of k $= \frac{1}{1-b} = \frac{1}{1\text{-MPC}} = \frac{1}{\text{MPS}}$ = the reciprocal of the marginal propensity to save (MPS). Since MPS is always less than 1, k is always greater than 1.

We had started out with the assumption that monetary policy is successful in lowering r and raising I by some ΔI. With the help of equation (13.12) we can work out the equilibrium effect of Δ I on Y. This is given by

$$\Delta Y = k.\Delta I. \quad (13.13)$$

More commonly, the above equation is called Keynes' multiplier equation. Since k > I, it shows that a change in I will lead to a greater change in Y, the extent of the change depending upon the value of k. This can be explained in a different way, too, which will bring out also the working of the multiplier process.

We start with a given ΔI (generated by, say, lower r). In the first instance, this will increase expenditure as well as income by ΔI. The income recipients will spend MPC times this extra income, i.e. $b.\Delta I$, on consumption and save the rest, i.e. $(1-b).\Delta I$. Then, $b.\Delta I$ will represent the second-round increase of expenditure and increase income by equal amount. Again, MPC times this extra income will be spent on consumption, i.e. expenditure as well as income will increase by $b^2.\Delta I$, which will represent third-round increase in expenditure and income, and so on in an infinite time sequence. All the terms of this infinite sequence of expenditure and income generated by an autonomous injection of ΔI can be summed up. For this, we write

$$\Delta Y = \Delta E = \Delta I\,(1 + b + b^2 + b^3 + \ldots \infty). \quad (13.14)$$

The terms within parentheses on the right-hand side of the above equation represent an infinite geometric series. Since the value of the common factor b lies between o and I, the sequence is convergent and the series has a finite sum. Using algebra, this sum is found to be equal to 1/1-b. Therefore (13.14) yields.

$$\Delta Y = 1/1-b.\ \Delta I, \quad (13.15)$$

which is the same thing as equation (13.13), remembering that we have already defined $k = 1/1-b$.

The series derivation of the multiplier gives exactly the same result as the earlier method of solving equation (13.10) for Y. The former has the additional advantage of highlighting the dynamic nature of the multiplier as a process over time and the manner in which, the MPC enters the picture in generating induced rounds of expenditure subsequent to the autonomous injection of ΔI. Therefore, we can easily see that the ΔY predicted by equation (13.13) or (13.15) is not realized all at once, but only in instalments over time. One should not be unduly concerned by the fact that equation (13.15) results from the sum of an infinite series, because most of the predicted increase in income will be realized in the first few rounds. More important is the presumed stability of the multiplier k, which may not be fully dependable. Equally important is the question whether additional real output will be forthcoming in response to additional rounds of expenditure. There may be supply-side bottlenecks or capacity constraints may be reached sooner in some industries than in others. These considerations are more important in LDCs like India (see Rao, 1952) than in developed economies. But even for the latter, Hicks (1974, lecture 1) has raised similar problems. If the supply of real output is not easily forthcoming in response to demand as assumed in Keynes' theory, the multiplier will operate only in money terms and not in real terms (Rao, 1952).

The above discussion is represented diagrammatically in Figure (13.3).

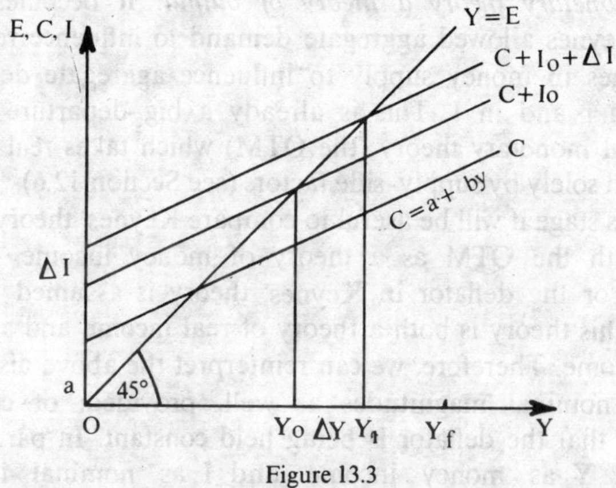

Figure 13.3

Determination of Income in Keynes' Theory

(Without Government Sector)

In Figure 13.3, Y is measured along the horizontal axis and E, C, and I are measured along the vertical axis. The 45° line is the locus of points at which E = Y. All magnitudes are measured in rupees of constant value in (say) crores. The upward-sloping C line represents the consumption function of equation (13.6). Its slope = b = MPC. Since I is assumed to be autonomous of Y, I_0 when added to the C line gives C+ I_0 line parallel to the C line. The perpendicular distance between the two lines represents I_0. The intersection of the C+ I_0 (or total E) line with the 45° line gives the equilibrium level of income at Y_0. At Y_0 all the output supplied will be demanded in full, neither less nor more. At any other level of Y, given C+ I_0 line as the aggregate demand line, there will be either excess demand or excess supply and market forces will operate to move the system to Y_0. Thus Y_0 represents stable level of income. However, this need not be full-employment level of income Y_f, which, in the figure, lies to the right of Y_0. Y_f is supposed to be given from outside. It shows the short-run maximum level of output an economy is capable of producing.

Now suppose ΔI occurs. This will shift the aggregate demand curve upward from its C + I_0 position to C+ $I_0+\Delta I$ position. The vertical distance between the two lines represents ΔI. The inter-section of the new demand line **with the 45° line gives** a new equilibrium value of income at Y_1. $Y_1 - Y_0$, then, is the value of ΔY by which total income increases due to ΔI. $\Delta Y > \Delta I$ due to the multiplier effect.

The above discussion extends by one more step Keynes' analysis of the effect of (say) an increase in money supply. Now, we see how it may even increase Y under conditions of unemployment. *This makes Keynes' monetary theory a theory of output.* It becomes possible because Keynes allowed aggregate demand to influence real output and changes in money supply to influence aggregate demand via changes in r and in I. This is already a big departure from the neoclassical monetary theory (the QTM) which takes real output as determined solely by supply-side factors (see Section 12.6).

At this stage it will be useful to compare Keynes' theory of *money income* with the QTM as a theory of money income. Since the *numeraire* or the deflator in Keynes' theory is assumed to remain contant, this theory is both a theory of real income and a theory of money income. Therefore, we can reinterpret the above discussion to apply to nominal magnitudes as well, provided, of course, we remember that the deflator is being held constant. In particular, we shall read Y as money income and I as nominal investment. The Keynesian theory of money income (in simplest form without government sector), then, is given by equation (13.12) or equation (13.13). The former gives this theory in level form, the latter in first-difference form. The QTM was discussed in the previous chapter. Its comparable equations are equation (12.12) and equation (12.13).[6]

The above comparison is made to answer the question: which of the two competing theories explains the observed behaviour of Y. The empirical evidence does not favour conclusively any of the two theories over the other. This book cannot go into a detailed examination of the finer points of the debate. We only note that the Keynesian theory and the QTM are two competing theories of Y or of aggregate money expenditure or of aggregate money demand for output. If for the latter, stability of V (income velocity of money) is important, for the former the stability of k is important, besides other things.

13.6 Income, Output, Employment, and the Marginal Productivity of Labour

In Keynes' theory it is the aggregate demand for output that is assumed to determine actual output and real income. This is the result of his assumption that in a developed economy under conditions of unemployment the supply of output will be perfectly adaptive to the demand for it, i.e., that firms will be perfectly willing to produce whatever output is demanded of them. The 'developed economy' qualification tells that there is no dearth in the economy of land, fixed capital, and other inputs that are used with labour to produce output, so that it is not the shortage of these non-labout inputs which may act as a hindrance to full employment, as is the case in many LDCs. What governs employment in developed economies is the level of output to be produced, itself determined by aggregate demand.

The link between output (Y) and employment (N) is supposed to be provided by the aggregate production function:

$$Y = f(N; K_o), \quad \frac{\partial f}{\partial N} > o, \quad \frac{\partial^2 f}{\partial N^2} < O \qquad (13.16)$$

The above is a *short-run* production function. As such, the stock of capital is taken as given at Ko. The functional form given by f (.) is supposed to represent the prevailing technology. The two additional qualifications say that the marginal productivity of labouris supposed to be positive but diminishing as more labour is combined with the given amount of capital K_o. Once we know the value of Y to be produced, then, given K_o, (13.16) can be used to determine N. All this is shown diagrammatically in Figure 13.4

In Figure 13.4 the upward-sloping f $(N;K_o)$ curve represents equation (13.16), given a certain quantity of capital K . It is drawn concave downward to show diminishing marginal productivity of

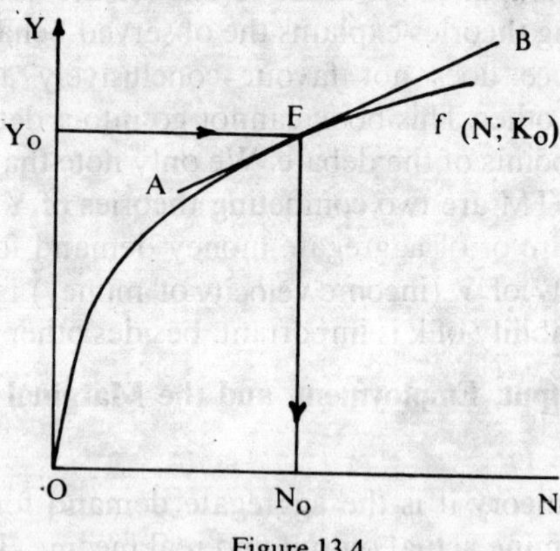

Figure 13.4

Production Function, Employment, and the Marginal Product of Labour

labour. Suppose the demand conditions induce firms to produce Y_o level of output. Given the particular production function, this will require that N amount of labour services is used (per unit of time). Thus, the level of employment offered and taken in the economy will be N_o. The directional arrows in the figure show that the causation runs from Y to N.

From Figure 13.4 itself we can also show the determination of the marginal producțivity of labour (MP_L). As per the hypothesis already embodied in equation (13.16), this will be a diminishing function of N, and so will vary from point to point on the f (.) curve. At N_o, this will be given by the slope of the tangent AB to the f (.) curve at the point F where the vertical through No meets the curve.

13.7 Marginal Productivity of Labour ana the Price Level

Finally, we arrive at the end of Keynes' sequence of effects, namely the effect on the price level (P), which was left implicit in his *General Theory* (1936). Despite his several strong departures from the neoclassical theory, Keynes did not reject the marginal productivity theory of wages, which says that, in equilibrium,

$$\frac{W}{P} = MP_L . \qquad (13.17)$$

The above equation gives the value of P, because MP_L is determined as soon as N is determined (see the previous section) and W is assumed by Keynes to be a given datum $\overline{W}$:

$$P = \bar{W}/MP_L \qquad (13.18)$$

The above equation makes P an increasing function of $\bar{W}$ and a decreasing function of MP_L. A change in $\bar{W}$, other things being the same, will lead to an equiproportionate change in P in the same direction. This shows the autonomous role of changes in $\bar{W}$ in bringing about changes in P. Where does the effect of a change in M on P appear? As was stated above in Section 13.2, it appears at the end of a long sequence of effects when a change in M is able to influence MP_L via a change in r, I, Y, and N. The effect is highly circuitous and not direct. The analysis of it is not as simple as the OTM makes it out to be.

It is worth noting that the above analysis gives an upward-sloping supply curve of output with respect to P. This is the consequence of the assumption of the diminishing marginal productivity of labour made in equation (13.16), so that when to produce a larger output more labour is employed, MP_L declines and, given $\bar{W}$, P rises. This means that fixed W does not imply fixed P in Keynes' model, as is carelessly made out in some of the macrotheory text-books. The possible source of the careless error will become clear from the following discussion.

Keynes of the *General Theory* (1936) had assumed W to be short-run sticky and as such given from outside. It was, therefore, natural for him to use W as his *numeraire* or deflator for converting nominal values into real values. But most Keynesian economists have found P as a more representative deflator than W. The switch from W to P as the deflator was further facilitated by the growing short-run stickiness of most industrial prices in the downward direction. Therefore, formal Keynesian models came to be specified with P (rather than W) as the deflator, supported by the assumption that P was short-run sticky. In this 'fix-price model' (in the language of Hicks, 1965), the supply curve of output of Keynes' theory became perfectly elastic upto the point of full-employment output (Y_f) and perfectly inelastic at Y_f with respect to P, giving the now-popular reverse L-shaped supply curve of output.

One important consequence of this switching of assumptions for Keynes' theory should be noted. If all other features of Keynes' model are retained, it should be clear from equation (13.17) that both W and P cannot be assumed to be (short-run) constants, because then W/P will become a constant and so will MP_L have to be. The constancy of

MP_L will clash with the assumption of the diminishing marginal productivity of labour made with equation (13.16). If the latter is to be honoured, only one of the two of W and P can at best be assumed to be given from outside and allow the other to be determined by equation (13.17). In Keynes' own model where W is assumed to be given from outside, (13.17) is used to determine P. In Keynesian models where P is assumed to remain constant at its initial level of the period, W must be allowed to be determined by the relation of equation (13.17).

13.8 Hicks' IS-LM Model

Until now we had restricted our discussion to Keynes' monetary theory. In Section 13.3 we had pointed out a serious analytical flaw in the formulation of Keynes' theory of r. To recapitulate, it arose because Keynes tried to determine r with the help of the equilibrium equation for the money market (13.2) alone, which contained besides r another unknown Y in his M^dfunction. This is invalid becuase unless we know already the value of Y, the equilibrium equation (13.2) cannot be used to determine r. As the subsequent discussion of Section 13.4 showed, Keynes' solution procedure involved him into circularity of reasoning, because in his model r was supposed to influence I and the latter Y. Thus r both influences Y and is influenced by Y. This represents a case of joint determination of r and Y and not of sequential determination first of r and then of Y, given in Keynes' model.

Hicks (1937) removed this analytical flaw in Keynes' model. Ever since Hicks' IS-LM model has overtaken that of Keynes to represent Keynes' theory. Following Leijonhufvud (1968) and others and to distinguish Keynes' model from the following, we shall call the latter Keynesian (in place of Keynes') monetary theory. The key feature of Hicks' (or Keynesian) model is the joint determination of r and Y. It also shows the interaction of the commodity market and the money market. Keeping in view the space constraint and the fact that this is not a textbook in macro theory, we shall be brief in discussing Hicks' model.

Following Keynes, Hicks also used W as the *numeraire* and assumed it to be a short-run constant at its historically-given value. He made the following departures from Keynes' model to accomdate some of the neoclassical hypotheses without discarding Keynes' behavioural hypotheses and the key feature of Keynes' theory which makes Y determined by Y^d (aggregate demand for output) alone and allows for the possibility of unemployment equilibrium:

(1) That savings are an increasing function of r; and

(2) That investment expenditure will also be higher at a higher level of income.

Combining the above two hypotheses with Keynes' hypotheses, Hicks thus gave a more general specification of the savings and investment function:

$$S = S(Y, r), \quad \frac{\partial S}{\partial Y} > o, \quad \frac{\partial S}{\partial r} > o, \tag{13.19}$$

$$\text{and } I = I(Y, r), \quad \frac{\partial I}{\partial Y} > o, \quad \frac{\partial I}{\partial Y} < o. \tag{13.20}$$

For stability, Hicks assumed that $\frac{\partial S}{\partial Y} > \frac{\partial I}{\partial Y}$, i.e., that the marginal propensity to save (with respect to income) is greater than the marginal propensity to invest (with respect to income). In simple words it means that a small increase in income induces a larger increase in savings than it does in investment. Diagrammatically, it means that, in a diagram which shows both savings and investment as increasing functions of income, the savings curve intersects the investment curve from below. If this were not so, any departure from equilibrium in the commodity market will not be self-correcting.

In the absence of the government sector (ignored for simplicity), the commodity market will be in equilibrium when savings = investment. This will require that

$$S(Y, r) = I(Y, r) \tag{13.21}$$

This is one equation in two unknowns Y and r. Therefore, it cannot give the equilibrium values of both Y and r, though it can be used to solve for one of them in terms of the other variable. To solve for the equilibrium values of both Y and r, we need another (independent) equilibrium equation in Y and r. This equation is provided by the equilibrium equation of the money market. Hicks modified the form of Keynes' demand-for-money equation (11.2)which makes the demand for money an additive function of $L_1(Y)$ and $L_2(r)$. As already pointed out (Section 11.4), the latter makes too sharp a distinction between transactions-precautionary balances and speculative balances. Assetholders do not treat them as two separate assets and both kinds of balances are influenced by both Y and r. On this view, a more general form of the demand-for-money function is that given below:

$$M^d = M^d (Y, r), \frac{\partial M^d}{\partial Y} > 0, \frac{\partial M^d}{\partial r} < 0. \qquad (13.22)$$

Hicks retained the assumption of equation (13.1) which says that the supply of money is exogenously given. Thus the condition of equilibrium for the money market can be written as

$$M^d(Y, r) = M. \qquad (13.23)$$

This is also one equation in two unknowns Y and r. As such, it alone canot give us the equilibrium values of both r and Y or of either without knowing the value of the other variable.[8] But, when combined with equation (13.21), the two equations can be used to solve for the equilibrium values of both Y and r. The simultaneous solution of the two equations captures the interaction of the two markets—the commodity market and the money market. Hicks' well-known IS-LM model gives the diagrammatic method of solving two simultaneous equations in two unknowns Y and r. This is explained briefly below.

First consider the commodity market and its two behavioural relations (13.19) and (13.20). They are plotted in Figure 13.5

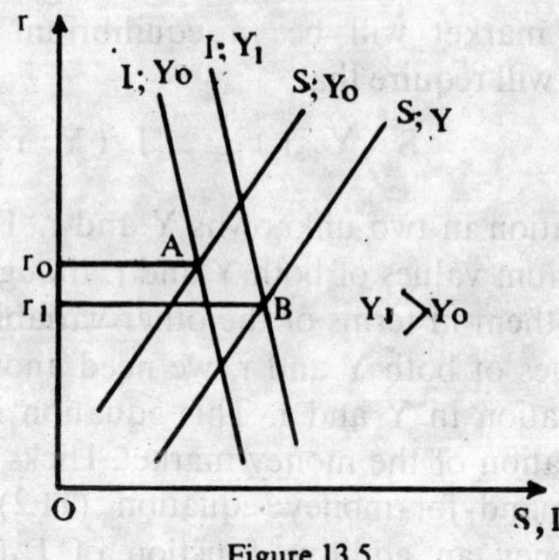

Figure 13.5

Saving-Investment Equilibrium

In figure 13.5 savings (S) and investment (I) are measured along the horizontal axis and the rate of interest (r) along the vertical axis. Both S and I are also functions of Y. But in a two-dimensional diagram, a third variable (Y in the present case) cannot have its independent axis. Therefore, it is shown as a parameter of the S and I lines. The S lines are drawn upward sloping, because savings are hypothesised to be an increasing function of r. But since savings are also influenced by Y, there is a whole family of such rising S lines, one for each value of Y. Only two such S lines are drawn in the figure—one for Y_0 and the other for Y_1. Since savings are hypothesised to be an increasing function of Y and since Y_1 is assumed to be greater than Y_0, the S line for Y_1, is shown to lie to the right of the S line for Y_0. The horizontal distance between the two S lines at any rate of interest shows by how much S increases when Y increases from Y_0 to Y_1. The ratio of the two values will give the value of the marginal propensity to save, which cannot be shown in this figure. A similar explanation holds for the I lines for which two things have to be remembered : ((*a*) I is a decreasing function of r : (*b*) the rightward shift in the I line for the given increase in Y from Y_0 to Y_1 is smaller than that for the S line. The latter follows from our assumption that the marginal propensity to save is greater than the marginal propensity to invest.

The above figure also shows two alternative points of equilibrium A and B between S and I. The point A shows that if the level of income is Y_0, S–I equilibrium will be attained at r_0: the point B shows that if the level of income chosen is Y_1, S–I equilibrium will be attained at r_1. If we had chosen other levels of income, there would have been other values of r which would clear the commodity market, that is, make S = I. When this equilibrium relation between Y and r is plotted in Y-r space, as in Figure 13.7, we shall get a downward-sloping curve, called IS curve. This curve is the locus of alternative combinations of Y and r at which the commodity market is in equilibrium. At all other points (not lying on the IS line), the commodity market will be in disequilibrium. At points to the right of the IS curve, this market will have excess of S over I or deficiency of demand. This will induce Y to fall (Keynes'theory) and/or r to fall (classical theory). In the opposite case of the points to the left of the IS curve, the commodity market will have excess demand or excess of I over S, which will induce Y to rise and/or r to rise.

The money market can be analysed on similar lines. Because of the fixity of M_l^s, the analysis is simpler. We go straight to equation (13.23) and represent it diagrammatically in Figure 13.6.

From equation (13.22), the demand for money (M^d) is an increasing function of Y and decreasing function of r. The latter relation is shown by the downward-sloping M^d curves in Figure 13.6.

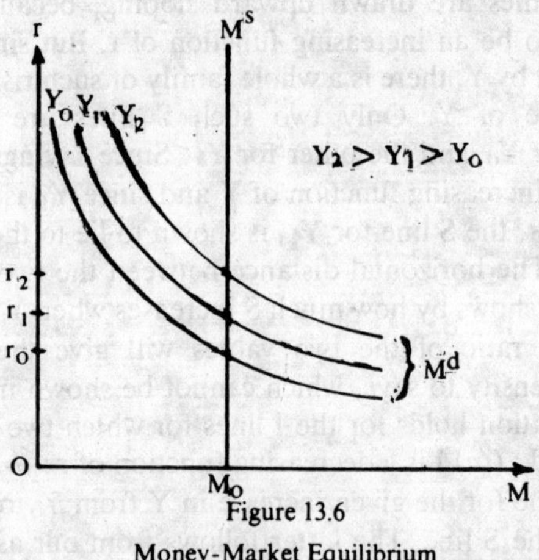

Figure 13.6

Money-Market Equilibrium

Three such curves have been drawn in the figure, one each for a different level of Y, shown as Y_0, Y_1, Y_2. Since M^d is hypothesised to be an increasing function of Y, holding r constant, the M^d curve for a higher level of Y is shown to lie to the right of that for a lower level of Y.

If the exogenously-given supply of money is fixed at M_0, the figure shows three alternative equilibrium points, one for each level of Y. These alternative equilibria are given by the pairs of Y and r: (Y_0, r_0), (Y_1, r_1), and (Y_2, r_2). This means that, for money-market equilibrium, a higher level of Y is associated with a higher level of r. This makes sense, because at a higher Y more M will be demanded; given the fixed supply of money, the money market can clear only if r rises to choke off the excess demand for M. When the equilibrium relation between Y and r is plotted in the Y-r space of Figure 13.7, we get an upward-sloping LM curve.[9] This curve is the equilibrium path for the combinations of Y and r at which alone the money market will be in equilibrium. Points to the right of the LM curve will show excess demand and points to the left of the curve will show excess supply in the money market. In the first case, r will tend to rise and Y tend to fall. In the second case, the reverse will happen.

We are now in a position to operate with Hicks' IS–LM apparatus, as depicted in Figure 13.7. Since the two curves (IS and LM) intersect at point E, this point lies on each of these curves. Therefore, Y_0 and r_0 associated with point E clear simultaneously both the commodity market and the money market and as such are the

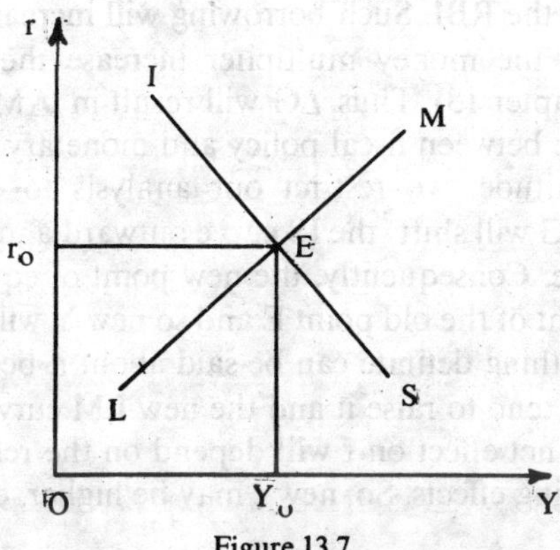

Figure 13.7
IS–LM Equilibrium

required equilibrium values. Since the two curves interesect in only one point E, the equilibrium shown by it is unique. Given Mo (and other parameters), at any other point in the diagram, one or both the markets will be in disequilibrium. Then, market forces will operate to bring it into equilibrium at point E. The exact path of adjustment will depend upon the dynamic-adjustment model postulated and the relative speeds of adjustment of the two dependent variables Y and r.

The above model gives simultaneous equilibrium values of only Y and r. For the rest, it is like Keynes' model. For example, this model, too, takes output to be demand-determined till the point of full-employment output is reached; it is a fix-price model; given W, employment and P are determined as in Keynes' model.

Three comparative-static exercises of the above apparatus are now given. They will show how the equilibrium effects of any autonomous change affecting either LM or IS curves or both on Y and r (and through them on other endogenous variables) can be easily worked out. Take the case of an autonomous increase in the supply of money. This will shift the LM curve outward. The IS curve remaining unchanged, the new equilibrium will be at a larger Y (assuming new Y is still less than Y_f) and a lower r. If the conditions governing the LM curve remain unchanged, but the IS curve shifts outward instead (due to, say, autonomous increase in I or government expenditure G), the new equilibrium will be in the north-east of the old equilibrium point E. This will mean that both Y and r will be higher than before.

Let us take a more interesting case of the outward shift of both the IS and LM curves. Such a case will arise when we assume that the increase in government expenditure (ΔG) is financed entirely by borrowing from the RBI. Such borrowing will increase high-powered money and via the money multiplier increase the total supply of money (See Chapter 15). Thus, ΔG will result in ΔM. This shows the interdependence between fiscal policy and monetary policy. Since ΔG is a flow magnitude, we restrict our analysis to only one-period increase in G. ΔG will shift the IS curve outward and ΔM do the same to the LM curve. Consequently, the new point of equilibrium will lie surely to the right of the old point E and so new Y will surely be larger than before. Nothing definite can be said about r, because the new IS curve alone will tend to raise it and the new LM curve alone will tend to lower it. The net effect on r will depend on the relative strength of these two opposing effects. So, new r may be higher, equal to, or lower than the old r.

In recent years, the above model of Hicks has come in for severe criticism for its comparative-static nature (Leijonhufvud, 1968, Chapter 1; Chick, 1977, Chapter 3). Hicks' model, it is said, deals with only once-and-for-all changes in the equilibrium values of endogenous variables as they respond to exgogenous change. But, in the real world, adjustments take time, so that lags in adjustments of various kinds are involved. These lags and the time path of endogenous variables generated by them are said to be of the very essence for economic analysis as well as policy making. The IS-LM model abstracts from them. It also ignores the role of expectations. Truly speaking, this kind of criticism is applicable to a large part of macroeconomic theory, most of which is cast in comparative-static mould; it is not a special weakness of Hicks' model alone.

NOTES

1. In Keynes' model all level magnitudes (like I, Y, M, etc.) are measured in wage units and the wage unit or the wage rate (W) is assumed to be a historically-given constant. Thus all the level variables are real variables, though the symbols used are the same that stand for nominal magnitudes elsewhere in the book. In fact, the assumption of constancy of W used as the *numeraire* makes the distinction between nominal and real values completely unnecessary in Keynes' model.

2. It is long-term r in which Keynes was mainly interested because in his theory the r effect on Y was conceived to operate through I in fixed capital. This point will be discussed in the next section.

3. Most Keynesians use the general price level or the price index number (P) as the deflator, instead. Which of W or P is used as the deflator and is assumed to be historically given is important for the determination of the other variable (P or W). But for the rest of Keynes' theory, the choice of the deflator does not make any difference. In the text we are sticking to Keynes' parctice of using W as the deflator.

4. Keynes had used the term 'marginal efficiency of capital' instead, though he had meant MEI (see Learner 1943, Chapter 19).

5. It is assumed that at the end of n 'years' the machine has no scrap value.

6. For comparison along these lines, see Friedman and Meiselman (1964) and for references on subsequent debate, see Friedman (1968, References).

7. It is interesting to note that by the time Keynes wrote his little book *How To Pay For The War* (1940) and put forward his theory of the inflationary gap (demand-pull inflation), he had also hypothesised that the supply conditions in the commodity market could be taken to be represented by the reverse L-shaped curve. Keynes' theory of the inflationary gap will be discussed in the next chapter.

8. Keynes' liquidity preference theory of the rate of interest (Section 13.3) is as much a special case of the more general theory embodied in equation (13.23) as the Cambridge theory of money-income determination (equation 12.13). The former assumes implicitly that Y is determined elsewhere so that it can be treated as a datum for the money market, the latter assumes that r does not play any role in the M^d function.

9. For simplicity, we leave out special cases of liquidity trap or perfect inelasticity of M^d to r.

CHAPTER 14

Inflation

14.1 Introduction

Inflation means *persistent rise* in the general level of prices. It is usually measured as a rate per cent per unit time, say, a year or a month. Thus while talking of inflation, we speak of prices rising at the average rate of 15% or 20% or 100% per year (or per month).

Everywhere inflation is now regarded as a major economic problem. In some countries (such as Argentina, Brazil, Chile) the problem is chronic. But in recent years, inflation has taken hold of many more countries, whether developed, like the USA, the UK, and Japan, or the LDCs. The two alarming features of the current world-wide phase of inflation are: *(a)* acceleration in the rate of inflation over time and *(b)* high (even rising) rate of unemployment in the face of high (even accelerating) rate of inflation. The feature (b) has already earned new names such as stagflation and slumpflation and posed serious challenge (for explanation) to the received macro-economic theory. In this introductory book, we cannot even summarise all the work that has been done on various aspects of inflation and related problems in recent years. To keep our discussion within narrow bounds of space, we have to be necessarily selective. In this chapter, therefore, we shall discuss mainly the major explanations of the sources (or causes) of inflation that have been offered from time to time.[1]

14.2 Demand-Pull Inflation

It is also called excess-demand inflation. In the excess-demand theories of inflation, excess demand means aggregate real demand for output in excess of maximum feasible, or potential, or full-employment, output (at the going price level). Since the level of output is taken as a given datum, the excess demand is supposed to be generated by forces operating only on the demand side of the commodity market. Hence also the appellation 'demand-pull inflation' which simply says that inflation has occurred because aggregate demand has been 'pulled' above (or in excess of) what the economy is capable of producing (or even supplying) in the short run.

On the question of forces responsible for 'excess demand' or demand-pull, we have two competing theories in the field: the Keynesian and the monetarist. We shall study the two separately—the former in this section, the latter in the next.

14.2.1 Keynesian Inflationary-Gap Analysis

Keynes gave his theory of the inflationary gap in his little book, *How To Pay For The War* (1940). Basically, it is an application of the static aggregate demand model of his *General Theory* (1936) to the situation of inflation. The notion of the inflationary gap can be explained easily with the help of the 'Keynesian-cross' diagram in Figure 14.1.

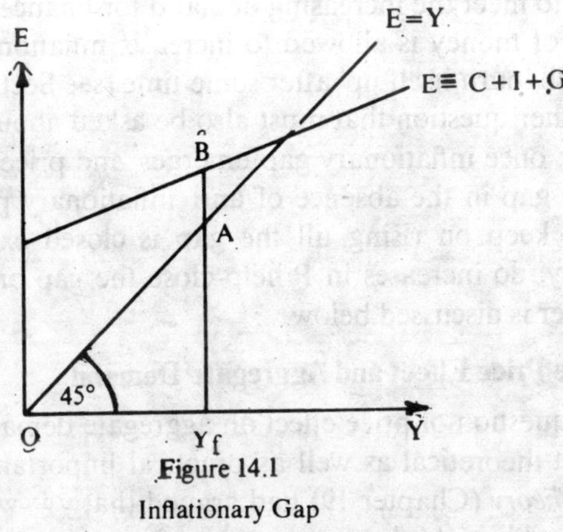

Figure 14.1

Inflationary Gap

Figure 14.1 is essentially similar to Figure 13.3 except that now we have allowed government expenditure G to stay in as a component of E. Y_f represents 'full-employment output', the maximum output the economy can produce in a given short period. But the position of the total expenditure (E) line is such that at Y_f aggregate demand is greater than aggregate supply by the amount AB. This AB is also the measure of the inflationary gap, which is another name for excess demand *measured at* Y_f If the economy is placed in this situation, the excess demand will cause prices to rise, because by assumption output cannot increase beyond Y_f in response to higher demand for it. The result is demand-pull inflation—an inflation caused by excess demand. Keynes argued that in order for inflation to stop, the E curve must be shifted downward to make it intersect the 45° line in point A. For this, appropriate policy measures such as lowering G or raising taxes or other measures will have to be taken.

The key distinguishing feature of this theory of inflation is that it is out and out a non-monetary theory. It does not assign any role whatsoever to increases in the supply of money in its explanation of inflation, whether its origin or continuance. Naturally, therefore, questions arise about the true role of money in Keynes' theory of inflationary gap: is the supply of money assumed to remain constant; if yes, how is a given level of real economic activity financed at rising prices? The latter can happen only if V (the velocity of money) is rising *pari passu* with P (see Chapter 12). The 'Keynes effect' discussed below does indicate that a rise in r (caused by rise in prices) will be accompanied by a fall in the demand for money or a rise in V. But even the Keynesians admit that such a rise in V will normally be not sufficient to meet the increasing demand for finance. Therefore, unless the stock of money is allowed to increase, inflation cannot go on too long; it will 'burn itself up' after some time (see Section 14.11).

Another question that must also be asked about this theory is the following: once inflationary gap emerges and prices start rising, what closes the gap in the absence of anti-inflationary policy measures or do prices keep on rising till the gap is closed exogenously? More specifically, do increases in P help close the gap or not? If yes, how? The answer is discussed below.

14.2.2 The Price Effect and Aggregate Demand

The question of price effect on aggregate demand for output (y^d) is of great theoretical as well as practical importance. Keynes in his *General Theory* (Chapter 19) had argued that y^d was independent of P. This would imply that no amount of price increase could close the inflationary gap. But, when it came to analysing inflation, Keynes took a different stand. He argued that if increases in money wages lagged behind increases in prices, the resulting reduction in real wages (and consumption) from persistent inflation will close the inflationary gap. In other discussions several other effects of rise in prices on y^d are pointed out. All these effects are discussed briefly below.

1. *Wage-Lag Effect.* As said above, Keynes laid maximum emphasis on this effect. His assumptions were *(i)* that inflationary gap raises commodity prices (P) in the very first period, without raising

money wages (W) in the period, thus lowering real wages (W/P) and causing redistribution of real income in favour of the profit-earners. Wages are adjusted upward only in the next period, when prices rise again, and so on. The one-period wage lag is maintained always, though, after the first period, both P and W rise at the same rate; *(ii)* that savings propensities as well as tax liabilities of profit-earners are much higher than those of workers. Consequently, the resulting redistribution of income lowers real consumption, raises savings, and fills the inflationary gap.

2. *Other Redistribution Effects.* Keynes' earlier discussion of the subject (see Keynes, 1923) had spoken of several other kinds of redistribution—of real wealth and real income—due to inflation as, for example, between creditors and debtors. These redistributions arise because some prices (such as interest payments and rents) are contractually fixed in nominal terms for long periods, while some others are adjusted upwards partially and with varying time lags (see Gupta, 1972c). The redistributions induce extra spending by the gainers from inflation and some reduction in spending at the margin by the losers from inflation. The general *presumption* is that, in the aggregate, some reduction in total spending does take place.

3. *Keynes Effect.* If M is held constant, increases in P will tend to raise r which will tend to lower I (and possibly shift the C function downward).

4. *Wealth effect.* Higher prices may reduce C (and also I) by reducing real wealth held in the form of government money and government bonds (see Appendix C). Also, to the extent that r rises, bond prices will fall, wealth of bond-holders go down and their consumption reduced.

5. *Fiscal Effect.* If tax collections rise faster than prices, the real disposable income of the public at any level of y will decline and the C function will be shifted downward. C will be reduced further because the real value of transfer payments fixed in rupee terms will decline due to inflation. If government expenditure is fixed in money terms (or allowed to rise less than the rise in prices), real G will also decline.

6. *Balance-of-trade Effect.* In an open economy, higher domestic prices will tend to encourage import and discourage exports.

7. *Price expectations Effect.* If rising prices generate expectations of further rise, consumers, investors, and speculators are likely to step up their purchases of storable goods. This will widen the inflationary gap. On the other hand, if the current rise in prices is expected to be temporary, the expectations effect will operate in the opposite

direction. In the current state of persistent rise in prices, inflationary expectations (rather than the reverse) have taken hold of the public (see Appendix D).

8. *Money-Illusion Effect.* If some spenders (whether workers, firms, or the government) suffer from money illusion and at least a part of their expenditure is fixed in money terms independently of P, inflation will reduce the real value of such expenditure and close the inflationary gap. [2]

14.3 Quantity Theory of Money (QTM), Excess Demand and Inflation

An alternative theory of excess demand inflation is that provided by the QTM (Chapter 12) which was born as a theory P. The monetarist explanation of inflation is a simple extension of it. As in the Keynesian inflation analysis, the QTM also takes potential output as given with, however, one important difference. Whereas in the neoclassical theory (of which the QTM is a part) actual output is always equal to potential output which is determined endogenously by the employment-production conditions of the economy (Section 12.7), in the Keynesian theory, potential output serves only as the notional short-run maximum of feasible output.

The crucial difference between the two theories is in respect of the sources of excess demand. Whereas the Keynesian theory identifies them with the autonomous components of expenditure, mainly G (government expenditure) and I (private investment expenditure) in a closed economy (and also exports if foreign trade is taken into account), the QTM holds excess increases in the quantity of money responsible for increases in prices. This is easily explained with the help of the QTM (Chapter 12).

First consider the case of a static economy with a given level of y (potential as well as actual). With constant V (assumption), P in it can rise only if M is increased. Alternatively speaking, increases in M alone are responsible for increases in P. On the assumptions of the QTM, P increases in the same proportion as M is increased, so that

$$\dot{P} = \dot{M}, \tag{14.1}$$

where $\dot{P}$ and M are proportionate rates of change (per unit time) of P amd M respectively. Since M is a policy-determined variable, the rate of inflation (under strict QTM) also becomes policy-determined.

Now consider the case of a growing economy—an economy is which y is growing over time due to the working of various growth factors. In the theories of excess-demand inflation, any general deficiency of aggregate demand is ruled out by definition. So, demand deficiency cannot inhibit growth, and all potential growth feasible from the operation of supply-side factors is realized. In a growing economy the real demand for money will also be growing over time. In the QTM model (see section 11.3) the rate of growth of the real demand for money will be equal to the rate of growth of y, since in the simple QTM demand for money equation (11.2) the income elasiticty of demand for money is necessarily unity. This growth rate in the demand for money gives the rate at which new money is (or can be) absorbed in the economy at constant prices. Only excess increases in the stock of money will lead to increase in prices, so that, for a growing economy, the rate of inflation is given by

$$\dot{P} = \dot{M} - \dot{y}, \tag{14.2}$$

where $(\dot{M} - \dot{y})$ gives the excess rate of increase in the supply of money.[3]

How can excess increase in the quantity of money $(\dot{M} - \dot{y})$ be interpreted as giving excess demand for output relevant for demand-pull inflation? The answer is provided by the QTM of y (Section 12.5), which translates excess supply of money into excess demand for output at given prices.

The limitations of the strict QTM model of P which we studied in section 12.7 are equally also the limitations of the QTM explanation of inflation. It is now generally admitted (even by monetarists, including Friedman) that the simple QTM model does not give a good enough explanation of the behaviour of prices or of inflation from one short period (of even one year) to the next. It is also generally admitted by all shades of economists that increases in the supply of money are necessary for inflation to continue for any length of time—that endogenous increases in V (with M^S constant) can help finance ever-increasing money value of transactions due to inflation only upto a point.

14.4 Cost-Push Inflation

Theories of cost-push inflation (also called *sellers'* or *mark-up inflation)* came to be put forward after the mid-1950s. They appeared largely in refutation of the demand-pull theories of inflation, and emphasised, instead, *autonomous* increases in some important component or the other of cost as the true source of inflation. The three common ingredients of such theories are : *(i)* that the upward push in costs is *autonomous* of the demand conditions in the concerned market; *(ii)* that the push forces operate through some important cost component such as wages, profits (mark-up), or materials cost. Accordingly, cost-push inflation can have the forms of wage-push inflation, profit-push inflation, material-cost-push inflation, or inflation of a mixed variety in which several push factors reinforce each other; and *(iii)* that the increase in costs is passed on to buyers of goods in the form of higher prices, and not absorbed by producers. We now discuss the three major kinds of cost-push inflation identified above.

14.4.1 Wage-Push Inflation

It has been widely argued in the USA and several other western countries that the growth of trade unionism in them and increases in money wages secured by unionised labour since the 1950s has been the main force (push factor) behind inflation, that non-unionised labour has gained wage increases mainly as a consequence of wage increases in the unionised industry, and that, consequently, if inflation is to be controlled successfully, an 'incomes policy' or 'wages policy' limiting increases in money wages to gains in productivity must be adopted and enforced strictly.

The hypothesis of wage-push inflation, in its simple form given above, when closely scrutinised, can be seen to suffer from several weaknesses. Merely because in unionised industry money-wage contracts are arrived at through a process of collective bargaining does not by itself prove that all wage increases gained by trade unions are autonomous of demand conditions in the labour as well as commodity markets. For all we know, a part or whole of the wage increase gained may be *induced* by the operation of demand-pull factors in the economy. At least, three important cases of induced wage increases are worth noting: *(i)* increases induced by an excess demand for labour, which may be the result of excess demand conditions in the commodity market and so demand-pull inflation; *(ii)* increases induced by (prior or anticipated) increases in the cost of living. They only help restore or protect real wages of workers. Such wage increases are clearly the result and not the cause of inflation; and *(iii)* increases induced by increases in the productivity per worker. Some or all of such increases can be price-stabilising rather than inflationary. This is explained below.

Let us start with the following equation:

$$P = W/x\,(1 + R), \tag{14.3}$$

where P = average price per unit of output,
W = money wage rate per unit time,
x = output per worker per unit time, and
R = 'mark-up' factor (a pure number).

In the above equation, W/x gives labour (wage) cost per unit of output, and the mark-up factor when applied to W/x gives non-labour cost, including profits, per unit of output. Equation (14.3) is P-determining equation of the 'fixed mark-up' type, very commonly used in explanations of cost-push inflation. It may, however, be pointed out that this sort of price determination is not necessary for price inflation to take place whenever wage-push inflation occurs, because even when output prices are competitively determined, an increase in wage cost will shift upwards the supply curve of output, and, other things being the same, will raise prices (and lower output, resulting in reduced employment of labour).

Coming back to the model of equation (14.3), now suppose that the working of growth forces (such as capital accumulation and technical progress) are increasing productivity per worker at a certain rate per unit time, denoted by $\dot{x}$. Denoting the rate of increase in money wages per unit time by $\dot{W}$, consider the following equation :

$$\dot{W} = \dot{x}, \tag{14.4}$$

which, in words, says that money wages increase at the same proportionate rate at which the productivity per worker is increasing. Going to equation (14.3), it can now be easily seen that if R remains unchanged, increases in W according to the rule given in equation (14.4) will leave P unchanged, and so will be non-inflationary. It follows that only increases in W in excess of increases in productivity per worker (in percentage terms) can lead to increases in P, assuming R is kept constant. In this model, the rate of inflation is given by the following equation :

$$\dot{P} = \dot{W} - \dot{x} \tag{14.5}$$

and only the excess increases in W given by $\dot{W} - \dot{x}$ will be called autonomous, because the increases in W given by equation (14.4) will be induced by increases in the productivity of labour. The latter increases in W represent one of the possible methods whereby workers share in the gains in productivity without altering relative factor shares in income distribution.

Next, we must understand that for wage-push inflation to occur, it is *necessary* that trade unions exercise substantial control (market power) over the the supply of labour. Therefore wages can, at best, be increased autonomously in only such industries in which labour is highly unionised, and not throughout the economy. The weight of such labour in the economy thus becomes important. This consideration has much relevance for the Indian economy, where the bulk of the labour force is not unionised, has weak bargaining power due to the excess supply of labour, and even in organized industry (including banking, finance, and government) trade unions are strong in only a few industries. Even in countries where trade unions are very strong and militant, their wage demands are not totally autonomous of demand conditions, but are influenced positively by the level and growth of employment as well as profits. The first factor represents demand conditions in the labour market; the second is taken as an indicator of demand in the commodity market. Both factors make employers more agreeable to money-wage increases. The Phillips curve highlights the observed relation between the rate of increase in money-wages and the rate of unemployment as a measure of tightness in the labour market (see next section).

A factor particularly held responsible for wage-push is the attempt of labour in low-paid industries to catch up with other workers in better-paid industries by demanding 'parity wages', by denouncing excessive wage differentials across industries in the name of equity and social justice. High wage settlements in a few 'key industries' are used as a guide for wage settlements elsewhere irrespective of variations in demand, profits, or productivity across industries. The resulting wage inflation has been called *wage-wage spiral.*

Monetarists have rejected wage-push as an explanation of inflation on the ground that unless the monetary authrotity acquiesces in excessive increase in money wages and increases appropriately the supply of money, increased unemployment rather than inflation will result which will sober down militant trade unions and wage-push will tend to disappear except in the short period. Several economists, taking a counter view of reality, have argued instead that governments publicly committed to the policy of full employment do actively increase money supply and use other policy measures to counter threats to employment even at the cost of inflation. Therefore, it has been suggested that many countries are now on 'labour standard' (of money) and not on gold or some other currency standard, under which as much increase in the supply of money is engineered or permitted as is required to validate higher money wages and prices.

As in the case of several other theories of inflation, the analytical problem is not merely one of explaining once-over 'excess' increase in money wages (and so of prices), but of persistent excess increase period after period, so that inflation does not come to a stop. One popular answer will be discussed in Section 14.7. (See also Appendix E.)

Having discussed the case of wage-push inflation in some detail, we discuss the other two sources of cost-push inflation more briefly, as analytically they raise the same kind of questions as does the wage-push inflation.

14.4.2 Profit-Push Inflation

The explanation of direct profit-push inflation is offered only with respect to such prices as are administratively fixed and not market-determined to clear the market. In fixing 'administered prices', businesses are assumed to apply a 'mark-up' factor to their labour and material cost per unit of output in the manner of equation (14.3) to earn a target rate of return. Such price fixing is said to be common practice with all oligopolistic firms or firms enjoying some market power in their respective industries. In the case of such administered prices, when mark-ups or profit margins are pushed up, without any increase in costs or in demand, the resulting increase in prices is called profit-push inflation. Once started by a few powerful firms, other firms in the economy enjoying some market power also tend to mark-up their profit margins, partly following the example of leading firms and partly because through inter-industry relations their material costs might have gone up. The speed of such price increases has been called *'profit-profit spiral'* to distinguish it from 'wage-wage spiral'.[5] Once started, the inflationary process can spread to other areas of the economy as well where prices are market-determined, because even competitive firms will find that their cost curves have shifted up, necessitating reduction in their output which is also accompained by higher prices.

The above model has been called into question on several counts. First, the model of 'full-cost pricing' or 'mark-up pricing' does not explain how the 'mark-up factor' itself is determined. Further, it is argued that the so-called mark-up factor is never rigidly fixed, but something variable which varies up or down with market demand conditions. Even oligopolistic firms enjoying sufficient market power whittle it down in various ways during periods of slack demand and firm it up when the demand for their products is brisk. In the public sector, administered prices are often revised upward in lagged adjustment to increases in prices elsewhere in the economy. Then, to explain any continued inflation (which in recent years has been proceeding at accelerating rates) in terms of profit-push inflation will require that mark-up factors (or profit margins) are pushed up continually, irrespective of the demand conditions in the product market. This implies that firms gloat in mark-up factors *per se* and not in total profits or total sales, which is not true of most businesses. The error in analysis possibly arises due to insufficient distinction between high levels of profit margins and continual increase in them. During boom conditions profits and profit margins improve substantially, but this can as well be due to better demand conditions and not necessarily because firms artificially boost their profit margins up.

14.4.3 **Material-Cost-Push Inflation**

As a variant of general cost-push inflation, it has also been suggested that the prices of some key materials (such as steel, basic chemicals, oil, etc.) may get pushed up either due to the working of autonomous push factors domestically, as discussed above, or due to autonomous international developments, as has happened with oil prices since October 1973. The crucial importance of these prices derives from the fact that these materials (including oil as an important source of energy) are used, directly or indirectly, in almost the entire economy. Therefore, increases in their prices affect significantly the cost structure in almost all industries, though not to an equal extent. Consequently, whether other prices are competitively determined or determined administratively by using a 'cost plus' formula, all prices are revised upward. Periodic increases in the prices of basic materials (as has happened with oil in recent years) then give continual boost to the general price level through the spread mechanism spelled out above.

That some products and their prices are more important than others cannot be denied. As an example, one may compare steel with hairpins or shoelaces. What has been questioned is the general model of cost-push, irrespective of demand conditions. Autonomous price push abroad such as of oil by oil-exporting countries as a cartel can also not be denied by importing countries. However, in all such cases generally only a part of the actual inflation is attributable to imported inflation.[6]

14.5 **Income-Shares Inflation**

Some economists such as Reder (1948), Duesenberry (1950) have interpreted the process of cost-push inflation (wage-profit-price spiral) as income-shares inflation. The basic idea is that when, at full employment, some income groups in the population attempt to raise their real incomes and so their shares in the total by raising their money incomes, while others attempt at least to maintain their real incomes, prices rise as a consequence when inflated money income claims are passed on as higher product prices. Then all groups necessarily experience some frustration in seeking their objectives, because total real income (in the sense of rewards, not output) demanded by them add upto more than total real income generated in the economy even at full employment. The process can be repeated period after period, generating fresh inflation each time. It comes to a stop only when the power to make excess income claims ceases or when those who have no power to change their incomes are sufficiently expropriated or through money illusion. After some time, the process can get started all over again.

As an interpretation of the inflationary process, this theory makes a lot of sense. The anti-inflationary 'incomes policy' under which annual increases in money incomes (more particularly wage claims) are kept within narrow limits is at least partly inspired by this kind of theory. However, the theory says precious little about the factors that determine or influence income claims of various groups and hence has very little predictive content.

14.6 Demand-Shift Theory of Inflation

Some economists, notably Charles Schultze (1959), have argued that in an economy with downward rigidity of money wages and prices (administered prices), shifts in demand (at any given level of aggregate demand) have inflationary effects, raising prices and wages in sectors to which demand shifts, but leaving them substantially unchanged in sectors from which demand is shifted. Though this theory does contain an element of truth and does contribute to our understanding of the inflationary process as well as inflationary bias of modern economies, it does not offer a complete or even a substantial explanation of continuous inflation, for which a much stronger force in the form of demand-pull and or cost-push is required than mere shifts in demand.

14.7 The Phillips Curve

The Phillips curve is the curve that shows the empirically fitted relationship between the rate of change of money wages (W) and the rate of unemployment (U) (see the curve PP in Figure 14.2 ignoring for the time being the vertical axis $\dot{P}$ on the right-hand side.) The curve has been so named after the British economist, Professor A.W. Phillips (1958), who was the first to identify such a relation in the annual data of the UK for the period 1861–1913.

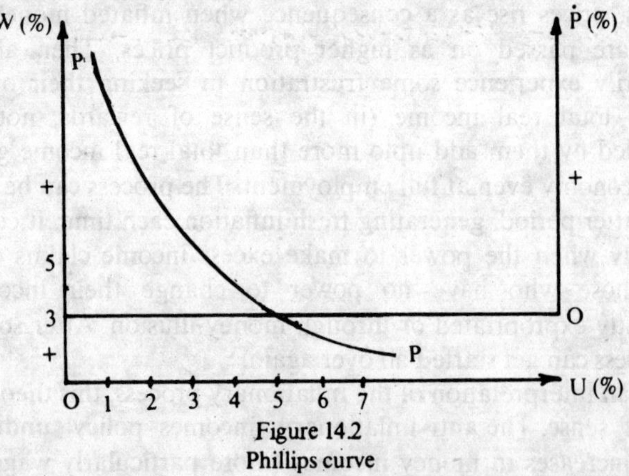

Figure 14.2
Phillips curve

In Figure 14.2 it is shown that *(a)* $\dot{W}$ is a declining function of U and *(b)* that the empirical relation between $\dot{W}$ and U is non-linear—that $\dot{W}$ rises faster as U declines. Phillips had fitted the curve using informal methods. Soon after, Lipsey (1960) fitted the relationship to Phillips' data using standard regression techniques and obtained similar results. Both Phillips and Lipsey had rationalised feature *(b)* noted above by saying that $\dot{W}$ was also a declining function of $\dot{U}$ — — that at any level of U a fall in U (as during business expansions) tends to raise $\dot{W}$ and a rise in U (as during business contractions) tends to reduce $\dot{W}$. Phillips (as well as Lipsey) had found the relationship between $\dot{W}$ and U fairly stable over the period in question.

The Phillips-curve analysis became rapidly popular, both among academic economists and policy makers. By the end of 1960's such curves had been fitted for most major countries. The idea of a fixed trade off between U and $\dot{W}$ (or $\dot{P}$) was found very appealing. It made the problem of policy choice between U and inflation look relatively simple. But the events of the 1970s have proved the presumed stability of the 'Phillips curve' trade off a delusion. More on this a little later.

Though the original Phillips curve was a relationship between U and $\dot{W}$, it can be and has been adapted to show the relationship between U and $\dot{P}$ (the rate of inflation). This has been shown in Figure 14.2 when we consider the PP curve with reference to the vertical axis

$\dot{P}$ on the right-hand side of the figure. The figure has been drawn on the assumption that the relation between $\dot{P}$ and $\dot{W}$ given in equation (14.5) (section 14.4.1) holds and that the average value of $\dot{x}$ = 3% per year. In the figure as drawn zero rate of price inflation (or $\dot{W}$ of 3% per year) will require 5% rate of unemployment in the economy; a lower U can be had only at a positive rate of inflation. To know the trade off between $\dot{P}$ and U, therefore, the position as well as the form of the Phillips curve are of crucial importance and also the question whether the curve is stable or shifts from time to time.

As said in the beginning, the Phillips curve is merely a statistical relation or an empirical phenomenon. What is its theory? What explains its existence, shape and position? The best-known answer has been given by Lipsey (1960), who derived the Phillips curve by making $\dot{W}$ an increasing function of the excess demand for labour.

More specifically, Lipsey hypothesised that

$$W = f\ \frac{(D-S)}{S} \qquad (14.6)$$

where D and S stand for the demand and supply of labour respectively and f (.) was an increasing function. In (14.6) $\dot{W}$ would be zero, if D = S or there was no excess demand for labour. This did not necessarily mean zero U, because the Phillips curve was seen to give zero $\dot{W}$ at a positive value of U (5% in Figure 14.2). Therefore, Lipsey measured the excess demand for labour by only the excess of the number of vacancies over the number unemployed. Thus defined, zero excess demand for labour can (and in actual economies does) occur at positive U. After this point, as the demand for labour grows, vacancies will increase and the number unemployed will go down. That is excess demand for labour will emerge and wages will start increasing. Also the higher the excess demand for labour, the higher the $\dot{W}$. Lipsey also assumed that the wage-adjustment function of equation (14.6) was non-symmetrical, so that negative excess demand for labour produced only a slow wage decrease, whereas an equivalent positive excess demand for labour produced a faster wage increase. When these hypotheses are put together, the resulting relation between U and $\dot{W}$ is the simple Phillips curve.

Lipsey's explanation is not fully satisfactory. It has been said that the wage - adjustment process in to-day's (advanced) economies is not a simple market-clearing process as hypothesised by Lipsey, that trade unions (and other institutional factors) necessarily intervene in the labour market, that it is necessary to recognize that a decline in U raises the market power of organized labour, which then is used to push W upwards. The recognition of this additional factor of the unionisation of labour is important because it has not remained constant over time; rather it has grown over time and the union wage demands have become increasingly aggressive. This factor, therefore, has become increasingly important in determining the shape and position of the Phillips curve, and can also be used to explain recently-observed upward shifts in the Phillips curve (see Appendix E). In contrast, Lipsey's wage-adjustment equation (14.6) is only an empirical rule-of-thumb. It does not tell (a) what determines the level of employment beyond which further increases in aggregate demand begin to create rising prices and (b) what determines the rate at which W will increase at a certain level of U. Both the questions lie at the heart of macro theory and policy.

The period of 1960s was the heyday of the Phillips-curve analysis and policy based on it. Thereafter, the march of events has shown that the presumed stability of the Phillips-cuve trade off between U and $\dot{P}$ was a short-lived phenomenon. The inflation of the 1970s in country after country seems to have no systematic relation with levels of U. In the USA only for the 15-year period 1955–69 the data on U and $\dot{P}$ traced a regular text-book-type Phillips Curve. Both before and after this period the observations do not fall around any single Phillips curve (Ackley, 1978, Chapter 14). This has brought into disrepute the Keynesian policy of aggregate demand-management for curing the problem of U in developed economies. It has also caused a serious 'crisis in Keynesian Economics' (Hicks, 1974) of a magnitude no other development, empirical or theoretical, did in the past. For, the problem of growing inflation coupled with higher (not lower) levels of unemployment cuts at the root of both the Keynesian theory and the Phillips-Curve analysis. The new phenomenon of 'growing inflation with growing (or higher) unemployment' is identified by such terms as 'stagflation' or 'slumpflation', which till recently would have been ruled out of court as contradiction-in-terms. This has necessiated serious reconsideration of the simple Phillips-curve analysis. Attempts in this direction will be discussed in Appendix E.

14.8 Structural Inflation in the LDCs

The theories of inflation discussed so far have all been developed with particular reference to the developed economies of the west. Do they have equal applicability to the inflationary experience of the LDCs ? Most of the time, such a question is not asked, and one or the other theory or theories are used to explain inflation in LDCs, too, on the implicit assumption that the stage of development does not make any difference to the nature and causes of inflation.

There is also another 'theory' (or view), called the 'structural theory' of inflation, which explains inflation in the LDCs in terms of the structural features of the LDCs. It is found in the works of Myrdal (1968), Streeten (1972) and several Latin American economists (see Kirkpatrick and Nixon, 1976). This view is explained briefly in this section.

Both Myrdal and Streeten have argued against the straightforward application of the orthodox aggregative analysis to the LDCs. According to them, this kind of analysis necessarily presumes balanced and intergrated structures, where substitutions in consumption and production and intersectoral resource flows in response to market signals are reasonably smooth and fast, such that we can legitimately talk in terms of aggregate demand and agreggate supply. But the situation is different when we come to analyse the working of the economies of the LDCs, which are structurally backward, unbalanced as well as highly fragmented due to market imperfections and rigidities of various kinds. Consequently, often times, substantial under-utilisation of resources in some sectors coexists with shortages in other sectors. These features of the LDCs make the application of fully aggregative analysis to the LDCs 'misplaced' (Streeten). They suggest that the simple notion of aggregate demand and aggregate supply should be rejected in favour of disaggregated analysis and of sectoral demand and supply balances[7]; that the given structural composition of the economy defines sectoral constraints—constraints that are slow to change and that get easily converted into sectoral bottlenecks, which then generate as well as exaccerbate inflation. Therefore, to understand the true nature (the origin as well as propagation) of inflation in the LDCs, one must go behind the forces that tend to generate bottlenecks or gaps of various kinds in the normal process of development, study how the bottlenecks lead to price increases and how these increases spread to the rest of the economy.

The above kind of 'structural view' of inflation has found maximum advocacy from several Latin American economists since the early 1950s. The essentials of their arguments can be summed up in two main propositions:

1. That whereas inflation in developed countries (DCs) is associated with full-employment policies and the labour-market

response to these policies, inflation in LDCs is bound with the developmental effort and the structural response to this effort expressed through bottlenecks or gaps of various kinds in these countries; and

2. That the socio-economic-political structure of a LDC determines the source and character of inflation by determining the particular kinds of sectoral demand-supply gaps or bottlenecks that emerge in the process of development. A study of these gaps or bottlenecks is, therefore, essential for understanding inflation in these countries and for devising appropriate anti-inflationary policies.

The gaps or bottlenecks that have attracted maximum attention in the literature are discussed below.

1. *Resources Gap.* Most of the LDCs are trying to industrialise themselves rapidly through the public sector. But the socio-economic-political structures are such that the government is not able to raise enough resources from taxes, borrowings from the public and profits of public-sector undertakings to meet rapidly-growing public-consumption expenditure, waste and corruption, and also save enough for investment. Under popular pressure, there is excessive dependence on 'deficit financing' (or borrowing from the central bank) which results in excess increases in the supply of money year after year. Thus, though the latter may be the proximate cause of inflation, one should not stop at saying only this much and must go to the operation of forces which tend to generate such excess increases in the supply of money. The resources-gap in the private sector puts further pressure on the institutional mechanism leading to the excess expansion of money supply and bank credit (see Krishnaswamy, 1976).

2. *Food Bottleneck.* Due to various structural factors, such as the defective system of land ownership and tenancy, technological backwardness and low rate of investment in agriculture, obtaining in LDCs, the domestic supply of food does not keep pace with increase in the demand for food coming from increasing population and urbanisation. The extreme dependence of agriculture on weather produces acute shortage of food from time to time due to drought, wide-spread floods, etc. In years of food shortages prices of foodgrains rise very fast, boosted further by speculative hoarding of foodgrains by traders. Foodgrains being the key wage-good, increase in their prices tends to raise other prices as well. Therefore, some economists consider foodgrain prices the kingpin of the whole structure of prices in LDCs, and analyse their behaviour separately (see Pandit, 1978).

3. *Foreign Exchange Bottleneck.* The industrial development of the LDCs requires heavy import bill on account of import of capital goods, essential raw materials and semi-manufactured goods, and in several cases also import of foodgrains and other consumer goods. Since 1973, due to periodic hefty increases in the price of oil, the import bill of oil-importing LDCs has been shooting up further. But due to low exportable surplus, restrictive trade practices the world over, and relatively poor competitive power of the exports of the LDCs, their export earnings do not increase as fast. Therefore, most of the time, the LDCs face serious shortages of foreign exchange on their trade account. So, the domestic availability of goods in short supply cannot be easily improved through imports, the prices of such goods increase, and the increase spreads to other prices. In Latin American countries, periodic devaluations of currencies to correct overvaluations so as to improve foreign exchange position have led inevitably to rise in domestic prices, which again overvalues their currencies and necessitates their further devaluation.

4. *Infrastructural (Physical) Bottlenecks.* Due to resources and foreign exchange gaps, rampant inefficiency and corruption, and faulty planning and plan implementation, most LDCs have come to face severe infrastructural bottlenecks in the fields of power and transport. This holds back the development in other sectors, creating under-utilised capacity in the economy, which, in turn, discourages further investment in the economy. Since most of the infrastructural facilities lie in the public sector, and due to the resources gap already considered, the government is not in a position to devote enough resources for adequate growth of these facilities, the rate of development of the entire economy gets arrested. Therefore, even small increases in expenditure get converted into excess demand pressures and generate inflation.

5. *Other Structural Factors.* It has also been said that capitalists in LDCs do not possess adequate spirit of enterprise, adventure, and innovation and that they prefer safe and conventional investments. Also, merchant capital is still relatively strong as compared to industrial capital. Socially unproductive private investments in land, precious metals, etc. fritter away a sizeable part of investible resources. These behaviour patterns hold back growth and prepare the ground for inflationary forces to operate successfully.

According to the structural approach to inflation, the above factors and similar other structural features of a LDC best explain inflation in that country.

14.9 Money and Inflation

One question most commonly asked by economists, policy makers, and the public concerns the nature of the relation between increases in money supply and inflation : more specifically, whether increases in money supply are the cause of inflation or they are merely permissive or passive response to increases in the demand for nominal money occurring in an economy, the causes of inflation lying elsewhere. In a way, we have already answered this question with respect to each theory discussed in the previous sections. But keeping in view the importance of the question and the regularity with which it keeps on cropping up in all discussions of inflation, we take it up in its essentials.

We may start with Milton Friedman, the leading exponent of the modern or sophisticated QTM, who has said that '*Inflation is always and everywhere a monetary phenomenon* and can be produced only by a more rapid increase in the quantity of money than in output' (Friedman, 1970, p. 24).

Many economists do not agree with Friedman, even though they may agree that more often than not inflation is *accompanied by* excess increases in the quantity of money. This statement says nothing about the *origin or initiating cause* of inflation, which can be any one or more factors other than money. At most, it says that for inflation to continue for any length of time excess increases in the quantity of money are necessary. Even the staunchest anti-monetarist economists do not deny the validity of this statement. For, what it means is that, automatic increases in V being limited, rising prices will require increasing quantities of money to finance even the same volume of real transactions or to meet increasing demand for nominal money.

Once the necessity of excess increase in M is accepted, in order to understand the role of money in inflation, we must enquire into the mechanism whereby these excess increases are brought about. More specifically, we must ask whether the mechanism is 'automatic' in the sense that whatever factor 'causes' inflation to occur in the first instance also induces required increases in the quantity of money through the working of market forces or whether changes in money supply are a control variable of the policy-making authorities.

No acceptable theory of money supply has so far been put forward which can explain satisfactorily any endogenous mechanism whereby increases in the demand for money lead automatically to equal increases in the supply of money without the authorities being in a position to control substantially such increases. Even most non-monetarists, therefore, only assume that the authorities knowingly permit accommodating increases in the quantity of money to validate whatever autonomous pressures cost-push factors bring to bear themselves on P. Alternatively, those who follow the Phillips-curve analysis have asserted that popular governments knowingly choose lower unemployment at the cost of inflation as a trade off and so follow an expansionary monetary policy. Similarly, the structuralists in LDCs insist that excess increases in the quantity of money (and so inflation) is a necessary price for promoting a high rate of economic development.

The basic contention of all kinds of non-monetary argument, thus, is that though the monetary authority does exercise 'technical control' over money supply, broader social concerns (of fuller employment in DCs and faster rate of economic development in LDCs) and various kinds of socio-political pressures force the hands of the authorities to adopt a permissive stance. It is in this latter sense that excess increases in the supply of money are interpreted, at best, as a proximate and not the utlimate factor responsible for inflation. To locate these ultimate forces, it is argued, one must dig deeper, beneath the surface or behind the scene. Many monetarists will not deny this, but then will stress that looking at the behaviour of money supply should at least serve as a good starting point or an indicator for knowing the intensity of inflationary pressures/forces operating in the economy and the submission of the authorities to these pressures. We should also examine how far the proclaimed concern for social weal is no more than a smoke screen to benefit the gainers from inflation at the cost of losers from inflation.

NOTES

1. For social costs (or the effects) of inflation, see Gupta (1979, pp. 16–20).

2. K.N. Raj (1966) who attempted a Keynesian inflationary-gap explanation of price behaviour in India, *implicitly* assumed complete money illusion on the side of demand.

3. Note that, on the assumptions made in the text, it represents the rate at which the real demand for money is growing in the economy.

4. For the applicability of the QTM model to India, see Gupta (1979, pp. 41–3).

5. Profit-push inflation can induce wage-push inflation if workers hike up their wage demands to partake in the higher profits of their employers.

6. At times this proportion is measured by multiplying the relative weight of the commodity (say oil) in the price index number with the autonomous hike in its price. Suppose the weight is .08 and the price hike is 50%. Then the product of the two, which will equal 4%, will give only the *direct* impact on P of the hike in oil prices, assuming all other prices remain constant. But this is an unwarranted assumption, because other prices do not remain constant when the price of such an important commodity as oil goes up markedly.

7. For an application of this view to the Indian experience, see Pandit (1978).

CHAPTER 15

Theory of Money Supply

15.1 Introduction

So far we have assumed money supply to be policy - determined. This is not true, because the supply of money is determined jointly by the monetary authority, banks, and the public. No doubt, most of the time, in this determination the monetary authority plays the active and also the dominant role. But the role of the public and banks cannot be ignored, nor even taken for granted. Proper recognition and understanding of this role is important for a successful policy of monetary control. All this will become clear as we study the theory of money supply in the present chapter.

As a preliminary to the study of the theory of money supply, it is essential to understand the distinction between two kinds of money: *(a)* ordinary money (M) and *(b)* high-powered money (H). In Section 1.6 we have already discussed alternative empirical measures of money. They are all measures of ordinary money (M), or money as generally understood. There it was also stated that in this book we shall define M 'narrowly' as the sum of currency and demand deposits of banks (including the RBI) held by the public; and that since 'other deposits' of the RBI included in the measure of M are a very small proportion (less than one per cent) of the total supply of M, no harm will be done if in our future discussion we ignore these 'other deposits' of the RBI. For simplification of our theoretical discussion, this is what we shall do. Accordingly, for our theoretical analysis, we define

$$M = C + DD. \qquad (15.1)$$

High-powered money (H) is money produced by the RBI and the Government of India (small coins including one-rupee notes) and held by the public and banks. The RBI calls H 'reserve money'. H is the sum of *(i)* currency held by the public (C), *(ii)* cash reserves of banks (R), and *(iii)*'other deposits' of the RBI (OD). Again, for simplicity, we leave out of our theoretical analysis OD, as they constitute only about one per cent of total H. Accordingly, for our theoretical analysis, we define

$$H = C + R. \tag{15.2}$$

The empirical definition of H in (15.2) is by its uses or by its holders, not by its producers (the RBI and the government). At a later stage, we shall find it fruitful to look at H from the latter angle.

On comparing equations (15.1) and (15.2) we find that C is common to both M and H and that the only difference between the latter two is due to the second component of each, namely DD in M and R in H. This difference is of crucial importance for the theory of money supply. It arises from the presence of banks as the producers of demand deposits, which are counted as money at par with C. But to be able to produce DD, banks have to maintain R, which is a part of H, produced only by the monetary authority and not by banks themselves. Since in a fractional-reserve banking system, DD are a certain multiple of R, which are a component of H, it lends to H the quality of high-poweredness (as compared to M)— the power of serving as the base for the multiple creation of DD. For this reason, H is also called 'base money'. All this will be discussed in some detail in the sections to follow.

15.2 The H Theory of Money-Supply

There is near-unanimity among monetary economists around the theory of money supply that says that the single most important and dominant factor that determines money supply is H. For short, we shall call it the H theory of money supply. For reasons that will become clear in the sequel, it is also called the 'money-multiplier theory of money supply'. But we prefer to call it the H theory, because the entire theory is built around the demand and supply of H and the money-multiplier is only an outcome of this approach, not its starting point. Calling it the H theory focuses attention on the key variable in the whole drama of money-supply changes. It also provides the theory the standard technique of demand-supply analysis.

We shall discuss the H theory in a very simple form. This will be enough to bring out the main contours of the theory and its basic analytical thrust. For the present book, this is all that is required.

As a first approximation and provisionally, it is assumed that the supply of H (H^s) is policy-determined. Later on, we shall examine how far this is a correct assumption to make in the Indian context and in what sense. This assumption gives us

$$H^s = \bar{H}, \qquad (15.3)$$

where the bar above H signifies that it is given exogenously to the public and banks.

The analysis of the demand for H (H^d) is much the more important for the H theory. The key insight of the theory is to relate it to DD or M. Let us see how this is done.

We have already said above that H is demanded partly by the public as currency (C) and partly by banks as reserves (R). These are the only two sources of demand for H in our model. The demand for C (C^d) as a component of M is affected largely by the same factors as affect the demand for M, such as the level of income and the rate of interest, among other things. The same is true of the demand for DD (DD^d). Therefore as a first approximation, it is reasonable to assume that C^d and DD^d will be highly correlated—that C^d will be (say) a proportional function of DD.[1] This may be expressed as

$$C^d = c.\ DD. \qquad (15.4)$$

c, then, is the ratio of C^d to DD. For short, we shall call it the (desired) currency-deposit ratio of the public. c itself will express the preferences of the public as between currency and demand deposits of banks. As such, this itself will be affected by several factors which in turn reflect the relative advantages (and costs) of the two forms of money. Consequently it can vary over time, not only secularly but also from one season to the other. Therefore, c is a behavioural ratio. But for simple exposition of the H theory, we shall assume it to be a constant.

What about the bank's demand for reserves (R^d)? The reserves of banks are usually divided under two heads : *(a)* required reserves (RR) and *(b)* excess reserves (ER). Required reserves are reserves which banks are required *statutorily* to hold with the RBI. Banks have no choice about them. Under the law, the RBI is empowered to stipulate the statutory reserve ratio, which may be varied between 3 per cent and 15 per cent of the total demand and time liabilities of a bank. Every scheduled bank is required to maintain all its RR as balances with the RBI. All reserves in excess of RR are called ER

Banks are free to hold them as 'cash on hand' (also called 'vault cash') with themselves or as balances with the RBI.

Banks hold ER voluntarily. They are held to meet their currency drains (i.e. net withdrawal of currency by their depositors) as well as clearing drains (i.e. net loss of cash due to cross-clearing of cheques among banks). These drains may be partly expected and partly unexpected, giving rise to what may be called banks' transactions demand and precautionary demand for cash reserves. Thus, the standard theory of the demand for money can be applied to the banks' demand for excess reserves as well, which alone is their disposable cash. Our objective here is not to go into a detailed discussion of the banks' demand for excess reserves (ER^d). We only hypothesise that ER^d will be determined largely by the banks' total liabilities.

Thus, both RR and ER^d and so R^d become increasing functions of the total demand and time liabilities of banks. We can introduce a further simplification here. The demand and time liabilities of banks are predominantly (about 92 per cent of them) due to the demand and time deposits from the public. Moreover, this ratio between liabilities and deposits has remained stable over the past 20 years. Therefore, as a simplification, we can revise our earlier hypothesis and say that R^d is largely a proportional function of the total deposits of banks:

$$R^d = r.\,D. \tag{15.5}$$

r, then, is the ratio of R^d to total deposits of banks. For short, we shall call it the reserve-deposit ratio.

Let us now introduce in our model the important fact that bank deposits are of two kinds — demand deposits (DD) and time deposits (TD) (see Section 1.5.1). The former are counted as money; the latter not. Since we are interested in developing a theory of money supply, we must decide how to treat TD. The division between DD and TD is decided by the public, given the terms and conditions on which banks are willing to sell the two kinds of deposits to the public. In other words, it is the public who decides how much TD to hold in relation to DD.[a] Again, as a simplification, we hypothesise that TD^d is an increasing proportional function of DD:

$$TD^d = t.\,DD. \tag{15.6}$$

t, then, is the ratio of TD^d to DD. For short, we shall call it the time-deposit ratio. Since, by definition, D = DD + TD, the use of (15.6) gives us

$$D = (1+t)\,DD. \tag{15.7}$$

From (15.5) and (15.7) we have

$$R^d = r\,(1+t).\,DD \tag{15.8}$$

Recalling that $H_r^d = C_r^d + R^d$, from (15.4) and (15.8) we have

$$H_r^d = [c + r(1+t)]\,DD \tag{15.9}$$

Thus, $H_r^{d'}$ has been expressed as a function of DD and three behavioural ratios c,t, and r.

The market for H will be in equilibrium when $H^d = H^s$, or from (15.3) and (15.9) when

$$[c + r\,(1+t)].\,DD = H.$$

The above equation can be solved for DD to give

$$DD = \frac{1}{c + r\,(1+t)}\,H. \tag{15.10}$$

The above equation gives us the equilibrium value of DD in terms of H and the three behavioural ratios c,t, and r.[3] In the literature on money supply, the expression $1/c + r(1+t)$ is called the demand-deposit multiplier.

Next, from (15.1) and (15.4) and assuming that $C = C^d$ we have

$$M = \frac{1+c}{c + r\,(1+t)}\,H. \tag{15.11}$$

The above, ultimately, is the key equation of the H theory of money supply. It makes the supply of money a function of H and the three behavioural ratios c,t, and r. The expression $\frac{1+c}{c+r(1+t)}$ gives the value of what is known as the money multiplier. We shall denote it by m. Then, equation (15.11) can be more simply written as

$$M = m\,(\,)\,H. \tag{15.12}$$

The above equation sums up briefly, but very well, the main message of the H theory of money supply. From its form it can be seen why this theory can be and has been more popularly called the money-multiplier theory of money supply. More important, the equation says that the determinants of the supply of M can be meaningfully classified under two main heads: *(a)* those that affect H and *(b)* those that affect m. Thus, in the first instance, the equation serves well one of the useful functions of a theory—that of providing a filing or classificatory device for various factors affecting a dependent variable, as, for example, is done by the well-known theory of demand and supply of price determination under perfect competition. Whether the classificatory device suggested by the theory of equation (15.12) is empirically meaningful or not can be known only after a detailed examination of the factors governing H and the factors governing m and the extent to which the former can be meaningfully separated from the latter. We have already summed up the proximate determinants of m in equation (15.11). They are the three behavioural ratios c, t, and r. We shall say a little more about them later in the chapter and also about the factors governing H. From this discussion we shall see that whereas changes in H are largely policy-controlled, changes in m are largely endogenous, i.e. are such as depend mainly on the behavioural choices of the public and banks. This is a useful distinction, analytically as well as for monetary planning. It implies that, for policy purposes, the monetary authority will do well to take the behaviour of m as something outside its control and to concentrate its efforts on controlling H to control M.

We shall comment on equation (15.12) later in this chapter, because it is high time that we explain the economics of what we have already done. We shall do so with the help of diagrams. The discussion will throw much-needed further light on the forces determining money supply and its correlates (such as currency, demand deposits, and time deposits held by the public and reserves held by banks), given the supply of H.

Either of the two Figures 15.1 and 15.2 can be used to show the determination of money supply under the H theory. First consider

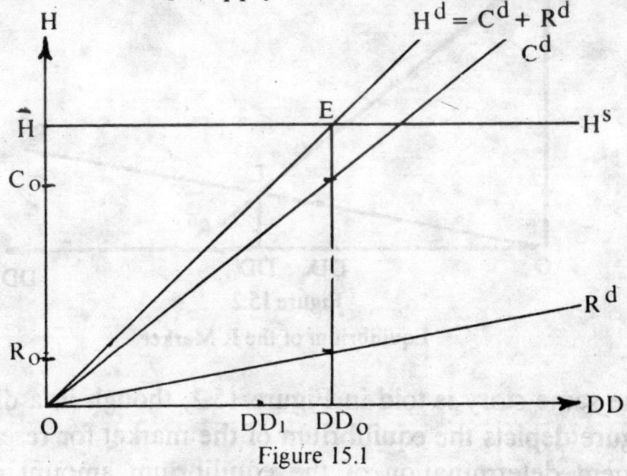

Figure 15.1
Equilibrium of the H Market

Figure 15.1. In it H is measured vertically and DD are measured horizontally. Since the supply of H is assumed to be given exogenously by the monetary authority at $\bar{H}$ (equation 15.3), the H^s curve is drawn parallel to the horizontal axis at the height $\bar{H}$, showing that H^s is perfectly inelastic to DD. The three demand curves in the market for H are upward-sloping straight lines going through the origin in accordance with the hypotheses of equations (15.4), (15.8), and (15.9). The C^d curve represents equation (15.4), with its slope equal to c. (In India at present the value of c is about one. So the C^d curve has been drawn to make an angle of about 45° with the horizontal axis.) the R^d curve represents equation (15.8). Its slope has the value of $r(1+t)$. The H^d curve is simply the vertical summation of the C^d and R^d curves. Thus, it represents equation (15.9).

The intersection of the H^d curve with the H^s curve gives the equilibrium of the H market. That is, at this point the public and banks are fully happy to hold all the amount of H the monetary authority chooses to place in the H market. In this situation, the equilibrium amount of DD, is that shown by DD_0 ; the public holds C_0 amount of currency and leaves the balance of H, that is, $\bar{H}-C_0 = R_0$ for banks to hold. For DD_0 amount, this is exactly equal to banks' R^d. It will also be noted that, given the C^d function, C_0 is exactly the amount of currency the public would like to hold when $DD = DD_0$.

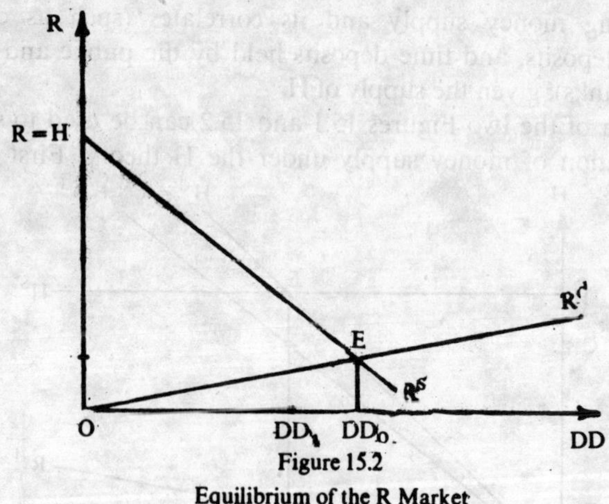

Figure 15.2

Equilibrium of the R Market

The same story is told in Figure 15.2, though in a different way. This figure depicts the equilibrium of the market for reserves and the consequent determination of the equilibrium amount of DD. The participants in this market are also the monetary authority, the public, and banks. On the demand side, the demand for reserves coming from banks is represented by the R^d curve (equation 15.8), as in Figure 15.1. The supply of R to banks is determined jointly by the monetary authority and the public. The monetary authority does so by fixing the total supply of H. Given $\overline{H}$, the public determines how much of H it would like to hold in the form of currency and how much to leave for banks to serve as their reserves. The decision is reflected in the C^d function (15.4). It is reasonable to assume that the public has first claim on H to meet its demand for currency, because banks always stand ready to convert their demand deposits into currency at par. Therefore, it is assumed that actual C held by the public is equal to their C^d. This makes banks only residual claimants for reserves. Consequently the supply of reserves to them is simply the excess of M^s over C^d.

$$R^s = H^s - C^d. \tag{15.13}$$

This is represented in Figure 15.2 by the downward - sloping R^s curve which is the vertical substraction of the C^d curve from the H^s curve in Figure 15.1 The intersection of the R^d and R^s curves in E (Figure 15.2) gives the equilibrium of R market. This equilibrium is attained when the amount of DD is DD_0— the same equilibrium amount of DD we had in Figure 15.1. This is as it should be, because Figure 15.2 has been derived from Figure 15.1 as explained above. In the former figure the amount of C is not shown. It has to be determined with the help of equation (15.4), given the equilibrium amount of DD_0.

Neither of the two figures shows the equilibrium amount of M produced or supplied. In Figure 15.1 it can be easily inferred, because we know the equilibrium values of C_0 and DD_0 that will be produced, given $\overline{H}$, and $M_0 = C_0 + DD_0$.

The crux of the above demonstration is the role the secondary expansion of money supply plays via the production of DD. The role of banks in money-supply changes also inheres in this. This will come out well when we study the money-multiplier process. But preparatory to this discussion and also to throw further light on what has preceded, we undertake the stability analysis of the equilibrium of the markets for H and R. This will also bring out clearly one crucial assumption of the H theory.

The stability analysis offers an opportunity for studying the disequilibrium behaviour of the system. For this, let us ask what will happen if, other things being the same, the public comes to hold DD_1 amount of demand deposits which are less than the equilibrium amount DD_0. At this value of DD, both R^d and C^d, and so their sum H^d will be lower than before (see Figure 15.1). H^s remaining the same, there will be excess supply of H in the H market. Correspondingly, there will be excess supply of R in the R market, as can be easily seen in Figure 15.2. What will be the consequences of this excess supply of R ? Before answering this question, it needs to be pointed out that the excess supply of R is not the same thing as excess reserves (ER), because desired excess reserves at each level of DD are already included in the R^d function. Therefore, the excess supply of R is called *undesired* ER.

Excess reserves, whether desired or undesired, do not earn banks any interest income. Therefore, banks try to get out of undesired excess reserves and move into earning assets (EA) as fast as they can. Earning assets are broadly sub-divided under two heads: *(i)* investments and *(ii)* loans and advances (see Section 5.4.3). Investments are made in marketable securities, whether government or private. The implicit assumption of the H theory of money supply is that the supply of earning assets to banks is very highly elastic around prevailing rates of interest and that banks are generally not deterred from moving into earning assets out of undesired excess reserves. In sum, one important assumption of the H theory is that banks restore equilibrium to their reserve holding pretty fast.

There was a time when the bulk of earning assets of banks consisted of loans and advances and investments in securities were negligibly small, because such securities had not grown in volume. The latter was the result of low level of corporate development as well as of government debt and securities market. In such a world, during depressions the demand for bank loans and advances could decline sharply and banks could stay loaded with undesired excess reserves. They did not have enough bankable earning assets to buy. The situation has been substantially different in recent times. For various reasons, most of the time, the market for bank loans suffers from excess demand rather than excess supply. Then, the investment market has grown significantly. Even if good corporate securities are in short supply, government bonds and bills are not. Ever since the government adopted the policy of planned economic development through the public sector in the early 1950s, it has been hard pressed for funds. That is, it has stood virtually ever ready to borrow from banks and others in the open market. The RBI as the manager of public debt has tried hard to widen the market for government debt as much as it can. To that end it has tried to keep orderly conditions in the market for government securities, avoid fluctuations in the prices of such securities, and even support it in time of need. This has meant virtual perfectly elastic supply of government securities of different maturities. Therefore, without any risk of capital loss in the short run, banks can afford to invest large amounts of funds in at least short-term government securities, especially treasury bills. This means that even if the demand for bank loans and advances slackens significantly, banks are not constrained to stay in undesired cash reserves; they can move into government securities as earning assets. Because of the stable conditions in the market for government securities (and the borrowing facilities against government securities as collateral extended by the RBI to banks), banks are not even encouraged to hold on to their surplus cash on grounds of speculation.

All this is confirmed strongly by relevant empirical evidence for India. The ratio of excess reserves to total demand and time liabilities of scheduled commercial banks declined continuously over the period of the 1950s from the high of 6.84 in 1950–51 to the low of 2.91 in 1960–61. The reasons of this decline were many and we need not go into them here. But the fact of continuous decline in the said ratio is important for our argument. Further, over the period 1960–61—1973–74, this ratio stabilised around the mean value of 2.73, with only minor fluctuations. It fell continuously over the next three years — from 2.58 in 1973–74 to 1.97 in 1976–77. All this goes to support our theoretical assumption about the capacity of banks to move into earning assets when they have undesired excess reserves and keep actual excess reserves equal to desired excess reserves. If this were not true we would have found large fluctuations in the excess reserves ratio.

After this rather lengthy digression spread over three paragraphs, we come back to our question of the fourth preceding paragraph : what will the banks do with their *undesired* ER ? Now we can confidently answer that they will invest and/or lend such ER. The borrowers from banks as well as sellers of securities (the government and others) will spend the funds received from banks. The recipients of funds so spent will retain a part in the form of currency and deposit the rest with banks, partly in demand deposits and partly in time deposits. How this division is made will depend upon the c ratio and the t ratio. The interesting thing to note is the consequent increase in DD, R^d and C^d. Thus, there will be a movement towards DD_0 from

DD_1. This movement will continue so long as banks possess undesired excess reserves. The movement will stop and the process of adjustment completed only when the original equilibrium is restored at DD_0 level of demand deposits. The reverse will happen when the banks are short of reserves.

15.3 The Money-Multiplier Process

Now we are in a position to discuss the money-multiplier process embedded in the H theory. It is called the multiplier process, because it is a process over time which ultimately results in multiple expansion or creation of bank credit, deposits and money from a given increase in H. It explains 'how banks create credit or deposits' when their reserve base increases. Thereby it also explains the source of the high-poweredness of H. We offer only a heuristic explanation of the process.[4]

For analytical simplification of the multiplier process, we shall first make a few simplifying assumptions and conduct the analysis with the help of a numerical example. Afterwards, we shall breathe greater reality in our discussion by removing the assumptions one by one and bringing out the role of each assumption in the analysis.

The simplifying assumptions are given below:

Some Simplifying Assumptions

1. That banks offer only one kind of deposits, namely, demand deposits (shown by D);
2. That the earning assets of banks comprise only loans to commercial borrowers (shown by L);
3. That the average as well as marginal value of the desired currency-deposit ratio (shown by c')=.5,
4. That the desired reserve-deposit ratio of banks (which includes both the required reserve ratio and their excess reserve ratio)=.1; and
5. That there is no dearth of the demand for bank loans at the going lending rate of banks, so that banks can remain 'fully loaned up' all the time. This, then, gives only the maximum value of the multiplier, not necessarily its true value.

The underlying basis of the multiplier process is the fractional reserve system of commercial banking, which is itself based on the common experience of banks (a) that not all depositors come to withdraw all their deposits at the same time—a matter of faith in the continued liquidity and solvency of banks and (b) that if there are outflows of some deposits, there are inflows of fresh deposits every day, so that a bank need keep only a certain fraction of total deposits in the form of cash reserves and the rest can be either loaned out or invested to earn income.

Now suppose that the public comes in possession of Δ H worth Rs. 60 crores, because (say) the government spends this amount on the purchase of goods and services from the public. Further suppose that all this payment is made in the form of cheques drawn on the RBI. The public deposits these cheques with their banks for collection. The banks, after collection, credit the deposit accounts of their clients. Thereby, each of the D of the public and R with banks increases by Rs. 60 crores. But, by our assumption of constant currency-deposit ratio (c) of .5, the public withdraws Rs. 20 crores from banks in currency and leaves only Rs. 40 crores worth of D and R with banks. Alternatively, we could have started the story by simply saying that the public comes in possession of additional currency (or Δ H) worth Rs. 60 crores, Rs. 20 crores of which they keep with themselves in the form of currency and deposit the rest (Rs. 40 crores) with banks, so that they maintain the value of their desired c at .5.

The crucial point is that either way the banks come in possession of Δ R worth Rs. 40 crores through their sale of deposits of equal value. Such deposits that bring in new reserves to banks are called *primary deposits*. The multiple creation of credit, deposits and money starts with the receipt of the new reserves—Δ R of Rs. 40 crores in the example. Till now nothing of the sort has happended.

Now, the banks find it neither necessary nor profitable to hold on to all the Δ R of Rs. 40 crores, as these reserves do not earn them any interest income. According to their desired reserve ratio (r) of .1, they need keep only Rs. 4 crores with them, and lend the rest (Rs. 36 crores) to the borrowers on interest. (We have already assumed above that the demand for bank loans at the going lending rate of banks is perfectly elastic.) When the banks lend Rs. 36 crores, this constitutes the first round of their credit creation. Since the deposit liabilities of banks are a part of money supply in the economy, the banks do not (have to) pay their borrowers in the form of cash. All that they do is to allow their borrowers to draw cheques upon their loan/credit accounts with concerned banks upto the maximum amounts of loans or credit granted.

This is where another feature of commercial banking comes to the fore. When the borrowers spend the loan amount in the market, the recipients of payments withdraw in currency only a part of these payments and deposit the rest with banks. How much they withdraw in currency will depend on the desired value of c of the public. In the example, we have assumed it to be 0.5. So, the public withdraws Rs. 12 crores in the form of currency and deposit Rs. 24 crores back with banks. (The usual form of realizing payment of a cheque is to deposit it for collection in one's account with a bank. This way, though individual banks are subjected to clearing drains, most of the cash—except that represented by currency drain—stays with banks as a whole. This is a unique feature of the chequable deposits of banks—a feature which makes them serve as means of payment.)

The currency withdrawal from banks is called *currency drain* (for banks) and the return flow of deposits represents accretion of *secondary deposits*. These deposits are different from primary deposits in that they do not bring in any new reserves to banks. Rather they have been created out of loans (or credit) extended by the banks themselves, as should be clear from the above example. (For individual banks or depositors, however, the distinction between primary and secondary deposits is of no significance or relevance, as they have no means of knowing which is which, most of the time. For example, instead of writing a cheque on my account and depositing it with another bank, I may withdraw cash from one and deposit it in another bank. But, for understanding the process of multiple creation of credit, deposits and money for the banking system as a whole, the distinction is of great analytical significance.)

With the accretion of secondary deposits of Rs. 24 crores, the second-round increase in deposits and money has taken place. (It had started with loan-making or credit extension by banks.) When the banks receive Rs. 24 crores of (secondary) deposits, this indicates that out of the first-round credit of Rs. 36 crores, they have lost only Rs. 12 crores as currency drain to the public. That is, if they have Rs. 24 crores of new (or additional) deposit liabilities, they are also left with Rs. 24 crores of Δ R with them. But not all of it can be lent out. Against Δ D of Rs. 24 crores they have to keep Δ R of Rs. 2.4 crores (at the value of .1 of reserve-deposit ratio). Then, the surplus or undesired excess reserves with them will be of the value of Rs.21.6 (=24–2.4) crores. Banks lend this again, which represents second-round creation of credit for them. Again, as the loan proceeds are spent by the borrower, the recipients of payments redeposit with banks only Rs. 14.4 crores and withdraw from banks Rs. 7.2 crores in cash to add to their holdings of currency. This currency drain reduces the surplus excess reserves with banks from Rs. 21.6 crores to Rs. 14.4 crores, the amount exactly equal to third-round gain of deposits by banks.

The above process goes on in several rounds of credit creation and creation of deposits and money. But in each round the amounts of credit, deposit, and money become smaller and smaller. As in the Keynesian theory of expenditure multiplier, each series of expansion of credit, deposits, and money is an infinite geometric series. But since each involves a positive common factor of the value of less than one, each series can be summed up. The summation gives the value of the relevant multiplier (see Gupta, 1979, Appendix D).

In our example, the rounds of expansion of D will be (in Rs. crores) 40, 24, 14.4.... They will sum to $\frac{1}{c+r} \cdot \Delta H$ or $\frac{1}{0 \cdot 5 + 0 \cdot 1} \times$ Rs. 60 crores = Rs. 100 crores.

The rounds of expansion of bank credit (in Rs. crores) will be given by 36, 21.6, 12.96... They will sum to $\frac{1-r}{c+r} \cdot \Delta H$ or $(1-r) . \Delta D$ = Rs. 90 crores.

Similarly, on summation, the expansion of money supply will be given by $\frac{1+c}{c+r} \cdot \Delta H = 2.5$. Rs $\times$60 crores = Rs. 150 crores.

In the above example, the respective multipliers are

(a) deposit multiplier $= \frac{1}{c+r} = \frac{1}{.6} = 1.667$

(b) bank credit multiplier $= \frac{1-r}{c+r} = 1.5$ and

(c) money multiplier $= \frac{1+c}{c+r}$ 2.5.

We should also note that the multiplier process is a process over time—that the several rounds of expansion of deposits and credit are not completed in one day. Then the changes in H—its injections and withdrawals through (say) budgetary and other operations—take place all the time. Consequently, the expansion in deposits as well as in bank credit over any short period is also the cumulative effect of several short-period Δ Hs, past and present.

We may now explain briefly the consequences of relaxing the assumptions made above one by one.

1. *When banks also offer time deposits* (or TD). This is also true of real life. In this event, we may simplify the whole discussion by assuming (a) that the desired currency ratio of the public relates not merely to demand deposits but to total deposits. We represent this ratio by c^* and assume its value to be only .3. The star ($*$) on c is used to indicate

that, due to the presence of TDs, c^* is different from c. Whereas c was defined above as the ratio of currency to only demand deposits—the only kind of deposits allowed so far—c^* is defined here as the ratio of currency to total deposits which include time deposits as well. To emphasise this point, we have also assumed a different (lower) value of c^*. (We have used c^* in place of c, because it simplifies greatly the explanation of the multiplier process in the presence of TDs. Due to the redefinition of c as c^*, we do not require separately the t ratio, i.e. the ratio of time deposits to demand deposits, of the previous section.

Thereby, of course, the expressions for multipliers also change, as they do not involve the t ratio. Novertheless, the simpler explanation of the multiplier process holds. Only its analytical richness is reduced somewhat. A lower value of c^* is assumed, because time deposits attract more savings of the public than merely demand deposits. It is further assumed that money is defined broadly as $M_3 = M_1 + TD$ of banks, and that the reserve ratio of banks does not undergo any change, since in India, the cash reserve ratio (CRR) is the same for all kind of deposits.

Then, the deposit multiplier will still be given by $1/c + r$, though, with change in the value of c $(=c^* = .3)$, its numerical value will increase to $1/.4 = 2.5$. Along with this, the value of the bank credit multiplier will increase to $.9 \times 2.5 = 2.25$ and the money multiplier $(= (1+c/(c+r))$ will attain the value $(1.3)\ (2.5) = 3.25$.

2. *That banks also invest in securities.* Banks do so mainly in government and 'other approved securities' and thereby provide credit to these parties. Thus, earning assets include both loans and investments. This widens greatly the demand for bank credit and makes the satisfaction of assumption 5 in India much easier.

The purchase of government securities, new or old, requires one modification in the verbal explanation of the multiplier process offered above. It arises from the fact that all transactions with the government or the RBI are settled in H—the only kind of money in which these agencies deal. Since neither the government nor the RBI operates any kind of loan or deposit account with banks, the latter have to pay to the RBI for purchases of government securities made in terms of H, that is, by drawing cheques of appropriate value on their deposits with the RBI. Thereby, the banks incur drain of reserves, rupee for rupee.

However, as in the case of bank loans to commercial borrowers, as and when the government spends the proceeds of bank credit to it, the public comes in possession of new H or Δ H. It was at this point that we had started our story of the multiplier process. It may also be noted that the budgetary operations of the government (the central as well as state governments), involving receipts from several tax and non-tax sources and expenditures of a wide variety go on all the time. Therefore, the flows of H into and out of the public and banks to government account are also a regular occurrence. What matters is the net position of individual banks each day and bankers keep a close watch on it and take remedial measures in time.

(4) *Borrowed reserves.* One special case of credit creation deserves separate mention. This refers to the extra power of 'borrowed reserves' (BR)—i.e., the reserves banks borrow from the RBI—to create credit. Suppose banks borrow Rs. 60 crores from the RBI. Under the rules, banks are not required to deposit any cash reserves with the RBI against such borrowed reserves. So, all of them serve as loanable resource for banks and they use them as such. This (full value of BR), then, represents the extra amount of bank credit which BR help create. At this stage, there has been neither any drain of cash in reserves of banks nor in the additional currency holding of the public. The latter arises only when the borrowers spend additional bank credit and the public comes in possession of BR as so much Δ H (of which it decides to withdraw a part in currency and deposit the rest with banks for which banks keep cash reserves). The earlier story of the multiple expansion of D, M and bank credit starts from this point onwards and it still holds true thereafter. Consequently, the values of the deposit multiplier and the money multiplier stay unchanged; it is only the value of the credit multiplier that undergoes a change. The latter increases by the value of 1. In the example, with only one kind of deposits, it increases from the value of 1.5 to 2.5. (When TDs are offered by banks and currency is taken as a ratio of total deposits with the value of .3, the bank-credit multiplier worked out was 2.25. Now this will have the value of 3.25.)

The above analysis is similar to the distinction between expenditure multiplier and tax multiplier of the well-known Keynesian income-expenditure theory, in which the expenditure multiplier is greater than the tax multiplier by the value of 1, giving the balanced-budget-multiplier the value of 1.

(3) *If no currency drain.* If currency drain is either totally ruled out or neglected, it will be seen that the initial amoun of Δ H of Rs. 60 crores will all be deposited with banks and increase their reserves. The only cash drain will be in the form of additional desired reserves given by the ratio of .1 as *r*. Then, the deposit multiplier will be equal to $1/r = 10$, giving Δ D = 10 × Rs. 60 crores = Rs. 600 crores. The credit

multiplier will be equal to $(1-r)/r$, i.e., = 9, giving $\triangle$ BC = 9 × Rs. 60 crores = Rs. 540 crores.

4. *Assumed values of c and r.* From the formulas for various multipliers it should be clear that their values depend upon the values of *c* and *r*. If the assumed values of *c* and *r* are different from their true values, the predicted value of each multiplier will also be in error. So, the behaviour of *c* and *r* needs to be analysed in terms of their respective determinants to be able to predict as correctly as possible the true values of *c* and *r*. (see the next Section on this point.)

(5) *Inadequate demand for bank* credit. Banks at times may be loaded with undesired excess reserves, if the demand for bank loans and advances from acceptable parties is not adequate to make the banks fully loaned up. (For this, we may further assume that banks hesitate investing surplus funds in marketable securites for fear of incurring capital losses from sales of such securites to be able later to lend the funds so realized.) This will raise actual r and lower the realized value of each of the multipliers below its maximum value.

15.4 Determinants of the Money Multiplier

We have already said above that the money multiplier (m) is a function of three behavioural asset ratios: c, t, and r. In the literature on money supply they are called the *proximate determinants* of m. Since they are behavioural asset ratios, they are themselves functions of other variables, such as several rates of interest, the spread of banking facilities in the country, especially rural areas, holdings of black money, etc. These last-mentioned factors are the *ultimate* determinants of m, and impinge on it by affecting first one or more of the asset ratios. This provides a well-ordered structure to the theory of the money multiplier and a systematic way of analysing the influence of myriad of forces influencing the supply of money (see Gupta, 1979, Appendix D).

15.5 Factors Affecting H

So far we have assumed H as policy-determined and so exogenously given. It is not as simple as that in actual life. To know the truth, we examine the factors affecting H in this section. The whole discussion relates to India of 1970s.

We recall that H is money produced by the monetary authority (the government and the RBI) and held by the public and banks. Speaking concretely, it is government currency plus the Reserve Bank money (RBM hereafter)—all held by the public and banks. Government currency comprises one-rupee notes and coins and small coins. The RBM comprises all currency notes other than one-rupee notes, deposits of banks with the RBI, and 'other deposits' of the RBI. Of the total stock of H, government currency constitutes a rather small proportion (only 7.3 per cent in 1975–76); the RBM is its dominant component. Then, changes in government currency are determined by changes in the RBM, as they are governed by the public's demand for small coins in relation to currency of higher denominations issued by the RBI. Therefore, changes in the RBM are virtually responsible for all the observed changes in H. We analyse below the factors governing the RBM, since the RBI does not change it completely arbitrarily. What is given here is a purely accounting analysis. This is only a necessary first step in understanding the complex of forces operating on H, not the final analysis.

We begin with the balance-sheet identity for the RBI in the following form:

$$\text{monetary liabilities} + \text{non-monetary liabilities} = \text{financial assets} + \text{other liabilities.}$$

Let us define 'net non-monetary liabilities' (NNML) as the excess of non-monetary liabilities over other assets. Then, the above identity can be rewritten as

$$\text{monetary liabilities} = \text{financial assets - net non-monetary liabilities.} \tag{15.14}$$

Monetary liabilities of the RBI are the same thing as the RBM. Therefore, the factors governing the RBM are the same that govern the entities on the right-hand side of (15.14). Financial assets are what the RBI acquires as a result of its transactions with others in discharge of its central-banking functions. So they can be broken down sector-wise. A similar sector-wise breakdown of the net non-monetary liabilities is not available in the books of the RBI. So, the RBI does not unscramble them.

To identify the proximate factors governing H, all the RBI's transactors may be divided into four sectors, viz. *(1)* the government *(2)* banks, *(3)* development banks, and *(4)* the foreign sector. The RBI provides them its credit, acquires its financial assets, and creates RBM in the process. Therefore, using this four-sector classification of the RBI's financial assets (or net credit) and denoting Reserve Bank credit by RBC, (15.14) can be rewritten as:

RBM = (1) net RBC to government
+ (2) RBC to banks
+ (3) RBC to development banks
+ (4) net foreign exchange assets of the RBI
− (5) net non-monetary liabilities of the RBI. (15.15)

Then, the five factors (with appropriate algebraic signs) listed above are the *proximate* factors governing the RBM.

Each of these proximate factors is explained briefly below:

(1) Net RBC to government. As banker to the government, the RBI provides credit to both the Central Government and state governments through investment in their securities (including treasury bills of the Central Government) and through short-term advances to state governments. The Central Government is empowered to borrow any amount it likes from the RBI. The state governments do not enjoy such unlimited borrowing power. Yet often times they do borrow above authorised limits and thus give birth to the problem of unauthorised overdrafts. The Central and state governments keep their deposits with the RBI. The value of these deposits is deducted from the gross RBC to the government to arrive at the net figure for this RBC. Increase in the net RBC to the government is a rough (not exact) measure of the deficit financing of the government. Among the factors affecting H, this factor has been the most important, contributing more than three-fourths of the increase in H.

(2) RBC to banks. The RBI provides credit to banks through loans and advances against government securities, usance bills or promissory notes as collateral, and through the purchase or rediscounting of internal commercial bills as well as treasury bills. The RBI, however, does not regard its purchase or rediscounting of bills for banks as a part of its credit to banks. Instead, it classifies it as RBC to whatever sector, commercial or government, which issued these bills in the first instance. This is not a defensible procedure, because thereby a part of the Reserve Bank accommodation provided directly to banks is not counted as such.

(3) RBC to development banks. A number of development banks (see Chapter 8) have been established in the country through the initiative and help of the RBI for the provision of long and medium-term finance to industry and agriculture. The RBI provides them credit by investing in their securities and through loans. This also leads to the generation of H.

(4) Net foreign exchange assets of the RBI. These assets which are net holding of the RBI represent RBC to the foreign sector, because they are financial liabilities of the foreign sector. Most of these assets are held abroad in the form of foreign securities and cash balances. The RBI comes to acquire them as the custodian of the country's foreign exchange reserves. As the controller of all foreign exchange transactions, whether on private or government account, it regularly buys and sells foreign exchange against Indian currency. All such transactions have a direct impact on H. When the RBI buys foreign exchange, it pays for it in terms of its own money and the supply of H in the economy increases. When the RBI sells foreign exchange, it receives payment from the buver of foreign exchange or its bank in the form of H and the supply of H goes down. Since the buying and selling of foreign exchange by the RBI goes on all the time, what matters for a change in H is the difference between the two. Thus, a deficit in the balance of payments decreases the supply of H, whereas a surplus in it increases the supply of H, other things being the same. That is why, the vast accumulation of foreign exchange reserves (mainly due to large inward remittances from Indians working abroad) in recent years (after 1975) had led to substantial increases in H and thereby in M. For the same reason, if the accumulated foreign exchange reserves are drawn down by spending abroad, the result will normally be anti-inflationary on two counts. On the one hand, the supply of H and so of M and therefore of the aggregate money demand for output will go down: on the other hand, the import surplus will increase the supply of goods in the market.

(5) Net non-monetary liabilities of the RBI. The net RBC to various sectors that we have been talking about under the above four points is financed by the RBI partly by creating its monetary liabilities (RBM) and partly by its net non-monetary liabilities (NNML), which financed as much as 25 per cent of the net RBC during 1976–77. The NNML, in large part, are owned funds of the RBI (capital and reserves and accumulated contributions to National Funds) and compulsory deposits of the public. Obviously, the larger these non-monetary resources of the RBI, the less it has to depend upon the creation of new H to finance its credit to various sectors. Hence this factor enters equation (15.15) with negative sign.

15.6 Adjusted H.

So far we have been talking about H and the statutorily required cash reserve ratio (CRR) for banks without asking what changes in the latter do to the former. It is, however, clear that, given the amount of total H, such changes affect the amount of *disposable* H available to the public and banks, because these changes either impound or release reserves of banks. When the CRR is revised upwards, some reserves are impounded by the RBI and when the CRR is revised downwards, some reserves get released. Obviously, impounding of reserves reduces and release of H adds to the amount of disposable H. In the literature on money supply analysis, such disposable H is generally called *adjusted* H. In this book we shall denote it by H*. In the presence of changes in CRR, it is H*, not H, which is relevant for the theory of money supply spelled out above.

15.7 Is H an Autonomous Policy-determined Variable ?

Now we are in a position to ask and answer a very important question concerning the H theory: Is H an autonomous, policy-determined variable ? While developing the H theory, in equation (15.3), we had assumed that H was exogenously determined by the monetary authority. This is only partially true, as we shall see in this section.

First of all, we should define carefully the term 'monetary authority'. Quite often it is used synonymously with the central bank of a country. This might be a correct view for a country like the USA where the central bank (the Federal Reserve System of the USA) is autonomous of the government. But this is not a correct view for India, where the RBI as the country's central bank is not autonomous of the government. In particular, as we have already said above, the RBI is obliged to lend whatever amount the Central Government chooses to borrow from it; even the state governments can go on drawing unauthorised overdrafts from the RBI with impunity. Thus, for all practical purposes, the RBI has no control over the deficit financing of the government. In other words, the government shares monetary authority actively with the RBI. Therefore, in the Indian context, it is imperative to define the term monetary authority broadly to comprise the RBI and the government.

H is not a fully policy-determined variable, because it is the decision of both the authorities and the public as well as banks which lead to the generation or destruction of H. For example, banks and development banks can change H within narrow limits by varying their borrowing from the RBI; net purchases or sales of foreign exchange by the public also change H. Despite all this, it is not wrong to say that, because of the vast powers of monetary control enjoyed by the RBI and the government, net variations in the stock of H* (i.e., adjusted H) are directly within the close control of the authorities, so that H* can be claimed to be a policy-controlled variable, though not a direct policy or control instrument.

We may classify all changes in H under two broad heads: *(1)* autonomous or discretionary changes and *(2)* endogenous or non-discretionary changes. Symbolically we represent the former by ΔH_1 and the latter by ΔH_2, so that

$$\Delta H_1 + \Delta H_2 = \Delta H. \tag{15.16}$$

Autonomous changes in H are determined directly by the policy-making authorities— the government and the RBI. Among the sources of change in H studied in the previous section, they are *(1)* changes in the RBM due to the government *(2)* changes in the discretionary component of the RBM due to banks and development banks, and *(3)* net purchases or sales of foreign exchange (and gold) by the government.

Endogenous changes in H are decided by the public, banks, and development banks, given the terms and conditions under which the RBI is willing to produce such changes. They arise as a result of the performance of certain central-banking functions by the RBI towards the public and banks: for example, its transactions with the public as the controller of the country's foreign exchange reserves or its function as bankers' bank. Thus, among the sources of change in H discussed in the previous section, endogenous changes in H are *(1)* changes in government currency held by the public—they are decided by the public and not by the government because the public has the option of converting at par government currency into the Reserve Bank currency without any restriction, *(2)* changes in the non-discretionary component of the RBM due to banks and development banks, and *(3)* net purchases or sales of foreign exchange by the public.

The above discussion shows that not all of H or ΔH is an autonomous, policy-determined variable; only H_1 or ΔH_1 is. In traditional economic analysis, therefore, it is taken as given. But in a 'political-economic' analysis, it will deserve to be explained. H_2 and ΔH_2 are endogenous variables. As such, their behaviour can be analysed in accordance with traditional economic theory. We do not undertake any of these tasks, because in this introductory discussion of the H theory, it will mean going to far. What is important to recognise is that it is the presence of ΔH_2 which creates the need for monetary control by the monetary authority. If all ΔH is ΔH_1, there will be very little left for the monetary-control measures to control, because, by assumption, all ΔH will be desired ΔH. It is here that the distinction between the RBI and the government as two seperate agencies constituting monetary authority becomes important. The government on budgetary considerations may resort to excessive deficit financing—by now a normal feature in India. Then, the RBI may be called upon to take offsetting measures to contain the excessive expansion of H and thereby of M.

15.8 Reserve Bank's Analysis of Money Supply

The RBI does not follow explicitly any theory of money supply either in its verbal explanations or in its data presentation. Instead, it publishes every month a purely accounting analysis of what it calls factors affecting money supply, or 'sources of change in money supply' in the form of a table in its *Bulletin*. All the so-called money-supply analysis of the RBI, other official agencies, and unfortunately also of most academic economists follows uncritically this table. Thus, a purely accounting analysis has usurped the place of any theory of money supply. This is most unfortunate for a proper understanding of the forces operating on money as well as for the correct formulation of any monetary policy. Before offering a fuller explanation of these points, let us see what the RBI's accounting analysis is. This is reproduced below.

Sources of Change in Money Supply

1. *Net bank credit to government* (A + B)
   A. RBI's net credit to Government (i - ii)
   (i) Claims on government
   (ii) Government deposits with RBI.
   B. Other banks' credit to government.

2. *Bank credit to commercial sector* (A + B)
   A. RBI's credit to commercial sector
   B. Other banks's credit to commercial sector

3. *Net foreign exchange assets of banking sector* (A + B)
   A. RBI's net foreign exchange assets
   B. Other bank's net foreign exchange assets

4. *Government's currency liabilities to the public*

5. *Net non-monetary liabilities of banking sector* (A + B + C)

A. Time deposits with banks

B. Net non-monetary liabilities of RBI

C. Other net non-monetary liabilities of banks.

In terms of the above factors, then,

$$M = 1 + 2 + 3 + 4 - 5.$$

The above table is derived by taking the consolidated balance sheet of the banking sector as a whole (the RBI and banks) and breaking down its financial assets sector-wise in the same manner as we did for our discussion of the 'factor affecting H' in Section 15.5.

The main points of criticism of the aforesaid (accounting) analysis of money supply are summed up below.

1. Since the RBI's analysis is a purely accounting or *ex post* one, it has no explanatory power of its own. That is, it cannot 'explain' the consequences (for money supply) of various policy and non-policy autonomous changes, such as the open market operations of the RBI, or changes in the statutory reserve requirement for banks, or changes in net foreign aid, etc., much less explain how and why such autonomous changes affect the supply of money. All that it does is measure changes in the stock of money after they have occurred (not predict them beforehand) and allocate the measured change to different sectors, factors, or sources according to a particular scheme of classification.

But a mere classification of the data provides no explanation. Nor is a particular accounting scheme of data presentation any substitute for theory. Nor does it obviate the need for a theory, however crude, for understanding the money supply mechanism or the way several forces operate to bring about changes in the supply of money, and for monetary planning. Obviously, before the RBI uses a particular monetary-control measure, it must know how this measure is likely to function and its likely effect on the quantity of money supply.

We may support the above argument by an analogy drawn from the well-known fields of national income measurement and determination. It is well accepted by now that national income measurement is a problem of (social) accounting and that national income determination is a problem of economic theory. Since *ex post* total income is identically equal to total expenditure in a closed economy, one way to measure national income (Y) is to measure total national expenditute. Among several possibilities, the latter can be taken as the sum of private consumption expenditure (C), private investment expenditure (I), and government expenditure (G). This gives Y= C+I+G. Thus, income is measured in terms of the components of expenditure. From the income-expenditure identity if follows arithmetically that, *ex post,* increase in any one of the component expenditures, C,I, or G, will be matched by an equal increase in Y.

But this is a purely tautological statement, true by definition, and thus devoid of any explanatory content. It does not tell us whether *ex ante* it is the increase in C which leads to an increase in Y, or *vice versa,* or it is the increase in some other factor which lies at the root of increase in both C and Y. But this is what a genuine theory should explain. For example, the Keynesian theory of national income *determination* explains what factors lead to changes in Y and why. In its simplest form, both I and G are assumed to be autonomous of Y. Together they are called autonomous expenditure (A). C is assumed to be an increasing function of Y. Since A is assumed to be autonomous of Y, changes in A can occur independently of changes in Y. It is these changes in A which bring about induced changes in Y and C via the well-known multiplier process. Thus, changes in both C and Y are explained by autonomous changes in A.

These arguments are fully applicable to the analysis of factors affecting money supply. We have stated earlier that the RBI analysis is only an exercise in *ex post* measurement and therefore cannot serve the purpose of a theory. But if we are genuinely interested in explaining changes in money supply, we must have recourse to some theory of money supply. One such theory has been spelt in Section 15.2. In the first instance, such a theory attempts to explain changes in M in terms of changes in H and in m. In addition, it tells us what lies behind changes in m and how to explain them in terms of their determinants — proximate and ultimate. Changes in H were traced to their several sources, using only accounting analysis. In a fuller study, the nature of each source can (and should) be examined and explained either as a policy variable, as an endogenous variable, or as an exogenous variable.

2. The RBI's accounting analysis adds up components of H and M, ignoring the dependence of the latter on the former. The result has been a total denial of any money-multiplier process or of the 'secondary' expansion of money and credit by banks induced by reserves accretion— something which any monetary economist or even the RBI has never seriously denied. As a result, the accounting

table has been a rich source of erroneous propositions, some of which are examined below:

(i) that 'the government sector's total impact on money supply is equal to its total budget deficit minus its net purchase of foreign exchange from the RBI'. This is wrong, because what the latter sum measures is the effect on H, not on M. The supply of M increases by a certain multiple of the increase in H, depending upon the value of the money multiplier m;

(ii) that 'increase in other banks' credit to the government leads to an equivalent increase in money supply'. This is not correct, because increase in other banks' credit to the government only reallocates banks' credit in favour of the government at the cost of the commercial sector, leaving the total supply of M as well as banks' credit practically unchanged. The last part of this statement is explained under the next point;

(iii) that 'bank credit to the commercial sector is an important factor contributing to the expansion of money supply. Bank credit in such statements usually includes both the RBI credit and the credit from banks. The causal role of the former in the expansion of money supply is understandable; but not so the role of the credit from banks. The latter is as much a dependent variable as the total money supply. Therefore, to say that money supply increased *because* banks' credit (whether to the government or the commercial sector) increased is not true. Nor does it explain anything. It only moves the enquiry about the money-supply increase one step backward. Now, the question must be asked: how could banks increase their credit? Do they have unlimited power to increase credit or is it limited by something? To say that banks could increase their credit because their deposits grew clearly contradicts the earlier assertion that an increase in bank credit causes an increase in money supply (which includes demand deposits of banks). Also, it is no solution to say so, because then we have only to re-word our previous question and ask: why did the bank deposits grow[8]? Either way we must locate some autonomous change which induces banks to increase their credit and, in the process, deposits as well. The answer is provided by the H theory of money supply (Sections 15.2 and 15.3).

3. The RBI's accounting table suppresses completely the RBI credit to banks as a factor affecting money supply, because in consolidating the assets and liabilities of the banking system as a whole it gets cancelled out as an internal transaction. But this is patently wrong, because the borrowings of banks from the RBI do increase H and thereby M.

The only way open to the RBI to disabuse money-supply analysis in India from these and similar errors and consequent faults in policy-making is to jettison its accounting approach to money-supply analysis and its concrete embodiment in the accounting table given earlier in this section.

NOTES

1. Alternatively, the correlation of C^d with M can be used and the H theory built on it. We do not follow that route. The results of both the routes are the same. But we find the route adopted in the text pedagogically better. The later diagrammatic exposition of the H theory comes out better with it.

2. Since both TD^d and DD^d are affected mainly by the same factors of the level of income and the rate of interest, it is open to us to relate TD^d to DD and only via the latter to income and the rate of interest. As said earlier, this is also the key insight of the H theory of money supply—to relate H^d or its components to DD. Relating TD^d to DD will move us in that direction.

3. Using equations (15.7) and (15.10), we can easily solve for total deposits (D).

4. A more rigorous statement is given in Gupta (1979, pp. 207-9), where the deposit multiplier is derived explicitly as the sum of infinite rounds of expansion of deposits initiated by an autonomous injection of a rupee of H.

5. For a detailed discussion, see Gupta (1979, Chapter 4).

6. Accordingly, H_1 and H_2 will represent autonomous and endogenous components of H respectively.

7. This section is based on Gupta (1976a, 1976b, and 1979, Sections 3.4 and 3.5).

8. 'Do loans make deposits or deposits make loans'? is a well-known puzzle in banking theory. The answer is also well-known. At the level of an individual small bank, it would be broadly true to say that deposits make loans. But at the macro level both deposits and credit are jointly-determined (or interdependent) variables. Neither is a cause of the other; both are the results of H and the asset preferences of the public.

CHAPTER 16

The Supply of Credit and its Allocation

16.1 Introduction

This chapter is devoted to a discussion of two main topics : *(a)* the theory of the supply of total bank credit and *(b)* the factors governing the inter-borrower allocation of institutional credit. The former will be seen as a straight-forward application of the theory of money supply, discussed in the previous chapter. The multiplier analysis can be suitably extended to cover the supply of credit of non-bank financial institutions as well. But the assumptions for such an extension will be too heroic, which we are not prepared to make and defend. Bringing other factors into the analysis will complicate it too much for the general level of discussion adopted in this book. We shall, therefore, not go into the theoretical determination of the supply of non-bank institutional credit. Given the dominance of banks in India's organized financial sector, this will not be much of a loss.

The problem of the inter-borrower allocation of credit is no less important than that of its total size. Here we shall not distinguish between bank and non-bank institutional credit, but offer a general discussion of the main factors governing the allocation of all institutional credit. Broadly speaking, the discussion will hold good for the allocation of non-institutional credit as well.

16.2 The Theory of Bank Credit and Bank Deposits

To start with, we should note that bank credit and bank deposits are very closely related with each other; that they represent, roughly speaking, two sides of the same coin, the balance sheets of banks. In the past there has been some controversy among monetary economists on the nature of relationship between the two, on which of the two is the cause and which is the effect. This is best summed up in the puzzle: 'Do loans make deposits or deposits make loans?'

Two kinds of answers have been given for the puzzle. One says that from the point of view of a single small bank it is more true to say that 'deposits make loans', but from the point of view of the banking system as a whole or a monopoly bank it is more true to say that 'loans make deposits'. In other words, a single small bank lends what it collects as deposits, whereas the banking system as a whole collects what it lends.

The second answer is different from the first. Concentrating on the banking system as a whole, it views the relationship between bank deposits and credit as a circular one and not one-way, so that it is true to say both that deposits make loans and that loans make deposits. A parallel example is provided by the circular flow of income and expenditure emphasised in the Keynesian theory of income determination. In both cases, the variables in question (e.g., bank deposits and credit in the present case) are jointly-determined (or interdependent) variables; neither is a cause or effect. Both are determined by third (autonomous) factors and cretain behavioural relations of the system. The task of theory is to identify these third factors and behavioural relations and explain how the interaction of these factors and relations determine the dependent variables of our interest, bank deposits and credit. Our task of providing such a theory is greatly simplified by the 'H theory of money supply' and the 'H theory of bank deposits' discussed in the previous chapter, because the determination of money supply, bank deposits, and bank credit are highly correlated.

We spell out briefly what we may call the 'H theory of bank credit' or the theory of the bank-credit multiplier. For this, we retain the behavioural specifications of the H theory of money supply (Chapter 15): The main departures of the H theory of credit from the H theory of money supply arise on account of the difference between the definitions of money and of bank credit. Whereas money was defined 'narrowly' as the sum of currency and demand deposits held by the public, we define bank credit (BC) 'broadly' as the sum of such credit to both the government and the commercial sector. In balance-sheet terms, it is the sum of investments (I) and loans and advances (LA) of all kinds, including bills purchased and discounted. I and LA together are also called earning assets (EA) of banks. Thus, we have

$$BC = I + LA = EA. \tag{16.1}$$

For simplification, we assume that the consolidated balance-sheet of all banks can be written as

$$DD + TD = R + I + LA, \tag{16.2}$$

where all the terms are as defined in this and the previous chapter. In writing (16.2) it is assumed

1. that the net worth of banks (a liability item) is equal in value to their physical assets (an asset item), so that the two offset each other completely and need not appear in the balance-sheet identity; and

2. that all their liabilities to the public are in the form of deposit liabilities, which appear as DD and TD on the left-hand side of (16.2).

It will be noted that for banks as a whole all inter-bank transactions, such as inter-bank deposits, call loans, and other borrowings get cancelled and so do not appear in the consolidated balance-sheet of banks as represented by (16.2).

From our discussion of the theory of money supply (Section 15.2) we recall the following equations:

$$TD^d = t. DD, \tag{15.6}$$

$$D \equiv DD + TD = (1+t) DD, \tag{15.7}$$

$$R^d = r(1+t). DD, \tag{15.8}$$

$$\text{and } DD = [c + r(1+t)]^{-1}.H. \tag{15.10}$$

From (16.1) and (16.2) we get

$$Bc = I + LA = DD + TD - R. \tag{16.3}$$

Then, in equilibrium, so that $R = R^d$ and $TD = TD^d$, from (15.7), (15.8), and (16.3) we have

$$BC = (1-r) D = (1-r)(1+t) DD. \tag{16.4}$$

Using (15.10) in (16.4) we finally have

$$BC = \frac{(1-r)(1+t)}{c + r(1+t)} \cdot H \cdot \tag{16.5}$$

Equation (16.5) makes BC a proportional function of H, where the factor of proportionality is a function of three behavioural asset ratios c, t, and r. This factor may be called 'bank-credit multiplier' and will be denoted by b, so that (16.5) can be rewritten as

$$BC = b(.). H, \tag{16.6}$$

$$\text{where } b = \frac{(1-r)(1+t)}{c+r(1+t)}$$

The bank-credit multiplier process lying behind the equation (16.5) is the same as the money-multiplier process discussed in Chapter 15. If b (.) can be assumed to be stable over time, BC will be an increasing and proportional function of H. This is the whole crux of the H theory of bank credit. For policy planning it implies that to control the total supply of bank credit, H must be controlled.

On comparing equation (16.15) with the money-supply equation (15.11) of the previous chapter, we find a very close similarity between the two and so between the 'H theory of money supply' and the 'H theory of bank credit'. The same forces of H and the behavioural asset ratios of c, t, and r determine the two. The three asset ratios (c,t, and r) are the proximate determinants of both the money multiplier m and the bank-credit multiplier b. The only difference is in the solution values for the two multipliers in terms of c, t, and r. For all these reasons, our earlier discussion of the H theory of money supply (Chapter 15), of the factors determining m and H and of the autonomous (or endogenous) character of H is fully germane for the H theory of bank credit.

The theory of bank deposits is fully present in the above discussion. From equations (15.7) and (15.10), we immediately have

$$D = \frac{1+t}{c+r(1+t)} . H, \tag{16.7}$$

where the ratio multiplying H gives the value of the (total) deposit-multiplier. What we have said above about the factors governing bank credit is fully applicable to the case of bank deposits as well.

16.3 The Allocation of Institutional Credit as an Institutional Process

The standard theory on the general question of credit allocation is highly simplistic. It assumes one homogeneous credit market in which all 'promises to pay' of borrowers are perfectly alike. It is further assumed that perfect competition prevails on both sides of the market, so that a uniform rate of interest comes to be determined by the interaction of the market-wide forces of total demand and total supply. This market-determined rate of interest is, then, assumed to act as the single allocator of total credit among competing borrowers as well as lenders and among competing uses. In particular, it says that each borrower is able to borrow whatever amount he likes to borrow at the going market rate of interest — that there is no credit rationing in the system. The associated conditions of eligibility for borrowing are always kept implicit and not woven organically into the analysis.

The above vision of the functioning of credit markets is totally unrealistic. Neither the credit markets are perfectly homogeneous, nor is there perfect competition in these markets. On the supply side, big financial institutions dominate the scene. On the demand side, the 'promises to pay' of potential individual borrowers are not alike. They differ widely in a variety of ways. A large part of the decision-making by the financial institutions is concerned merely with the assessment of the degree of creditworthiness of individual borrowers. All these and related considerations have made the allocation of institutional credit an institutional process quite distinct from a market process.

The last point made above is so important that it will bear a little more explanation. The institutional process is different from the market process in that it does not operate entirely through the impersonal price mechanism. Non-price mechanism is often more important in both the selection of eligible borrowers and the determination of the amount of credit to be given to eligible borrowers. In contrast, under pure market mechanism, price alone is the arbiter of both. It separates the eligible from the non-eligible. Those who are willing and able to pay the market-determined price fall in the category of eligible buyers; others get automatically left out. The same rule also determines how much each eligible buyer will get—as much as he wants to buy at the market price. Technically speaking, he is perfectly free to travel along his demand curve, that is, he himself chooses the amount he would like to buy at a given price.

The institutional process, on the other hand, operates through non-price factors, practices and rules, market clearing not necessarily being one of them. It does admit of a price. But the price is not the sole equilibrating or market-clearing mechanism. More correctly speaking, the price itself is not determined by the market-clearing mechanism of demand and supply. This itself is determined by some kind of a non-market process, though the market conditions of demand and supply may impinge, directly or indirectly, on the fixation of a price. As a corollary, the price does not act as the sole rationing device. The practices, rules, and non-price factors share the job with price as only one of the factors responsible for rationing. Therefore, an understanding of these practices and non-price factors, the way they operate and impinge on credit allocation is very important for understanding the allocation of institutional credit in the economy. The discussion in the sequel will explain why the non-price factors tend to dominate the price factor in the allocation of credit.

The factors influencing the institutional allocation of credit may be divided under two heads :*(a)* financial and *(b)* non-financial. They are discussed below in that order.

16.4 Financial Factors in the Allocation of Institutional Credit

The key financial considerations that influence the allocation of institutional credit are *(i)* the risk of default and *(ii)* the net rate of return. Each of these two factors incorporates several other factors. We offer a brief and simple explanation of each of the two factors. For simplicity, we shall use the term loan and credit interchangeably. Wherever necessary, we shall feel free to refer to other forms (than loans) in which credit is made available. We dispose of first and briefly the factor of net rate of return. The bulk of the explanation of credit allocation as an institutional process concerns the factor of risk of default.

16.4.1 The Net Rate of Return

The net rate of return is given by the loan rate of interest minus the cost of servicing loans. According to the received theory, the loan rate of interest is the sole allocator of credit. As said earlier, this view is highly simplistic. In actual life, the institutional loan rate of interest is an administered price. What this rate does is to separate out the willing borrowers from the unwilling borrowers at this rate. Those who are unwilling to borrow at the autonomously-given rate of interest are automatically rationed out. In this limited sense the rate of interest does act as a rationing device. But among the willing borrowers the allocation of credit is done on considerations other than the rate of interest. And it is these considerations or factors which hold the key to the allocation of institutional credit; not the rate of interest. We shall study them soon. Here attention may be drawn to the cost of servicing loans. What services are associated with the loan business will be discussed below. It will suffice to note at this stage that the average cost of servicing small loans is higher than that of servicing big loans. Therefore, given a uniform rate of return, and other things being the same, the net rate of return to lenders from small loans turns out to be lower than that from big loans. This by itself discourages institutional lenders from catering to the borrowing needs of small borrowers. There are weightier reasons also which militate against small borrowers. They will come out later in the chapter.

16.4.2. **The Risk of Default**

A loan involves two kinds of 'promises to pay' of the borrower: *(i)* the promise to repay the amount borrowed and *(ii)* the promise to pay the interest due on the loan, and both as specified in the loan contract or the promissory note of the borrower. Both the promises to pay relate to the future. Therefore, there is a risk that either one or both of the promises to pay may not be fulfilled in full. This risk is called the 'risk of default', whether the default is in respect of the principal of the loan or in respect of interest due on it, whether it is partial or full. Normally, in a stable political environment, the risk of default on the government debt is taken to be nil (or nearly so), because it commands a vast power to raise funds by taxing public and borrowing further from it. It is for this reason that government securities are called gilt-edged securities, that is, securities of the highest quality.

But all loans to private parties (as well as non-departmental public-sector undertakings) involve some risk of default, whether low or high. Therefore, it is the first concern of a lender to assess this risk somehow and insure against it appropriately and adequately. The whole concept of *creditworthiness* of a borrower relates to this concern. The separation of the eligible from the ineligible and acceptable borrowing capacity of the eligible borrowers rests on this concern. The criteria of allocation of credit derived from this concern (for the risk of default) are not purely, even mainly, market determined, that is, they are not determined by a simple balancing of the forces of demand and supply. The market forces do matter, but in complex and indirect ways. Non-market forces such as the law of contract, its enforceability in the courts of law, the cost of law suits, the time delays involved in court procedings, etc. count a good deal. So, the criteria may vary from country to country, from time to time, and even from one kind of financial institution to another, depending on the kind of borrowers it deals with.

A distinction may be made between two sources of risk of default, namely, *(a)* personal (or moral) risk and *(b)* trade risk. The former relates to the honesty of the borrower who may choose not to honour his 'promise to pay'. This again is not a market phenomenon. The force behind this may be political or some other kind of influence, corruption, or sheer audacity or dishonesty of the borrower. The trade risk, narrowly viewed, arises from the riskiness of the enterprise for which the loan is being made. Broadly speaking, the trade risk will depend upon the 'repaying capacity' of the borrower. The latter, in turn, depends upon the current as well as the expected wealth and income position of the borrower over the life of the loan in relation to his total indebtedness (including interest liability) and the degree of certainty of these expectations. Therefore, before advancing funds, the lender evaluates complete financial position (balance sheet as well as profit and loss statement) of a loan applicant, including the firm's expected profitability projection over (say) the next 3 to 5 years. This is true not only of loans and advances, but also of underwriting of (or investments in) new issues, whether of bonds, preference shares or equity shares.

A particular mention may be made here of two among several summary measures or ratios which are generally used as indicators of the degree of 'trade-riskiness' (of default) of a borrower. One is the debt-equity ratio; the other is the ratio of total income to interest liability per year or simply the income-interest ratio, showing the relative size of the interest cover. One is the stock ratio; the other is the ratio of two flows per unit of time. Equity means total amount of owned funds invested in business, and debt usually refers to only long-term debt capital excluding any short-term working capital borrowed from banks and others (say, in the form of net trade credit).

The *debt-equity ratio* is a summary measure of the degree of security cover for debt capital. The higher the value of this ratio, the smaller the cover, and the lower the value of this ratio, the larger the cover. For example, the debt-equity ratio of the value of one indicates that even if the entire debt capital goes to waste, the borrower's equity in business can still provide full cover to the lender. (Of course, much will depend on the nature of the charge the lender holds against the borrower's equity, court proceedings, and such other things.) But if the debt-equity ratio is greater than one, the risk of default faced by the lender is that much higher. Therefore, financial prudence requires that, as a rough rule of thumb, the highest safe value for the debt-equity ratio is pitched at one and a higher value (of this ratio) is considered unsafe, both for the lender and the borrower. For the former, it is unsafe because the implied risk of default is too much. For the borrower, it is unsafe as well as unwise, because it increases too much the fixed interest charge.

The last argument relates to the composition or structure of capital. The total capital employed in business is divisible into two parts : borrowed capital and owned capital. The former is the same thing as the debt of the enterprise, the latter its equity. The property of debt capital is that it has fixed interest charge, whatever the current income of the enterprise. The property of owned capital (paid-up capital plus reserves) is that it does not have any fixed interest charge. The income return to it is variable. This return may be high or low, even negative. Any industry or enterprise can face bad times for any number of reasons when its earnings may take a sharp decline. If all the capital invested is owned capital, the low income or even loss is shared pro rata by total capital. But, if a part of the capital is debt capital, the interest charge on it is a fixed charge. This has to be honoured even in the event of a loss, if the firm wants to stay in business and maintain its goodwill. The payment of this interest accentuates the total loss borne by the owners of equity capital. Clearly, the interest burden will be high if the debt-equity ratio is high. A few (even 2-3) bad years in succession can be easily the cause of the undoing of a firm with too high a debt-equity ratio. This will be specially true of a young firm.

We have studied above (Chapter 8) that the industrial development banks in India have, by their financial policy, promoted excessively high debt-equity ratios. They consider the debt-equity ratio of 2 quite normal. The ratio of 4 or higher for certain industries financed by them are not uncommon. Thus, the capital structure promoted by them is very risky. No wonder, many of them are facing the problem of excessive overdues, and the problem of industrial sickness is on the increase in the country.

The second summary measure, the *income-interest ratio*, is yet another measure of the repaying capacity of the borrower. This ratio is not totally independent of the debt-equity ratio studied earlier. Even then it is important in its own right, because, besides the debt-equity ratio, its value will also depend upon the length of gestation lags, extent of capacity utilisation, and other factors affecting the gross profitability of individual business ventures. For the lender it obviously counts whether the borrower will have enough income or not to meet his periodic interest obligations. The bare minimum required will be income equal to the interest payments due. This will give an income-interest ratio or the interest cover of the value of one. A safe value for this ratio is taken to be two in India. For a lower value of the ratio, defaults in interest payments are more likely to occur.

In evaluating this ratio several term-financing institutions in the public sector follow the questionable practice of overestimating the true income of the borrower. This is done by computing income gross of depreciation. But depreciation is a part of the capital cost of production. Therefore, it should not be treated as a part of income. If the provision for depreciation is treated as something available for meeting interest obligation, this means that the financing agency does not care for the continued good health of its borrowers, which requires that the capital of the firm is maintained intact. By including depreciation in income a rosier picture of the income-interest ratio is painted than is warranted by the facts of the case. This is an unhealthy practice.

The key point to note here is that all this assessment before the loan/investment is sanctioned and disbursed is an institutional, and not a market, process. In the case of issues of securities to the public, the market comes into the picture at a much later stage when all the screening, evaluation, necessary changes, and dressing up of the new issues has already been done at the underwriting stage and the sanction of the authorities (controller of capital issues) obtained. In traditional credit theory built mainly around portfolio choice and asset-price (or interest-rate) determination, therefore, the lender's concern for the risk of default gets conveniently neglected and almost the entire attention devoted to the question of risk arising from the uncertainly of market prices of assets. Alternatively, in simple two-asset models with only money and government bonds, the risk of default again gets conveniently left out on the reasonable assumption that the government bonds do not suffer from such a risk. The net result is that the most important factor of risk of default which dominates all kinds of allocation of credit does not have any occasion to stand up and be counted. Things would possibly have been different if in the economist's dictionary 'promises to pay' or credit claims were not restricted to only marketable assets but were also to include explicitly non-marketable claims such as the loans and advances of banks.

16.4.3. Security (Primary and Collateral)

Even the experience of adequate 'repaying capacity' is not enough to induce a lender to lend, because this alone does not give him enough of a handle to recover his loan with interest in the event of actual default. Therefore, lenders usually insist on adequate, tangible security against the loan. The loans backed by tangible security are called secured loans. The loans not so secured are called unsecured or clean loans and are generally advanced for short periods to only well-established, prime borrowers only on the strength of their promissory notes. The basis of security-oriented credit is thus the risk of default, which is sought to be safeguarded against directly by having a charge against tangible security of good value and indirectly by restricting the borrower's ability to borrow further against the value of the same security.

The security itself is of two types—primary security and collateral security. Primary security is the security of assets that are created or acquired with the use of loan funds and on which the lender has first charge through the loan deed. Collateral security is additional security to supplement the primary security. It may be offered by the borrower himself or by a third party to ensure or guarantee that all the terms of the loan agreement will be honoured by the borrower. In the case of most personal loans, the aforesaid distinction is not of much practical relevance, as the lender usually takes firm possession of such movable tangibles as ornaments and proper mortgage of immovable property. Yet in the financing of consumer durables, the hire-purchase finance companies usually insist on adequate collateral security (even in the form of personal guarantee from a person of adequate means), because the borrower must be allowed the possession and use of the said consumer durables.

Similarly, business loans are supposedly taken for the creation or acquisition of productive business assets, whether factory building, machines, stock-in-hand or trade receivables which automatically serve as primary security for the lender. But to reassure himself against the possible risk of default and due to practical difficulties of effective policing of the end-use of credit, the lender may insist on collateral security as well. Does this mean excessive security consciousness?

Any answer to the above question is bound to have important implications for credit allocation. To begin with, it should be recognized that strict imposition of collateral-security requirement by institutional lenders such as banks can be obstructive of one of their basic functions—that of providing productive credit, because not all potential borrowers are ever in a position to offer adequate collateral security for all the credit advanced by banks, as this will require that they have already accumulated enough bankable assets to serve as collateral security. Bank loans advanced on the strength of only collateral security will then serve primarily to monetise illiquid assets and only secondarily to assist current production and investment by providing productive credit.

Equally important is the resulting discrimination against poorer owners of tangible wealth who otherwise deserve bank credit. And this is not an imaginary danger. For, whatever the declared credit policy of the RBI, in actual practice, even nationalised commercial banks still insist on adequate collateral security especially from new, small borrowers, and are not similarly insistent in respect of large and established borrowers. For example, in the case of big corporate borrowers, personal sureties of directors are considered good enough collateral for large sums of credit. This practice favours large and wealthy borrowers and penalises young entrepreneurs not born of wealthy parents. Therefore, it is best not to insist too strongly on collateral security and look for safety against the risk of default in the primary assets of good value, coupled with the assessed repaying capacity of the borrower. In what follows we shall speak of security only in the sense of primary security and not collateral security, though some general statements about security will be applicable to the latter as well.

Various kinds of assets may serve as security. They may be stock-in-trade (goods), machines, vehicles, real estate, gold and silver bullion or ornaments, documents of title to goods (warehouse receipts, railway receipts, bills of lading, etc.), stock exchange securities, life insurance policies, fixed deposit receipts, bills, and book debts. Collectively, they are called bankable assets, that is, assets generally acceptable to banks as security against loans.

To be acceptable as security against the loan, the tangible assets must possess certain desirable properties. For example, they must be durable, so as to last in value over the life of the loan, and easily storable. They must be easily marketable, stable in prices, and of adequate economic value to cover more than fully the loan repayment with interest and incidental expenses. In cases of real estate, life insurance policies, fixed deposit receipts, etc. the title deeds lodged with the lender as security must be prefectly in order in the eyes of the law.

It needs to be understood that when any asset is tendered as security against the loan, a proper charge of the lender must be created on the asset. The charge creation is an institutional, and not a market, process. The charge on security must be created according to the law of the land and prevailing business practices. The creation of charge is a legal transaction as a result of which the lender acquires certain rights over the security. The principal methods of creating a charge are lien, mortgage, hypothecation, and pledge. Each method has certain legal properties and is applied to particular kinds of security. For example, in the case of immovable property (real estate), mortgage of such property in favour of the lender is executed. In the case of movable properties, the methods of hypothecation, pledge, or lien may be used. Mortgages, then, are of various forms such as simple mortgage, equitable mortgage, legal mortgage, usufructuary mortgage, or English mortgage. Similarly, other methods of creating a charge are also of various forms.

The point of interest for us (as economists) in knowing all this is twofold. One is that for evaluating loan proposals, adequate competent staff is required. Related to this is the cost of servicing loan-making, which includes evaluation of loan proposals, sanctions, disbursals, and recoveries of funds, any law suits and subsequent sales of goods or assets acquired in the recovery proceedings.

16.4.4 Margin Requirement

Given even acceptable security, how much credit is a borrower allowed against it? Normally, banks do not advance full value of whatever bankable assets—whether machinery, goods or bills receivable —businesses offer as security and insist that a certain minimum percentage of total value of such assets is financed by the borrower from his own resources. Technically, this minimum percentage is called 'margin requirement' for a loan and the difference between the value of the security and the margin is known as the 'drawing power' of the borrower under the 'cash credit system (see Sction 5.5) prevalent in India, subject, of course, to a pre-determined maximum, called the 'credit limit'. In the case of new issues of shares, the margin requirement is fulfilled in the form of promoters' equity, that is, the investment in such shares initially made by the promoters of the issue/company. For debenture issues, adequate security of existing assets and new assets to be acquired with the help of debenture capital is created through a trust deed to take care of the repayment of the loan with interest.

The chief role of margin requirement is to create the borrower's stake in business financed by the loan. If the lender finances in full the business assets carried by a borrower, the borrower's stake in his business will be reduced to nil and the entire risk of business will be borne by the lender. The borrower's own investment in business (assets) provides the much-needed margin of safety to the lender against possible losses incurred by the borrower. In several countries, including India, central banks have used margin requirements as a tool of 'qualitative control of credit' (Section 19.10), as by manipulating the margin requirement, bank credit against particular kinds of security can be restricted or encouraged.

In actual practice, all these institutional arrangements against credit risks can be (and actually are) manipulated to their advantage by individual borrowers, because the values of security can be overstated, security not lodged with banks and in actual possession of the borrowers (as they must necessarily be in cases of hypothecated machines, vehicles, goods-in-process, etc) can be tempered with in various ways, and false returns can be filed with banks.

The above discussion would indicate the complexity of forces and institutional processes involved in the evaluation of the creditworthiness of a borrower and so in the process of loan-making. All these problems are conveniently neglected in the standard theory of credit allocation through the interest-rate mechanism. The interest rate is, no doubt, a price, a price paid by the borrower to the lender for the use of funds for a certain period. But the loan market is not like a simple commodity market of the orthodox economic theory in which once a transaction has been made, that is the end of the matter. In the loan market, the relation between the borrower and the lender continues throughout the currency of the loan and anything can go wrong during this period or at the stage of repayment of the loan Therefore, this feature of loan-making is of the essence and must be woven organically into any theory of credit allocation.

16.4.5 The Credit Supply Curve

Having studied economic considerations and institutional arrangements arising from the lender's concern to provide against the risk of default of borrowers, we are now ready to weave these factors into the standard demand-and-supply analysis. With one or two assumptions, the abovementioned factors can be captured in the notion of a credit supply curve facing individual borrowers. And it is the supply or availability of credit which is mainly affected by these factors. To the extent potential borrowers voluntarily take notice of these factors and the institutional norms and practices for extending credit, their demand for credit also gets influenced.

In the traditional theory, it is standard practice to assume that the supply curve of credit facing an individual borrower is perfectly elastic at the market-determined rate of interest. Taking first the question of slope of the supply curve, our discussion of factors derived from the risk of default suggests that this hypothesis cannot be true—that no individual borrower can possibly borrow any amount he likes. The counter-hypothesis derivable from our discussion will assert that the credit supply curve facing an individual borrower is upward-sloping.

The above hypothesis itself can take two forms: (a) smooth upward-sloping supply curve and (b) reverse L - shaped supply curve (see Figure 16.1). We discuss them one by one. In both cases it is necessary to assume that, given the creditworthiness position and character of the borrower as already discussed above, (i) the degree of riskiness (of default) of each amount of the loan can be estimated by the lender and that (ii) the lender will be willing to undertake that degree of risk if he can charge a determinate 'risk premium' at an appropriate rate per unit time over and above the pure (default-free) rate of interest. After a point, the assessed risk may be so high that the lender is not willing to lend at any rate of interest howsoever high.

Next, we introduce a very important hypothesis about loans or claims (or promises to pay or IOUs)[1] in the form of the 'law of declining economic quality of IOUs'[2]. Kalecki (1937) had called it 'the principle of increasing marginal risk' of loans and advances. More simply the hypothesis states that, given the net worth of the borrower, the risk of default on a loan is an increasing function of the amount of the loan. This is because in a world of uncertainty, due to any number of unfavourable developments not seen beforehand, the expected returns from an investment project may not materialise and may even turn into losses and, with the best of intentions, the borrower may not be in a position to repay the loan, if his owned capital (equity or net worth) is relatively small. Therefore, given the borrower's equity, the risk of default will increase as the loan amount increases or the debt-equity ratio rises. Alternatively speaking, this means that, other things being the same and at least after a point, the 'economic quality of a borrower's IOUs begins to decline as more of them are supplied (that is, as more and more loans are taken by him). Therefore, the lender will be willing to lend more to borrower only if he is duly compensated by a higher rate of interest for the increasing risk of deafult or the declining economic quality of the IOUs.

The two forms of supply curve (a) and (b) hypothesised earlier are shown in Figure 16.1 as LS_a and $\bar{r}AS_b$, respectively. (Temporarily ignore other things in the figure.) Each of the two supply curves is drawn on the assumption that factors other than the rate of interest (r) (such as the borrower's equity) that influence the readiness to lend are held constant. These other factors help determine the position of the LS curve. The LS_a curve shows that upto L_0 amount a higher r will

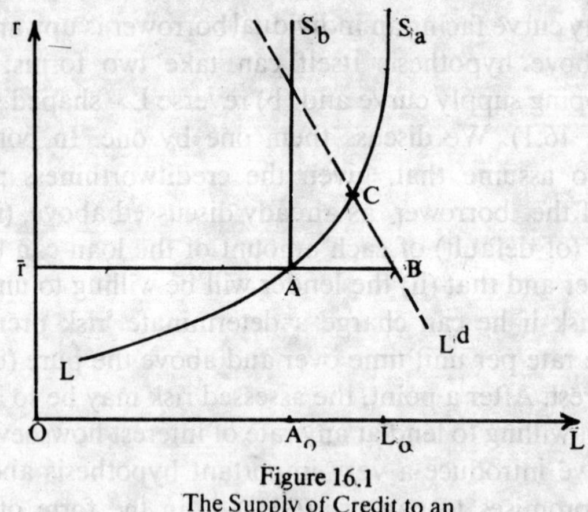

Figure 16.1
The Supply of Credit to an
Individual Borrower

bring forth a larger amount of credit supply. At L_o, this curve becomes perfectly vertical, showing that beyond L_o amount of credit, the lender does not consider any r high enough to compensate him for the risk of default assessed by him.

The reverse L-shaped curve $\bar{r}\,AS_b$ is drawn on the assumption that the rate of interest $\bar{r}$ is determined autonomously, whether by the monetary authority (as the RBI does in India) or by the bankers' association, or even by an individual financial institution (or lender), and not by the market-clearing condition in the credit market. This is quite true of the market for institutional loans and advances, at least in India. The sharp kink in this curve occurs at point A, which lies on the LS_a curve. This indicates the maximum amount of credit (A_o) which will be offered at the rate of interest $\bar{r}$. By assumption of model (b), any higher amount of credit will be offered only if the autonomously-determined $\bar{r}$ is revised upward. Then, the point A will move up along the LS_a curve. Thus, the two curves are inter-related, after all.

So long as the demand for credit represented by the downward-sloping L^d curve in the figure is greater than $\bar{r}A$ amount of credit at $\bar{r}$ rate of interest, the particular borrower is credit-rationed by the amount AB. Only when the L^d curve lies sufficiently inward so as to intersect the horizontal segment $\bar{r}A$ to the left of A is the particular borrower not credit-rationed, as he gets whatever amount he likes to borrow at the $\bar{r}$ rate of interest. Thus, the function of the demand side of credit in this model is only to determine *(i)* whether a particular borrower is credit-rationed or not and *(ii)* if credit-rationed, by how much.[3]

In model (a) of the supply curve of credit, if L^d and LS_a curves are market demand and supply curves, the credit market gets cleared at point C, which determines the equilibrium rate of interest and also the equilibrium amount of credit demanded as well as supplied. In this model of the traditional theory, no potential borrower is credit-rationed.

16.4.6 Inter-Borrower Allocation of Credit

We may now extend the analysis of the previous sub-section to explain the inter-borrower allocation of credit at an autonomously-given rate of interest. Our earlier discussion tells us that in the traditional security-oriented supply of credit the factor that matters most with lenders is the equity (or net worth) position of competing borrowers, which governs the latter's capacity to offer the required security and also meet the margin requirement. Other factors such as interest cover, the assessed riskiness of investment projects of borrowers, etc. are of relatively secondary importance. Further, the supply of credit is an increasing function of the equity position of borrowers — the larger a borrower's equity, the larger the amount of credit offered to him. Thus, the guiding principle of the security-oriented allocation of credit must necessarily be 'to him that has' and, as a corollary, 'the more one has, the more (credit) he may be given'. In the supply models of the previous subsection this means that the supply curve for a rich borrower will lie farther to the right than that to a poor borrower. (In Model (b) this will mean that the horizontal segment r A will extend farther to the right for a rich borrower than for a poor borrower. Thus, the supply of credit will not be borrower-neutral.)

Since the demand for credit curve L^d of a rich borrower is likely to lie farther to the right than that of a poor borrower, the actual amount of credit given to the former is also larger than what is made available to the latter. The degree of credit rationing among borrowers is, in general, not even proportionately uniform, and so not borrower-neutral. Most of the time, it differs across borrowers, and the differentiation mainly arises on the supply side of credit, given the demand for credit at a given r. This invests credit institutions with special powers of favouring some at the cost of others in making their credit available. The favoured parties are helped in numerous ways such as through overvaluation of security, liberal acceptance of assets of even dubious value as security, granting multiple credit against the same security, cutting red tape and delays in sanctioning credit facilities, etc, while others are subjected to all kinds of harassing rules and conditions.

16.5 Non-Financial Factors in the Allocation of Institutional Credit

If the allocation of institutional credit is an institutional, and not a market process, it must perforce be influenced by non-financial factors as well. The latter may be sub-divided under two broad categories of *(a)* social factors and *(b)* political factors.

(a) Social factors. Collectively, they represent considerations which arise from social relations in which the managers of financial institutions as a class are placed with the borrowers. The social factors encompass relations born out of family ties; social status, actual or aspired for; social intercourse through meetings, cocktail parties and dinners; the style of life and its social demands; values of life and aspirations shared with the rich; common perceptions of social reality and common beliefs in the meaning, goals and methods of social progress; corruption, direct or indirect, involving operations of the public relations staff of big borrowers; the lure of current "extra' rewards in cash or kind and the future prospect of finding a cushy job (after retirement) with today's borrowers; in short, the whole western-style corporate culture in which the top executive of financial institutions have been brought up all through their careers, and the resulting complete domination of their minds by the interests of big business. This results in preference for big borrowers, supported by the dictates of conventional wisdom discussed above. Modern financial institutions have, after all, grown with modern industry and commerce. Mercantile, industrial, and finance capital have a long and common history of growth. Thus, over time, the relations among them have got fairly streamlined, as evidenced by the financial securities produced by industrial and commercial borrowers, the organization of stock exchanges, the legal structure accompanying them, the methods of extending credit, and the like. Naturally, the financial managers find extending credit to big borrowers very comfortable. In this setting, it is not surprising if the small borrower generally loses out and is treated as more a headache than a welcome customer.

(b) Political factors. Most of the time the political influence also works in favour of big borrowers. Because of their economic power, the big borrowers also wield substantial political power. This is buttressed by their power to corrupt the political decision-makers,

both among the politicians and the bureaucracy. The processes of corruption are quite well-known and wide-spread. The extent of corruption, though not easily measurable, is generally admitted to be quite large. The small borrowers are not entirely without a supporting lobby. But this lobby is relatively weaker, less organized, less informed and less intelligent. Consequently, even if policy decisions have been taken in principle for greater institutional credit to the small borrower, the formulation of actual credit schemes and their actual implementation leave much to be desired. What is, therefore, needed is a correct specification of the preconditions for the success of such schemes and also the spelling out of the ways in which the preconditions can themselves be realized efficaciously as well as expeditiously (see Section 20.6).

NOTES

1. The term IOU is abbreviation of the full term 'I owe you', which means a 'promise to pay'

2. Such declining *economic quality* with increasing supply is a peculiar property of the IOUs, not shared by ordinary goods like wheat, cloth, radios, etc. However, a similar phenomenon is observed in the case of labour services, since due to increasing fatigue, the quality of labour service declines as more of it is supplied continuously by an individual worker.

3. For a fuller discussion, see Lindbeck (1963, Chapter 7).

CHAPTER 17

Interest Rates

17.1 Introduction

Interest is the price paid for borrowed funds. This price is generally expressed as a rate per cent per unit time such as per year or per month. When so expressed, it becomes a rate of interest. Since interest is cost to the borrower and return to the lender, it affects at the margin, among other things, borrowing and lending, investment and saving, portfolio composition, selection of projects and their lives capital-intensity of production techniques chosen, international capital flows, and distribution of income. Thus, interest as price affects decision-making in several spheres and has important other effects. In this chapter we shall study answers to two main questions: *(a)* how the general level of interest rates is determined in an economy and *(b)* what explains a large variety of interest rates prevailing in an economy. The first question is usually answered on the simplifying but admittedly unrealistic assumption that there is only one perfectly homogeneous and default-risk-free security and so only one uniform rate of interest, called *the* rate of interest, for all borrowers and lenders. The second question will be answered in two steps. In the first step, we classify rates of interest in India from different angles. The resulting classification will yield various structures of rate of interest. It will also suggest possible source of differences in rates of interest, which will be discussed in the second step.

17.2 The Loanable Funds Theory

The determination of *the* rate of interest has been a subject of much controversy among economists. The differences run along several lines. We shall not survey all of them. Broadly speaking, there are now two main contenders in the field. One is Keynes' theory of liquidity preference, the other is the loanable funds theory. The former was discussed in its original form in Section 13.3 and in the general-equilibrium form of Hicks' IS–LM model in Section 13.8, which explains the joint determination of the rate of interest (r) and real income. Keynes, in his theory, had asserted that r was a purely monetary phenomenon. With Hicks, the Keynesians admit that r is determined by the interaction of monetary and non-monetary (real) forces.

The loanable-funds theory of r is an extension of the classical savings and investment theory of r. It incorporates monetary factors with the non-monetary factors of savings and investment. The theory is associated with the names of Wicksell and several other Swedish economists and the British economist D.H. Robertson. We discuss it very briefly below.

According to the loanable-funds theory, *the* rate of interest is determined by the demand for and the supply of funds in the economy at that level at which the two (demand and supply) are equated. Thus, it is a standard demand-supply theory as applied to the market for loanable funds (credit), treating the rate of interest as the price (per unit time) of such funds. The theory is based on the following simplifying assumptions:

1. That the market for loanable funds is one fully integrated (and not segmented) market, characterised by perfect mobility of funds throughout the market;

2. That there is perfect competition in the market, so that each borrower and lender is a 'price-taker' and one and only one pure rate of interest prevails in the market at any time. The forces of competition are also supposed to clear the market pretty fast, sc that the single rate of interest is the market-clearing (or the equilibrium) rate of interest.

The theory uses partial-equilibrium approach in which all factors other than the rate of interest that might influence the demand or supply of loanable funds are assumed to be held constant. In other words, it *assumes* that the rate of interest does not interact with other macro variables.

In its popular form, the theory is stated in 'flow' terms, considering flow demand and supply of funds per unit time. As such, the theory hypothesises that it is the 'flow equilibrium' (or the equilibrium between two flows) of loanable funds which determines the rate of interest.

Given the above assumptions, the determination of r is easily explained, once the demand and supply of loanable funds is specified.

This is where the loanable-funds theory is claimed to be an improvement over the classical savings and investment theory of r, since, besides the real factors of savings and investment, it also takes into account the monetary factors of hoarding, dishoarding, and increase in money supply in the determination of r. In this sense it combines both the monetary and non-monetary factors.

The supply of loanable funds (LS) is usually taken to be given by

$$LS = S + DH + \Delta M, \tag{17.1}$$

where S = aggregate saving of all households and firms *net* of their dissaving,

DH = aggregate dishoarding (of cash),

ΔM = incremental supply of money.

Following standard economic theory, both S and DH are hypothesised to be increasing functions of r, ΔM to be autonomously given, and so LS also an increasing function of r.

The demand for loanable funds (LD) is usually taken to be given by

$$LD = I + \Delta MD, \tag{17.2}$$

where I = gross investment expenditure,

and ΔMD = incremental demand for money (or hoarding).

Following standard economic theory, each component of LD and so total LD is hypothesised to be a declining function of r.

Equilibrium r is determined at a level where LD (r) = LS (r), or where

$$I + \Delta MD = S + DH + \Delta M. \tag{17.3}$$

In contrast, in the classical theory, the r-determining equilibrium condition is given by

$$I(r) = S(r). \tag{17.4}$$

The above two equations are shown diagrammatically in Figure 17.1, where we have shown directly only LD, LS, I and S as functions of r. ΔMD is not shown separately, but can be derived as the horizontal distance between the LD and I lines. This distance increases as r falls, because ΔMD is hypothesised to be a declining function of r. The horizontal distance between the LS and S lines represents the sum of DH and ΔM. This distance is shown to increase with increase in r, because ΔM is taken as exogenously given and DH

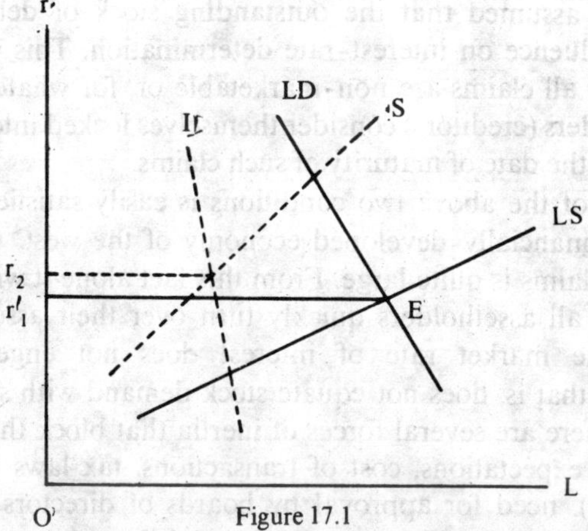

Figure 17.1
Interest Rate Determination—Loanable-Funus Theory and Saving-Investment Theory

is hypothesised as an increasing function of r. To keep the diagram simple, ΔM (or DH) is not shown separately. The equilibrium between LD and LS yields the equilibrium rate of interest r_1, whereas the S-I equilibrium of the classical theory will yield r_2 as the equilibrium r.

The loanable-funds theory (as stated above) has been criticised on several counts, discussed below.

1. The traditional statement of the theory misspecifies various sources of supply and demand of loanable funds (Gupta, 1974a). Take the supply side first. It is well known that not all savings are routed through the loan market; some are invested directly into physical assets by firms as well as households. Similarly, all dishoarding (of cash balances) is not lent to others; some is spent directly by the dishoarders. The demand side, too, is misspecified. All investment or hoarding is not financed by borrowed funds; a part of it is financed by owned funds. Then, funds are borrowed for several purposes other than investment and hoarding as well, such as for consumption spending, purchases of old financial and non-financial assets.

2. The 'flow-equilibrium' approach of the theory has been criticised on the ground that in the bond (or securities) market it is the 'stock equilibrium' that dominates the behaviour of the rate of interest, at least in any short period, because, in this market, the volume of outstanding bonds is many times over the flow of new demand and supply of bonds (loanable funds) during any short period of time. For the loanable-funds theory to be true, therefore, it must

somehow be assumed that the outstanding stock of debt does not exert any influence on interest-rate determination. This will be true only if either all claims are non-marketable or, for whatever reason, the claimholders (creditors) consider themselves locked into the claims they hold till the date of maturity of such claims.

Neither of the above two conditions is easily satisfied in actual life. In any financially-developed economy of the west, the stock of marketable claims is quite large. From this fact alone it will be wrong to infer that all assetholders quickly turn over their asset portfolio, whenever the market rate of interest does not engender stock equilibrium, that is, does not equate stock demand with stock supply of claims. There are several forces of inertia that block the way, such as uncertain expectations, cost of transactions, tax laws (concerning capital gains), need for approval by boards of directors (in case of corporate holders), etc. However, the inertial-forces argument should not be extended too far, because in well-developed financial markets there are speculators whose main business is to make money from portfolio switches or trading in stocks and in any active market such trading supported by the market transactions of investors is likely to be fairly large in relation to the new (flow) demand and supply of funds in any short period. Therefore, in any financial equilibrium, stocks cannot be neglected. [1] What is required is stock-flow analysis in which both stocks and flows interact with each other and jointly determine a rate of interest at which the conditions for stock equilibrium as well as for flow equilibrium are satisfied.

3. Criticising the partial-equilibrium approach of the theory, it is said that since the rate of interest affects all other macro variables like savings, investment, real income, prices, demand and supply of money and, in turn, is affected by them, it cannot be determined independently of all these variables. That is, for explaining the interest-rate determination, a general-equilibrium model should be used.

The importance of this argument becomes clear when we note that by ignoring the saving-investment equilibrium condition, the theory neglects the simultaneous clearance of the commodity market. In Figure 17.1, it can be seen that the economy cannot be in macro equilibrium at the rate of interest r_1, because at this rate, there is excess of I over S (or excess demand in the commodity market). (In the figure, the S–I equilibrium is attained at a higher rate r_2.) Wicksell had noted this problem and tried to resolve it through his well-known dynamic analysis of the cumulative process in which prices (not real income) continously rise or fall whenever the market (or money) rate of interest is different from the 'natural' rate (given by the S-I equilibrium). After Keynes' *General Theory* (1936), changes in real income are invariably brought into the analysis of dynamic adjustment.

4. All theories (including the loanable-funds theory) of *the* rate of interest necessarily postulate that all borrowing and lending is done through perfectly homogeneous bonds in one fully-integrated market. This is not true of even the most well-developed financial markets, where a wide variety of loan contracts and instruments are used in several imperfectly-competitive and segmented markets. Thus, the working of credit markets generates a bewildering variety of interest rates and loan contracts and not *the* rate of interest and *the* homogeneous (and perpetual) bond of economic theory. Either concept is an extreme abstraction.

17.3 Heterogeneity of Interest-Rate Determination

In the previous section we had assumed as if all borrowing and lending are done at one uniform rate of interest. This is not so in actual world. For example, it is well known that financial intermediaries of all kinds borrow funds at rates of interest which, on average, are lower than the average of their lending rates. That is why they are able to operate at profit in the market for funds. It is more important than this to understand that in the Indian economy a wide variety of social arrangements for interest-rate fixation and variation obtain. Here, the market for loanable funds is not one indivisible whole, but highly segmented. Funds do not flow easily from one segment to the other, as various kinds of barriers obstruct such flows. (This is much less true of the USA and several other economies.) Consequently, wide differentials of interest rates obtain between one segment and the other, though within one segment rates are more competitive. The last statement is not true of the unorganized sector of the credit market, which is quite large in itself, where even within that sector the interest-rate differentials are enormously large.

The important problem of interest-rate differentials will be discussed in the next section. In the present section we describe various forms of social arrangements under which rates of interest are fixed and varied.

We first distinguish between *(a)* administered interest rates and *(b)* market-determined interest rates. The latter are rates that are determined by the interaction of the forces of demand and supply in the market and as such can vary quite frequently with changes in demand and supply. The administered rates, on the other hand, are fixed autonomously by some authority or by borrower/lender alone; they are not formed from day to day by the market forces of demand and supply. These forces express themselves mainly and directly on the quantity side, in terms of quantity demanded or supplied. The variations in them have to be made by the authority or agency fixing them in the first place. Such administered rates are very important in the Indian economy.

The administered rates may be divided under two heads: *(i)* deposit rates and *(ii)* lending rates. The deposit rates of banks on savings deposits and fixed deposits of various maturities are fixed by the RBI and deposit rates on post office savings deposits and fixed deposits and rates of interest on various small savings certificates are fixed by the Government of India. And these (bank and post office) deposits are the dominant form of financial assets held by households in India. Then, public limited non-financial companies also solicit term deposits from the public at rates of interest administered by them. Other deposit-accepting institutions and firms also administer their own rates of interest, which may be linked loosely with other administered rates such as those of banks in the country. We may widen this category of administered deposit rates to include the treasury bill rate, which is administered by the RBI but which is not a deposit rate, because unlike deposits treasury bills can be bought and sold freely in the market. The lending rates of commercial banks for borrowers of different categories are administered by the RBI. Similarly, lending rates of co-operative banks, land development banks and the term-lending institutions such as the IDBI and the IFCI are all administered by the authorities concerned. The bank rate of the RBI and its lending rates for banks and others are all administered rates, fixed by the RBI.

Market-determined interest rates need to be sub-divided under two heads : *(a)* interest rates on marketable government debt and *(b)* interest rates on other marketable debt. For present purposes, the marketable government debt should be defined broadly to include not only the market debt of the Central and state governments (as is usual), but also that of local authorities, of development banks as the IDBI and the IFCI, and of such semi-official agencies as port trusts and state electricity boards. The reasons for adopting such a broader definition are: *(i)* the market debts of agencies other than the government listed above are guaranteed by the government both in respect of principal and interest so as to make them default-risk free; and *(ii)* the statutory investment requirements imposed on various financial institutions have created a large and growing captive market for such debt along with the government debt. The net consequence is artificially lower rates of interest on such debts. Though they are not administered rates, they partake very much of administered rates due to the two features listed above and strong market support to the government debt by the RBI. As a result, fluctuations in these rates are relatively small.

Other market debt is of several kinds and rates of interest on its several components have a wide spread. Therefore, we distinguish among its several categories. First, a distinction should be made between corporate debt and non-corporate debt. Corporations borrow funds in the open market by issuing bonds or debentures of various maturities and preference shares. All these papers are traded on organized stock exchanges in the country. Therefore, their prices (and yield rates) can vary from day to day, even hour to hour, under the impact of changes in the market demand-supply conditions. A special mention may be made here of the call money rate at which short-term call funds are traded in the inter-bank call money market, already discussed in Section 3.3.

Non-corporate firms (partnerships and individual enterprises) also borrow funds. Some of them issue *hundis* which are traded in the traditional sector of the Indian money market (Section 10.3). The rate of interest at which indigenous bankers discount these hundies or offer short-term accommodation to their customers is called the bazar bill rate.

Much of the borrowing by non-corporate firms and households is done in the unorganized sector of the money market in the form of negotiated loans that do not generate any market paper which may be bought and sold in the securities market. The loans are provided by varied agencies like indigenous bankers, moneylenders, finance companies, nidhis and chit funds (Chapter 10). The mode of operation of these several agencies and the cost of funds lent by them diverge greatly over a wide range. In certain cases the effective rate of interest may turn out to be as high as 100 per cent per year or even more.

Then, there is the large category of trade credit or book credit which cuts acorss the distinction of corporate and non-corporate firms and even households, as this type of credit is settled mutually between any two parties. Often times the cost of credit is not stated explicitly though the period of credit may be so stated; the cost of credit is often included in the over-all profit margin so that it is difficult to say what the acutal rate of interest charged is in a particular sale on credit.

The above discussion is summed up in the form of a chart in Figure 17.1. For the current structure of rates of interest in India, see RBI, *Report on Currency and Finance,* 1985-86, Vol. II, Statement 50.

17.4 Interest Rate Differentials

Wide differences in interest rates are quite common, and not the uniformity of them. What are these differences due to ? As we shall see in this section, several factors are responsible for them. But monetary economists have devoted excessive attention to only one of them, namely the term to maturity of an otherwise-homogeneous debt, to the near-neglect of others. The resulting discussion carried out under the caption of the 'term structure of interest rates' has, no doubt, offered economists an excellent opportunity for sophisticated analysis and empirical testability of competing hypotheses mainly with the help of the US data. But this excessive concentration on the term structure of interest rates has created a false impression as though the only difference in interest rates worth considering is that which may arise due to differences only in the term to maturity of debt, even though in fact differences arising from other sources may be relatively much more important. Also we can think of as many structures of interest rates as there are separate sources of differences in interest rates such as the default-risk-structure or the net-worth-structure of interest rates. The term-structure of interest rates is only one of these several structures which may coexist in an economy. Further, a rate of interest can be a member of more than one structure. For example, a short-term rate is obviously a member of the term structure, but whether the debtor is the government or a private firm will determine its place in the risk structure, and the net worth of the private debtor will determine its position in the net-worth structure, and so on. We shall not go into any exhaustive theoretical discussion of several interest-rate structures. Instead, we offer below a simple heuristic discussion of the major sources of interest-rate differentials as observed in India. Simultaneously we speak briefly of the associated interest-rate structure.

1. Differences in Risk of Default and Overdues

In the previous chapter we have studied that the first considera-tion in loan-making is to ensure against the risk of default of the loan

Figure 17.1

Classification of Interest Rates

(by mode of determination)

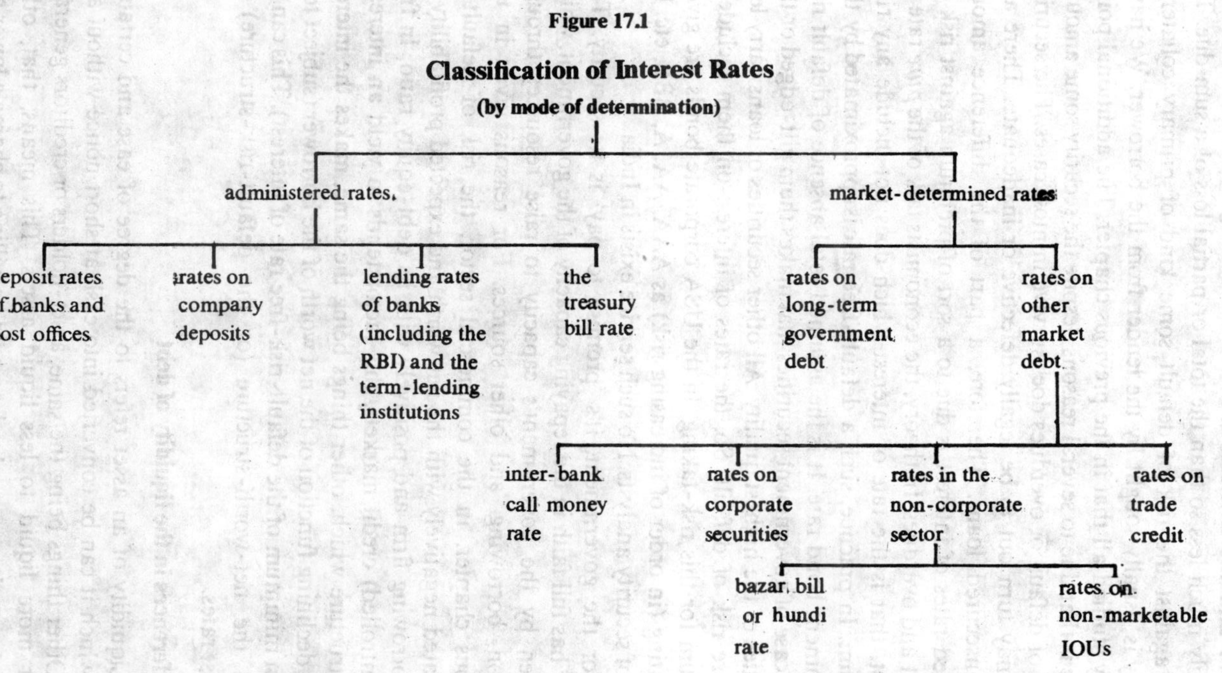

principal and the interest due. Overdues are also unwelcome, but relatively much less so than the total or partial loss of a sum due. To guard against the risk of default some kind of primary collateral security is usually sought by the lender from the borrower. We have already studied all that in the previous chapter. The additional point to note is that due to several reasons despite the security some amount of risk of default or overdues does survive in most cases. The security itself may turn out to be legally defective or inadequate. There are also unsecured loans. Therefore, a part of the difference among recorded rates of interest is due to a sort of premium against risk of default and overdues. In theory, the economists talk of the *pure* rate of interest, that is the rate of interest which does not include any risk premium. In practice, such a default-free rate is approximated by the government bond rate. It is the assumed total absence of default risk in the case of government securities that makes them gilt-edged or the securities of the highest quality. All other securities or loans carry less or more risk of default. So, the rates of interest on them include a premium for this risk-taking. In the USA corporate bonds are given risk rating (in order of increasing risk) as AAA, AA, A, BBB, etc. by firms of security analysts. No such service exists in India.

For the government, it's 'promise to pay' is its security. The lender has full faith in the repaying capacity of the government, which is given by the government's capacity to raise resources through taxation, borrowing, and other sources. For reasons given in the previous chapter, in the commercial sector, the risk of default is associated negatively with the net worth and expected profitability of the borrowing firm and positively with its debt-equity ratio. In free (uncontrolled) credit markets, this factor tends to yield an interest-rate structure which, other things being the same, makes the interest rate a declining function of the net worth of the borrower (subject to a certain minimum of the default-risk-free rate of interest). This can be called the net-worth-structure (or the default-risk-structure) of interest rates.

2. Differences in the liquidity of debt

Liquidity of an asset refers to the degree of ease and certainty with which it can be converted into cash at short notice without any loss. Other things being the same, asset-holders or creditors generally prefer more liquid to less liquid assets. This means, that, other things being the same, a lender would be willing to charge a lower rate of interest on more liquid debt than on a less liquid debt.

For non-money financial assets or debts, the two main determinants of their liquidity are their *(a)* marketability and *(b)* term to maturity. There are some IOUs or financial instruments, like bonds, preference shares, treasury bills, etc. which are traded in well-organized markets. They can be easily bought and sold in these markets at short notice. In itself, this ready marketability of these (marketable) financial instruments increases their liquidity as compared to similar other financial instruments, which are not marketable. such as loans and advances made by banks, moneylenders, etc.

The other factor affecting the liquidity of assets (debts) is their term to maturity. It is obvious in the case of non-marketable debts that the longer the term to maturity the less their liquidity, because a longer waiting period is required for their conversion into cash. In the case of marketable debt what makes longer-term debt less liquid than shorter-term debt is the greater capital-uncertainly of the former than of the latter. For, it is theoretically well-understood and empirically well-observed that the prices of long-term debt fluctuate over a wider range than do the prices of short-term debt. The factor of term-to-maturity of debt is discussed further under the next subheading.

3. **Differences in term to maturity**

Other things being the same, rates of interest also differ according to term to maturity (time-length) of debt. The resulting structure is called the term structure of interest rates and the curve showing the relation between yield and term to maturity is called the 'yield curve'. Much theoretical and empirical work has been done on the term structure of government debt in the USA. This work is of little relevance to the Indian scene, because, as explained in Sections 17.3 and 19.4, in the Indian gilt-edged market, the treasury-bill rate is an administered rate and other rates in interest are effectively controlled by the RBI.

Corporate market debt even in the USA is considered sufficiently heterogeneous for the term-structure analysis, so that the observed differences in rates on such debt of different maturity cannot be attributed to differences in term to maturity alone. In India, additionally, the market for this kind of debt is not well-developed; it is both narrow and shallow. Also, the institutional investors generally do not trade in securities and private dealers are small and unimportant. Therefore, full importance of differences in term to maturity for market-determined interest-rate differentials in the Indian context cannot be easily assessed.

In the sphere of RBI-administered (or controlled) rates, the yield curve is upward-sloping, with the short rate (on treasury bills) pegged at 4.6% per year and the long rate averaging at about 6.6%. There is much greater spread allowed on time deposits of banks, the rates currently varying from the low of 2.5% per year on fixed deposits of 15 to 45 days to the high of 10% per year on fixed deposits of more than 5 years. The rates of interest offered on company deposits also have a rising structure as one moves from one-year deposits to three-year deposits. Thus, in most cases, the rates of interest are higher on debts (assets) of longer-term maturity. Possibly, this is to encourage longer-term public savings or to attract longer-term funds.

The administered lending rates of financial institutions on loans and advances show a reverse term structure, as the rate of interest on term loans by development banks is generally lower than the rate of interest charged by commercial banks on their short-term commercial credit. Presumably, this policy has been adopted to encourage fixed-asset formation and to discourage excessive inventory-holding of goods in the general climate of shortages of several essential goods.

4. Differences in lender's cost of servicing loans

Lenders incur costs on several counts in servicing loans. They have to appraise each loan application, which involves appraising income-earning prospects of the project plan for which loan is sought, various other sources of funds for the project, the adequacy of the financing arrangement, the value, marketability, and capital-certainty of the security against the loan offered by the borrower, the personal integrity or honesty or the previous credit-record of the borrower, etc. The use of the loan and the security against it have to be supervised during the currency of the loan; the loan accounts maintained; regular interest payments and loan instalments or repayment of the principal at the maturity of the loan collected. In the case of accumulation of overdues or threatened default, special effort has to be made to recover maximum of the amount due. At that time, adequate security in the hands of the lender comes in handy as a safeguard. Some of these costs are fixed per loan transaction, whatever the size of the loan. This gives a higher cost per rupee of loan for small loans than for large loans. Then, the problem of timely recovery of loans may be specially acute in the case of small borrowers. They may also be inconveniently located from the point of view of institutional lenders like banks, as is true of rural borrowers. These factors increase further the cost per rupee of loan on small loans.

Presumably, relatively much higher servicing cost per rupee of loan on small loans is one factor which discourages banks from going in for small loans to small borrowers in a much bigger way than they have done so far, despite the social need to expand their loan operations in favour of small borrowers.

5. Differences in lending practices and extra-loan services

Finance companies in cities are in a position to charge higher rates of interest from their borrowers even when the latter are eligible to borrow from commercial banks at a much lower rate of interest. And yet finance companies are expanding their business. Why do such borrowers continue to borrow from finance companies than switch over to bank finance ? Two reasons are generally given. One is the informal lending practices of finance companies as compared to several formalities observed by banks in their loan-making, e.g., various kinds of disclosures about the state of business, loans outstanding from other sources, net worth, etc., strict adherence to margin requirements and length of the loan period, bank's charge on goods purchased with the bank loan, maintenance of proper books of accounts, etc. Some borrowers prefer to avoid all these formalities and restrictions even at the cost of paying a higher rate of interest. Then, finance companies provide fuller and more liberal finance. It is also more expeditious and assured. Rolling over from one term to another of debt is also easier. Some finance companies also provide additional trade services of various kinds to their customers. For example, they may have links with manufacturers or dealers of certain products and may offer to arrange delivery of goods from the manufacturer or dealer, arrange for insurance and other services to the customer at a small charge and also offer the necassary finance. Thus, there is a package of special services and facilities which finance companies offer to their borrowers, which banks do not, and for this package finance companies are able to include an extra charge in the rate of interest. Besides, all the customers of finance companies do not have bankable assets with them, or are otherwise not eligible for borrowing from banks. For them, finance companies are the easiest or the cheapest source of funds. In their case, the factor discussed next (monopoly gain) also becomes a relevant factor.

6. Differences in monopoly (or exploitative) gains

Rates of interest on loans and advances by private moneylenders, indigenous bankers, finance companies, etc. carry an element of monopoly (or exploitative) gain as well. Usually, these rates are much higher than the rates charged on loans and advances by banks or the rates of interest prevailing in the organized bond market. The excess of the former over the latter cannot all be easily explained in terms of the factors discussed above, namely, default risk, lower liquidity, term to maturity and lender's cost of servicing the loan. The small borrowers whom the private moneylenders serve usually have no alternative source of funds to turn to. In a village, a few local moneylenders may be the only source of credit. Thus, local money-lenders enjoy a position of monopoly or oligopoly. And being aware of it, they take full advantage of it.

Most small borrowers in villages and even in cities borrow under duress. Most often, with them profit calculus involving a comparison between the expected rate of return and the rate of interest on borrowed funds does not have much meaning. For, being self-employed (in agriculture, handicrafts, cottage industry, small trade, etc.), even the earning of labour income is entirely dependent on the availability of sufficient capital to carry on in their hereditary occupations. Therefore, such borrowers are in extremely weak borrowing position and often times submit to extortionist tactics of moneylenders. The position of medium borrowers is slightly better, because they can borrow funds from institutional sources, and can also afford to reject potential loan offers if the rate of interest is too high in comparison with the expected rate of profit from their planned investment. Under such conditions, the only way to protect the small borrower from the high-cost finance of the moneylender is to provide him institutional finance through banks and cooperative credit societies. On the one hand, such institutions would, then, meet a growing proportion of the credit needs of the small borrower, and on the other, help lower the stranglehold of moneylenders on small borrowers.

7. **Other reasons**

The lending rates of banks (whether commercial, co-operative, or other) are not uniform for all borrowers. Instead, under the policy directives of the RBI, credit is given to borrowers of priority sectors (Section 6.3) and weaker sections (under the Differential Interest Rate Scheme) at concessional rates. The same is also true of credit extended by other official credit agencies.

17.5 Equalising and Non-equalising Differences in Interest Rates

It will be useful to cross-classify the above sources of differences in several rates of interest under two heads as *(a)* equalising differences and *(b)* non-equalising differences.[2] The former differences are those that arise due to the presence of certain real costs on the lender's side over and above the mere lending of cash and represent market compensations for these real costs at competitive rates. The latter differences are purely the result of market imperfections and policy decisions and do not represent any reward or compensation for any additional service rendered to the borrower or any additional real cost incurred (or direct gains made) by the lender in making a loan.

Under the classificatory scheme adopted above, the differences in interest rates arising under the first five sources can be called equalising differences. If a lender undertakes any risk of default or overdues, or suffers greater illiquidity and market risk, or incurs any cost in servicing the loan, or renders any service to the borrower over and above that of ordinary loan-making, he should be entitled to an adequate compensation for these services, otherwise he would not be induced to combine these services with loan making. What constitutes adequate compensation is, however, not easy to say.

Monopoly (or expolitative) gains, by definition, represent a non-equalising difference in interest. They are neither a reward for any additional service rendered to the borrower, nor a compensation for any additional cost incurred by the lender. They are purely the result of a superior bargaining position of the lender in an imperfect market for loanable funds, where the alternative sources of such funds are few. If competition is introduced in these market, such gains will tend to disappear over time, whereas in competitive credit markets equalising differences in rates of interest will still survive, so long as the real cost (services) associated with them continue to be incurred (rendered) by lenders as before. With appropriate reorganizations of lending practices, institutions, and markets and with improvement in the working efficiency of banks and credit societies and reduction in their bad debts and overdues, these cost (equalising differences) can also be reduced. Policy-determined differences are, of course, a different matter.

17.6 Deficiencies in the Prevailing System of Administered Interest Rates

The RBI's Chakravarty Committee (1985) has examined the prevailing system of administered interest rates in India. It has highlighted its major deficiencies and come up with various recommendations for restructuring the system. In this section, we shall study only the deficiencies, the Committee's recommendations in this connection will be discussed in Appendix F.

The prevailing system suffers from the following well-known deficiencies:

1. *Relatively low yield on government securities.* The yield on government securities has been kept exceedingly low. For example, the rate on 91-day treasury bills has been kept fixed at 4.6% p.a. since 1974, whereas the other administered money market rates (e.g., the Bank Rate of the RBI, the commercial bills discount rate of banks) have gone up. Such low yield does not even cover the average cost of funds to banks and has been negative in real terms over most of the past 20 years or so. As a result, more than 90% of the outstanding treasury bills are held by the RBI alone as a captive holder; other holders of these bills, mainly banks, rediscount them with the RBI at the earliest opportunity.

Till recently, the same has also been broadly true of long-term and medium-term dated government securities which used to carry very low coupon rates. (Since 1982-83 these rates have been progressively revised upward. Now, the 20-year government securities carry a respectable 11.5% p.a. coupon rate.) The banks and other financial institutions (like L.I.C. and G.I.C. and subsidiaries) have been investing in them only to meet the Statutory Liquidity Ratio (SLR) requirement (see Section 18.6) imposed on them. Even then, a large part of the public debt has to be held by the RBI. This has led to a considerable monetisation of public debt, resulting in high levels of monetary expansion and inflationary pressures.

This phenomenon of the monetisation of public debt may be briefly explained. When the RBI buys treasury bills or other government securities, it pays for them ultimately by issuing its currency or deposits to the government. When the government spends it or them, the amount of H (high-powered money) with the public and banks goes up and through the money-multiplier process the amount of M in the economy increases. In technical language, the above process has monetised public debt, that is, has converted non-money public debt into money (through the intermediation of the RBI as the currency authority), leading to high levels of monetary expansion. Clearly, this (the high level of monetary expansion) is the price the economy has been paying for providing low interest debt to the government.

The policy has had other effects, too. It has hindered the growth of wide, deep, and active money market and capital market in public debt in the country. What market exists is the 'captive market' maintained by the *SLR-type* requirement where only financial institutions participate to meet their statutory requirement.[3] Funds from other sources, avoid this market, mainly because of low yield from government paper. All this has limited greatly the scope for the use of open market operations by the RBI. The low yield coupled with SLR requirement has adversely affected the profitability of banks. More importantly, the low rates of interest have encouraged inefficient use of credit (and other capital funds) in the government and the public sector in the selection of investment projects, long gestation lags in their completion, and careless operation afterwards.[4]

2. *Too Many Concessional Rates of Interest.* A complex system of multiple concessional rates of interest for priority sector and different categories of industrial projects, borrowers and regions, and that, too, for long-term loans as well has grown around administered rates. Thereby the government tries to favour or appease various interests, without ensuring adequate delivery of credit to target groups. Some of the concessional rates barely cover the cost of funds to banks and, in certain cases, are even lower than this cost. Availability of relatively cheap credit has had several deleterious effects, e.g., it has harmed effective use of credit, promoted poor quality of project preparation and inefficient project implementation and operation, heavy accumulation of inventories financed with bank credit, uneconomic creation of additional capacity and its consequent under-utilization, etc. Strange though it may sound, a large part of industrial sickness also is due to cheap institutional credit which has demoted cost conciousness among industrialists.

3. *Shortcomings in the Fixation of Deposit and Lending Rates of Interest of Banks.* Under the prevailing administered interest rate system, both the deposit rates of interest, the maximum lending rate of interest and concessional rates of interest for priority sector and other designated sectors are fixed by the RBI. Each set of rates suffers from shortcomings as explained below.

Fixed deposits of banks are an important medium of savings mobilisation of the public. But till the upward revision of rates of interest on them in 1982 even the maximum rate of interest on fixed deposits did not protect depositors fully against the erosion of the real value of their deposits by inflation. Thus, over the 14-year period of 1971-84, half the time, the real rate on them was negative. This must have discouraged their growth to some extent, though their recorded rate of growth has been impressively high and that, too, in the face of competition of higher rates of interest on unsecured deposits of companies, corporate bonds and other savings media. Possibly, this is due to relatively greater security and liquidity which fixed deposits with banks offer their depositors.

Another factor worth noting in this connection is that for the richer savers these deposits offer *effective* rates of interest that are much higher than the nominal rates. This is because of the tax exemptions (full or partial) allowed on interest income from banks, post offices and other tax-exempt savings media (upto a certain maximum). Obviously, the richer the saver and the higher his marginal income-tax bracket, the greater his tax saving from tax exemption and higher the effective rate of interest to them when tax gain is taken into account. On the opposite end, there are depositors with no taxable income even when interest income from banks has been taken fully into account. They do not gain anything from the aforesaid tax concession. Therefore, this policy of tax concessions is highly regressive and on the principle of social justice should be done away with. The irony is that the Chakravarty Committee (1985, para 10.29), after having recognized the element of social injustice embodied in the aforesaid tax-concession policy, has recommended its retention in the name of capturing larger financial savings in the form of tax-favoured financial assets (see Appendix F). A better and socially just way out would have been sticking only to a reasonable positive real rate of return. There is also a case for bringing about reasonable uniformity in effective rates of interest on various official savings media.

As to the non-concessional lending rates of banks, the system suffers from lack of flexibility in these rates in response to changing market conditions and the need for controlling better (through cost incentives) bank credit and its allocation. This can be accomplished better if banks are allowed to vary their lending rates of interest (subject to a certain minimum rate fixed by the RBI, but no maximum—see Appendix F). Greater interest rate competition among banks and with non-bank financial institutions can be expected to improve the working efficiency, selection of loan proposals, and customer service.

4. *Excessive Reliance on Quantitative Controls on Credit for regulating Aggregate Demand.* This kind of reliance has been prompted as well as necessitated by the system of relatively low administered interest rates which encourages excess demand for bank credit—that is, demand which cannot be met fully by banks from the resources they are able to mobilise from the public. Then, under this system, the interest rates are not changed frequently enough in response to changes in market conditions or for purposes of monetary manage-

ment of demands, In such a situation, the *supportive role* of price mechanism in regulating aggregate demand and in ensuring more effective use of credit needs to be explicitly recognized. This will require that a suitable interest-rate policy is evolved as a tool of monetary management. This, of course, should be kept fully compatible with the policy of monetary targeting discussed elsewhere (see Appendix F). It may be noted that proper use of short-term interest rates as a tool of monetary management can reinforce the anti-inflationary impact of monetary targeting.

NOTES

1. It might be added that, impressed by the importance of stock demand and stock supply of bonds, several neoclassical economists prefer to explain the determination of the rate of interest by the simple stock-equilibrium theory as applied to the market for bonds.

2. The distinction between equalising and non-equalising differences in rates of interest is analogous to the one often-times made in the case of wage-differentials (see Friedman, 1962, Chapter 11, pp. 211–25).

3. It should be remembered that the RBI is the single most important 'captive holder' of government securities (including treasury bills).

4. It must, however, be noted that the low cost of borrowed funds is only one of the factors (and not the most important factor at that) for the inefficient use of capital in the government, political corruption in decision-making and implementation being the relatively more important factor. If this were so, raising the cost of credit to the government in accordance with the recommendations of the Committee (see Appendix F) may turn out to be unrequited loss to it—its cost of credit may increase without yielding the anticipated benefits.

Part Three : Policy

The nominal supplies of money and bank credit are highly amenable to policy manipulation. Changes in these supplies and the allocation of bank credit influence much the level and composition of economic activity and their several correlates such as real output, employment, growth, prices, distribution of income and wealth, etc. For both these reasons, money supply and bank credit have been traditional concerns of actual policy-making as well as academic analysis. Our study of institutions and theory in the first two parts of the book has prepared the ground for studying various aspects of monetary and credit policies in the Indian context. This will be attempted in the next three chapters. In Chapter 18, the need and rationale of the usual distinction between goals, targets, and indicators of monetary policy are explained, and the choice and formulation of goals and targets for the Indian economy discussed. Chapter 19 is devoted to a systematic discussion of the several instruments of control, both quantitative and qualitative. Chapter 20 closes the discussion of this Part with a study of the planning of credit allocation at various levels.

Part Three: Policy

The nominal supplies of money and bank credit are highly amenable to policy manipulation. Changes in these supplies and the allocation of bank credit influence much the level and composition of economic activity and their several correlates such as that of output, employment, growth, prices, distribution of income and wealth, etc. For both these reasons, money supply and bank credit have been traditional concerns of actual policy-making as well as academic analysis. Our study of institutions and theory in the first two parts of the book has prepared the ground for studying various aspects of monetary and credit policies in the Indian context. This will be attempted in the next three chapters. In Chapter 18 the need and rationale of the usual distinction between goals, targets, and indicators of monetary policy are explained, and the choice and formulation of goals and targets for the Indian economy discussed. Chapter 19 is devoted to a systematic discussion of the several instruments of control, both quantitative and qualitative. Chapter 20 closes the discussion of this Part with a study of the planning of credit allocation at various levels.

CHAPTER 18

Goals, Targets and Indicators

18.1 Introduction

By monetary policy we mean policy concerned with changes in the supply of money. Correspondingly, it seems natural to define credit policy as policy concerned with changes in the supply of credit. But it can be and is much more than this and so for several reasons. First, unlike money, credit is not merely a matter of aggregate supply, but also, a matter of its allocation among competing uses and users. Then, there are different sources of credit, institutional and non-institutional, and even among institutional sources, banks are only one, though primary, source. Besides quantity, other aspects of credit such as its cost and other terms and conditions, duration, renewal, risk of default, etc. are also important for both the borrower and the lender. Thus, the potential domain of credit policy is very wide — much wider than that of monetary policy. (To make the discussion managable, in this chapter and the next two, we shall study only about policy concerning *(a)* total quantity of bank credit and *(b)* its allocation among competing uses and users.

We should also note other points of difference between monetary policy and credit policy (howsoever defined), which will throw further light on the nature of two policies. Fundamental among them is the point that money is an asset of the holding public but liability of the producers of money — the government and the RBI for currency and banks for deposit money, whereas bank credit is asset of banks and liability of the borrowing public and the government. This asset-liability distinction is not purely of accounting value. It underlies much of monetary theorising. In part Two of the book we have seen how the demand function for money serves as the foundation of monetary theory, whether of the 'quantity theory of money' vintage (in the Cambridge cash-balances tradition) or of the Keynesian vintage. Broadly speaking, given the stable demand function for money, an autonomous change in the supply of money leads either to a direct change in the level of money income (*a la* the quantity theory of money) or first to a change in the rate of interest which then leads to a change in the rate of investment and then to a change in the level of income *a la* the Keynesian theory. In either case the explanation of the transmission mechanism whereby a change in the supply of money induces a change in expenditure in the commodity market depends crucially on the nature of the public's demand function for money posited. A comparable theory of the 'supply of credit effect' which may explain why and how an autonomous change in the supply of (bank) credit will affect several endogenous variables has not been worked out.

Since in Keynes' monetary theory changes in the supply of money influence economic activity through prior effect on the market rate of interest, this theory is a 'cost of credit' theory. Accordingly, in the Keynesian monetary policy maximum emphasis is laid on the manipulability of the rate of interest (or the interest-rate structure). This distinguishes the Keynesian theory of monetary policy both from the 'monetarist' theory of monetary policy which emphasises the direct money-stock effect after the quantity theory of money, and from the 'credit' theory of monetary policy which emphasises the 'availabiltiy of credit' effect.

On the supply side of money and bank credit, however, there are several points of commonality: *(i)* the same authority, the central bank, administers both kinds of policies, *(ii)* the instruments of control *at the aggregate level* are the same, and *(iii)* the same forces determine the supply of money as well as the supply of bank credit (Section 16.2). Presumably, it is these common points which militate against any distinction between monetary policy and bank credit policy. But, for reasons given earlier such a distinction is very much warranted and is essential for analytical clarity, correct policy formulation and its proper evaluation. This should not, however, be misread to say that monetary policy and credit policy are totally unrelated. In fact, in this chapter and the next, most of the time, we shall study the two policies together. Only in Chapter 20, we shall study issues that pertain only to credit policy.

18.2 Goals, Targets, Indicators, and Instruments

In recent discussion on the theory of monetary policy, a

distinction is made among *(i)* goals, *(ii)* targets, *(iii)* indicators, and *(iv)* instruments of monetary policy. The distinction between goals and instruments is quite old (see Tinbergen, 1952). The newcomers on the scene of theoretical discussion are the concepts of targets and indicators. To fix ideas and to aid later discussion, we list below variables under each head which are currently treated as candidates for attention.

Goals

1. maximum feasible output,
2. high rate of growth,
3. fuller employment,
4. price stability (or 'optimal' rate of inflation ?),
5. greater equality in the distribution of income and wealth,
6. healthy balance in the balance of payments.

Targets

1. money supply,
2. bank credit,
3. interest rates.

Indicators

1. high-powered money (adjusted)
2. money supply,
3. bank credit,
4. interest rates.

Instruments

1. open market operations,
2. variations in reserve requirements,
3. Reserve Bank credit to bannks (including development banks) : cost, availability,
4. statutory liquidity requirement,
5. selective credit controls.

The relationship among the above variables is dominated by the following sequence:

instruments → indicators → targets → goals.

The reverse sequence in which the influence may run from the goal variables to targets and indicators and even to instruments in some cases is relatively much weaker. In this chapter we shall discuss only goals, targets, and indicators of monetary policy; the instruments of control will be discussed in the next chapter.

18.3 Goals of Monetary Policy [1]

In the previous section we had listed six commonly-accepted goals of economic policy, which also serve as goals of monetary policy/credit policy. In this section we discuss how monetary policy/credit policy may help or hinder the attainment of these goals. the relative effectiveness of monetary policy and of credit policy, and possible conflicts among the goals.

We have already said above that monetary policy operates through changes in the stock of money, which changes influence the level of *aggregate* demand for output in money terms, either directly (as in the quantity theory of money) or indirectly through the rate of interest (as in the Keynesian theory). Two features of it are noteworthy. One is that it is an aggregative policy; any allocational or sectoral problems are beyond its domain and lie within the sphere of credit policy; the other is that it operates on the demand side and not on the supply side of the commodity market; again, credit policy can affect even the supply side of output. This delimitation of monetary policy is too sharp; it is drawn to help appreciate the role and limitations of monetary policy better than is usually done.

What kind of monetary policy can serve best all the policy goals ? It's a tall order, because there are six goals and only one 'instrumental variable', the supply of money.[2] Yet the task can be done reasonably well, if the monetary authority follows a policy of *'long-run price stability at maximum feasible output'*. For short, we shall call it the policy of *'long-run neutral money'*. We discuss below the rationale, meaning and difficulties of such a policy.

For price-level stability it is necessary to avoid both inflationary and deflationary pressures. Moreover, we want this stability not at any level of output, but at the level of maximum feasible output, empirically defined as 'full-capacity output'. In the Indian context, given the structural imbalance between the supply of labour and the supply of the co-operating factors of production, such as land and capital, full employment of labour in the near future is usually treated as structurally infeasible. Without going into the normative aspect of this view, we accept it as a binding policy constraint in the present socio-political framework and economic organization so far as the employment-generating aspect of output management is concerned.

Accordingly, in the Indian context, full-capacity output is the appropriate counterpart of the concept of full-employment output used in western economies.

The concept of full-capacity output viewed as short-run maximum feasible output implies that, at the aggregate level, any increase in the demand for output beyond this ceiling level cannot lead to any increase in output and must result in pure inflation of prices only. When aggregate demand (at prevailing prices) falls short of ceiling output, we shall have deflation, which will surely reduce output and also reduce such prices as are flexible downwards. The neutral-money policy is designed to avoid both inflationary and deflationary situations.

The accent in our goal prescription is on *long-run* average stability of prices, and not on complete year-to-year stability of prices, which kind of price stability is much harder to attain. In other words, we are only prescribing against a price policy which has a positive inflationary trend built into it. In the present state of our knowledge of the Indian economy, we are also not aiming at any contracyclical role of the monetary policy (see Gupta, 1979, PP. 35–9).

14.3.1 Difficulties and Conflicts

Several structural difficulties can arise in the actual realization of the twin objectives of full-capacity output and price-level stability. One set of difficulties is associated with the phenomenon of 'stagflation', the other with the operation of cost-push forces. Each one is discussed serially below.

Stagflation refers to a situation of inflation combined with growing 'excess capacity' in the economy. The emergence of this phenomenon shows that in the prevailing situation increases in aggregate demand instead of increasing output in the face of excess capacity and unemployment only result in higher and higher prices. This shows clearly that the problem is not one of deficiency of *aggregate demand*, whatever else the situation may be the result of. Several causes are possible, of which only two may be briefly mentioned. On the demand side, the composition of demand may not be such as conforms to the installed productive capacity in the economy. For example, the government may ask cotton textile mills to produce a certain quantity of coarse cloth, but the poor households as potential consumers of such cloth may not have adequate purchasing power to buy such cloth. Equally or more important are the supply-side bottlenecks, which may arise due to acute shortages of key basic inputs, such as power (coal and electricity), transport, or some essential raw materials and spare parts imported from abroad, or serious labour troubles, or policy hurdles and uncertainties created by excessive government intervention in economic affairs. A detailed analysis of recent episodes of inflation will show how well these explanations are and how the importance of individual factors has varied from one episode to another and from one industry to another within the same episode of inflation. The lesson to learn from such experiences is that pushing up the aggregate demand through monetary policy is no substitute for correcting either structural imbalances in the composition of aggregate demand or the supply-side bottlenecks. If output is to be pushed up to the full-capacity level, specific measures to meet the difficulties of individual industries will have to be undertaken without generating excess aggregate demand.

The 'neutral money' policy of our conception combines two policy goals, viz. maximum feasible output and price stability, into one. It presumes that these two goals are consistent with each other, or that there is no inherent conflict between the two. This presumption will not be justified if strong autonomous cost-push forces are operative in the economy.

Three sets of such forces may be briefly examined. One which has received a lot of attention in the west is the demand for money wage increases in excess of the increases in productivity per worker. This phenomenon is captured in the celebrated Phillips Curve (Section 14.7) which gives a downward sloping relation between such excessive demands for the rate of increase in money wages and rate of unemployment. The hypothesis is that as the economy nears the point of maximum feasible output (full-employment output in developed countries), the autonomous money-wage demands get pushed up giving inflationary push to the price level. Therefore, it might be argued that maximum feasible output can be realized only at some positive rate of inflation.

Whatever the validity of the Phillips Curve hypothesis for the developed countries (see Section 14.7), it is not of much importance for the Indian economy. Apart from a high rate of chronic unemployment, by and large workers in India are not organized in strong trade unions to be able to demand *autonomous* wage increases. This is unquestionably true of the mass of agricultural workers and workers in the large unorganized sector of rural industries, cottage and small-scale industries and service industries in urban areas. The relative size of the large-scale organized sector (manufacturing industries and such service industries as banking, insurance, railways, and government establishments) in total wage employment is still quite small. In this sector also most of the money wage increases so far have been of a 'corrective nature', which compensate workers (in several cases only partially and with lag) for prior increases in their cost of living. To the extent some groups of workers are able to protect their real wages and may also gain some increase in them through increases in money wages and other workers are not so successful in gaining similar increases in money wages, the relative wage structure changes in favour of the former group and against the latter group and causes much heart-burning among those losing to the forces of inflation. But this phenomenon cannot be interpreted as evidence of wage-push phenomenon.

Another source of cost-push inflation can be increases in the prices of imported goods and services. To the extent India is a relatively small buyer in the world market, world prices are given data to it. Therefore, if the prices of essential imports such as oil, capital goods, spare parts, essential raw materials, and even essential consumer goods such as vegetable oil go up, some inflation gets imported into the country through them. (On this ground, much spectre has been associated with the sixfold increase in the price of crude oil since October 1973.) The contribution to inflation of such increases in the price level is not only direct, but also indirect through induced increases in the prices of other goods for whose production the imported goods serve as inputs. To the extent certain goods are imported on government account and, for reasons of social policy, are distributed to the public at prices which do not cover fully the rise in their import prices, their distribution has to be subsidised through the budget, which goes to enhance deficit in the government budget.

All the problems connected with the above phenomenon and its explanation cannot be discussed here for reasons of space. But one general point can be made. How much of a cost push an increase in the price of an imported good represents will depend upon three factors: *(i)* the weight of that good's import in the price index number, *(ii)* the combined weight in the price index number of the products of industries using the imported good as an input adjusted for the proportions of total costs of individual products which the imported good constitutes, and *(iii)* the annual percentage increase in the import price of the good. Detailed commodity-group-wise analysis of Indian data has not been undertaken. Therefore, the relative importance of imported inflation in India's inflationary experience cannot be assessed. However, we may illustrate the main point of the argument with the help of a hypothetical example. Suppose over a year unit value of imports, giving the weighted average price of imports, goes up by 10 per cent. We know that on average imports constitute about 8 per cent of India's GNP. We may *assume* that when indirect influence of import prices in the price structure is taken into account, the weight of import prices is double that of the direct weight of 8 per cent, that is, the full weight is 16 per cent. On this rough estimate, the 10 per cent rise in import prices will contribute 16 ×.1 = 1.6 per cent push to the general price level in the country.

The third source of cost-push can be 'autonomous' increase in administered prices — an upward push in such prices which is autonomous of not only excess demand conditions in the commodity market, but also of wage-cost push and imported inflation already discussed above. For example, if administered prices are revised upward to cover the increase in money-wage cost due to wage push, then considering increase in administered prices *in addition to* wage-cost push will mean double counting of the same phenomenon. Administered prices are now common phenomena in the organized sector of manufacturing industries, services and public utilities. Some of these are in the public sector, others in the private sector. In the former, almost all increases in prices are delayed adjustments to increases in cost of production. Therefore, such upward revisions in prices are, in no sense, autonomous, though when they are made, they do raise the general price level. But the point to appreciate is that they are not the cause of inflation; instead, they themselves are the result of past inflation in the economy. So far as administered prices in the private sector are concerned, they can be pushed up autonomously depending upon the degree of monopoly/oligopoly power firms enjoy in the market for their products. Such autonomous upward pushes are not unknown either. But no estimates are available about their relative weight in any inflationary episode. However, it can be asserted with confidence that most of the time even such upward pushes of administered prices are widespread and large only in a situation of excess demand in the commodity market, so that if excess demand conditions are avoided or kept within small limits, the scope as well as inducement for autonomous increases of administered prices will be small.

14.3.2 Neutral Money and Other Policy Goals

Our major contention is that monetary policy will serve best the other goals when it takes on the form of the policy of 'long-run neutral money'. That is, when monetary policy is conducted with a view to long-run price stability at maximum feasible output, other goals of economic policy, viz., fuller employment, a high rate of growth, greater equality, and healthy balance of payments are also promoted to the maximum extent. The alternative we have in mind is an inflationary monetary policy, which will be injurious to each one of these goals. This contention is briefly explained.

It is well known that inflation causes large-scale redistribution of income and wealth in a society. The losers are the fixed-income people (most wage-earners and rentiers) and monetary creditors (bond-holders, pensioners, depositors, holders of cash balances, etc.). The gainers are the variable-income people (profit-earners) and monetary debtors. The gains and losses from inflation arise because all prices and nominal values do not rise equiproportionately : some rise more or faster while others remain fixed for a long period. In most cases, the redistribution is in favour of the richer sections of the population. Thus, inflation is inequality-enhancing and highly iniquitous. The neutral-money policy by avoiding inflation will eliminate an important source of growing inequalities, tax evasion, black markets, and corruption.

Under neutral-money policy *excess* deficit financing by the government will have to be cut down totally. The government, therefore, will be compelled to raise more resources through taxes, which will require stricter tax vigilance and stamping down tax evasion, which enhances economic inequalities. Neutral-money policy will reduce tax evasion by inducing less of it and by requiring the government also to allow less of it. Thus, it will promote greater equality by lessening tax evasion.

Credit policy can play a positive role in reducing economic and social inequalities by giving preference to productive loan proposals coming from the weaker members of the society (see Section 20.6).

The relation of monetary policy to economic development is indirect through the effect it has on *(a)* the rate of saving and investment in the economy and *(b)* the allocation of resources. It is sometimes claimed in favour of an inflationary monetary policy that it is growth-promoting because by transferring income and wealth from low savers (workers) to high savers (profit-earners and the government) it increases the over-all saving rate in the economy. The latter is known as the doctrine of *forced saving*. It is true so far as the absolute poor as losers from inflation are concerned, because they are so poor that they are forced to reduce their consumption in full when their real incomes fall. And it is through reduction in consumption that real savings are generated. But there is another large group of losers from inflation who are not so poor and who have been saving voluntarily. When inflation erodes their real incomes, for some time at least, they do not reduce their real consumption and their savings fall instead. This argument is based on the 'hypothesis of asymmetrical consumption behaviour' or the 'hypothesis of downward stickiness of consumption standards' (Gupta 1979, Section 1.8). Simultaneously, the gainers from inflation do raise their consumption. Consequently, total real consumption may increase rather than fall, and the reverse will be true of savings. Therefore, it cannot be taken as axiomatic truth that inflation necessarily raises the saving rate.

The counter-proposition that neutral-money policy will encourage higher savings and greater institutionalisation of savings has much greater validity. For the bulk of household savers, financial assets such as deposits of financial institutions and non-financial corporations or cash balances and marketable securities (bonds and equities) are the best and the most convenient form of holding their savings (wealth). During inflation the real value of such financial assets (except equities) declines, because their face value is denominated in nominal terms. Thus their holders suffer capital losses in real terms. Once inflation comes to be foreseen, asset holders' demand for financial assets will tend to decline. To avoid foreseen real capital losses, they will be encouraged not to hold financial assets. In the absence of acceptable tangible assets with qualities of divisibility, low risk, no-need for personal supervision etc., most of the households will be encouraged to save less and consume more. This will tend to lower the saving rate. In addition to this, the institutionalisation of savings will decline, because the rates of interest on deposits of financial institutions are slow to be revised upward to compensate the depositors for capital loss from inflation and the rates of interest in the unorganized market move higher faster under the impact of inflation. Thus there is a diversion of funds from financial institutions to unorganized markets. This is not conducive to controlled allocation of funds/resources. More specifically, funds tend to flow into socially-unproductive and harmful activities of speculative hoarding of goods in short supply to reap quick and high private gains from inflationary increase in prices; genuinely productive activities suffer relatively for want of funds. Price stability does not encourage such maluse of scarce resources on a large scale. Then, by reducing uncertainties generated by inflation about the future behaviour of prices of products and inputs, their availability, labour discipline etc., price stability tends to encourage investment, too. Thus, neutral-money policy is highly conducive to growth, both by encouraging higher rates of saving and investment and by better allocation of resources.

Credit policy in its allocational aspect can augment the wholesome effects of neutral-money policy by making credit allocation production-oriented rather than security-oriented as it is at present.

The maximum that monetary policy *per se* can do for encouraging fuller employment in the economy is achieved when it pursues the goal of neutral money as defined above. In the short run, when maximum feasible output is produced, the associated employment will also be the maximum feasible under the circumstances. Over a longer run, a monetary policy which encourages a higher rate of growth will also increase employment opportunities. The neutral-money policy will promote employment further by encouraging less-capital-intensive industries and techniques of production. This is because the cost of capital which is made artificially low by inflation will be nearer its true value in a regime of price stability. What makes the cost of capital artificially low during inflation is the common experience of loan rates of interest not rising sufficiently by the full amount of inflation, so that the rate of interest (as cost of borrowed funds) when adjusted for the expected rate of inflation is lowered, which encourages more capital-intensive industries and techniques of production. This inflation-induced distortion in capital market, coupled with defective allocation of institutional credit and liberal tax concessions in the form of investment allowance have done much damage to employment expansion in India, with the result that over the past 20 years the rate of growth of emplyment has not even kept pace with the rate of growth of output in the economy, much less exceed it.

Credit policy can play a direct and more positive role in employment expansion if credit is made available much more liberally to labour-intensive enterprises and at concessional rates of interest. This is something not open to monetary policy, which is inherently aggregative in character.

The goal of promoting a healthy balance in the balance of payments will also be best served by the policy of price stability, as this will encourage exports, discourage imports into the country, and attract net capital inflows. If trading partners suffer from inflation, export duties can be used to siphon off at least a part of the difference between high export prices and low domestic prices.

Thus, the policy of long-run neutrality of money will best serve the several goals of monetary policy listed earlier.

18.4 Targets of Monetary Policy

The monetary authority uses various instruments of monetary control in order to influence the goal variables in desired directions and degrees. To decide optimally what to do next, it would like to know what effects its current policy actions are having on the goal variables. But in a dynamic world of uncertainty, these effects are not only delayed and distributed over time, the underlying lag structure and the determinants of it are also not known reliably. Then, there is always delay in getting full information about the true state of goal variables such as real income and employment, not to say of the distribution of income and wealth about which much is not known in quantitative terms for any period. We should also recognize that the processing and interpretation of information are time-consuming. Furthermore, the goal variables are affected both by policy measures and non-policy developments and the effects of the two cannot be easily separated, as our knowledge of the economic structure is incomplete and imperfect, that is, we do not have reliable estimates of the true values of various structural coefficients.

All these information gaps make the task of policy-making very difficult and hazardous. Therefore, policy-makers need, and in practice follow, some other variable or variables as proxies for goal variables and use them as their immediate policy targets or indicators or both to guide their policy steps. The proxy variables are also used to characterise policies as expansionary or contractionary, easy or tight, inflationary or neutral, etc. Recent discussions on targets and indicators examine critically the basis as well as soundness of such practice and characterisations. The issue is important because if the monetary authority follows false policy targets or indicators, its policy actions can do more harm than good to policy goals, howsoever well-intentioned the policy actions may be.

The target variables are endogenous variables which the monetary authority tries to control or influence so as to influence the goal variables in the desired manner. To serve the target function well, a chosen target variable should possess the following four qualifications

1. it should be closely related to goal variables and this relation should be well understood and reliably estimable,

2. it should be rapidly affected by policy instruments,
3. non-policy influences on it should be relatively small, i.e., small relative to policy influences, and
4. it should be readily observable (and measurable) with little or no time lag.

Traditionally, three variables have served as candidates for monetary-policy targets. They are: money supply, bank credit, and interest rates in securities market. Which one or more of them should be chosen as targets and why ? All the three satisfy equally well condition *(4)* listed above. There, the similarity among them ends. Both money supply and bank credit meet almost equally well conditions *(2)* and *(3)*, whereas interest rates do not fulfil these conditions satisfactorily. Not all market rates of interest change together and equiproportionately. Even when attention is concentrated on one rate treated as the key rate or on a weighted average of a few market rates, qualifications *(2)* and *(3)* are not met easily. This is so because non-policy factors impinge rather heavily on the behaviour of market rates of interest, much more so than such factors do on money supply and bank credit. Also, they are not affected by policy instruments as rapidly as the two other contenders for the status of monetary-policy targets.

Coming to qualification *(1)*, we should recall the dicussion of monetary theory in Part Two of the book. Of the two main approaches to monetary theory, the Keynesian macro theory emphasises the interest-rate channel and the neo-classical monetary theory emphasises the direct money stock effect (the quantity theory of money). Correspondingly, Keynesians prescribe interest rates as appropriate target variables and monetarists recommend money supply for this position. Practical central bankers and a minority of economists who are of the opinion that the availabiltiy of credit acts as a major constraint on the deficit spending of the public tend to follow or recommend bank credit as the best target variable. The theory as well as empirical evidence in support of the close causal link between bank credit and the level of economic activity (and other goal variables) are rather weak. Also, on the demand as well as the supply sides, money and bank credit (via bank deposits) behave similarly. Therefore, money supply scores over bank credit as a target variable. As between money and interest rates, money comes out as a superior target variable. Briefly, the reasons are:

1. money supply meets conditions *(2)* and *(3)* much better than interest rates. The weaknesses of the latter on these scores have already been noted above. Money supply also is an endogenous

variable and is affected by both policy factors and non-policy factors. But the discussion in Chapter 15 tells us that money supply is much more easily policy-manipulable than interest rates and that, most of the time, the weight of policy factors in money-supply variations is far more important than the weight of non-policy factors;

2. empirically the relation between changes in money supply and changes in money expenditure (as a measure of the level of economic activity and an essential link with various goal variables) is highly stable and well estimable. The same cannot be claimed in favour of interest rates. So, money supply meets condition *(1)* also better than interest rates.

On the above grounds, money supply (M^S), or the rate of growth of money supply ($\dot{M}$) in a growing economy, turns out as the single best target of monetary policy. That being so, the monetary authority must consciously choose the *target* rate of growth of money supply (represented by $\dot{M}^*$) that will best serve the chosen policy goal of price stability with maximum feasible output. The stated target value of M will then serve as the test of the degree of success or failure of the monetary policy as actually conducted. It has been argued that such a value of $\dot{M}^*$ will be given by the 'money-absorptive capacity' or the demand for money of the economy when it is growing along its path of maximum feasible output with stable prices (Gupta, 1979, Chapter 2)

On empirical grounds we state (*i*) that the best estimate of the income elasticity of demand for money in India is unity (Section 11.7), (*ii*) that the trend rate of growth of real income in India has been about 5% per year, and (*iii*) that factors other than real income (including monetisation of the Indian economy) do not or are not likely to exert significant influence on the demand for money in India (Section 11.7), the highest permissible value of $\dot{M}^*$ comes to 5% per year. Any value higher than this can be justified either on grounds of strong cost-push factors beyond the control of the authorities or on the ground that an inflationary monetary policy is positively beneficial for policy goals.[3] In either event it is incumbent on the authorities to lay bare their hand and state clearly the basis of their solution of $\dot{M}^*$. To the best of our knowledge, the RBI has not attempted such a task explicitly. Therefore, we are constrained to conclude that 'the stock of money has been (and is still) treated as a residual quantity of no major significance, variations in which are allowed to be the outcome of several other policy decisions, autonomous policy developments, and random changes' (Gupta, 1974 c, p. 265). The conclusion is reinforced by the actual behaviour of M, which had the average annual value of 3.65% during the 1950s, of 8.9 % during the 1960s, of 11.7 % during the 1970s, and 13.2 % during the 1980s.

18.5 The Indicator Problem

A monetary-policy indicator is needed to measure correctly the intensity of policy actions, so that by looking at it we can know how much of a change in the target variable already chosen (money supply as argued above) is due to policy actions. This should help evaluate, guide, and readjust policy actions quickly. The underlying presumption is that the indicator chosen will be at least one step closer to the authorities than the target variable, so that it will record policy actions much more honestly than the target variable which can get affected by other influences as well. On this criterion, the ideal indicator will be the one which is influenced by only policy actions. The existence of such an indicator will also presume that all policy actions can be translated into a single measure. Such an ideal indicator (on either of the above two counts) does not exist. All the available candidates for the indicator's position (listed in Section 18.2) suffer on both counts — each one is influenced by non-policy factors and no one can provide a single-measure translation of policy actions of all kinds. Therefore, whatever imperfect variable is used as an indicator, it must be supplemented by qualitative analysis.

However, the indicator problem is not a spurious one, because the authorities do use some indicator or the other, knowingly or otherwise, to gauge the intensity of their actions and to guide their steps for further action. And the use of a faulty indicator can result in perverse policy actions. An example will make the point clear. Assume an inflationary situation in which rates of interest go up due to all-round inflationary expectations. If the rate of interest is used as the policy indicator, the monetary authority will misinterpret the rise in the rate of interest as anti-inflationary and may not do anything to curb inflation. Worse policy actions can result, if the interest rate is also used as the policy target and its target value is arrived at without regard for inflationary expectations and what these expectations can do to the market-determined rates of interest. This example has much relevance for the strong inflationary climate prevailing currently in several countries including India and high and rising levels of rates of interest in them.

Of the four possible indicators listed in Section 18.2, the rate of interest is the poorest candidate, next best is bank credit, money supply is still better, and the adjusted high-powered money H^* is best of all. In the previous section we have already studied the properties of the first three as possible candidates for the target of monetary policy. The discussion is equally relevant for choosing the best indicator. Add to this the discussion of the previous paragraph on the faulty performance of the rate of interest as an indicator. The trouble arises due to dominant influence which non-policy factors exert on interest rates and also long and variable lags with which interest rates respond to changes in money supply.

Between money supply and bank credit we have already seen in the previous section that money supply scores over the latter. But as an indicator of monetary policy, money supply (M^s) is inferior to H^*, because the money multiplier which links M^s to H^s is largely an endogenous variable subject to non-policy influences of various kinds (Chapter 15). H^* itself is not totally policy-determined, though changes in it are much more within the control sphere of the monetary authority (defined broadly as the RBI and the government) than changes in any other monetary variable (Section 15.7). In this sense, H^*, though not a perfect indicator, is much better than all other monetary indicators.

NOTES

1. The discussion in this section and the next is based on Gupta (1975, 1979, Chapter 2).

2. *(a)* According to a well-known proposition of Tinbergen (1952), there must be at least as many independent instruments as goals to be achieved for a policy to be successful.

(b) In so far as the supply of money (M^s) can be successfully manipulated by the use of policy instruments, M^s can itself be called an instrumental variable vis-a-vis policy goals in the present context.

3. It can be legitimately argued that structurally the economy has developed a strong inflationary bias via excessive deficit financing by the government, necessitated by large-scale tax evasion, low profitability of public-sector enterprises, high and rising public-consumption expenditure coupled with declining efficiency and rising corruption in the administration. This is reinforced by excess deficit spending by commercial borrowers, financed by rapidly-expanding supplies of bank credit.

4. On the empirical relation between H^* and the supply of money in India, see Gupta (1979, pp. 215–7).

CHAPTER 19

Instruments of Control

19.1 Introduction

In the previous chapter we have talked about a target rate of growth of money supply. Since the supply of money is an endogenous variable, what can the monetary authority do to attain this target ? The answer will depend on our understanding of the forces determining money supply, of the various instruments of control in the hands of the authorities, and of the institutional conditions under which they are operated. Our study of the theory of money supply in Chapter 15 arms us with two important insights into the determination of money supply : (*a*) broadly speaking, the factors determining money supply can be sub-divided under two heads: (*i*) adjusted high-powered money (H^*) and (*ii*) the money multiplier (m); (*b*) m is determined largely by the behavioural functions of the public and banks, whereas H^* is *largely* policy-controlled. Monetary policy-making is built up (consciously or unconsciously) on these two insights. Accordingly, almost all policy actions are translatable into attempted changes in H^*. Thus, H^* can be treated as a good indicator of the thrust or intensity of monetary policy. While making such a judgment, however, we must separate the policy- engineered change in H from the policy-autonomous change in H. Obviously, to be successful, the former component must dominate the latter component

Keeping this important point in mind and the fact that, in India, the RBI, as the designated monetary authority, has no control over the deficit financing of the central government (which has been the major source of increase in H in India over the years) and only limited control over its foreign exchange assets, we discuss below the instruments of control wielded by the RBI.

19.2 Open Market Operations

The term 'open market operations' stands for the purchase and sale of government securities by the RBI from/to the public and banks on its own account. In its capacity as the government's banker and as the manager of public debt, the RBI buys all the unsold stock of new government loans at the end of the subscription period and thereafter keeps them on sale in the market on its own account. Such purchases of government securities by the RBI are not genuine market purchases, but constitute only an internal arrangement between the government and the RBI whereby the new government loans are sold 'on tap', not directly by the government, but through the RBI as its agent.

The theory of open market operations as an instrument of monetary control is quite simple. Every open market purchase by the RBI increases H by equal amount; every sale decreases it. Thereafter, the money-multiplier process takes over and affects the supply of M in the standard way. It matters little whether the RBI buys or sells securities from/to banks or the non-bank public except that in the former case the reserves of banks are affected directly, in the latter case indirectly. We are, of course, assuming that the banks remain fully loaned up all the time; that is, that their actual excess reserves are always equal to their desired excess reserves. There are side effects, too, via changes in the government bond rates of interest. But in India, because of the captive nature of the government bond market and the RBI's monopoly position, these effects are rather small. These features of the Indian gilt-edged market will be explained a little later in this section.

In the USA, the UK and other developed countries, open market operations are regarded as technically the most efficient instrument of monetary policy, because they are highly flexible, they can be used continuously in widely - varying amoumt, one way or the other as required, and at the option of the central bank, they are easily reversible in time, they involve no public announcement as changes in the bank rate or changes in the statutory reserve ratio or in the statutory liquidity ratio of banks do, and so do not carry 'announcement effects' with them. Their *direct* effect on H is immediate and the amount of H directly created or destroyed by them is determined precisely. These are all weighty advantages. We should, however, remember that these operations also have certain indirect effects in the form of interest rate changes and offsetting borrowing/repaying actions of banks from/to the central banks. These effects cannot be easily predicted or measured. But a central bank must take them into account as best as it can.

In India the open market operations of the RBI have not been a powerful instrument of monetary control. For such a role, at least three conditions must be satisfied : *(i)* the market for government securities should be well organized and developed, that is broad, deep and resilient; *(ii)* the central bank should have enough capacity to buy and sell securities and *(iii)* the central bank in its conduct of these operations should not be weighed down by weightier considerations than monetary control. Of these, only condition *(ii)* is well satisfied. The RBI has more than adequate authority and capacity to buy and sell securities. For example, at the end of March 1991, if the RBI were to buy all outstanding marketable central government securities including treasury bills with banks and the public, it could increase the stock of high-powered money (H) by about 100 per cent; if it were to make an open market sale of its entire holding of central government securities including treasury bills, it could buy up almost all of the outstanding H.

The other two conditions for the efficient use of open market operations as a tool of monetary control are not well satisfied. The Indian gilt-edged market is not well-developed. The treasury bill market representing the short end of the market is practically underdeveloped — it is limited largely to the RBI itself and scheduled commercial banks. The market for government bonds, on the demand side, is a largely-captive market, comprising mainly financial institutions such as commercial banks, the LIC, the GIC and subsdiaries, and provident funds. These institutions are required by law to invest a certain minimum proportion of their total liabilities in government securities and certain 'other approved securities.' It is this statutory investment requirement which creates a captive market for government securities, whatever the rate of interest on them. Moreover, it is a growing market which, given the statutory requirement, grows automatically with the growth in the liabilities of designated financial institutions. The extra voluntary demand of these institutions is rather small; the demand from other sources is also small. On the supply side, the RBI is the main reservoir of government securities and enjoys a near-monopolist position. The turnover in the market is also small, because most of the holders of government securities are investors who buy them for long-term holding and are not traders who may buy and sell for making quick capital gains. In fact, there is no private dealer in government securities who may buy and sell such securities on a large scale on its own account. All that we have are a few (about a dozen) firms of brokers who act as middlemen between the RBI and the rest. In this kind of market, the RBI is pretty much in a position to fix effectively the prices of government securities at whatever level it deems desirable and revise them up or down almost at will, subject to the RBI's judgement about fair return to the institutional investors on their investments.

The other reason for the relative unimportance of upon market operations as an instrument of monetary control in India is that they are weighed heavily by considerations of public-debt management. The RBI's prime objective has been to use these operations to assist the government in its ever-growing borrowing programmes by maintaining orderly conditions in the gilt-edged market and to keep the interest cost of debt to the government as low as possible. To this end, these operations have been used largely, in RBI's words, to 'groom' the market by purchasing securities nearing maturity before periodic floation of new loans. This puts cash in the hands of investors which they can use to subscribe to the new loan floations to follow. This also helps redemption of maturing loans and lengthens the average maturity of government debt outstanding. Besides, the Bank makes available 'on tap' all the time a large variety of old issues to meet the diverse demands of investors and to attract more and more investors to the gilt-edged market. The government securities are not sold aggressively to mop up excess liquidity in the economy, lest such a step should lower too much prices of government bonds, impose capital losses on the holders of such securities, shake public confidence in the relative stability of the government bond market, and make future borrowings by the government difficult and costlier. This explains how the debt-management objective with accent on more and more government borrowing all the time acts as a major obstacle in the path of using open market operations as an instrument of monetary control. The consequence has been greater and greater reliance on other tools of monetary control.

The gilt-edged market conditions as described above have been undergoing some important changes in recent years. We have already discussed them briefly above in sections 3.4 and 3.8. It is too early to look for their effects. It will take some time before the effects are well-established and become noticeable.

19.3 Variations in Reserve Requirement

Banks always keep a certain proportion of their total assets in the form of cash, partly to meet the statutory reserve requirement and partly to meet their own day-to-day needs for making cash payments. Cash is held partly in the form of 'cash on hand' and partly in the form of 'balances with the RBI'. All such cash is called cash reserves of banks. They are usually divided under two heads: (*a*) required reserves and (*b*) excess reserves. Required reserves are cash balances which a bank is required statutorily to hold with the RBI. They are calculated on average daily basis over a fortnight (formerly a week). Under the existing law enacted in 1956, the RBI is empowered to impose statutorily 'cash reserve ratio' (CRR) on banks anywhere between 3% and 15% of the net demand and time liabilities (DTL) as of the last Friday of the second preceding fortnight (previously—before March 29, 1985—it used to be of the preceding week). It is this authority of the RBI to vary the minimum CRR which makes the variable reserve ratio a tool of monetary control. Till 1973 the RBI used it only once in 1960 for a short period of ten months. Since June 1973 the RBI has used it several times as a major instrument of control to curtail excess increases in the supply of money. The latest position on the CRR is summed up here. It was 15 per cent of the scheduled commercial banks' NDTL in 1994-95, was lowered to 14.5 per cent in November 1995 and further to 14 per cent in December 1995. Later, in May 1996, it was lowered to 13 per cent of NDTL and in early July 1996 to 12 per cent. The CRR was reduced to 10 per cent for non-resident external (Rupee) (NREA) accounts in late 1995. It was removed fully on Foreign Currency NR accounts and on their repatriable deposits. Moreover, the incremental CRR of 10 per cent was removed. It may be noted that the RBI pays interest to banks on the additional required reserves over the minimum CRR of 3%.

Besides required reserves, banks also hold excess reserves, which are reserves in excess of the required reserves. It is only these (excess) reserves which banks as a whole can use to meet their currency drains (i.e., *net* withdrawal of currency by their depositors) as well as clearing drains (i.e., *net* loss of cash due to the cross-clearing of cheques among banks). A large part of the excess reserves banks hold in the form of 'cash on hand' or 'vault cash' with themselves. The remaining small part they hold as excess balances with the RBI. Excess reserves are very much a behavioural function of banks. Banks always try to so adjust their asset portfolios that their actual excess reserves are equal to their desired excess reserves. This simple but key point can explain much of the behaviour of banks and the money-supply mechanism (Section 15.2).

The control measure of variable reserve ratio attempts to affect the stock of money via the impounding or release of bank reserves. When the average CRR is revised upward, banks are required to hold larger reserves or balances with the RBI than before for the same amount of liabilities. This amounts to leaving the required reserve ratio unchanged but impounding of additional reserves by the RBI. Since reserves are a part of high-powered money (H), this amounts to a virtual withdrawal of a part of H from the public equal to the amount of additional reserves impounded. In the opposite case when the CRR is lowered or the incremental CRR withdrawn, this amounts to releasing of reserves which would have been otherwise impounded and so *virtual* increase in H. When account is taken of such virtual changes in H, what we get is called *adjusted* H (Section 15.6). The RBI may also choose to actually release the previously-impounded reserves under the incremental CRR as it did in instalments over the years 1984 and 1985.

It is this adjusted H which serves as the base of the unchanged money-multiplier. The money-multiplier itself is left unchanged, because, in our method of analysis, the impact of the change in the required reserve ratio is picked up through the impounding or release of reserves, assuming *as though* the reserve ratio has remained unchanged. From the change in adjusted H we can estimate the resulting change in M as well as bank deposits (using the appropriate multiplier analysis) attributable to the change in the required reserve ratio. (Some economists prefer to pick up the influence of changes in CRR through changes in the money multiplier and leave the measured H unadjusted.)

The above argument tells us that the esssential function of changes in the required reserve ratio is to bring about desired changes in the *effective* (or adjusted) amount of H and through it in the amount of money (and bank credit) and that, in this sense, the method of variable reserve ratio can act both as a supplement and as an alternative to other methods of monetary control such as the method of open market operations.

It is commonly alleged that changes in reserve requirement as an instrument of monetary control is inferior to the tool of open market operations in that it makes lumpy and discontinuous changes both in time and amount of reserves and deposits, and produces 'announcement effect', since changes in reserve requirement are newsworthy. This is true. But much should not be made of this argument. Banks can be given advance notice of changes and the changes can be introduced in stages so that banks have enough time to adjust their portfolios accordingly. Then, in a situation of accelerating or continuing inflation, H and reserves would normally be growing rapidly, and it would not be too hard on banks to meet a higher reserve requirement, if they want to co-operate with the monetary authority in checking excessive expansion of money supply. Further, since the RBI does not have much freedom to use open market operations for purposes of monetary control, changes in reserve requirement have to be resorted to from time to time as the situation may demand, if monetary stability is valued as a goal of economic policy.

As a control measure, the method of variable reserve ratio is not perfectly fool-proof. It has a its own leakages, just as other control measures have. And some of these leakages are common with those of other measures, especially of the method of open market operations. For successful monetary management, it is essential that the authorities understand well the true nature and working of these leakages and not get unduly perturbed at their presence. Instead, they should try their best to plug or offset these leakages as far as possible through other measures at their disposal. This only shows that the variable reserve ratio, by itself, is not a sufficient method of monetary control; it needs to be supplemented by other measures to make it effective.

When the required reserve ratio of banks is revised upward to impound bank reserves, a part of the 'impounded' H may leak back into the economy through the following actions of banks:

(i) Non-compliance or incomplete compliance of banks to the higher or additional reserve requirement. Over the three-year period of 1974–7, there was an average shortfall in required reserves of 25 per cent of the reserves sought to be impounded by the RBI. Heavier shortfalls have occurred in later years despite penalties imposed on the defaulting banks for these shortfalls;

(ii) Increased or compensatory borrowing by banks from the RBI and other sources; and

(iii) Increased or compensatory sale of government securities by banks to the RBI.

If the RBI means business about its policy of monetary control, it should take appropriate measures to plug these leakages to make the impounding of reserves truly and fully effective.

19.4 Changes in the Cost and Availability of Reserve Bank Credit (RBC) to Banks.

In terms of traditional central banking theory as well as practice, the caption of this section should have been 'Bank Rate Policy'. But the conditions governing the RBC to banks, an important source of change in H, in India are much more complex than what the simple theory of bank rate policy implies. These are explained along with the traditional theory of bank rate policy in the present section.

The RBI provides credit to banks in two forms : *(a)* as advances against eligible security, such as government securities and 'other approved securities' and *(b)* as rediscounts of eligible usance bills under its Bills Rediscounting Scheme of November 1970. Credit is provided to banks partly in fulfilment of the traditional central banking functions and partly for promoting certain new policy objectives. Under the former, we may place the 'lender of last resort' function and the provision of busy-season finance; under the latter, we may place refinance facilities and rediscounting under its Bills Rediscounting Scheme. As the 'lender of last resort' a central bank always stands ready to come to the rescue of a bank or banks in temporary need of cash when other sources of raising cash are practically closed or have become prohibitively costly. The RBI also lends to banks to help them provide busy-season finance to the economy during the months of November to April when the demand for funds traditionally increases to finance the marketing of major (kharif) crops and banks are subjected to currency drains as the public moves out of deposits into currency.

The RBI also uses its lending power to banks *(a)* to influence their credit allocation and *(b)* to develop a genuine bill market in India. It does the former under its refinance facilities to banks and the latter under its Bills Rediscounting Scheme, and both at concessional rates of interest. Refinance means providing finance to banks partly or wholly against credit extended by them to designated priority sectors.

Bank Rate Policy

Let us now study the traditional theory of bank rate policy. Formally, the bank rate is the rate at which the RBI should be prepared to buy or rediscount eligible bills of exchange or other commercial paper. But the bill market in India is not well developed and the RBI makes advances to banks mainly in other forms (against government securities and as refinance). Moreover, the bank rate itself is not the key lending rate, though it does form the basis for the multiplicity of the RBI's lending rates charged for various types of advances.

The theory of the bank rate is divisible into two parts. Part one is concerned with the operation of the bank rate as a weapon of control of money supply. According to it, an increase in the bank rate by raising the cost of borrowed reserves, other things being the same, discourages bank borrowings from the central bank. The reverse is supposed to happen when the bank rate is lowered. This varies the rate of expansion of H and so of M, assuming the money multiplier to remain unchanged.

In actual practice, however, it is extremely difficult to predict precisely the effect of a change in the bank rate on the amount of bank borrowings, let alone on M. For, this effect will depend on several factors such as *(a)* the degree of banks' dependence on borrowed reserves, *(b)* the sensitivity of the banks' demand for borrowed reserves to the differential between their lending rates and borrowing rates, *(c)* the extent to which the other rates of interest have already changed or change subsequently, *(d)* the state of the demand for loans and the supply of funds from other sources, etc. Much will also depend on the refinance facilities made available by the RBI at concessional rates and the extent to which borrowing by banks is treated as a right, not a privilege, freely available to banks on specified terms.

The experience in India and most other countries is that even as an instrument for controlling only the amount of bank borrowings the bank rate is not very efficient. The most important reason is that by varying merely the bank rate, the RBI does not vary the interest-rate differential between the lending rates of banks and the cost of borrowed reserves, the factor which determines the extent of profitability of banks from borrowing, because the RBI does revise upward simultaneously various lending rates of banks, now administered by it. Therefore, an increase in the bank rate does not discourage banks from borrowing. The market, in turn, may be in a position to support a higher level of interest rates, if, under the impact of inflationary expectations generated by an on-going inflation, it expects much higher nominal rates of return from the use of borrowed funds.

Further, in order even to maintain a given control over the borrowings of banks, in a period of rising market rates and the lending rates of banks, the bank rate must also be increased continuously in step. But the bank rate is, usually, much more sticky than other rates. Changes in it are always discontinuous. Since bank rate changes have 'announcement effects' (i.e. effects or market reactions produced by the mere announcement of a change in the bank rate), central banks avoid making frequent changes in the bank rate, even though changing conditions may warrant such changes. Another defect of the bank rate policy of monetary control is that under it the initiative lies with banks, who determine how much funds they would like to borrow at a given bank rate. Consequently, the RBI loses control over the amount of borrowed reserves and so of H and M. To overcome such a situation, the Bank has been compelled to take additional measures of various kinds, discussed later in this section.

The other part of the bank rate theory relates to the effect of the bank rate changes on the domestic level and structure of interest takes and thereby on the level of economic activity and the balance of payments of the country. An increase in the bank rate is supposed to be followed by a rise in the market rates of interest all along the line—more so and rapidly on the end than on the short end than on the long end of the interest - rate spectrum. This happens because the lending rates of banks are likely to be revised upward, partly to absorb the higher cost of borrowed reserves and partly to take in the slack in their lending rates which, being sticky, might have become too low than what the market could pay and because the banks' supply of credit tends to be reduced consequent on their reduced borrowing from the central bank. The other market rates rise in sympathy or as the effect of costlier as well as tighter bank credit spreads through the market for loanable funds. The 'announcement effect' of changes in the bank rate is supposed to hasten the spread process, as the market has come to interpret an increase in the bank rate as the official signal for the onset of a period of relatively dearer as well as tighter money, and the reverse in the case of a reduction in the bank rate.

Bank rate changes in India have been rather infrequent. For the first 16 years of the RBI's operation upto November 1951, the bank rate was kept pegged at 3% per year; for the next $5\frac{1}{2}$ years it was held at 3.5% and at 4% for the next $5\frac{1}{2}$ years till December 1962. Thereafter, the bank rate has been varied (mostly raised) more frequently till it was raised to 12% per annum in October 1991. Besides, the Bank's refinance/rediscounting facilities open to banks continue to be discretionary and selective (with respect to the object of refinance that the RBI wants to promote).

19.5 Changes in the Cost and Availability of Reserve Bank Credit (RBC) to Development Banks

The RBI provides credit to not only scheduled commercial and state co-operate banks but also to development banks (chapter 8). In the RBI's analysis of sources of changes in money supply or in reserve money (H), RBC to development banks does not appear as such but is counted as a part of the RBC to the commercial sector. This is not a happy practice, because thereby the RBI's link with development banks gets obliterated. For monetary analysis as well as policy, this link should be explicitly recognized, because the RBC to development banks is a source of increase in H and since 1970–71 this source has become sizeable and has been expanding at a fast pace. The RBC to development banks must be viewed as a control instrument of the RBI, since the RBI can vary it in its own discretion. In practice, of course, there are several limitations on this discretion arising from the pressures of powerful borrowers from the development banks. The only way to resist these pressures, like those from the deficit financing of the government, is to operate via the 'incremental H budget' (see Gupta, 1979, pp. 99- 102).

19.6 The Statutory Liquidity Ratio

The Statutory Liquidity Ratio (SLR) for banks is yet another tool of monetary control in the hands of the RBI. For aggregative monetary control, it works indirectly rather than directly. Therefore, its role as a tool of monetary control is not fully understood. The chief direct role of the SLR is to govern, howsoever imperfectly, the allocation of total bank credit between the government and the commerical sector. The indirect role of monetary control is played through this direct role.

There are two distinct ways in which the SLR operates as an instrument of monetary control : one is by affecting the borrowings of the government from the RBI ; the other is by affecting the freedom of banks to sell government securities or borrow against them from the RBI. In both the ways the creation of H is affected and thereby variations in the supply of money.

Banks in India are subject not only to cash reserve requirement ; they are also subject to statutory liquidity requirement. Under the latter, each bank is required statutorily to maintain a prescribed minimum proportion of its daily total demand and time liabilities in the form of designated liquid assets. These liquid assets consist of (*a*) excess reserves, (*b*) unencumbered government and 'other approved' securities, and (*c*) current-account balances with other banks. Thus, the statutory liquidity ratio (SLR) of a bank is defined as follows :

$$SLR = \frac{ER + I^{*} + CB}{L}, \text{ where}$$

ER = Excess reserves,

I^* = Investment in unencumberd government and 'other approved' securities,

CB = Current-account balances with other banks, and

L = Total demand and time liabilities.

Excess reserves are defined as total reserves (cash on hand plus balances with the RBI) minus statutory or required reserves with the RBI. Securities are unencumbered if loans have not been taken against them from the RBI. Other approved securities are securities that enjoy government's guarantee in respect of payment of principal and interest. Important examples of such securities are bonds of IDBI, NABARD, and other development banks, co-operative debentures, debentures of state electricity boards, state road corporations, port trusts, etc.

The SLR was first imposed on banks in 1949 and was fixed at 20%. It remained unaltered at this level for almost 15 years, till in September 1964 it was raised to 25%. The next change came in February 1970. Since then it has been stepped up successively and quite frequently till it was raised to 38.5% in September 1990. For scheduled commercial banks the RBI is empowered to raise it upto 40%.

The higher SLR and rapidly growing DTL of banks have provided an expanding captive market for government securities and also served as a means of allocating a growingly larger share of banks' resources to government and specified public sector agencies.

Since April 1992, the SLR is being gradually reduced to 25 per cent of the NDTL of banks. To that end, the SLR on incremental net domestic demand and time liabilities (NDTL) has been reduced from 38.5% in 1991-92 to 25%. As a result, the average effective SLR declined from 29.5% in March 1995 and is expected to decline further.

19.7 Moral Suasion

Moral suasion is a combination of persuasion and pressures which a central bank is always in a position to use on banks in general and errant banks in particular. This is exercised through discussions, letters, speeches, and hints thrown to banks. For example, the RBI issues periodically letters to banks making clear its policy positions and urging banks to fall in line. Moral suasion can be used both for quantitative control of credit and money supply and for qualitative control of credit, i.e., control over the distribution of bank credit. In respect of the former, moral suasion can be used by the RBI to urge banks to keep a large proportion of their assets in the form of government securities, lend their helping hand to develop a broad and active market in treasury bills and other government securities, and not borrow excessively from the Bank when it is engaged in fighting the forces of inflation. It is also a standing practice of the RBI to advise banks at the beginning of the slack reason (May-October) each year to reduce gradually their indebtedness to the Bank over the slack-season period. All these actions are different ways of controlling the expansion of H, and so of M. But it is very difficult to say how far such advice is heeded by banks. Nor can we measure its contribution to monetary-control mechanism. Nonetheless, it cannot be denied that moral suasion measures do offer some scope for the RBI to exercise control over money supply.

19.8 Selective Credit Controls

The instruments of control discussed so far are commonly known as *general* or *quantitative* methods of credit control, while the regulation of credit for specific purposes is termed as *selective* or *qualitative* credit control. Whereas the general credit controls relate to the total volume of credit (via changes in H) and the cost of credit, selective credit controls operate on the distribution of total credit. The latter can have two main aspects: positive and negative. On the positive front, measures can be used to encourage greater channeling of credit into particular sectors, as is being done in India in favour of designated priority sectors (see Section 6.3). On the negative side, measures are taken to restrict the flow of credit to particular sectors or activities. Most of the time, the term selective credit controls is used in this latter sense.

Selective credit controls (SCCs) are used in the western countries for such purposes as regulating stock market credit or credit for consumer durables. In India such controls have been used mainly to prevent speculative hoarding of essential commodities like food grains and agricultural raw materials to check an undue rise in their prices. The underlying theory of such controls is very simple: if the availability of bank finance for purchasing and holding some commodities is restricted, the capacity of traders to hold their stocks will get restricted, the market supply of these commodities will be easier than otherwise and their prices will not rise as much as they would have done otherwise.

Thus stated, the degree of success of SCCs will depend upon several factors, discussed below.

1. *The extent of effective credit restrictions.* Since SCCs are generally security-oriented and not purpose-oriented, influential borrowers can manage to escape the bite of these measures by borrowing against the security of other collaterals and using the funds so borrowed for indulging in the speculative holding of stocks. Therefore, the effectiveness of SCCs is likely to improve if they are fully supported by general credit controls.

2. *The availability of non-bank finance.* To the extent traders do not depend upon banks for financing their inventories and have other sources of finance (their own and of the unregulated credit markets), they will again escape the constraints of the SCCs. With 'black money' rapidly multiplying in the economy, this factor is becoming more and more important over time so that even if the bank credit is effectively restricted in particular directions, speculative hoardings may not be curtailed much. Obviously, much will depend on the cost and availability of non-bank finance to the parties concerned.

3. *The degree of shortfall in supply in relation to normal demand* The greater this shortfall, the more will the speculative fever rise. In cases of acute shortages, credit controls should be imposed well in time without waiting for the prices of sensitive commodities to actually rise.

From the above brief discussion it can be inferred that SCCs can, at best, serve as useful supplements to general credit controls and will be more successful in company with the latter than without them. Even then, they should be viewed as only short-term and not long-term measures. In any longer-run planning, the supply position must be improved and brought in better balance with demand. Also, the SCCs can only moderate the price rise and not arrest it completely.

In India, SCCs were first introduced in May 1956. Since then they have been expanded in coverage, scope and content. At present, the commodities covered by the SCCs include foodgrains, major oilseeds and vegetable oils, cotton and kapas, sugar, gur and khandsari, cotton textiles, including cotton yarn, man-made fibres and yarn and fabrics made out of man-made fibres (including stock-in-process).

The RBI operates the SCCs under the directive powers conferred on it by the Banking Regulation Act. The techniques of SCCs used genrally are :

(*a*) minimum margins for lending against securities. The margins vary from the low of 20% (for certain varieties of cotton) to the high of 85% (for stocks of major vegetable oils) ;

(*b*) ceilings on maximum advances to individual borrowers against stocks of certain commodities ;

(*c*) minimum discriminatory rates of interest prescribed for certain kinds of advances ;

(*d*) prohibition of clean advances for financing hoarding of sensitive commodities; and

(*e*) probibition of the discounting of bills covering sale of sensitive commodities.

As the SCCs are focussed mainly on credit to traders for financing inventories, the RBI generally ensures that credit for production, movement of commodities and exports is not adversely affected by such controls. The RBI has made frequent changes in its SCC directives with changing market conditions. No definitive informatin is available about the degree of success or failure of the SCCs. However, there is a general presumption that they do moderate speculative pressures on the prices of sensitive commodities to some extent.

19.9 Credit Monitoring Arrangement (CMA)

The CMA has been in operation in place of the Credit Authorisation Scheme (CAS) since October 10, 1988. Between November 1965 and October 1988, the CAS was the main instrument of credit control used by the RBI for regulating directly bank credit to individual borrowers in amonts in excess of prescribed credit limits. Under the CAS, prior authorisation by the RBI of credit above these limits was required. These limits and the conditions of credit were revised from time to time. Initially, the CAS was viewed as a measure for preventing pre-emption of scarce credit resources by a few large borrowers. Later, the Tandon Group and Chore Committee recommendations (See Section 5.6) were also incorporated in the CAS scrutiny of credit proposals by banks. The authorisation by the RBI usually involved long delays, which were disliked by both the banks and their large customers. Also,there was no system of monitoring the bank credit disbursed.

Under the CMA, banks have been authorised to sanction credit proposals of large borrowers after thorough appraisal as in the past. They are also required to submit large credit proposals to the RBI for post-sanction scrutiny. These are proposals which involve working capital limits of Rs. 5 crore and above and/or term loan in excess of Rs. 2 crore. Since January 1991, only a certain percentage of such proposals (in place of 100 per cent of them) has to be submitted for scrutiny. Banks are also advised to monitor their credit more closely and carefully than before. Thus, the appraisal as well as monitoring of credit to large borrowers have devolved increasingly from the RBI to banks themselves.

NOTES

1. For detailed discussion, see Gupta 1979, Chapter 6-10).

2. Technically speaking, rediscounting means purchase of bills by the RBI from banks and not lending to them. But the purpose as well as the effect of rediscounting are to provide accommodation or credit to banks.

3. For empirical evidence, see Gupta (1979, pp. 218-20).

4. For later developments with respect to CRR and SLR, see sec 20.3.

CHAPTER 20

Monetary-Credit Policy of the Reserve Bank of India

20.1 Introduction

It is hard to come by a well-articulated statement of the monetary policy of the RBI or of its credit policy with its underlying rationale. Probably, the closest approximation to it may be culled from Chakravarty Committee (1985) and Rangarajan (1985 and 1987). We shall draw upon these sources for the said purpose. To avoid possible confusion, we shall discuss monetary policy separately from credit policy : the former will be discussed first in the next section and will be followed by a discussion of monetary policy measures in Section 20.3. We shall discuss some aspects of credit theory and policy in the last Section 20.4.

20.2 Monetary Policy

Monetary policy is primarily concerned with the management of the supply of money or, in a growing economy, with managing the rate of growth of money supply per period. At least three questions need be discussed here: (i) what is the appropriate empirical measure of money, (ii) in the context of India's growing economy, what will be the 'optimal' rate of growth of money supply per year and (iii) how has the actual money supply behaved over the past four decades since 1951 and why ? The first question basically relates to the choice between M_1 and M_3 as two most important alternative measures of money. We shall discuss this question separately in Appendix G, entitled 'M_1 or M_3 ?' The other two questions are discussed in the present section.

We begin with the determination of the 'optimal' rate of growth of money supply per period (say, year) for India, which the RBI should pursue as the 'target' rate of growth of money supply. (See also Sec. 18.4 for a discussion on monetary targeting.) We need this target rate to guide RBI's monetary policy and to serve as a criterion with which to compare the actual rate of growth of money supply. Such a comparison will allow us to assess easily the degree and direction of the departure of actual money supply from its socially-desired time path.

In a growing economy, the optimal conduct of monetary policy requires that the supply of money is grown to subserve certain well-defined social goals. Talking in terms of the annual rate of growth of money supply, the optimal monetary policy requires that this rate of growth, on average, is such as to be consistent with the attainment of the desired social goals. It is universally admitted that the best combination of these social goals is growth with stability and equity. Stability here means over–all economic stability, but, for all practical purposes, is generally equated with general price stability. It has been argued congently that, in the Indian context, the pursuit of the above set of goals will mean maximum feasible output and employment in every short run and also promotion of a healthy balance-of-payments position (see Gupta 1979, Chapter 1 for a fuller discussion) in the medium run.

How are money-supply changes related to the attainment or otherwise of the foresaid social goals ? The key to the explanation is provided by the public's demand for real money or cash balances (see Chapter 11 above). This demand indicates the public's absorptive capacity or willingness to hold money in real terms, given the values of the several specifiable key determinants of the public's demand for money. This point is central to the whole concept of 'monetary targeting' or monetary policy-making. Yet in policy-making circles, it is not given enough emphasis or attention. The serious consequences of such an attitude will be pointed out later in the discussion.

It is the concept of the public's demand for money combined with policy goals which yield the optimal rate of growth of money supply (see Gupta 1979, Ch. 2.). Two solution values have been put forward in the literature. The first was derived explicitly for the first time by Gupta. It was put at 5 per cent per annum, (a) drawing on the statistically derived most common result that the real income elasticity of demand for real money in India is unity; (b) that the best estimate of the expected rate of growth of the Indian economy may be put at 5 per cent per year and (c) that the planned/desired rate of inflation should be put at zero. Using these values and assumptions, Gupta had arrived at the optimal or target rate per annum for India.

The Chakravarty Committee (1985, Chapter 9) did follow Gupta's method of analysis. But, in its empirical specification, it departed from the above exercise in two important respects. First, it did not refer to an empirically-estimated value of the real income elasticity of the demand for real money ; instead, it arbitrarily chose the value of 2 for it and said that it was doing so only as an illustration. With 5 per cent annual rate of growth of real income, this gave it the rate of growth of money supply per year of 2 × 5 = 10 per cent.

The Committee further assumed that a 4 per cent rate of inflation will be socially tolerable and also conducive to growth. Thus, in its illustration, the Committee arrived at the target rate of growth of money supply of 10 + 4 = 14 per cent per year. As the Committee never went beyond its illustration, it is said to have recommended this 14 per cent annual rate of growth of money supply as the target rate. The Committee, in its further discussion, did not stick to even this 'high' rate as the upper limit, but recommended further relaxation in the name of flexibility of monetary policy and thereby justified the actual as the optimal (as we shall see later in the present section) and torpedoed entirely the monetary discipline needed for a healthy Indian economy. This is a sure sign of a 'soft' state and its policy-making and policy-recommending agencies. Normally, flexibility should be two-way, both up and down. But, in India, this has been practised as only upward flexibility so far as the annual rate of money-supply expansion is concerned, seasonal changes in money-supply notwithstanding.

This calls for some comments which we offer below. A more detailed discussion will be taken up in Appendix F (Section F.2).

First, we take up the Committee's allowance for 4% annual average rate of inflation. In the words of Rangarajan (1987 : 702), who was a very influential member of the Chakravarty Committee, "absolute price stability is not feasible in a large and complex economy undergoing structural transformation. Imbalances to some extent are inevitable." Such an assertion is not necessarily correct. For, it is not at all self-evident or axiomatic that "in a large and complex economy undergoing structural transformation" stability of absolute price level will not be feasible. Much depends on the kinds of policies pursued and the flexibility (both ways) of individual prices. Historical evidence of reasonable price stability with growth and structural transformation in several countries is surely available. Moreover, for monetary targeting for price stability, what we mean is long-run average stability, not absolutely stable price level for every year. Providing for an average annual rate of 4% inflation will be an invitation to a progressively higher and higher rate of inflation, because, as our experience of the past 30 years amply shows, the ever-indigent government in India resorts to inflationary finance, unless checked seriously. After all, since the middle of 1991, to gain large enough loans from the IMF and assistance from the World Bank, the Government of India has been operating under pressures and conditions, of these institutions for reducing its fiscal deficit–GDP ratio, reining the high rate of monetary expansion and of domestic inflation, along with other structural reforms. It is a pity, the government did not follow them on its own and in good time till the country reached the stage of grim foreign exchange crisis and the prospect of default on its foreign exchange obligations. This is despite repeated urgings of the RBI in its annual reports, that growing large deficits of the government and their automatic monetisation through the RBI should be severely curtailed in the interest of price stability. For example, in the Annual Report for 1988-89, it had said 'the level of fiscal deficits as a proportion of GDP needs to be much lower than what is now.' (p. 114). This is exact anticipation of the IMF prescription. The former finance minister has made the latter the cornerstone of his policy, whereas the former coming from the RBI had not been paid any heed. Why? The intelligent reader can find his/her own reasons.

The following two additional reasons were also advanced by the Chakravarty Committee (1985 : 170 and also Rangarajan 1985 : 1043) for believing that, in the Indian context, absolute price stability may not be a feasible objective :

(i) In the context of differential rates of growth of various important sectors of the economy and the inter–sectoral resource transfers implied in the planning process, some price increase would be inevitable in the process of growth. But, correctly speaking, the said resource transfer requires appropriate changes in relative prices and not increase in absolute prices for growth industries. A correct policy could allow increase in some prices with decrease in prices for declining industries. It should not try to protect the latter to necessitate higher prices for growth industries to attract resources. Normally, changes in technology and in tastes and preferences of the public as well as in the distribution of income and wealth are responsible for the growth of 'sun-rise' industries, whereas opposite factors induce decay of some other industries. Prices play a second fiddle in the drama, unless the government chooses to intervene and protect prices from falling; (ii) External shocks such as droughts may cause sharp declines in agricultural output and may raise their prices. However, such a picture has already undergone significant changes due to extension of irrigation facilities in the country, buffer stock (especially of wheat and rice and also of sugar and cotton), operations of the government and public distribution system. They can be strengthened further.

Before we look at the actual monetary performance of the Indian economy, we should understand the meaning of the important concept of 'excess' increases of money supply. Excess here means 'in excess of the rate of growth of money supply which an economy is able to absorb at stable prices and at maximum feasible output.' We need this concept to find out how the supply of money has been behaving in an economy-- in its optimal or excess mode. To find out , we look at the annual average rate of growth of money supply in India. This rate during the 1950s, was 3.65 per cent, about 7.6 per cent during the 1960s, about 11.75 percent during the 1970s and 13.16 per cent during the 1980s. To find out the excess rate of growth of money supply, we look at only the experience of the last two decades of the 70s and the 80s as an illustration. According to our model, using the unitary elasticity of demand for real money with respect to real income, the expost excess rate of growth of money supply will be given by the difference between the average annual rate of growth of money supply and the average annual rate of growth of real income realized, measured for each decade. We have measured real income by GDP at factor cost at 1980–81 prices. The average annual rate of growth of real income for the 1970s was 3.0 % and that for the 1980s was 5.76%. We have already noted above the average annual rates of growth of money supply for the two decades. Therefore, the excess rate of growth of money supply can be found out easily. For the 1970s, it comes to 8.75 (*i.e.*, 11.75–3.0) per cent and for the 1980s, it comes to 7.40 (*i.e.*, 13.16-5.76) per cent.

It is interesting as well as instructive to note that, as a long-run phenomenon, as predicted by the Quantity Theory of Money, the excess rate of growth of money supply is absorbed by increase in prices. That is, it entails a prediction for the annual average rate of increase in prices, which may be compared with the realized annual average rate of increase in prices. For the decade of the 1970s, the two respective (predicted and realized) rates were 8.75% and 9.4%. For the 1980s, the two rates turned out to be 7.4% and 8.1%. Such closeness in predicted and actual rates should not be expected for year-to-year changes. The model is expected to hold only for longer periods. That is why we chose two decades. But this gives only two observations. The way out of this limitation will be to take 10-year (even 5-year) moving averages of data and then use regression analysis on the increased number of observations.

The IMF Prescription and Monetary Policy. One of the important conditionalities of the loan assistance granted by the IMF to India since 1991–92 has been to lower its fiscal deficit as a proportion of the GDP over the next three years. Fiscal deficit is defined as the excess of total (government) expenditure over revenue receipts, grants and non-debt capital receipts. This deficit is met by loans of all kinds and from all sources–domestic and foreign (and is inclusive of all lendings by the Centre to the states and others). These loan funds were raised from the open market loans, subscribed by banks and other financial institutions under the pressure of statutory requirement (such as the SLR for banks), small savings and, most all, the net RBI credit to the government, which led to automatic monetisation of the government debt and thereby to increase in money supply and in prices. Moreover, the government debt was raised at relatively low administered rates, which induced high fiscal proligacy. The commercial sector was starved of ample bank credit and this credit was too costly. The monetary policy was reduced to the status of a hand-maid confined to financing fiscal deficits at administered rates so as to minimise the interest cost to the government. Thus, high and growing fiscal deficits lay at the root of several of India's economic ills, including its serious balance-of-payment problems. Therefore, it was imperative to lower significantly as soon as possible the fiscal deficit–GDP ratio, without which all loan assistance by the IMF would have gone down the drain. It is ironical that the same advice had been tendered several times by the RBI in its annual reports. But the government did not pay and heed to it. However, coming from the IMF, it was a dictate. *i.e.*, an essential condition for loan assistance, and the Government of India fell in line readily.

Over the following two years, using a combination of revenue-raising and expenditure-control measures, the government has been able to bring down significantly the fiscal deficit—GDP ratio. Thus, this ratio (at current market prices and in percentage terms) had the value of 8.4 for 1990–91 and had been brought down to the value of 6.2 for 1991–92 and the value of 5.0 for 1992–93.

The concept of fiscal deficit is much broader than that of 'monetised deficit', which means only the net Reserve Bank credit. The latter leads to equal increase in H and thereby increase in money supply through the money-multiplier process. As we have studied earlier at several places, in the past about three decades of the Indian economy, net Reserve Bank credit to government has been the major source of increase in H and thereby of M. The fiscal deficit has many more effects which we have already indicated above.

Beyond the above, the IMF specification has nothing more to say for monetary policy. For a discussion on the control of money supply, see Gupta (1979 : Ch. 5).

20.3 Monetary Policy Measures

Till recently, the RBI was greatly handicapped by the government's fiscal policy in its role of regulating the rate of growth of money supply. As pointed out in the previous section and at several places in the book, 'excess' deficit financing by the government has been a major source of increase in H, which, in turn, has been largely responsible for excessive increases in money supply year after year. The RBI, in its annual reports, had been pleading unsuccessfully for several years that the government must exercise checks on its very large budget deficits in the interest of monetary stability. But to no avail. Unfortunately, as explained in the previous section, the Chakravarty Committee (1985) had recommended a high annual rate of growth (of 14%) of money supply. The external I.M.F.- World Bank pressure on the government since June 1991 to cut down its deficit and carry through other structural reforms has opened the gate for monetary policy reforms as well. These reform measures are in their infancy. We shall study them in some detail in Appendix H.1. We have already studied above in Sections 3.4 and 3.8 and also in Sections 19.3 and 19.6 the operations of CRR and SLR till the end of 1994-95. These measures have been adopted with a view to developing an active market for Government securities, the gilt-edged market is being reorganised in such a way that the Government reduces its dependence on credit from the RBI and he banks.

20.4 Some Aspects of Credit Theory

To start with, it will be instructive to examine critically some of the questionable notions held and propagated by senior RBI economists. As illustrations, we take up below four authoritative statements from Rangarajan (1985, 1987) for evaluation.

1. 'The process of money creation is a process of credit creation. Money comes into existence because credit is given either to the Government or to the private sector or to the foreign sector' (p. 703).

It states, in words, what the RBI has been publishing regularly in its monthly *Bulletin* in a statistical table, entitled "Sources of change in Money Supply." It masquarades as an analytical table, summing up the 'Factors affecting Money Supply'. Several years ago in 1976. I had criticised it severely and called it "theoretically faulty and emprically empty". (For details of my criticism see Gupta 1979, Ch. 3, especially, pp.51–62. Also, see Section 15.8 above.) Speaking differently, the above statement oversimplifies the process of money cretion by equating it to the process of credit creation, which, in turn, is interpreted merely as identification of the parties to whom (bank) credit is given. But, classification of credit by categories of its beneficiaries is by no means a process of credit creation or of money creation. It amounts to the total rejection of any theory of money supply, so assiduously developed in the literature (*e.g.*, see Ch. 15 above). The second sentence in the statement commits the error of conflating two kinds of credit : The Reserve Bank credit to the government and the foreign sector (through the holding of foreign exchange assets) and the ordinary bank credit to the commercial sector (wrongly restricted to the private sector, neglecting the public sector). Whereas the Reserve Bank credit normally results in the generation of H, the high-powered money, ordinary bank credit is the result of a complex process involving the public's decision about the holding of currency vis-a-vis bank deposits, the decisions of banks about the holding of cash reserves, the mobilisation of non-deposit resources by them in the market, borrowing of reserves in the inter-bank call money market and the RBI, their varying defaults relating to the CRR and the SLR administered by the RBI. The whole process is not as simple as it has been claimed to be in the quoted statement. This will get amplified further in the discussion of the next point. (Also see Section 16.2 above, where bank deposits and bank credit are like twins that are produced and extinguished together, consequent on a change in H.)

Moreover, whatever the degree of simultaniety in the processes of creation of money and credit, the two end products are not one and the same thing. Otherwise, why speak of money and credit separately ? Whereas money is an asset of the holding public, credit is liability of the borrowing entities. Money has a specifiable demand function, and this function plays a crucial sole in both the keynesian and the neoclassical monetary theory. A comparable demand for credit theory has not been spelt out in monetary - credit literature or in the RBI papers.

2. While discussing the choice between the narrow definition of money (M_1) and the broad definition of money (M_3), Rangarajan has argued that 'the concept of broad money has this advantage that *in balance sheet terms, it has a direct link to the expansion in credit*' : (p. 704, italics mine). We may recall that M_1 stands for the sum of currency and demand deposits of banks and that $M_3 = M_1$ + time deposits (TD) of banks. Therefore, leaving aside the presence of currency in both M_1 and M_3, it is the presence of TD in M_3 and its absence in M_1 that makes the crucial difference.

By itself, Rangarajan's statement is devoid of any explanation. However, it does suggest a fundamental question in monetary theory as well as the theory of bank credit which has generally escaped the attention of the traditional monetary theory : What is it that monetises bank credit ?

To set the stage for our discussion, we admit straight away that since TD are not generally–accepted means of payment to their holders, they should not be included in any empirical measure of money supply. The mere presence of TD on one side of the balance sheet, which on its other (assets) side has credit (broadly defined as loans and advances to the commercial sector and credit to the government through investment in its securities and other approved securities) and thus finances a part of the bank credit does not impart moneyness to TD, unless it can be shown or argued convincingly that bank credit monetises TD. Such a proposition is not implied by the balance sheet, which is merely an expost accounting identity. Yet, Tobin (1965 : 467) has spoken approvingly of the alchemy of monetisation of commercial loans (of banks). Therefore, it is worth our while to pursue this subject of the monetisation of bank credit.

To understand properly the process of monetisation of bank credit, the following basic features of bank credit must be remembered : (a) When banks extend credit, they do not part with cash and give it to the borrowers; instead, they open cash credit or loan accounts in their books in the names of borrowers and allow them drawals upto agreed amounts. Normally, most borrowers borrow in order to make payments to others in the normal course of their business transactions. They do this by issuing cheques to their payees. Payment by cheque is an accepted safe mode of payment in modern times. The payee deposits the cheque with his bank for collection. On any day, every bank receives several cheques from its depositors for collection. At the same time, its account-holders have drawn several cheques for payment to others, which are submitted by the latter to their banks for collection.

A necessary part of the payments mechanism through bank cheques is the organisation and working of 'clearing houses', where all cross payments among banks (which generally constitute a substantial proportion of total payments through banks cheques) are settled through book entries, where much of cross payments through cheques cancels itself out. In cases, where total receipts and payments for a bank do not match and individual banks end a particular day with surpluses or deficits, the deficit banks are said to face a 'clearing drain', and they are required to meet this drain from their cash reserves, owned or borrowed. Short-term funds are raised by deficit banks in the inter-bank call money market or from other sources, including the RBI, which acts as the 'lender of last resort.'

Besides the above, banks have also to be prepared for 'currency drains' which arise when currency withdrawals from a bank exceed fresh deposits of currency with it on any day. To meet currency drains also, every bank maintains cash reserves with itself or raises funds from the market at short notice.

Thus, as we have explained above briefly, it is the property of chequing deposits of banks, whether owned by depositors or created by banks through their loans and advances (credit) to their borrowers that makes them serve as means of payment under the modern banking system. In working this system, the role of cash reserves is paramount. The reserves, owned or borrowed, make it possible for banks, to meet all 'clearing drains' and thereby honour all 'good cheques' drawn on them. This inspires confidence in the public (payees) that 'good cheques' are almost as good as money. The alchemy which some economists speak of and which is said to monetise commercial bank credit is not a simple, direct and transparent process. It is unlike the way the RBI monetises government debt : the RBI simply pays its money to the government to acquire the latter's debt. More importantly, the RBI is authorised to issue its currency to the public on the strength of government securities acquired by it. Monetisation of commercial bank credit, on the other hand, is a result of the complex processs of making payment through bank cheques, their clearing, the support of cash reserves and the institutional arrangements for the ready availability of such reserve to deficit banks of 'good standing'.

The following points may be added to the above. Firstly, consider time deposits (TD) of banks. It is true that they are not money in the sense of 'generally acceptable means of payment' to their holders. It is also true that they lead indirectly to the creation of 'bank money'. This may be understood by asking : Why do banks seek TD, when such deposits cost them interest ? The chief explanation is that TD serve as an important source of funds/reserves to banks. Moreover, their service cost as compared to demand deposits is much lower to banks and the risk of their sudden withdrawal is also much lower.

How do TD serve as source of funds to banks ? The answer is straight forward. The public buys TD from banks by making cash payment in currency or by way of cheque drawn on the same or some other bank. Currency is a part of H and directly boosts the cash reserves of banks. Demand deposits (DD) converted into TD with the same bank does not bring any extra funds to the bank, but is welcome to it nevertheless for the auxiliary gain of TD over DD pointed out in the previous paragraph. Cheques drawn on other banks either serve to offset the liability of the bank in question in 'clearing' the cheques drawn upon it by its parties or add to its cash reserves. Thus, TD are an important vehicle for banks to gain reserves from the public.

Secondly, only a part of TD (as also of demand deposits) is available to banks for lending to the commercial sector (private and public sectors), because one part has to be deposited by them with the RBI as CRR and another part has to be invested in government and other approved securities under the SLR requirement. It is worth noting that the CRR as well as investment in government securities are paid in H, as neither the RBI nor the government holds any account with commercial banks. Thus, a part of H gained by banks through the sale of TD to the public gets impounded by the authorities under the CRR and SLR requirements. Consequently, only a part of TD is left with banks for extending credit to the commercial sector, and it is this which gets monetised under the modern banking system. This first-round effect of loan-making out of TD (and non-deposit resources of banks) can be expected to generate subsequent rounds of money effects as the bank credit allowed is paid back in the borrower's account with the bank and drawn upon again and again to make payments. as is customary under the cash credit. A related but separate effect arises from the real income and real wealth produced by the credit-financed business activity, which lead to further accretion of deposits over time to banks, other things being the same. However this kind of real income/wealth-induced effect for the accretion of deposits is not peculiar to banks only, but is also true of non-banks, depending on the properties of their liabilities to the public.

Thirdly, banks raise resources from varied non-deposit sources, such as non-bank financial institutions (NBFIs such as the LIC, the GIC and its four subsidiaries, IDBI, NABARD, etc.), whether as contributions to 'participation certificates' issued by banks (see Sec. 5.4.2) or refinance and other advances from term-lending institutions (or what we have called as development banks). The credit extended by commercial banks on the strength of these sources also partakes of the monetisation process applicable to the rest of banks credit based on the deposit sources of banks. In either case the monetisation of bank credit is the outcome of the working of the modern commercial banking system already discussed above.

Fourthly, the process of monetisation of bank credit gets better explained and appreciated when we note that a similar monetisation does not occur in respect of non-bank credit. This is entirely because of the operation of chequing facility in respect of the demand deposits of banks and the associated payments mechanism. This is a peculiar property of banks, not shared by non-banks. The latter only lend whatever they mobilise from the public. They do not create credit or their credit does not enjoy the property of money.

3. Another point worth of our consideration is the *relation between credit and output* and the correct interpretation of the role of credit. It is true that credit 'facilitates' production. But this does not mean that real credit is at par with the traditional factors of production of land, labour, capital and organization or entrepreneurship. If, following Rangarajan (1985 : 1039), real credit or money is entered in the production function, besides the [traditional] factors of production, the estimated results (statistically good or poor) will be hard to interpret. Even if the marginal coefficient of real credit in the estimated production function is statistically significant and positive, it will not be correct to call this co-efficient the marginal product of real credit, holding other factors of production constant. This is because real credit is not a factor of production in itself. In a monetised economy, real credit only places real purchasing power (or funds) in the hands of deficit spending units, say producers, with which to hire or buy physical productive inputs, including technology. The productivity, then, is of these productive inputs, whatever the return for credit, which is a matter for factor pricing in market economies.

Similarly, 'the elasticity of output with respect to credit' spoken of by Rangarajan (1985 : 1039) is essentially the elasticity of output resulting from the increase in the use of productive units made possible by the increased availability of credit. This is not so in a neo-classical model-world because of the assumption of full employment of resources even in a short period. This is not necessarily so in any real-word economy as of India. Therefore, a better deployment of credit can, no doubt, promote real output. But, even in this case, additional output is due to the utilisation of the hitherto unworked resources made possible by the availability of credit. Without the availability of unused productive inputs, the mere availability of credit would be of no use. In other words, credit *per se* is not a productive input.

Pursuing this point further, another assertion by Rangarajan (1985 : 1039) needs to be contested : that when bank credit is increased, it has two effects :, on the one hand, it increases nominal demand for output; on the other hand, it promotes real output. The second part of the assertion in not fully corect. It is correct only when the economy suffers from Keynes–type deficiency of aggregate demand and increase in nominal credit increases this demand. This increase in demand will induce corresponding increase in real output, provided the economy does not suffer from supply–side bottlenecks, arising from, say, infra–structural shortages such as of power, labour troubles, etc. In other words, real output will be promoted, if there existed ample balanced un-utilised capacity in the economy or if some firms or industries were credit–rationed and could not produce in full due to the non–availability of adequate finance. In the latter case, additional output will result, if additional credit is provided to these credit–rationed firms/industries. By itself, credit does not promote output. If it could, it would be very easy for the RBI to promote output to any extent by only increasing nominal credit to the required extent !

4. The last point we discuss relates to the demand for money function. The meaning and role of the public's demand function for real money balances in 'monetary targeting' have been, unfortunately, totally misunderstood and misinterpreted by the RBI high-ups (*e.g.*, see Chakravarty Committee Report, 1985 : 141 and Rangarajan (1985 : 1035–39). It is generally well accepted that the said function is a behavioural or structural relation. Therefore, it is highly erroneous to claim that 'the demand function for money can be restated as a price equation.' To solve for the equilibrium value of the price level (P), we need, besides the demand function for money, specification of the supply of money and equilibrium between the demand and the supply of money for given values of real income and the rate of interest (see Section 12.6 above).

It is equally erroneous to say that 'the demand function for money ....ignores the link between output and credit inherent in the process of production' (Rangarajan 1985 : 1039), because real income as well as other explanatory variables enter the behavioural demand function as exogeneously given. So, real income is free to be determined by labour, capital, technology or credit. The demand function for money is not supposed to dwell on the relation between credit (and any other factor) and production.

Appendix A

The QTM, Monetary Velocity and the Commodity Market

A.1 The QTM and the Commodity Market

In this appendix we explain how the famous Quantity Theory of Money (QTM) equation:

$$MV = Py \tag{12.5}$$

of Chapter 12 can be interpreted as the demand-supply equilibrium condition of the commodity market. This will bring out better the logic as well as the assumptions of the QTM as a theory of P and also help answer better the uncharitable criticism that the QTM is nothing more than a tautology. The above equation will be used to show that even under the QTM, P, after all, is determined by the equilibrium of aggregate demand and aggregate supply in the commodity market.

As explained in the main text, MV in equation (12.5) gives the total money value of final expenditures and hence the money value of aggregate demand for output. Keynes (1936, p. 258) was fully familiar with this interpretation of MV, though he rejected it as an acceptable theory of aggregate demand for output, mainly on ground of the instability of V. The question of the stability of V or otherwise, too, has been discussed in the main text (Section 12.7) and need not detain us here, because at this stage we are not discussing how good the QTM is a theory of P, but only the validity of its status as a theory of P.

Coming back to equation (12.5), let us divide both sides of it by P to get

$$\frac{MV}{P} = y. \tag{12.5.1}$$

It is easy to read the right-hand side of the above equation. This shows output produced and supplied (y^s). In all neoclassical theory it is assumed to be given independently of P (Section 12.6). Suppose it is some quantity y_o. The really interesting part of equation (12.5.1) is its left-hand side. We have already said that MV represents money value of aggregate demand for output. Let us denote the latter by y^d. For any given amount of $M = M_0$ and assuming V to be a constant, Y^d is also uniquely given by $Y_0^d = M_0V$. What about the real demand for output, y^d? Is it also a constant when P is allowed to vary? No. Since, by definition, $y^d = Y^d/P$, fixing Y^d at (say) Y_0^d, makes y^d an inverse function of P. Not only this; given Y_0^d the y^d curve will be a rectangular hyperbola in the y-p space. All this is shown graphically in Figure A.1.

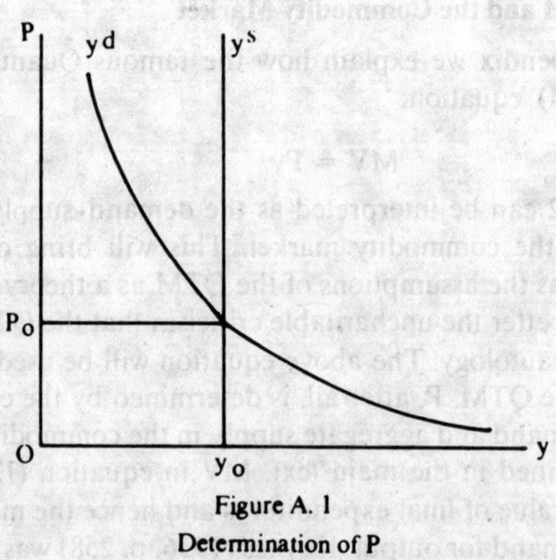

Figure A. 1
Determination of P

Since y^s is assumed to be autonomous of P and given, the y^s curve in the figure is a vertical line through (say), y_0. The y^d curve in the figure shows the kind of inverse relation between y^d and P derived in the previous paragraph. The intersection of the y^d and y^s curves, then, determines the equilibrium value of P—in this case P_0. Given other things, it is only at P_0 that the commodity market is in equilibrium. That is, the two sides of equation (12.5.1), derived from equation (12.5), are not always equal *ex ante; ex ante* they are equal only in equilibrium. At any other value of P, there will be either excess demand or excess supply in the commodity market and market forces will operate to push P up or down towards P_0.

The comparative statics of the QTM can now be easily explained. If the quantity of money in the economy were to be increased from M_0 to (say) M_1, y^d curve in figure 12.1 will shift upward, because Y^d = MV will increase (proportionately). But y^s will stay unchanged at y_0, because it is assumed to be determined independently of M. The point of intersection between the new y^d curve and the fixed y^s curve will shift upwards and P will rise. The rectangular hyperbola form of the y^d function (with a constant y^s) will ensure that P rises in the same proportion as M is increased. This is simpler to deduce from equation (12.5).

The above interpretation of the QTM as a macro theory of the commodity market is formally correct. It is also an interesting and useful way of looking at the QTM. But it has its own shortcomings, most of which have already been discussed in the main text. The output-supply assumption may be defended by reinterpreting it to say that y_0 refers to the maximum feasible output an economy is capable of producing in any short run. But the real problem arises in giving behavioural meaning to MV/P as the real demand for output. As explained in Section 12.5, it can be shown how MV gives the money value of total expenditure. The statistical results of the application of the theory to observed data may also be good. Still the QTM as a theory of aggregate demand (Y^d) does not carry easy conviction with most readers, because it does not explain *directly* spending decisions of various spending units and their determinants in behavioural terms, something which Keynes' theory of aggregate demand does so well and simply. At best, the QTM accomplishes this task indirectly by looking at the money-holding decisions of the public.

Then, in the above demonstration, y^d as an inverse function of P has been derived purely definitionally by deflating Y^d (or MV) by P, and not on behavioural grounds. In a behavioural explanation, one must show why the *aggregate demand* for output will be a declining function of P, what effects a change in P produces on aggregate demand, and why should the P elasticity of demand for output be unity as implied in the rectangular hyperbola y^d curve in Figure A.I. All these are important questions, which the QTM *per se* neither poses nor answers (see Gupta, 1972 c).

A.2 Monetary Velocity as a Multiplier

It will be highly instructive to see that the following equation:

$$\Delta Y = V.\Delta M \qquad (12.13)$$

in the main text has the structure of a multiplier equation, analogous to that of the multiplier equation (13.13) of the Keynesian theory.

To show this, we explain briefly the multiplier process underlying equation (12.13). We start with an initial increase in the quantity of money by M. Starting from a position of equilibrium in the money market, all of it will appear as excess or undesired M in the hands of the public. Therefore, in the simple QTM-world, to get out of the excess quantity of M, the public spends all of ΔM in the commodity market. This gives first round increase in money expenditure and so of money income (ΔY_1) equal to ΔM. (The subscript 1 with ΔY is used to indicate that ΔY_1 is only first-round, and not total, increase in Y. Similarly, ΔY_2 will indicate second-round increase in Y, and so on). Increase in Y leads to an increase in the demand for money. From equation (12.11) in the main text, this increase (in M^d) will be equal to $K. \Delta Y$, where K is the 'marginal propensity to hold money', measured in time unit (see Section 11.3).

Since at this stage $\Delta Y = \Delta M$, ΔM^d is also $= K. \Delta M$. This increase in M^d reduces the excess supply of money to $(1-K) \Delta M$. Again, this induces another round of expenditure in the commodity market $= (1-K) \Delta M$, so that the public can get out of the remaining excess quantity of money. This produces a second-round increase in expenditure and income which gives $\Delta Y_2 = (1-K). \Delta M$. Again, this leads to a further increase in the demand for money and a consequent reduction in the excess supply of money $= K. \Delta Y_2 = K(1-K). \Delta M$. This will produce a third-round increase in expenditure and income, given by $\Delta Y_3 = (1-K)^2 \Delta M$, and so on till the entire ΔM has been fully absorbed by the economy, that is, it comes to be held willingly by the public. The public is induced to hold more of M, because, through the adjustment process explained above Y has gone up.

The total increase in income due to ΔM will be given by the sum of the successive rounds of increase in income explained above. This can be written as

$$\Delta Y = \Delta M. [1 + (1-K) + (1-K)^2 + \ldots \infty]. \qquad \text{(B.1)}$$

The terms within square brackets in the above equation represent an infinite geometric series, which will converge only if the common factor (1-K) lies between 0 and 1, i.e., if K is a positive fraction. This is easily fixed, once we take Y as annual income, because it is known empirically that, in modern economies, the stock of M is a certain fraction of annual Y. This means that the aforesaid geometric series necessarily converges and its sum will be equal to $1/K$, so that equation (A.1) yields

$$\Delta Y = 1/K.\Delta M. \qquad (B.2)$$

Since 1/K is the same thing as the income velocity of Money (V), equation (B.2) is identical with equation (12.13). Thus, V (or 1/K) also is of the nature of a multiplier (money-income multiplier). Traditionally, V is called the 'income velocity of money'— the average number of times per period a unit of money changes hands in income transactions. And this name has stuck. But there is no reason why the multiplier interpretation of V should be ignored

APPENDIX B

The Real-Balance Effect

So far we have ignored completely an important construct of the neoclassical monetary theory—the real-balance effect. Introduced by Pigou (1943) to defend Say's Law (that supply creats its own demand) against Keynes' attack, the real-balance effect in the commodity market has been raised to the status of *sine qua non* of monetary theory by Patinkin (1965).

Briefly, the real-balance effect refers to the effect which a change in the value of real cash-balances held by the public produces in the economy. Real balances are defined as $\bar{M}/P$, where $\bar{M}$ is 'outside' money, that is, money (currency) issued by the government or the central bank, who are not counted as a part of the public. $\bar{M}$ is liability of the government but asset of the holding public. Therefore, $\bar{M}/P$ is a part of the real net wealth of the public, the other part being physical capital. Since $\bar{M}/p$ is part of the real wealth of the public, any change in it will produce wealth effect. In particular, it will affect consumption-savings of the public: if $\bar{M}/P$ goes up, other thing being the same, households are wealthier than before and they will be induced to consume more (save less) out of the given level of real income. The reverse will happen if $\bar{M}/P$ goes down. This, in sum, is the real-balance effect for consumption-savings decision. Being a part of the wealth effect, it will be operative in all other spheres where real wealth counts.

It is obvious that $\bar{M}/P$ changes whenever either $\bar{M}$ changes or P changes. The first kind of change is generally taken as a policy change, the other kind of change as an endogenous change. Patinkin has made much use of the real-balance effect of a change in P in (i) showing how price flexibility will lead to full employment by eliminating any demand deficiency (Patinkin 1948) and also in (ii) showing how this effect serves as the link between the monetary sector and the real sector (Patinkin 1965, Chapter 8). The real-balance effect of a change in $\bar{M}$ can also be invoked to explain why $\Delta\bar{M}$ affects expenditure and thereby Y and P. It must be noted that this explanation (of the transmission mechanism) is different from the explanation given in Section 12.5. The latter explanation is independent of the net wealth character of M and is not confined to government money alone. Its key argument revolves around actual M being equal or unequal to desired M and the consequent effort of the M-holding public to get back into equilibrium.

The real-balance effect of a change in P is of a class of several real effects produced by a change in P, when there are several nominal magnitudes which do not change equiproportionately with P (see Gupta 1972c). These several effects have been discussed in Section 14.2.2

Appendix C

Monetary Transmission Mechanism

The question of monetary transmission mechanism, that is, the mechanism or channels whereby monetary influences are transmitted to the commodity market is of paramount importance in monetary theory. Much controversy among monetary economists (as, for example, between the Keynesians and quantity theorists) ultimately concerns, among other things, the empirical importance of the presumed channels of such transmission. Yet a consolidated statement of it at one place is not easily available. What we do get are theories of individual channels of transmission. Since there are several such channels, we have discussed individually each of them at its appropriate place. As the resulting discussion is scattered at several places, the full focus on the transmission mechanism gets diffused. To overcome this problem, we sum up briefly below four different channels of transmission. The first two emphasise the asset effect of money, the two the credit effect associated with money. The several channels can and do operate simultaneously, but the influence of individual channels varies across countries and over time.

(1) *Quantity Theory Mechanism.* The oldest explanation is associated with QTM. The earlier economists used to explain it by emphasising that money as general purchasing power when increased will flow into all other (non-money) markets and push upward the demand for both bonds and goods and services. Thus, markets for money, bonds and commodities were seen to be linked, but very loosely. The exact nature and form of the relationship were never clearly specified. Fisher's equation of exchange gave QTM an overly simple and mechanical equational form, always true *es post.* The Cambridge QTM did imply a transmission mechanism linking a discrepancy between actual and desired stocks of money with adjustments through changes in flows of expenditure (see Section 12.5). But it was never carefully spelled out. For a time, Keynes' attack on QTM sounded

almost a death knell for it and the associated direct transmission mechanism, substituting indirect interest-rate transmission mechanism in its place. Finally, Friedman resurrected QTM and gave it a new lease of life under modern QTM. We have already studied its transmission mechanism in Section 12.7 (under point (3)).

(2) *The Real-Balance Effect Mechanism.* Another explanation of the transmission mechanism is provided by the theory of the real-balance effect. This has been discussed briefly in Appendix B.

(3) *The Interest-Rate Mechanism.* The theory of this mechanism is associated with the name of Keynes (1936), though pre-Keynes classical and neo-classical economists were also aware of it. Keynes had used it to demolish the validity of QTM and to highlight the chief source of ineffectiveness of monetary policy (see Sections 12.7 and 13.3). The key point emphasised by Keynes was that money influences commodity market, not directly as stressed by QTM, but indirectly through the bond rate of interest as the cost of credit in the credit market.

(4) *Credit-Availability Mechanism.* This mechanism emphasises the availability of credit to deficit spenders in addition to its cost (of the interest-rate mechanism) as an important channel of transmission of monetary influence to the commodity market. Because of the risk of default and relative fixity of the lending rates of banks and other financial institutions, the negotiated loan market generally suffers from much credit rationing (see Chapter 16). Therefore, when the availability (supply) of credit is eased, the financial resource constraint on deficit spending is relaxed, and 'autonomous expenditure' in the economy goes up with multiplier effect. We also know that a change in the quantity of money is accompanied by a change in bank credit in the same direction (see Section 16.2)—in fact, the bulk of new money enters the economy via credit to the government or business firms. So, the first-round effects of increase in the quantity of money are often directly the credit supply effects. Further, since the outstanding amount of credit, like money, is also a stock and as such can be used repeatedly (giving its own velocity of circulation) so long as the borrowers keep on repaying to the lender, a certain part of the aggregate expenditure is credit-financed/induced spending by deficit units and as such is influenced positively by the availability of credit.

Another way of looking at the above argument is to say that since much of bank credit is supported by deposits (demand and time) with banks, the former transmutes even time deposits into ready purchasing power in the hands of borrowers, though holders of time deposits themselves, cannot use them as ready cash or means of payment. This argument, however, should not be misinterpreted as an argument for the inclusion of time deposits in an empirical definition of money or of the adoption of M_3 as the correct measure of money supply. For, this argument only says that though time deposits do not affect spending directly as money, they do affect it indirectly as bank credit and thereby the velocity of circulation of money. (This has the advantage of opening up a way of bringing in non-bank credit at par with bank credit as an influence on deficit spending, or, looked at from the other side of the balance sheet, as non-bank financial assets which act as substitutes for money in the asset portfolio of the public. Either way, a change in such credit or assets will influence the value of V.)

APPENDIX D

Inflationary Expectations

In this book at various places we have referred to inflationary price expectations. They are discussed briefly in this section.

Price expecations of any kind are expectations about the future course of prices (P). They are more conveniently cxpressed in terms of the 'expected rate of change of prices', denoted by $\dot{P}^e$ per unit time (say, per year). When $\dot{P}^e > O$, expectations are said to be inflationary. They will be deflationary or for stable P, when $\dot{P}^e < O$ or $= O$, respectively. In any on-going inflation, price expectations also tend to be inflationary. They influence economic behaviour in various ways, some of which have been discussed in various sections of the book. They are summed up briefly below.

1. $\dot{P}^e$ *and Demand for Money and Other Financial Assets.* In Section 11.6 it was noted that Friedman includes $\dot{P}^e$ as one of the opportunity cost variables in his specification of the demand function for money. The argument is that when the public expects prices to (say) rise in the future, it will like to hold less of cash balances than otherwise, because price rise will decrease the real value of such balances. The hypothesis has been supported in a number of empirical studies relating to cases of hyperinflation (Cagan, 1956), of high rates of inflation (Deaver, 1970) and even of relatively mild inflation in India (Trivedi, 1980).

The above argument and results can be easily extended to non-money financial assets (NMFAs) whose nominal values and/or coupon rates of interest are fixed in terms of money. Examples are bonds, fixed deposits, provident fund contributions, life insurance policies, UTI units, etc. Collectively they are called 'monetary assets' (to distinguish them from 'real assets' comprising all physical assets and equities), because, like money, they suffer or gain in real value due to changes in P, whereas real assets generally do not. For this reason, the demand for all monetary assets is affected adversely, and that for real assets favourably, by inflationary price expectations.

Also, the higher the $\dot{P}^e$, the greater the reduction in the demand for monetary assets in real terms, other things being the same. This tends to discourage both the rate and institutionalisation of savings (see Gupta, 1979, Chapter 1).

2. $\dot{P}^e$ *and Inflation* $\dot{P}^e$ is not only influenced by inflation, it also influences inflation. It does so by reducing the demand for money at any level of income (Y) and so raising the income-velocity of money V, which is given by the reciprocal of M/Y (Chapters 11 and 12). This raises $\dot{P}$ further. Therefore, at the theoretical level, it raises the question whether inflation once started will feed upon itself by generating inflationary price expectations, raising V, causing further inflation, and so on. The answer to this is in the negative (Cagan, 1956), though, as monetarists have themselves pointed out, during the period of adjustment when the public is reducing its real demand for money in response to a certain $\dot{P}^e$, $\dot{P}$ will be greater than $\dot{M}$. But since, *ex hypothesis*, corresponding to each $\dot{P}^e$ there is a certain amount of M/P demanded *ceteris paribus,* once the latter amount has been attained, the public will stop shifting out of money, rise in V will stop, and further inflationary pressure arising from rise in V will disappear. The inflationary pressure of only excess increases in the supply of money will remain, so that, in equilibrium, once again $\dot{P} = \dot{M}$. This means that inflation cannot be self-financed through induced increases in V; to sustain it, excess increases in the supply of money must be maintained period after period. It might also be added that if for any reason $\dot{P}^e$ is revised upward, $\dot{P}$ will again be greater than $\dot{M}$ for the reason given above. But, as explained above, this phenomenon will again be temporary.

3. $\dot{P}^e$ *and Money Rates of interest.* For the reason of real-value depreciation of monetary assets and no such depreciation of real assets under the impact of rise in P, when the public comes to anticipate inflation, lenders will claim and borrowers will be willing to pay higher and higher rates of interest than before to reflect at least a part of $\dot{P}^e$. This is the major answer to why rates of interest in countries experiencing inflation have been going up. The adjustment in the market rates of interest is, no doubt, slow and partial, depending on various institutional and other factors. That is why, the administered rates of interest in India (e.g. government bond rates, deposit rates of banks and post offices, and lending rates of banks) have not risen as fast and as much as the market-determined rates.

The above consideration has very interesting implication for the relation between money supply and r. In Keynes' theory, increase in money supply (outside the liquidity trap) reduces r (Section 13.3); in classical theory, it is held that changes in the supply of money leave the equilibrium r unchanged or that money is comparative-statically neutral (towards r and other real-sector variables) and r is taken to be a real-sector phenomenon (see Patinkin, 1965, Chapter 10). In contradiction of both the above positions, the recognition of the relation between $\dot{p}^e$ and r suggests that inflationary increases in the supply of money by generating inflationary price expectations raise r (see Friedman 1968; Gupta, 1974d).

4. *Anticipated Inflation and the Distribution of Income and Wealth.* In monetary literature a distinction is usually made between unanticipated inflation and anticipated inflation. A strong hypothesis is then put forward, which says that it is only unanticipated inflation which causes redistribution of income and wealth, and that once inflation comes to be (fully) anticipated, it generates behavioural reactions and policy measures that guard against the aforesaid redistributions except those that arise in the form of 'inflation as a tax on cash balances'. Strictly speaking, the hypothesis is not true, because full anticipation is only a necessary and not a sufficient safeguard against the inflation-generated redistribution. It is also necessary that the potential losers from inflation should be able to protect themselves against the lossess from anticipated inflation by forcing appropriate measures (full escalation clauses) on the contracting parties (potential gainers). This condition is not easily satisfied in actual life. Nor is inflation fully (or exactly) anticipated.

5. $\dot{P}^e$ *and the Phillips Curve.* This will be discussed in the next appendix, where we shall explain briefly the role which price expectations play in Friedman's critique of the simple Phillips Curve.

Estimating $\dot{P}^e$

$\dot{P}^e$ is not directly observed; it has to be estimated from observable data. This requires an expectations- formation model. The model which has been most widely used is called the 'adaptive expectations model' or the 'error-learning model'. It says that the public learns from experience and that, starting from a certain $\dot{P}^e$, the public revises (adapts) its expectations up or down in proportion to the discrepancy between the actual and the expected rate of change of prices (Cagan, 1956). The model yields $\dot{P}^e$ as a weighted moving average of the current and past values of $\dot{P}$ only, where weights decline geometrically as one goes into the past.

In several cases, the model has yielded good results. But it has the limitation that it makes $\dot{P}^e$ a function only of realized $\dot{P}$s and has no means of utilising any other information that might be pertinent for the formation of price expectations.

APPENDIX E

The Phillips Curve, Expectations and Other Factors

In Section 14.7 of the main text it was pointed out that after the end of the 1960s the simple Phillips curve in the USA and several other countries has been found to be shifting upwards. This shows that there does not exist any *stable* trade off between the rate of unemployment U and the rate of wage inflation $\dot{W}$ or of price inflation $\dot{P}$. As already noted in the main text, this development has posed a serious crisis in Keynesian economic theory and policy. Several explanations of this phenomenon have, therefore, been offered. Only a brief summary of the main lines of analysis is offered in this appendix. For simplicity, any growth in labour productivity will be negelected completely, so that we can talk about wage inflation ($\dot{W}$) and price inflation ($\dot{P}$) interchangeably.

E.1 Cost-of-Living Influence on Wages

Over the years since the first appearance of Phillips' article in 1958, it has been pointed out by several economists (with supporting empirical evidence) that $\dot{W}$ is not a simple function of only U or that the *simple* Phillips Curve is not *generally* true. We have already noted in the main text that both Phillips and Lipsey had admitted the additional role of U. Besides, Lipsey (1960) had found that for selected years of the period 1913–57, $\dot{W}$ in the UK was related positively to $\dot{P}$. Some other economists have singled out, among other things, business profits as an additional variable affecting $\dot{W}$ positively. The resulting multiple regression equations were so specified as to give better fit to the data.

Of these elaborations, the relation between $\dot{W}$ and $\dot{P}$ is worthy of special attention, because it is a two-way relation: $\dot{W}$ both affects $\dot{P}$ and is affected by $\dot{P}$. In our discussion leading to equation (14.5) in Section 14.7, we had seen how $\dot{W}$ influenced $\dot{P}$. But whenever P increases, cost-of-living of workers also increases and, in order to protect their real wages, workers demand (and employers concede) compensatory increase in W, though with some time-lag and may be only partially. The important point to note is the (lagged) feedback from $\dot{P}$ to $\dot{W}$, which leads to further inflation and so on. This results in what is known as *Wage-Price-Spiral.* A large part of the 'new inflation' and the instability of the *simple* Phillips Curve in recent years is, no doubt, due to the aforesaid cost-of-living influence on W. What this means is that expansionary monetary policy and associated inflation can 'buy' reduction in U for only a short period till the resulting rise in the cost of living induces workers to demand still higher $\dot{W}$, thus shifting the Phillips Curve upwards (see Figures E.1 and E.2). Such shifting has necessitated a distinction between short-run and long-run Phillips Curve, discussed below.

In each of the aforesaid two figures, a family of *short-run* Phillips Curves has been drawn, one each for a particular value of $\dot{P}_{t-1}$, the rate of inflation experienced during the previous period. (For simplicity it is assumed that realized P influences W after a fixed lag of one period.) The cross-cutting steeper curve in Figure E.1 and vertical curve in Figure E.2 are long-run Phillips Curves, which show the long-run relation between U and $\dot{W}$. This relation will depend on the degree of impact $\dot{P}_{t-1}$ has on $\dot{W}$. Briefly, if this effect is less than

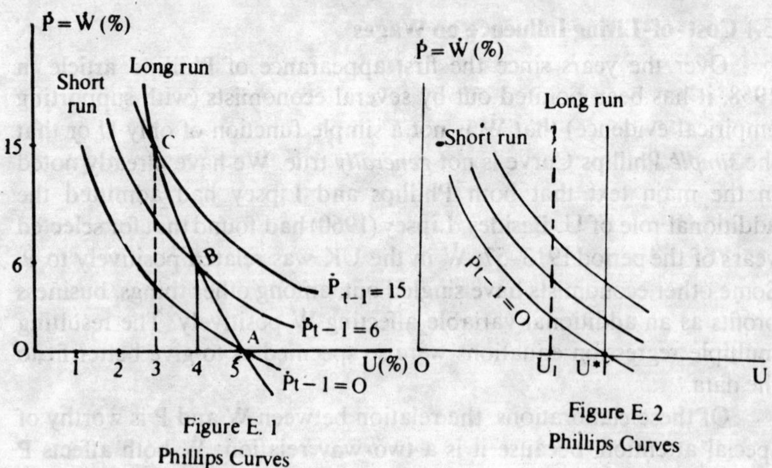

Figure E. 1
Phillips Curves

Figure E. 2
Phillips Curves

equiproportionate, that is, if a 1% increase in the cost of living results in less that 1% increase in P via an increase in W, the upward shifts in short-run Phillips Curve will tend to die down and yield a *stable* long-run equilibrium $\dot{W}$ (or $\dot{P}$) at a *particular value of U,* as shown by points like A, B and C in Figure E.1. The result will be a stable long-run Phillips Curve, downward-sloping, but steeper than any short-run Phillips Curve (Figure E.1). If the increase in cost of living raises $\dot{W}$ and then $\dot{P}$ equiproportionately, the long-run Phillips Curve will be vertical (Figure E.2). Only at an unique value of U (shown by U* in Figure E.2) any rate of inflation, once attained, will continue without change. But at any value of U less than U* (e.g. at U_1), the rate of inflation will accelerate without limit along the vertical long-run Phillips Curve through U_1.

These propositions can be better understood with the help of a little algebra, which is analogous to that given towards the end of the next section, surrounding Equations (E.2) and (E.3). For adaptation of the algebraic explanation to the present case, all that is required is to substitute $\dot{P}_{t-1}$ for $\dot{p}^e$ in each of the two equations. Even otherwise, the explanation of the present section will bear comparison with that discussed in the next section.

E.2 Price Expectations and the Phillips Curve

The cost-of-living feedback from $\dot{P}$ to $\dot{W}$ and back to $\dot{P}$ is only one of several types of feedback that may contribute to the process of inflation and shifts in the simple Phillips Curve. Milton Friedman (1968, 1976) (also Phelps, 1967) have expounded the theory of another feedback based on the role of price expectations in the process of inflation.

Fundamental to Friedman's theory is his concept of the '*natural rate of unemployment*' (U*). This rate is the rate of unemployment which the free working of market forces, with all the attendant imperfections and other structural features, will generate in an economy. Alternatively, it can be viewed as the exact counterpart of the neoclassical concept of full employment. According to Friedman, actual U can possibly be reduced below U* through demand-expansionary policies involving excess increases in money supply and inflation, but only for a *short period.* If such a policy is persisted with, the rate of inflation will go on accelerating due to the operation of *price-expectations effect*, and the short-run Phillips Curve will keep on shifting upwards tracing out a *vertical long-run Phillips Curve.* A stable short-run Phillips Curve with a *stable* rate of inflation ($\gtrless$ O) will obtain at U* only. These propositions of Friedman's theory are explained briefly below.

1. As a preliminary we first note that Friedman's model relates to flex-price world where all prices (and wages) are determined through a market-clearing process and where both buyers and sellers in all markets take into account their expectations of future prices, such that if they expect them to rise by (say) 10%, both the demand and supply will so behave that actual P will rise by 10%. In the event $\dot{P} \neq \dot{P}^e$, the

latter will be revised up or down in the manner of the 'adaptive expectations model' (Appendix D). When $\dot{P} = \dot{P}^e$, inflation becomes fully anticipated and inflationary equilibrium is attained in the sense that the rate of inflation becomes stable at the particular $\dot{P} = \dot{P}^e$, other things being the same.

2. If we start with the following equation of the simple Phillips Curve:

$$\dot{P} = f(u), \frac{d\dot{P}}{du} < 0, \quad (E.1)$$

Friedman's theory given in the previous paragraph requires addition of an extra explanatory variable in the form of $\dot{P}^e$ (the expected rate of change of prices) to the above equation to vield

$$\dot{P} = f(U) + \dot{P}^e \cdot \quad (E.2)$$

The above equation will yield a whole family of short-run Phillips Curves, one for each value of $\dot{P}^e$. The higher the P^e, the farther to the right will an individual Phillips Curve lie (see Figure E.3). The vertical distance between any two curves measures simply the difference between two $\dot{P}^e$ s associated with them. Each Phillips Curve will be valid for only a short period for which the associated $\dot{P}^e$ stays unchanged.

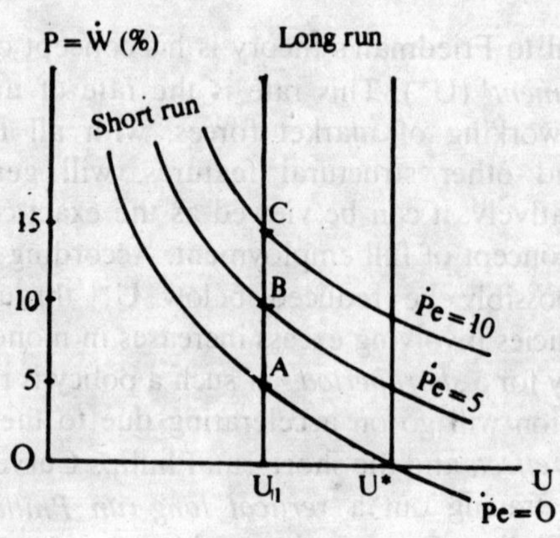

Figure E. 3
Phillips Curves

3. Acceleration in the rate of inflation may be explained thus. Suppose the economy starts with $U = U^*$ and $\dot{P} = \dot{P}^e = 0$, so that the appropriate Phillips Curve in this situation is the curve labelled $\dot{P}^e = 0$ (Figure E.3). Now suppose that accepting the trade off between U and $\dot{P}$ given by this curve, the government moves the

economy to a lower level of unemployment U_1 at the cost of 5% per year of $\dot{P}$, given by the $\dot{P}^e = o$ curve (point A). The simple Phillips Curve stops here. But, according to the expectations hypothesis, this situation will be short-lived, because with realized $\dot{P}^e = 5\%$ per year, the old price expectations of stable P will also come to be revised upward. Following Friedman, let us assume that, after a time, actual inflation comes to be fully anticipated, so that the revised $\dot{P}^e$ also is 5% per year.

The crucial assumption made here by Friedman is that the actual P will also soon rise by the full value of $\dot{P}^e$ (see equation E.2). But when this has happened the short-run Phillips Curve will have shifted up to the position of the Curve labelled $\dot{P}^e = 5$ in Figure E.3, now giving 10% rate of inflation at U_1. In the next period, the public finds itself cheated once again, because $\dot{P} > \dot{P}^e$. Therefore, it again revises upward its $\dot{P}^e$, which again shifts the short-run Phillips Curve upward, giving a still higher rate of inflation at U_1, and so on. Thus, the rate of inflation keeps on accelerating. It does not come to a stable value so long as the assumptions of the model explained above hold.

4. The resulting time-path of $\dot{P}$ at U_1 traces out a *long-run Phillips Curve* which is necessarily *vertical* in Friedman's model. Such a curve demolishes the very concept of a (long-run) trade off between $\dot{P}$ and U, so that, in the long run, the public through the government cannot buy a little less U (than U*) even at the cost of a stable rate of inflation.

5. There is *a whole family of long-run vertical Phillips Curves,* too—one for each level of U, with one crucial difference among them. The vertical through U* has the property that at any point on it $\dot{P}$ will be stable. This means that U* can be combined with any constant value of $\dot{P}$. The accelerationist hypothesis does not apply to it, though at any other value of U, this hypothesis will hold. Hence the importance of U* in Friedman's theory.

Friedman's theory has had only limited acceptance. It is, of course, conceded that expectations play an important role in any on-going inflation and that any satisfactory theory of inflationary process must take due cognizance of it. What is denied is the strong hypothesis of vertical long-run Phillips Curve (implying no long-run trade off between U and $\dot{P}$), itself derived from the strong assumption that the price expectations variable, $\dot{P}^e$ enters equation (E.2) with the coefficient of unity. This is neither true on *a priori* grounds nor supported by firm empirical evidence. This question is of crucial importance, because it can be shown that if the co-efficient of $\dot{P}^e$ in equation (E.2) is significantly less than unity, a long-run trade off between $\dot{P}^e$ and U will exist or that the long-run Phillips Curve, too, will be downward-sloping, not vertical.

To show this, assume that the coefficient of $\dot{P}^e$ in equation (E.2) is h where h lies in the interval $0 \leq h < 1$. Then, equation (E.2) will read as

$$\dot{P} = f(U) + h\dot{P}^e. \qquad (E.3)$$

What will be the equilibrium value of $\dot{P}$ when inflation is fully anticipated, i.e. $\dot{P} = \dot{P}^e$? Using this condition in (E.3), we solve for $\dot{P}$ to get

$$\dot{P} = f(U)/(1 - h). \qquad (E.4)$$

The above equation gives the eventual rate of inflation as a function of U when any discrepancy between $\dot{P}$ and $\dot{P}^e$ has disappeared. This rate of inflation will, then, have no tendency to get revised. It represents long-run trade off between $\dot{P}$ and U and is also the equation of the long-run Phillips Curve. By comparing it with equation (E.1) and remembering that h is positive but less than 1, it can be seen that the slope of the long-run Phillips Curve will be steeper than that of a short-run Phillips Curve. However, if h = 1 (as implied by Friedman), $\dot{P}$ will not have any unique value. Thus, the value of h becomes crucial to the whole argument and this value is an empirical matter that cannot be decided on *a priori* grounds.

Besides the above criticism, it has also been said that Friedman's models of price formation as well as expectation formation are only partly true, that, in actual life, price expectations influence directly wages and prices that are fixed 'administratively', the time-length of wage contracts, escalation clauses, etc., and not through their prior effect on quantities demanded and supplied as in a market-clearing model. Then, the 'adaptive expectations model' only extrapolates the past behaviour of $\dot{P}$ into the future, without taking into account any additional information relevant for the formation of $\dot{P}^e$.

E.3 Institutional Influences on the Inflationary Process

Each of the previous two arguments relates the spiral character of the inflationary process to the basic economic fact that, despite some degree of money illusion, all economic units are interested in 'real' returns from their endeavours and that accordingly increases in prices of final products must ultimately lead to increases in factor prices and *vice versa* (after adjusting for productivity changes). One major difference between the two explanations is that whereas the first allowed the *direct* effect of actual increases in product prices on factor prices and thereby on product prices, with appropriate lags at each stage, the latter routed this effect through *prior* changes in price expectations and thereby on product as well as factor prices.

There is yet another view which holds that, given the state of aggregate demand in the economy, the actual character of the inflationary process, including the time-rate of inflation and its structural composition, is affected greatly by a number of institutional factors relating to the manner in which wages and prices are set and changed. For example, in the western developed economies, where an increasingly large proportion of the work force is unionised, the duration and character of wage contracts, whether they are fixed-term or for an unspecified term, whether they include escalator clauses or not, whether escalator clauses are universally used and provide for 100 per cent compensation for increases in cost of living or not and how fast are important considerations. They provide either inertia or speed to the inflationary process, generalise and perpetuate upward movements of prices anywhere in the economy or abroad (through import prices), or contain inflationary pressures in the sector of their origin. We have already said in Section 14.3 of the main text that the use of wage comparisons in setting wages produces a bias towards faster wage inflation, because low-wage workers always try to catch up with higher-wage workers. The social and political forces, operating through minimum-wage legislation, wider coverage of social security and higher levels of support to workers on social security have also imparted a net inflationary bias. Recent studies in the USA have also found that changes in the *composition* of demand for labour and the supply of it (that necessarily arise from the working of numerous factors in a dynamic world) have also imparted an upward pressure on the average wage rate at any level of unemployment, because of downward rigidity of money wages and the use of wage comparisons in wage setting.

Thus, inflation is neither monocausal nor a simple process. Instead, it is a highly complex dynamic process in which several institutional and market forces interact with varying speeds and lags and which lend inflation, once started by whatever factor, a life of its own and make it a self-maintaining process.

Appendix F

Chakravartv Committee Recommendations
(Restructuring of Monetary System in India)

F.1 Introduction

In this appendix we discuss briefly the main recommendations of Chakravarty Committee—the 'Committee to review the Working of the Monetary System' set up by the RBI under the chairmanship of Prof. S. Chakravarty—that reported in 1985. These recommendations are designed to improve monetary regulation so as to promote price stability, 'the dominant objective of monetary policy' (para 9.25). In its view, such stability is essential for promoting growth with social justice, viable balance of payments and other social objectives.

The term monetary regulation has been defined broadly to include

1. controlled increases in money supply through 'monetary targeting' and
2. 'credit budgeting' to determine
   - (a) the permissible level of bank credit for the commercial sector and
   - (b) a broad profile of the sectoral deployment of such credit (para 9.90).
3. For the above, the Committee has advocated much greater reliance on the instrumental role of organised-sector *administered rates of interest* than at present. This is to be gained by relaxing appropriately the straight jacket of the prevailing complex system of administered rates of interest and introducing 'controlled competition' or flexibility in their midst. The suggested price competition is supposed to supplement and facilitate and not supplant entirely the system of quantity rationing in the spheres of monetary targeting or credit budgeting and also promote much-neglected effective use of credit.

The above three sets of recommendations incorporating monetary targeting, credit budgeting and controlled flexibility of administered interest rates constitute the kernel of the Committee's conception of the 'restructured monetary systems'. Each one of the triad will be discussed briefly in this appendix.

Besides, the Committee has also recommended restructuring of the loan system at micro level for individual borrowers and made several recommendations for the development of the financial system in India such as (i) the development of treasury bills as a money market instrument, (ii) widening of the inter-bank call money market by including non-banks as the suppliers of short-term funds, (iii) promotion of bill market, (iv) gradual replacement of the cash credit system by loans and bill finance, etc. These and other secondary or supporting recommendations have been discussed elsewhere at appropriate places in the book.

F. 2 Monetary Targeting[1]

Monetary targeting refers to fixing *ex ante* the optimal target rate of growth of money supply (or its narrow range) as the foundation of the policy of monetary regulation. This is done to help attain certain well-defined policy goals. In keeping with received monetary theory and large empirical evidence (including the Indian experience), the Committee has rightly advocated that the growth of money supply should be so regulated as to promote price stability at planned levels of output even though prices are affected significantly by several non-monetary factors as well.

The Committee has interpreted the goal of price stability liberally and said that an average annual increase of no more than 4% per annum in the wholesale price index number should be treated as 'acceptable' (para 12.23). The basis for this number is rather weak. Two arguments have been advanced. One simply says that the economy has lived with a higher average rate of inflation of the order of 7% per annum over the nine years 1974-75 to 1983-84. So, it is argued that, in comparison, the limit of 4% per annum should not look formidable (para 12.23). The other argument views this much inflation 'acceptable', as 'reflecting changes in relative prices necessary to attract resources to growth sectors' (para 9.88). The argument should have been developed further. For, as argued by Datta (1986, p. 75), it is not clear how to discover a unique rate of general inflation that will ensure the attainment of a targeted change in relative prices in a concrete historical situation. Also, there always lurks a danger in a policy stance that allows for even a low rate of inflation in a managed paper currency system of the Indian variety that this maximum acceptable rate of inflation is taken for granted and tends to be converted into the minimum rate for any fight against inflation. Also, it will strengthen inflationary price expectations of the public, which factor the Committee has not taken fully into account.

The basic approach to the determination of the target rate of growth of money supply is the same as that spelled out in Gupta (1979, ch. 2). In brief, it has said that, optimally, the growth in money supply should be adapted to the expected growth in the demand for money[2] associated with the expected growth in real income at stable prices. This gives a simple rule of guidance for determining the target rate of growth of money supply. All that it requires is (a) to project the rate of growth of real output and (b) to estimate the real-income elasticity of demand for real money. Then, the product of the two will give the optimal target rate of growth of money supply. Most estimates of the said elasticity put it at unity. That being so, if the projected value of the growth rate of output is 5% in the forthcoming year, the optimal target value of $\dot{M}$ (the rate of growth of money supply) also comes to 5% for the next year.

The Chakravarty Committee has departed from this number in two respects (para 9.88):

(i) It has not put forward any estimate of its own of the income elasticity of demand for money, but, *as an example*, has used the value of 2 for it;

(ii) In the same example, it has also opted for an 'acceptable rate of inflation' of 4% per year (in place of our zero per cent rate of inflation). As discussed above, the Committee has also justified the necessity of this much annual rate of inflation.

With these two changes, the optimal target value of the rate of growth of $\dot{M}$ arrived at in the example comes to 14% (=2×5%+4%) per year. Presumably, this is also the Committee's preferred value for M. On the basis of past experience and most empirical estimates of the income elasticity of demand for money (defined broadly as M_3), it can be safely predicted that such a high rate of monetary expansion will surely result in higher than 4% per annum average rate of inflation and strengthen further inflationary price expectations of the public.

Further, the Committee has advocated a *narrow range* for $\dot{M}$ around the target value of 14% per year and not the specific magnitude of 14% per year— not even as an average annual rate over a longer period of (say) 5 years, not to speak of it as the maximum rate.

How narrow should be the range is not indicated. For, in its anxiousness to impart sufficient flexibility to monetary policy (or sufficient discretion to the RBI and the government), the Committee has recommended that even the target range for $\dot{M}$ announced earlier may be revised up or down later during the year 'in the light of emerging trends in output and prices.' (para 9.88). It has called such flexible monetary targeting as '*monetary targeting with feedback*'.

But, such excessive flexibility in monetary targeting, by making any $\dot{M}$ target excessively short-lived and subject to revision even before the results of the pursuit of the previous $\dot{M}$ target have fructified fully, will render monetary targeting an exercise in futility, as it will not be able to exercise any discipline on excessive monetary expansion. Besides, imperfections and lags in information, in the processing of information, in decision-making, and lags and slippages in the effect of monetary policy measures are quite well-known and experienced every year by the RBI. Also, the empirical evidence about the relation between money, prices and output in India presented in the Report by the Committee amply show that these relations are not contemporaneous for even annual data. For all these reasons, any attempt at instant monetary treatment of small short-period fluctuations in output and prices is not warranted except for feasible reallocations of credit and pro-seasonal small variations in money and credit. In other words, too much short-period fine-tuning of the monetary system should be avoided and the emphasis should be on ensuring longer-term monetary stability.[3]

The Committee has hoped that its kind of 'monetary targeting with feedback' "would bind the Reserve Bank and the Government of India in a common effort to achieve the desired rate of growth in money supply" (para 9.88). But, to most observers of the Indian scene, this would appear as just so much pious hope on the part of the Committee, because unless some kind of statutory constraint is imposed on the power of the Government of India to borrow from the RBI, no amount of monetary targeting or the like can contain excessive budgetary deficits (correctly defined) and so of the excess creation of H and M beyond a pre-set monetary target.

Two other features of the above design of monetary policy should be noted.

(i) with the Committee, M_3 is the favoured measure of M, not M_1. (For the distinction between M_1 and M_3, see Section 1.6 above). The

Committee has not given the basis for its preference. But it needs to be stressed that it is M_1 that is, money narrowly defined, that serves as the means of payment, that fixed deposits of banks (which are the major component of time deposits, which when added to M_1 yield M_3) are *not* the means of payment, as they are neither chequable nor easily withdrawable without incurring some cost. Generally, therefore, the bulk of the deposit holders treat fixed deposits for one year or more as the medium for holding their savings. Then, the bulk of monetary theory, whether of the Keynesian or the monetarist vintage, explains the relation between M and Y (and so P) for M viewed as M_1 (money as the means of payment) (see chapters 12 and 13 above). The theory of the relation between M_3 and Y (or P) is yet to be worked out. The RBI or the Chakravarty Committee also have not attempted such a task.

(ii) Though the Committee accepted the H (or the money-multiplier) theory of money supply and the empirical judgement and evidence that the money multiplier in India is highly stable, it did not exploit systematically and fully the crucial role of H and of the sources of changes in H in the formulation of monetary and credit policy. For example, it chose not to draw upon the useful concept and policy tool of 'ΔH-budgeting',[4] which brings the constraint on the shares of various competing claims on target ΔH into sharp focus, if target ΔM is to be realized. Without the organizing concept of 'Δ H-budgeting', the Committee's recommendations about the management of ΔH lie scattered at several places through the Report's chapters 9-13 and lose some of their impact as well as clarity as some recommendations are combined with the sectoral allocation of commercial bank credit.

F. 3 Credit Budgeting

The second main component of the restructured monetary system of the Committee's conception is credit budgeting.[5] The stated objectives of the credit budget, as said earlier, are to determine.

(a) "the permissible level of bank credit to the commercial sector" and

(b) "a broad profile of the sectoral deployment of credit" (para 9.90).

The above statement does not distinguish between stocks and flows. From the context, however, we may infer that it refers to incremental (and not total) bank credit for both objectives (a) and (b) and that for (b) no wholesale restructuring of total bank credit is envisaged every six months of policy review. We, therefore, discuss the determination of (a) and (b) in incremental terms.

(a) *Determination of the Permissible Incremental Level of Bank Credit for the Commercial Sector.* Two important steps as explained below are involved in this determination.

(i) Having determined the target value of $\triangle M_3$ for the next year (as explained above under 'Monetary Targeting'), the derivation of incremental bank credit for all the sectors from this magnitude (or range) is easy. For, given the estimated marginal value of $\hat{c}^*$ (i.e. the currency-deposit ratio), $\triangle \hat{D}$ will be equal to $\triangle \hat{M}_3 / (1+c)^*$, *since*

$\triangle \hat{M}_3 = \triangle \hat{C} + \triangle \hat{D}$ and

$\triangle \hat{C} = c^* \ \triangle \hat{D}$. (paras 9.92) and so, the maximum incremental supply of bank credit ($\triangle \hat{BC}^s$), will be equal to

$\triangle \hat{D}$ + other resources of banks — $\triangle \hat{R}$.

In the above explanation the symbol $\wedge$ indicates that the hatted amounts are predicted amounts for the next year, superscript *s* stands for supply, and symbol R stands for total cash reserves of banks.

From the above it should be clear that having agreed on target $\triangle M_3$ (i.e., having adopted 'monetary targeting'), there is no freedom left *with the monetary authority* to determine either $\triangle$ D or $\triangle$ BC (because each of them is co-determined with $\triangle M_3$), though banks may vary $\triangle$ BC within narrow limits by varying $\triangle$ other resources. However, having opted for an optimal $\triangle$ BC (or its range), the monetary authority is reasonably free to alter its allocation among sectors and individual borrowers;

(ii) The amount of incremental bank credit for the commercial sector will then be determined residually by taking out the share of $\triangle$ BC going into government securities (of both the Central and state governments) and 'other approved securities'. Such statutory investment will be given by the prevailing SLR (see Section 19.8 above) and the total net liabilities of banks, provided banks do not default in this regard and they are not carrying any undesired excess investment in such securities.

(b) *Broad Profile of the Sectoral Deployment of Credit.* Presumably, this relates only to the deployment of credit within the commercial sector, as the credit going to the government and 'other approved sectors' has already been determined as in the previous paragraph. Here, the Committee has said the following three things:

(i) The sectoral allocation of credit (in the credit budget) will be decided in the light of Plan priorities (para 9.98);

(ii) If $\triangle M_3$ (target) is revised in the course of the year in the light of output trends and the behaviour of prices, the credit budget will also be appropriately modified (para 9.98); and

(iii) $\triangle BS^s$ for the commercial sector (as arrived under *(aii)* above) should be compared with the estimates of the demand for such bank credit (independently arrived at) to estimate 'the likely extent of recourse to RBI refinance by banks which in turn should be cross-checked with the estimated expansion in the other components of reserve money' (para 9.96).

The last point (iii) deserves careful attention as the Committee's discussion does not throw any light on what is discussed in the sequel. So long as the estimated $\triangle BS^s >$ the estimated $\triangle BC^d$, it will only call for relaxation in credit allocation and will not pose any serious problem. But a very difficult problem in monetary targeting and credit budgeting will arise, if the estimated $\triangle BC^s <$ the estimated $\triangle BC^d$ by a large enough margin.[6] Such problems will also arise if the changed situation warrants downward revision of credit allocation, as visualised by the Committee in the case of agro-based industries when the estimate of agricultural output is revised downward (para 12.29). And all this because of relatively low downward flexibility in credit allocations because of numerous structural features, not least of which is the frequent exercise of political pressure at various levels. In all such situations, expanding the RBI finance to banks, other things being the same, is sure to jeopardise monetary targeting and through it price stability.

It will not be out of place to mention here that in the past the RBI, presumably, has been pursuing such a demand—accommodating policy for bank credit expansion to a large extent, and this has resulted in excess increases in the supply of bank credit and money year after year, whatever the seasonal bank credit ceilings announced by it (see Anoop Singh *et. al.*, 1982, pp. 22-27).

To justify *ex post* such expansion of bank credit for the commercial sector on the 'needs of credit for increase in output' argument is questionable. This is because all the anticipated increase in output has been duly allowed for while drawing up the initial or revised target for $\triangle M_3$. Besides, and more importantly, much over-expansion of H has been occuring anyhow due to over-financing of the government through the Reserve Bank credit. Presumably, such over-financing will continue even under the 'restructured monetary system' as recommended by the Committee. So, the inescapable result of the aforesaid over-expansion of credit and M_3 will be, as it always has been, rise in prices.

F. 4 **Flexible Interest Rates**

The third important component of the scheme of monetary regulation recommended by the Committee and which marks an important departure from the prevailing monetary-policy practice in India relates to significant relaxations in the prevailing system of administered rates of interest. The Committee has highlighted several deficiencies in the latter, which we have already discussed in Section 17.6 above. Here we concentrate on the major recommendations of the Committee on the subject.

In general, the Committee is against pricing credit too low, whether for the government or the commercial borrowers in public or private sector. This is because, as discussed elsewhere (see Section 17.6 above), low rates of interest

(a) encourage too much borrowing by the government from the RBI and so too much monetisation of government debt,
(b) leave too little for the RBI's refinance of banks,
(c) discourage effective use of credit by borrowers (government and others),
(d) discourage financial savings and
(e) reduce profitability of banks and other financial institutions.

Therefore, in most cases, the Committee has recommended upward revision of several rates of interest, 'controlled competition' among banks, both for attracting deposits (within an 'administered spread') and for lending to commercial borrowers above a RBI-fixed 'basic (minimum) lending rate' to reap the benefits of price rationing (in addition to quantity rationing) among potential borrowers. The main ideas are discussed below.

For analytical convenience, the several recommendations of the Committee are discussed under the following three main heads:

(i) Interest rates and the expected rate of inflation ($\dot{P}^e$);
(ii) Interest rates on government securities and
(iii) Interest rates on deposits and loans of banks.

F.4.1 **Interest Rates and Expected Rate of Inflation** ($\dot{P}^e$)

One fundamental innovation in policy-recommendation made by the Committee is to link administered interest rates with appropriate P^e. This clearly draws upon Irving Fisher's well-known hypothesis about the relation between money (nominal) and real rates of interest which says that, in a risk-free world, in equilibrium, we would have

$$i = r + P^e,$$

where i = money rate of interest and
r = real rate of interest.

The Committee's recommendation regarding the fixation of an administered *i* translates this equation into actual practice. To that end, it has suggested from its own side what target *r* the RBI should aim at for a particular administered *i* and that it should estimate on its own the appropriate $\dot{P}e$—short-term or long-term—as required. Using these values in the above equation will give the appropriate value of *i* of a particular administered *i*.

This approach has given birth to specific recommendations in respect of particular administered *i's*. They are discussed below. The general question of the relation between *i* and $\dot{P}^e$ will be evaluated critically later.

F.4.2 **Interest Rates on Government Securities**[7]

The Government of India borrows funds through two main kinds of market instruments (apart from non-marketable instruments of small savings schemes, like post office savings and fixed deposits, National Savings certificates, etc.): treasury bills (T bills hereafter) and marketable debt of medium and long-term maturities. Of these, more than 90% of the T bills and more than 30% of dated securities are held by the RBI. Thus, the RBI has been the major 'captive holder' of central government debt and dominantly so of T bills. That is how and because the rate of interest on these bills has been kept fixed at the low level of 4.6% per annum (p.a. hereafter) since 1974 and the rate of interest on dated government securities also kept relatively low till 1982-83. The low rates have had practically dried the voluntary or non-captive demand for government securities.

The Committee's chief recommendation is for the upward revision of all these rates, so that they become competitive with other rates in the open market to attract enough voluntary investment in government securities.[8] The criterion of revision is stated in terms of (a) the real rate of interest and (b) the expected rate of price inflation ($\dot{P}^e$) The recommended structure of nominal interest rates is given below (para 10.35, Table 1):

	Security	**Nominal Interest Rates**
a)	T bills	Short-term $\dot{P}^e$ + a marginally positive real return.
b)	15-year dated securities	Short-term $\dot{P}^e$ + a positive real rate of return of 3% p.a.

For other maturities of less than 15 years, the real rate may vary between 1% and 3% p.a. The Committee has also advised that the maturity should be not more than 15 years, because the capital market will find it hard to form price expectations beyond 15 years.

About the T bills, it is the committee's view that (a) they 'should be developed as an active monetary instrument and should constitute the ideal short-term paper in the money market' (para 10.11); (b) that for this, the yield (discount rate) on T bills should be raised substantially and (c) that T bills (a short-term financial instrument) should be used only to meet the unanticipated short-term deficit in the budget and not as a cheap source of long-term funds for the government in place of long-term market loans, as has been the practice for long.

The chief motivation for the upward revision of the yield structure of government securities is derived from the Committee's concern for excessive annual increase in H (high-powered money) resulting from excessive dependence of the government on the net Reserve Bank credit[9] to meet its *fiscal* deficit.[10] The 'excess increase' in H[11] results in too much increase in M (through the money-multiplier process) relative to increase in real output (and in the demand for real money) and puts upward pressure on prices, thus jeopardising monetary targeting and associated price stability.

What then is the best way of checking excess increases in H, which occurs primarily through excessive reliance of the government on the Reserve Bank credit? The Committee's recommended solution is much greater reliance on open-market borrowing than heretofore on the strength of higher competitive rates of interest, after allowing for greater attraction to the investing public of the government securities because of their greater security and liquidity in comparison with private corporate securities of comparable maturity. It is the Committee's strong hope that higher rates of return on government securities will increase greatly voluntary demand of the financial institutions and the public for such securities.

The effects of the above recommendation are examined briefly below. They are both positive and negative.

On the *positive side,* the Committee has claimed the following.

(i) That its proposal will help reduce greatly the dependence of the government on the Reserve Bank credit and so on the monetisation of its debt;

This hope will not fructify if the increased market borrowing is offset fully by the increase in fiscal deficit occasioned by (say) increases in unproductive expenditure of the government. Such increases are largely a function of political mismanagement — a factor generally ignored by economists — and not purely a function of economic calculus. Therefore, concerted political effort to curtail unproductive expenditure, among other things, to curtail fiscal deficit is more important than the effort to find ways and means of meeting financially the increasing fiscal deficits;

(ii) That the higher cost of credit (capital) to the government will lead to more effective use of credit by it, to better project selection, speedier project completion and better utilisation of capacity.

The argument, though relevant for private sector enterprises, is of only marginal significance for the government. For better project selection, completion and operation, if the authorities use social cost-benefit analysis, it is the shadow price and not the actual cost of capital that should be used. If political considerations and corruption dominate the scene, the cost factor will take the back seat and the government will not hesitate incurring even costlier unproductive debt, so long as it can borrow funds;

(iii) That the higher yields on government securities will raise the incomes and so profits of the 'captive investors' like banks, insurance companies, provident funds, etc.

To an extent this may be considered desirable for the financial health of the concerned financial institutions, most of which fall in the public sector. But much more important is the distribution of costs and benefits among members of the society at large in their capacities as tax-payers, beneficiaries of government expenditures, interest-earners, insurance-policy holders, employees, etc. The subject is vast and complex and the Committee has not referred to these considerations even in passing.

The arguments on the *negative side* of the Committee's recommendation are examined next.

(i) The Committee's recommendations will *raise interest cost* to the government and its several agencies and undertakings. On a quick estimate for the year 1984-85, the Committee has estimated the *additional* interest burden of about Rs. 250/- crores. It has also admitted that in subsequent years, this burden will go on increasing, if the yields are maintained at higher levels.

The Committee has expressed the hope that the restructuring of the monetary system as suggested by it will lead to 'reasonable price stability' via reduction in 'excess increases' in the supply of money generated by too much net Reserve Bank credit to the government. It further hopes that this will have 'beneficial impact on government expenditures' and 'a part or even the whole of the additional interest burden might well be offset by saving in government expenditure (para 9.54). Therefore, though initially interest cost to the government will increase as successive tranches of its borrowings carry higher coupon rates, in the Committee's assessment, 'the net impact on the government budget *need not be large in the long run* to the extent that relative price stability is achieved' (para 9.54).

The Committee has further noted that if reasonable price stability is maintained over a period of time, this will induce downward revision in inflationary expections of the public and thereby lowering of the money rates of interest, leaving the real rates broadly unchanged.

All this is wishful thinking (Dandekar, 1986, p. 170), as there is no firm basis for the Committee's expectations.

(ii) It is feared that higher interest rates on government (and other approved) securities will merely lead to portfolio substitution in their favour from other assets (namely, private-sector securities) without increasing significantly the total size of savings, as such savings are not known to be much interest-rate-elastic. In particular, it is feared that the stiffer competition from government (and other approved) securities will tend to 'crowd out' the private-sector securities and thus hurt capital formation in the private sector and the investment target set for it in the plans. But, as a counter to this argument, we should admit that for promoting effective use of credit in the capital-scarce economy of India, there is a strong case for bringing the private organized sector, too, under the interest-rate discipline.

(iii) It has been argued by some (e.g. see Dandekar, 1986; Patil, 1986) that the government does deserve cheaper (or subsidised) credit, as the borrowed funds are used in building up the economy's infrastructure and for financing other kinds of development expenditure, the fruits of which are reaped by the whole economy.

This kind of argument is much too general, offers blanket support to all kinds of government expenditure, ignores social priorities and wastes in government expenditure and also the fact that a part of borrowings is used to finance unproductive expenditure of the government.

In conclusion we may say that the case for releasing the T bill rate (discount) from the straight jacket of 4.6% p.a. is quite strong and so is the case for bringing the level and structure of all the rates of interest on government securities into reasonable conformity with other organized-sector rates of interest, when due allowance has been made for the greater security and liquidity of government paper than the private IOUs. The steps taken recently by the government and the RBI in this direction have already been pointed out in Sections 3.5 and 3.9.

But, the higher interest-cost factor alone is not likely to induce the government to curtail its fiscal deficits. The best way to reduce the government's reliance on the RBI credit is not to recommend another costlier source of funds, but to impose a statutory restriction on its authority to borrow from the RBI—it may best be stipulated in the form of a maximum proportion of the target ΔH.

F.4.3. **Deposit and Lending Rates of Banks.**

The Committee's main recommendations on the above rates are summed up below:

1. The maximum deposit rate applicable to deposits with a maturity of 5 years and above should be fixed at long-term $\dot{P}^e$ + a positive real *r* of not less than 2% p.a.

2. One-year deposit rate should be marginally positive in real terms (implying that it should be = short-term (1-year) $\dot{P}^e$ + a small positive real *r*).

These two rates should be fixed by the RBI. (The Committee does not say anything on how frequently these rates should be changed if the RBI's price expectations need to be revised when actual prices change differently.)

Other deposit rates on deposits with varying maturity between 1 and 5 years should be left to be fixed by banks themselves, within the limits of the above two rates. The Committee also allowed the RBI similar flexibility in regard to deposit rates for maturities of less than one year, subject to the ceiling of the 1-year deposit rate (para 18.20). In early April 1986, the RBI tried this suggestion out, but had to beat hasty retreat after only 6 weeks of experiment, as the banks soon offered the maximum deposit rate of 8% p.a. on all term deposits of 15 days or more upto one year, with further attraction of automatic renewal, causing a sudden scramble among banks for short-term deposits and real danger to the RBI's policy of credit control. Besides, the holders of savings deposits had justly started to feel cheated and before long there could have been large-scale diversion of funds from savings deposits (with 5% p.a. rate of interest) into 'short-term' deposits (with 8% p.a. rate of interest).

The Committee has recommended that the rate of interest on savings deposits may stay at 5% p.a. and has not recommended any neutralisation of $\dot{P}$ even on the minimum balance held in a savings account for (say) a year.

The Committee has spoken approvingly of the fiscal incentives (tax exemption on interest income from bank deposits upto a stipulated maximum) as this has led to phenomenal increase in the volume of fixed deposits over time. The Committee has recognized that small savers cannot be benefited from such fiscal incentives, as they do not earn high enough incomes to be taxable. It also admitted strong justification for devising suitable deposit scheme for small depositors, but, instead of doing so itself, has left it to 'the imagination and innovative spirit of banks'. This means doing nothing in this direction.

In respect of the lending rates of banks, the Committee has made the following recommendations.

The RBI should fix only the basic (minimum) lending rate to serve as a floor to the non-concessional lending rates of banks and leave the rest to market competition among banks. This basic lending rate should be fixed at 3 percentage points higher than the maximum rate on deposits. (Since the maximum deposit rate recommended = long-term $\dot{P}^e$+2% p.a., the basic lending rate will come to long-term $\dot{P}^e$+5% p.a.). Then, 3% p.a. will constitute the minimum *'administered spread'* between the lending rate and the rate on deposits for banks. The actual spread will be higher on average, because the average rate of interest on deposits will be lower than the maximum and the weighted average rate of interest charged by banks on non-concessional loans and advances will be higher than the basic minimum. The Committee has also explicitly opposed any ceiling rate for non-concessional loans and advances. All this will introduce what the Committee has called *'controlled competition'* among banks. This is expected to promote better use of credit by borrowers and prompt them to improve their credit-rating so as to gain more favourable terms from their bankers and, in turn, make bankers more cost and profit conscious and also more responsive to the genuine needs and problems of their customers.

As regards *bank lending to the priority sector*, the Committee has emphasised the need to rationalise the number of concessional rates. To that end, it has recommended only two concessional rates: (i) one equal to the basic (minimum) lending rate and (ii) the other somewhat below this rate. The latter should also be determined by the RBI in consultation with the government. Further, the credit delivery system to the priority sector should be appropriately strengthened.

Finally, the Committee has recommended that the current ceiling (of 10% p.a.) on *inter-bank cell money rate* should be removed and to broad-base the call money market new institutional members who generate sizeable short-term surplus funds should be permitted to participate in the call money market.

The above recommendations are designed to simplify the complex system of administered rates.

F.4.4. Interest Rates and $\dot{P}^e$—A Critical Evaluation

Now we evaluate critically the general basis of the Committee's recommendations about the level and structure of administered nominal rates of interest, discussed in the preceding two sub-sections. The main difficulties with the Committee's recommendations are discussed below.

(1) The Committee has recommended that each of the nominal rates to be administered by the RBI should be a sum of (i) a target real rate of interest (r^*) suggested by the Committee and (ii) an appropriate (short-term or long-term) $\dot{P}^e$. The underlying assumption seems to be that thereby actual real r will turn out to be equal to the target real r. Clearly, this will be so if and only if $\dot{P} = \dot{P}^e$. But, this kind of perfect or error-free prediction of $\dot{P}$ is not easily realizable. Also, the RBI's price expectations may diverge much from the public's price expections. This will be all the more so, because, in general, to play safe and not to lend official confirmation to the public's $\dot{P}^e$, the RBI will tend to underestimate $\dot{P}^e$.

If the Committee's true objective is to ensure a certain positive real r in specified cases of borrowing and lending, it can be achieved unambiguously only if the money rates are fully 'indexed', that is, linked to a price index number (as the payment of dearness allowance to government employees is linked to the cost-of-living index number), not by bringing in the troublesome factor of $\dot{P}^e$. Like the Committee's recommendation, our suggestion, too, will, of course, not safeguard the asset-holder against loss through erosion of real value due to $\dot{P}$ of the capital sum deposited, invested or lent.

(2) It should be relatively easy for the RBI to fix the nominal rates on the terms deposits for one year and five years and above and also basic (minimum) lending rate for banks, if they are not to be revised too frequently. But, managing the market for government securities so as to maintain a certain chosen interest rate structure (as recommended by the Committee) and yet ensure enough voluntary (non-captive) demand for government bonds and bills will not be that easy. It will still have to stand ready to support the market for government securities at the chosen rates of interest. This will make Reserve Bank

credit to government highly volatile, signifying a conflict between the targets of public debt management and monetary management.

We should also remember that, in a reasonably free capital market, fixing the coupon rate of a security does not fix its yield, because the market price of the security can deviate from its issue price for any number of developments in the market and, as already noted, the capital market's estimate of $\dot{P}^e$ may be quite different from the RBI's estimate of it. Also, in the absence of the RBI's support, the government bond market will lose its steadiness, the risk of capital loss on government bonds will grow and so voluntary investors will not be easily attracted to it.

(3) The Committee has linked the treasury bill rate with short-term $\dot{P}^e$ and all other *r*'s (except the one for 1-year fixed deposits) with long-term $\dot{P}^e$, without assigning any reasons for its recommendation. (For the *r* on 1-year fixed deposits, the Committee has not specified the kind of $\dot{P}^e$—short-term or long-term—to which it should be linked). Now, making these two types of price expectations is not an easy task, unless one simply projects the past experience into the future of appropriate time-length and does not worry too much about the degree of error involved in such prediction. Then, if the divergence between short-term and long-term $\dot{P}^e$ is too large, the task of administering the *r*-structure for the RBI will become very difficult. For example, if the short-term $\dot{P}^e$ is (say) 20% p.a. and the long-term $\dot{P}^e$ is (say) 8% p.a., the RBI will not find it easy to sell 15-year government bonds with 11% p.a. as the coupon rate when it is selling 91-days treasury bills which yield a discount rate of more than 20% p.a.

(4) How often or when should the nominal *r*'s be revised? The Committee has not offered any guidance.

(5) It is not clear what is the Committee's own estimate for the long-term $\dot{P}^e$. We may try to infer it from a few administered nominal rates. For example, when the Committee reported, the *r* on fixed deposits for 5-years was 11% p.a. If, as recommended by the Committee, the real *r* in this case is taken as 2% p.a., the balance of 9% p.a. gives one measure of long-term $\dot{P}^e$. Before the Committee had submitted its report in April 1985, the new issues of 20-year government loans were carrying a coupon rate of 10.5% p.a. implying long-term $\dot{P}^e$ of 7.5% p.a. (with real *r* of 3% p.a.). The Committee had considered it a little low. So, later issues (of 30-year maturity) have carried coupon rate of 11.5% p.a., giving a higher estimate of long-term $\dot{P}^e$ of 8.5% p.a. These estimates are far above the maximum acceptable $\dot{P}$ of 4% p.a. the Committee had put forward in its exercise on monetary targeting (para 9.88).

(6) Though the policy-maker should surely take the public's price expectations into account, it is inadvisable to link administered nominal r's schematically with any particular measure of these expectations in a tight formula. The inadvisability arises for several reasons. First, the public's price expectations are never precise; they involve differences of opinion, are never held with confidence, and are unlikely to coincide with the policy-makers' $\dot{P}^e$. Then, even in a free-market economy, nominal r adjusts to $\dot{P}^e$ over a fairly long period, and always with distributed lags. It should not, therefore, be the policy-maker's task to hasten this process, as this is likely to strengthen rather than weaken the inflationary price expectations. Also, if it becomes widely known that banks are anticipating a particular rate of inflation, that anticipation will tend to be generalised as the minimum $\dot{P}^e$, with expectation of a higher not lower rate of inflation. This will tend to strengthen inflationary expectations in the economy.

F.5 Conclusion

In the end, we may collect here the main points of the above discussion bearing on the rate of growth of money supply ($\dot{M}$)—the key target variable of monetary regulation. In our assessment, the Committee's full set of recommendations will not help contain excessive $\dot{M}$ for reasons already discussed above. These reasons are recounted very briefly below:

(1) Under monetary targeting, if the value of the income elasticity of demand for money is placed at 2 (as done in the example in para 9.88 of the report) by policy-makers, this will result in over-expansion of $\dot{M}$ every year, because the true value of this elasticity is generally estimated to be in the close neighbourhood of 1. With the average rate of growth of real output taken at 5% p.a., this elasticity factor alone will lead to extra $\dot{M}$ of 5% p.a.

(2) On top of the above, the Committee has also provided for the general rate of inflation of 4% p.a.

(3) The Committee has recommended a range rather than a target or the maximum for annual $\dot{M}$. This provision is likely to be interpreted liberally by the government which is always short of funds and the RBI will concur. So, the extra danger of the excess expansion of M is built into this recommendation.

(4) The Committee has provided for further flexibility in the target range for $\dot{M}$ by recommending 'monetary targeting with feedback', which says that the target range for $\dot{M}$ announced earlier may be revised up or down later during the year 'in the light of emerging trends

in output and prices'. This will render any $\dot{M}$ target excessively short-lived and dilute further whatever monetary discipline 'monetary targeting' is designed to infuse in the authorities.

(5) Under credit budgeting, the recommendation that the RBI should provide additional refinance to banks when the estimated demand for legitimate credit cannot be met fully with banks' own resources raised under 'monetary targeting' constraint opens up yet another door for excess expansion of M.

(6) The recommendations concerning administered interest rates indicate P^e of 9% p.a. built into them, though the maximum acceptable (to the Committee) rate of inflation was stated to be only 4% p.a. This estimate for $\dot{P}^e$ is easily derivable from the current structure of administered interest rates, as shown in Section F.4.2 above. Incidentally, this figure also approximates very closely the actual average annual rate of inflation in recent years.

NOTES

1. The discussion is based on ch. 9 of the Committee's report. Also see Gupta (1979, chs. 1-5) on the subject for a fuller and more systematic discussion.
2. The misinterpretations of and the charges against the demand function for money in the Report (paras 9.4 and 9.5) are, to say the least, gratuitous. Presumably, the Committee's target of attack was the grossly-misinterpreted model of the Quantity Theory of Money.
3. Also see Gupta (1979, Section 2.6) for a fuller discussion of the issues involved here.
4. In contradiction of the Committee's observations on the 'credit effect' (paras 9.5-9.8), it needs to be noted that whatever increase in output is expected to occur due to increase in real credit (or due to improvement in credit allocation and several other factors) is supposed to be picked up fully in the estimate of the next period's output, so that no more of real-credit effect on output remains to be picked up separately or again. Then, the distinction between 'partial' and 'total' credit effect on output should also be kept in mind.
5. See Gupta (1979, Section 5.3).
6. Also see Gupta (1979, Section 2.5.2).
7. See also Sections 3.5, 3.9 and 17.6 above.
8. This will also lead to upward revision of all the linked administered rates such as those on the state government securities and 'other approved securities' (e.g. bonds of state electricity boards, port trusts, etc.).
9. See Section 15.5 above.
10. Fiscal deficit is defined more broadly than budgetary deficit to include all government borrowing even through dated securities, whether bought by the public, banks and other financial institutions or the RBI and small savings schemes.
11. The excess increase in H is given by the excess of actual increase in H over that which is considered sufficient to meet the expected increased in the demand for nominal money at the expected level of real income with stable prices.

Appendix G

M_1 or M_3?

In Section 1.6 we had seen that the RBI now publishes four different, but inter-related, measures of M. Two of them, namely M_1 and M_3, generally called narrow and broad empirical measures respectively of M are of special significance. Most monetary economists like to define M narrowly in the sense of M_1, that is, as something which is generally accepted as means of payment. In this book, we have also taken the same position. But Friedman and others of his persuasion use M in the broad sense of M_3, largely on ground of statistical measurement. In recent years, the RBI also has shown marked preference for it over M_1 and so has the Chakravarty Committee (see Appendix F). Since the empirical definition of M is of much significance for theoretical as well as empirical work and for policy analysis and formulation, we discuss briefly the arguments surrounding the choice betweeen M_1 and M_3 in this appendix. Towards the end we also give annual data on M_1 and M_3 since 1970-71.

The key arguments generally advanced in favour of M_3 are given below.

(1) In measurement, M_3 does not suffer from the problem of arbitrary division of savings deposits between the demand deposit portion and the time deposit portion. Since M_1 does, M_3 is a neater total than M_1.

(2) In the 'credit approach' to monetary policy preferred by the RBI and 'credit budgeting' practised by it in policy making, it seems natural to prefer total D (and M_3) over only demand deposits (and M_1), because total bank credit is closely connected with total deposits (and not merely demand deposits) of banks.

The arguments in favour of M_1 (and so against M_3) as the appropriate measure of M are given below.

(1) Money as generally acceptable means of payment has been the basis of all monetary theorising, even when it is also viewed as a store of value as in Keynes as well as Friedman. And these two properties of money are possessed by only M_1, not by M_3. In the latter, the additional component of time deposits (TDs.) serves only as a store of value, not as a means of payment. So, in the two-asset portfolio choice of Keynes, it is perfectly liquid M_1 (not imperfectly liquid, interest-bearing M_3) which is pitted against bonds. Similarly, in the generalised

asset demand for money of Friedman's theory, it is the demand for M_1 in the face of competition from non-money assets of all kinds (including interest-bearing time deposits) which, strictly speaking, is the subject of analysis. (Friedman's preference for M_3 over M_1 in empirical work relating to the US economy is based on other considerations.) For this very reason, the monetarist as well as the Keynesian theory of monetary transmission mechanism (see Appendix C) views M narrowly as M_1.

(2) Time deposits of banks as store of value have more in common with other interest-bearing financial assets like non-bank deposits (e.g. of post offices and other companies) than with M_1. All these 'non-money financial assets' (NMFAs) are near-money in varying degrees and affect the overall liquidity and thereby economic activity in the economy. But liquidity is a magnitude very hard to measure, though we all talk about it. Therefore, most monetary economists prefer to analyse the influence of these NMFAs via the demand function for money (or via the income-velocity of money) than via broadening the definition of money and including some of these assets in it.

(3) Another useful way of looking at the role of NMFAs is not via the asset side or what these assets do to the spending decisions of their holders, but via the credit side, i.e., via the credit made available to deficit spenders by various institutes whose liabilities NMFAs are. This credit aspect of the financial system is undoubtedly very important. But this importance of credit or of time deposits (and other financial assets) that are used to mobilise financial savings of the public for supplying credit to deficit spenders is not contingent on the inclusion of these deposits (and other financial assets) in any empirical measure of M. Credit is important in its own right and should be emphasised as such, not via M. Moreover, credit is a much broader category than money and includes bank as well as non-bank credit. Also, credit involves a complex market and institutional mediation between the borrower and the lender and this mediation should be studied as such, not through the inclusion of some of the aforesaid assets in the definition of money.

(4) For 'credit budgeting', too, the adoption of M_3in place of M_1 as the empirical measure of M is not necessary. This is because the growth of TDs and so total deposits will be predictable from the planned growth of M_1 and H (high-powered money). So, the optimal amount of incremental bank credit, so critical to 'credit budgeting' at the macro level, will also be known. Then, the RBI cannot have any extra degree of freedom in fixing the optimal size of the credit budget to meet any unsatisfied demand for credit simply by defining M as M_3 in place of M_1. Of course, allocation of this budgeted amount of credit

among the competing uses and users can still be done in any manner the RBI and banks decide.

(5) TDs as asset are not one uniform asset, but many, depending on their time to maturity. The shorter-term TDs are closer to M_1 than the longer-term TDs. But, in any aggregative measure of M_3, this difference in maturity and relative closeness to M_1 must necessarily be ignored and all TDs entered symmetrically in the measure.

For all these reasons, M_1 seems to enjoy a balance of advantage over M_3 as a measure of M. But, the empirical definition or measure of M is very much an empirical question. So viewed, the ultimate test of the usefulness of any empirical definition of M must rest on its power to explain and predict better than any other alternative measure of M the course of key variables of our interest such as nominal income and prices, on relatively greater stability of its demand function and supply function and on relatively greater ease in its policy manipulability. The discussion must rest here till we come up with reliable and well-tested empirical evidence on the subject.

APPENDIX H

New Financial Developments

H.1 Narasimham Committee : Financial Reforms

This is discussed in two steps : first, we discuss deficiencies and problems of India's banking system, then we take up the recommendations of the "Narasimham Committee on the Financial System", followed by the steps taken uptodate by the authorities.

H.1.1. Deficiencies and Problems of India's Banking System

The Narasimham Committee (1991) has offered a highly incisive and frank (open) discussion of the main reasons for steep decline in productivity and efficiency of India's banking system, leading to a serious erosion of its profitability. About the poor state of the profitability of banks, the Narasimham Committee (22-3) has recorded that : "gross profits (*i.e.*, surplus before provisions) have been declining for the banking system over the past decades and in 1989–90, such profits (before provisions) were no more than 1.10 per cent of working funds." If adequate provisions were made for sticky advances and against loan losses, the situation would be a cause for serious concern. While this represents the average for the system as a whole, "there are several banks in whose case the incremental cost of operation per rupee of working funds is higher than the incremental income per rupee of working funds".

The factors responsible for this state of affairs are discussed briefly below. They have reduced the income of banks and/or increased their expenditure; some are the products of macro-policy decisions of the authorities and others are internal to banks -- their organisation, staffing and branch expansion, etc.

1. On macro-policy front, the "system of directed investment" and the "system of directed credit programmes" have gone a long way in depressing banks' potential income. The former has come in the form of the minimum "statutory liquidity ratio" (SLR) and the minimum "cash reserve ratio" (CRR). We have discussed them already in Chapter 19. Here, it is sufficient to note that today the two together preempt well over half of the total resources mobilised by the banking system. The SLR till March 1992 was 38.5 per cent of net demand and time liabilities (lowered to 30 per cent thereafter for any increase in such liability). In addition, the CRR is 15 per cent of these liabilities plus a 10 per cent incremental ratio (withdrawn in April 1992). This had made a total of 63.5 per cent at the margin and somewhat less than this on the average. It has been argued that the SLR has diverted too much of the household savings mobilised by the banking system to finance the government expenditure -- capital as well as current. This could possibly be justified so long as the bulk of the funds so raised were used for public investment. But with large revenue deficits in recent years, the SLR is helping finance current expenditure of the government, while" crowding out" the private sector's access to bank funds for more productive activities.

It is important to note that the SLR investments have affected adversely the profitability of banks, because the coupon rates of interest on government bonds were too low—much lower than what banks could earn on alternative deployment of their funds. In recent years (since 1985), the coupon rates of interest on government borrowings have, no doubt, been progressively raised. But, it should be remembered that in respect of long-dated (say, 20-year) bonds, this has several effects. First, it augments earnings of banks only at the margin from new issues only; but the average earnings do not increase much, weighed as they are by past investments. Second, even though higher than before, the new coupon rates are still much lower than competing market rates of interest. Third, the rise in the coupon rate of interest on new issues of government bonds depresses the market prices of old dateds, imposing accrued capital losses on their holders. Provisioning for such capital losses spoils the balance sheets of banks, which they do not like. But, raising the cost of their credit to other borrowers as another alternative has contributed to making the Indian economy a high-cost economy.

2. **The CRR.** The high CRR also depresses income of banks, because the interest paid by the RBI on deposits above the basic minimum of 3 per cent is below the opportunity cost of funds of banks. The RBI has been paying interest on additional deposits impounded at the rate of 10.5 per cent on eligible cash balances as on March 1990 and 5 per cent on

incremental cash balances thereafter. But these rates are below the current rate for one-year term deposits with banks. With well over half of bank deposits as term deposits, the loss in potential income to banks from the reserve requirement tax has adversely affected profitability of banks.

3. **The system of directed credit programmes**, has come in for severe criticism at the hands of the Narasimham Committee (27–33). Such programmes were adopted under the developmental credit policy of the government enunciated at the time of the nationalization of banks in 1969. They involved extending bank credit facilities geographically as well as functionally--geographically, over the hitherto unbanked regions such as the rural hinterland; functionally, by expanding bank credit to agriculture, small industry and the professionals -- the so-called priority sectors of the economy. We have already discussed about the priority-sector credit in Section 6.3.2 above. Leaving out the export sector and the food-procurement sector, this kind of credit was equal to the targeted figure of 40 per cent of the total bank credit in 1991. It may be noted that a part of the increase in priority sector credit has been on account of accumulated interest arrears which are added by banks to outstanding credit amounts.

Quantitatively the redeployment of bank credit has been, more or less, as per the policy directions. But, as emphasized by the Narasimham Committee, this achievement has been at the cost of the quality of loan portfolio of banks, the growth of overdues and consequent erosion of profitability of banks. In the desire to attain credit targets, the banks paid inadequate attention to the qualitative aspects of lending. Norms of supervised credit and of credit-worthiness of borrowers were not followed seriously. Consequently, loan delinquencies have been very high. Even the institution of credit guarantee has had the unintended effect of the primary lender not undertaking the needed loan-appraisal in the mistaken belief that the loan recovery was, after all, guaranteed to the bank. Other loan conditions such as adequate collateral and margin requirements, productive use of credit and post-credit supervision have also been lax.

4. **Concessional Lending rates on priority sector credit.**

This involves an element of subsidy, which is given by the excess of the normal lending rate of banks over the concessional rate. This also cuts into the profits of banks. Two points are worth bearing in mind here. One : the timely and adequate access to credit is much more important than its cost or the subsidization thereof. After all, institutional finance, even at normal cost, is much cheaper then the informal-sector finance. Two, subsidized credit to the selected beneficiaries is at the expense of those unfortunate ones who are denied bank credit, because no bank can possibly meet the credit needs of all potential borrowers.

5. **Political and administrative interference.** According to the Narasimham Committee (p.30), by far the most serious damage to the credit system of banks and one which has contributed greatly to the decline in the quality of the loan portfolio of banks has been the political and administrative interference in their credit-decision-making. The following grave cases of such interference are worth recording. :

(i) In many cases of IRDP lending, banks have virtually abdicated their responsibility in undertaking need-based credit assessment and appraisal of potential viability of aspirants for loans, and have, instead, tended to rely on lists of identified borrowers prepared by government authorities;

(ii) The phenomenon of loan meals was quite contrary to the principles of a professional appraisal of bank credit needs;

(iii) Loan waivers have added an additional element of politicization of banking. They have also done serious damage to credit discipline among borrowers by encouraging defaults. The political element has condoned overdues of defaulters without any regard for the social obligation of banks towards their deposit-holders.

The problem of infected loan portfolios is quite sizeable. It is estimated that over 20 per cent of agricultural and small-industry credit is not recoverable. In the field of non-priority sector, too, the problem of 'sick industries' is grim and large. On top of it, under government pressure, banks are made to extend further credit to sick units in attempts at their rehabilitation. Unfortunately, this is not fully reflected in reported results due to inadequate provisioning for bad loans and overdue of accumulated interest. This hurts the self-revolving character of bank credit and locks up bank funds with the defaulters.

6. The squeeze on the profitability of banks has also come from the side of expenditure. The latter has gone up on several counts. Firs , the interest cost of raising funds for the banks has been going up as a result of higher interest rates on deposits and a shift in the maturity pattern of deposits towards longer-term deposits. Second and perhaps the single

most important cause for the growth in expenditure has been the phenomenal expansion of branch banking (see Section 6.2.4). This has raised several problems. The bulk of the new branches have gone to rural and semi-urban areas, where loans are given largely for agriculture and small industries and at subsidized rates. But, the unit costs of administering such loans tend to be relatively higher as compared to the costs of servicing loans to large industrial borrowers. Add to this the factor of high overdues, already discussed above. Further, as pointed out by the Narasimham Committee (34-5), extensive geographical spread of banks has tended to weaken the central office supervision of far-flung bank branches and any system of internal control, balancing of books, reconciliation of inter-branch and inter-bank entries and timely audit of all bank accounts.

7. **Man-Power problems**. Another problem area for banks is their man-power. With rapid growth of banks, their offices and diversification, has come the rapid growth in the number of staff, accompanied by overmanning at various levels. Accelerated promotions have diluted the quality of supervisory and managerial staff. Trade unions, besides looking after the legitimate grievances and service conditions of their members, have also contributed to the proliferation of restrictive practices in terms of work norms, resistance to mechanization and computerization and obstacles to rational policies in respect of promotions and staff transfers. Some of these practices have affected adversely discipline and work culture and, in the process, also affected productivity and efficiency. The technology of bank operations has, over the past few decades, shown little improvement, despite manifold expansion of business. This has come in the way of providing efficient customer service in an industry which is essentially a service industry. Moreover, emoluments of bank staff and their revisions have no relation to either productivity of staff or profitability of banks, either individually or in the aggregate. This has aggravated the position of some of the weaker banks. Therefore, there is a strong case for curtailing yearly expansion of bank staff and for their suitable redeployment as among several centers.

8. **Other Shortcomings**. Declining profitability of banks has affected adversely their capitalization, as they are not able to add sufficiently to their own resources in the form of reserves. The ratio of capital funds of Indian banks to their risk-weighted assets is low on the average by international standards. Moreover, we are saying this on the basis of published balance-sheets, when the truth is that these documents conceal much.

The concealment is attempted generally by making inadequate provision for loan-losses and bad and doubtful debts in their accounts.

H.1.2 Recommendations of the Narasimham Committee on the Financial System

In this sub-section, we study briefly the main recommendations of the Committee for improving the financial (especially banking) system. At appropriate places, we have also inserted our own comments and critical observations placed within square brackets.

1. The Committee's approach to financial sector reform is to ensure that the financial services industry operates on the basis of operational flexibility and functional autonomy with a view to enhancing efficiency, productivity and profitability. A vibrant and competitive financial system alone will be able to sustain the ongoing structural reforms of the real sector economy.

[The recommendations based on this approach, as discussed below, betray excessive zeal for the profitability of banks to the total neglect of broad social objectives, which also deserve to be kept in mind by banks and other financial institutions.]

2. One major factor responsible for depressed income of banks identified by the Committee is the system of directed investment in terms of the SLR requirement and the relatively low rate of interest paid/received on these investments. Accordingly, the Committee has recommended that the SLR should be brought down in a phased manner to 25 per cent (the minimum prescribed under the law) over a period of about five years. In the budget proposals for the year 1992–93, a beginning was announced (effective from April 1992) and the SLR for incremental net demand and time liabilities of banks has been reduced from 38.5 per cent to 30 per cent. This reduced the effective average SLR to 36% during 1992–93.

[This is a step in the right direction, party because it leaves an increasingly larger proportion of funds with banks for proper deployment among productive borrowers and partly because it curtails easy and captive finance-- the public's financial savings mobilized by banks available to the government to overspend. This had encouraged much of excess deficit financing by the government.

Some of the Committee's points in respect of the rates of interest on SLR investments need to be controverted. First, these rates have been steadily revised upward in recent years. If a rise in the rate means higher interest return on new issues of government securities (bonds), it also inflicts capital losses on the holdings of old dateds with lower coupon rates. This is a well-known effect of rise in the rate of interest. The accrued capital losses, however, need not be realized and can be avoided if the securities are held to maturity. But, in recent years of the "securities scam", several banks had tried to play the market through interested brokers in an effort to make extra gains. The results, in general, have been disastrous for many banks.

As a policy option, it is much better for the authorities to try their level best to control the forces of inflation with a view to bring the rate of inflation down to a manageable level. This will be highly beneficial for the all-round working of the economy. By reigning in inflationary price expectations, it will make further rise in money rates of interest totally unnecessary. On the contrary, some lowering of the money rates of interest will become necessary. Therefore, in the context of continued success in keeping the forces of inflation under firm control, the current coupon rates on the recent issues of government bonds will become quite attractive to banks.

Even in a freely competitive market economy, the government bond rate of interest is likely to be significantly lower than the average rate of interest on bank loans extended to the traditional sector. The main reason is practically nil risk of default in respect of government bonds and a positive (low or high) risk of default in respect of the loan portfolios of banks (even for the traditional sector). Moreover, banks value highly regular and timely flow of interest receipts from their investments in government securities. The interest receipts from their loans are not fully dependable. A part of the loan portfolio always suffers from overdues and irregular accounts. This factor has not been given its due weight by the Narasimham Committee.]

3. The Committee has rightly pointed out that, at present, the CRR for banks is much too high. In fact, since July 1, 1989 it had been pitched at its statutory maximum of 15 per cent of the net demand and time liabilities of banks. The RBI's justification for such a high CRR has been its perceived need for keeping the growth of money supply in the economy under control, in the face of much deficit spending by the Government, resulting in excess increases in H year after year. With the Government's resolve to reduce its fiscal deficit, the Committee has recommended progressive reduction in the CRR from its present high level. It has also said that with the deregulation of interest rates, there would be more scope for the use of open market operations as a monetary control instrument

by the RBI. Consequently, there would be less dependence on variations in CRR as a measure of monetary control.

In addition, the Committee has recommended that the interest rate paid to banks on their impounded reserves (under the CRR) above the basic minimum (of 3 per cent) should be increased : it should be broadly related to bank's average cost of deposits. It has added that, during the present regime of administered interest rates, this rate may be fixed at the level of bank's one-year deposit rate. [The recommendation is fully in line with the Committee's concern for banks' profits. But, it is counter-argued by some that the yield from a significant part of required reserves is simply compensation to the RBI for free services rendered by it to banks such as supervision, clearing facilities, etc. The Committee has not taken note of this point.]

4. The most debatable recommendation of the committee is that for scaling down the priority sector credit from the present high level of 40 per cent of aggregate credit to 10 per cent. We have already discussed about priority sector credit in Ch. 6 above. This credit is what the Committee has called " directed credit programme", *i.e*, credit allocation under government direction, not by the commercial judgement of banks under a free market competitive system. The Committee admits that such directed credit has contributed much to the growth of agriculture and small industry. But, it is of the view that such programmes should be re-examined at least in respect of those who are able to stand on their own feet and to whom these programmes with an element of concessionality in the rate of interest charged has become a source of economic rent. The Committee has also observed that the objective of redistribution through banking and credit policies pursued so far may better be accomplished through fiscal measures.

In view of the above, the Committee has recommended that the directed credit programmes should be phased out. Recognizing the need for their continuation for some time, it has recommended the following revised programme :

(a) The priority sector should be redefined to comprise the small and marginal farmer, the tiny sector of small industry, small business and transport operators, village and cottage industries, rural artisans and other weaker sections;

(b) The credit target for this redefined priority sector should now be fixed at 10 per cent of aggregate credit, which would be broadly in line with the credit flows to these sectors at present. (The Committee has

proposed that a review may be undertaken at the end of three years to see if directed credit programmes need to be continued;)

(c) As regards medium and large farmers, and the larger among small industries, including transport operators, etc., the Committee has recommended that the RBI and other refinancing agencies should give preferential refinance to banks to encourage them to provide credit to the forementioned sectors who would not constitute a part of the redefined priority sector.

[The above recommendation will be the hardest to implement politically. The reasons may be easily surmised. The chief *raison d'etre* for the nationalization of 14 major commercial banks in 1969 was the provision of bank credit to hitherto neglected sectors of the economy such as agriculture, small industries, etc., designated as the priority sectors for credit. These sectors continue to be creditworthy for their contribution to growth in output and employment. If the overall net rate of return to banks from loans to these sectors is relatively lower, the Committee has not diagnosed the main causes and then recommend suitable remedies. Instead, by simply recommending phasing out the bulk of such credit, it has thrown the baby with the bath-water.

What will be the social cost of it ? The Committee has not undertaken any social cost-benefit analysis. Taking an accountant's approach, it has shown its concern for only the net profits of banks.]

5. The Committee has recommended further deregulation of interest rates to reflect emerging market conditions. However, for this, a reasonable degree of macro-economic balance through sufficient reduction in the fiscal deficit is necessary. Meanwhile, concessional interest rates should be phased out. Interest rates on bank deposits and the spreads between the key rates may continue to be regulated by the RBI.

6. Banks (and financial institutions) in India suffer from capital inadequacy in relation to their risk-weighted assets. This should be removed within the next three years.

The banks whose operations have been profitable and which enjoy a good reputation in the market should raise fresh capital from the public through the capital market. In respect of other banks, the Government should meet the shortfall in their capital requirements by direct subscription to capital or by providing a loan which should be treated as subordinate debt.

7. Two very important recommendations of the Committee concern the system of income accounting and loss provisioning followed by banks and other financial institutions in India. The Committee has strongly recommended that the balance sheets (and income statements) of these institutions should be made transparent with full disclosures made in them according to international accounting standards. In regard to income recognition, the Committee has recommended that the institutions following the accrual system of accounting should not recognise any income in their accounts in respect of "non-performing assets". They are defined as assets on which interest remains due for a period exceeding 180 days on the balance sheet date.

For the purpose of provisioning, the Committee has recommended that the assets of banks and other financial institutions should be classified into four categories, namely, standard, sub-standard, doubtful and loss assets and provisioning done accordingly. Accepting the recommendations with certain modifications, the RBI issued appropriate guidelines to banks " on income recognition and asset classification for determining provisions for loan losses" in early September 1992. This may be given due recognition by the tax authorities.

8. Banks at present experience considerable difficulties in recoveries of loans and enforcement of security charged to them. The Committee, therefore, has recommended strongly the setting up of Special Tribunals to speed up the process of recovery.

9. A novel recommendation of the Committee is the establishment of a new financial institution called the Assets Reconstruction Fund (ARF), which would take over from banks and financial institutions a portion of their bad and doubtful debts at a discount, and subsequently follow up on the recovery of the dues owed to them from the primary borrowers. The Fund would pay for the acquisition of these (bad and doubtful) assets from banks/DFIs at a discounted price (based on the realisable value of assets) in the form of five-year bonds which would bear interest at market-related rates and which would be guaranteed by the Central Government and thus would qualify as SLR assets. The share capital of this Fund would be subscribed by the Government of India, the RBI, public sector banks and DFIs. The Fund is proposed as an emergency, and not a continuing measure. Banks, in future, should pay due commercial attention in loan appraisal and supervision and make adequate provision for assets of doubtful realisable value.

10. The Committee has made some suggestions (not operational recommendations) about the reorganization of the structure of the banking system and of rural credit. [The suggestions have not been well worked out.

Moreover, they are not fully consistent with the Committee's overall emphasis on the deregulation of the financial system.]

11. The Committee has proposed that the Government should indicate that there would be no further nationalization of banks, that new banks in the private sector would be welcome subject to the normal requirements of the RBI, that branch licensing should be abolished and that the policy towards foreign banks should be more liberal.

12. The Committee has said that the internal organization of banks is best left to the judgment of the management of individual banks and that they should be free to make their own recruitment of officers, instead of having a common recruitment system with other banks except at the clerical level. The Committee has stressed the need for a radical change in work technology and culture and greater flexibility in personnel policy. It has favoured computerization.

13. In the Committee's judgment, the Indian banking system, at present, is over-regulated and over-administered. Instead, supervision should be based on prudential norms and regulations, with greater emphasis on internal audit and inspection.

14. The Committee was firmly opposed to the duality of control over the banking system by the RBI and the Banking Division of the Ministry of Finance. Ending this, the RBI should be made the primary agency for the regulation of the banking system. Going a step further, the Committee has recommended that a separate authority should be set up under the aegis of the RBI for the supervisory function over banks and DFIs [-- an unnecessary creation of yet another agency in our view.]

H.I.3 **Follow-up-action**

The government and the RBI have taken follow-up action summed up blow on a number of foresaid recommendations. Some more action is yet to follow.

1. The action taken so far with respect to the SLR and the CRR has already been indicated in the previous sub-section and in Section 20-3.

2. Regarding the Committee's suggestion that the interest paid to banks on impounded reserves (through high CRR) above the basic minimum should be increased, the RBI has not favoured the suggestion. It has argued that the CRR is essentially a monetary instrument for impounding liquidity. The payment of higher interest on CRR by reducing the amount impounded dilutes the very purpose of imposing/raising a CRR. Therefore, from the viewpoint of monetary control, it is preferable to have a lower CRR with less or no interest paid than to have a high CRR and pay a high rate of interest.

3. In April 1992, the RBI introduced a risk-assets ratio system for banks (including foreign banks) in India as a capital adequacy measure and prescribed risk weights to assets of banks. Banks will have to achieve a capital adequacy norm of 8 per cent by specified dates for different categories, but positively by March end, 1996 by all banks. However, foreign banks operating in India will have to achieve this norm by March 31, 1993 and banks with international presence will have to achieve it by March 31, 1994 at the latest.

4. The RBI has issued in 1992 new prudential norms relating to income recognition, classification of assets and provisioning for bad debts. The new income recognition norms ensure that interest not actually received cannot be shown as accrued, a practice which exaggerates profitability of banks. Norms have also been specified for categorising non-performing accounts and for making provisions for substandard, doubtful and loss–making assets.

The finance minister has clarified that there would be 'no immediate outgo from the budget, as the government contribution is in the form of government bonds. But the interest payment on these bonds, and their ultimate redemption, will be a real burden on the budget in future.' The finance minister said that this was the price one had to pay for having long tolerated management practices in the banks and types of lending which paid inadequate attention to portfolio quality and recoveries. He said that, while undertaking such a large injection into the banks, specific commitments would be required from each bank to ensure that their future management practices ensure a high level of portfolio quality, so that the earlier problems did not recur.

To meet the additional capital needs of the banks, all of which cannot be serviced by the budget, the government had decided that the SBI and other nationalised banks, which were in a position to do so, would be allowed access to the capital market to raise fresh equity to meet their shortfall in capital requirements over the next three years. This would also help the banks to expand their lending. It was clarified that the government would continue to retain majority ownership and, therefore, effective control in public sector banks.

5. The balance sheet and profit and loss account formats have been revised to reflect the true financial health of banks. These formats were made effective from the bank accounting year 1991–92.

6. As of April 1992, banks attaining capital adequacy norms and prudential accounting standards can set up new branches without prior approval of the RBI. Banks now have the freedom to rationalise their existing branch network by relocating branches, opening of specialised branches, spinning off business of other locations, setting up of controlling offices/administrative units, etc.

7. In regard to regulated interest rate structure, a series of reform measures have been put in place:

(a) Considerable rationalisation has been effected in banks' lending rates with the number of concessive slabs reduced and some of the rates have been raised thereby reducing the element of subsidy;

(b) The regulated deposit rate structure has been replaced by a single prescription of not exceeding 13.0 (revised to 12.0 and then to 11.0) per cent per annum for all deposit maturities of 46 days and above ; and

(c) Rates of interest on Government securities have been raised and all Treasury bills (of 91-day, 182-day and 364-day) and 5-year and 10-year securities are auctioned. Other deposit-raising instruments of commercial banks carry market-related rates of interest.

8. The RBI has announced guidelines for the setting up of private banks as public limited companies. The guidelines have stipulated that the banks in the private sector should be financially viable and avoid such shortcomings as unfair preemption and concentration of credit, cross-holdings with industrial groups, etc.

In view of the above, the following developments may be noted:

1. Recapitalisation of less strong public sector banks through budgetary support of about Rs. 15,000 crore was taken till 1994-95. These banks have promised the RBI to strengthen bank management and improve efficiency;

2. As already explained in a footnote to Chapter 5, the SBI and some other nationalised banks have been allowed to seek capital market access;

3. 13 public sector banks have already attained the capital adequacy by reaching the target level of 8 per cent of capital to risk-weighted assets. In the case of foreign banks, all of them have already attained this norm;

4. For early recovery of overdue bank debts, Debts Recovery Tribunals have been set up. Besides, a Board for Financial Supervision has also been set up and a list of large defaulting borrowers is being prepared and updated from time to time.

As a result of all these measures, the commercial banking system in the country has been strengthened and in 1994-95, the public sector banks as a whole had net profits of more than Rs. 1,100 crore.

H.1.4. Capital Market Reforms

Besides the banking sector reforms discussed above, a process of **capital market reforms** has also been initiated since 1991–92. The need for such reforms arises from the fact of impressive increases in the quantity of funds raised in the capital market since 1985–86, but without any improvement in this market. The functioning of stock exchanges shows many shortcomings with long delays, lack of transparency in procedures and vulnerability to price rigging and insider trading.

The key measure adopted in this field is the according of statutory status by an Act of Parliament to the Stock Exchange Boards of India (SEBI) with effect from March 31, 1992. We shall discuss the main function of the SEBI separately in the next sub-section. Here we sum up briefly other significant reforms.

1. The Capital Issues Control Act, 1947 was repealed in May 1992 and the office of the Controller of Capital Issues (CCI) was subsequently abolished. With the abolition of CCI, prior government permission is no longer needed by companies to access the capital market. Companies are now free to approach the capital market without prior government permission subject to getting other documents cleared by SEBI. Control over price and premium fixation has also been removed and most issuing companies are free to fix the issue price of their securities for the public as well as rights issues.

2. Indian companies have been permitted to raise capital for modernization and import requirements in international capital market through Euro-equity issues. Several companies have been given such permission. Upto the end of January 1993, two companies had raised around Dollar 250 million from the Euro-market.

3. Companies issuing capital in the primary market are now required to disclose all material facts and specific risk factors associated with their projects.

4. As a significant liberalization measure, all restrictions on interest rates on debentures and public sector bonds other than the tax-free PSU bonds were rescinded in August 1991.

5. Foreign pension funds have been allowed to invest in the Indian stock market, subject to certain safeguards.

Thus, almost all the capital market reform measures are intended to achieve a blending of market freedom and regulation of the market for investor protection. The process of reforms, however, has only just begun. It needs to be deepened further along the charted lines.

H.2 New Financial Institutions and Instruments

Since 1988 the financial sector in India has been undergoing a process of structural transformation. New institutions have been established to serve the increasing financial needs of commerce and industry in the area of venture capital, credit rating and leasing, etc. Technology Development and Information Company of India (TDICI) Ltd., a technology venture finance company has been sanctioning project finance to new technology ventures in diverse fields since 1989. Risk Capital and Technology Finance Corporation (RCTFC) Ltd. has been providing risk capital to new entrepreneurs and technology finance for technology-oriented ventures since 1988. Infrastructure Leasing and Financial Services (IL and FS) Ltd., which commenced its operations in 1988, focuses on leasing of equipment for infrastructure development. As yet, the amount of finance provided by each of these companies is rather small. But, each has made a new beginning in a new field.

H.2.1 Some Important New Financial Institutions are Discussed Below

1. Discount and Finance House of India (DFHI), Ltd.

The DFHI, which commenced its operations in April 1988, has been set up as a specialised money market institution. It is a subsidiary of the RBI. Its basic objective is to stimulate activity in the money market by providing liquidity to money market instruments. It does so through its dealings. Treasury bills and rediscounting of commercial bills and thereby developing a secondary market in them. The endeavour of the DFHI has been to increase the turnover of money market assets rather than becoming a mere repository of these assets. It is this high turn over which is the key to increased liquidity of money market assets and institutions. The DFHI also operates in the inter-bank call money market as well as in the inter-bank term deposit market.

All these operations of the DFHI have been increasing year after year in nominal (as well as real) terms. During the fiscal year 1994-95, the cumulative turnover in the call and notice money market was Rs. 5,29,000 crore, turnover of treasury bills was about Rs. 31,000 crore and turnover of dated government securities was about Rs. 12,500 crore.

2. Shipping Credit and Investment Company of India (SCICI)

In recent years, a new development bank by the name of SCICI has been established for providing finance to the shipping companies for the development of shipping and fisheries in the country. During 1994-95, it disbursed finance of about Rs. 3,800 crore and Rs. 1,440 crore, respectively. The cumulative assistance at the end of March 1995 was Rs.

7,700 crore of sanctions and Rs. 3,700 crore of disbursements. It is in the process of diversification. As yet, these plans have not taken a definit shape.

3. Small Industries Development Bank of India (SIDBI)

It has been set up as a wholly-owned subsidiary of the IDBI. It started its operations in April 1990. Its main objective is to ensure larger flow of financial and non-financial assistance to the small scale sector. To that end, it has chosen to concentrate its immediate thrust on (i) initiating steps for technological upgradation and modernization of existing units; (ii) expanding the channels for marketing the products of the SSI sector in domestic and overseas markets; and (iii) promotion of employment-oriented industries, especially in semi-urban areas, to create more employment opportunities and thereby checking migration of population to urban and metropolitan areas.

The financial assistance of SIDBI to the small-scale units scattered throughout the country is being channelized through the existing delivery mechanism comprising SFCs, SIDCs, commercial banks, co-operative banks and RRBs which have a vast network of branches in the country. The total number of institutions eligible for assistance from SIDBI is close to 1,000.

The major activities of SIDBI are : (a) refinance of loans and advances; (b) discounting and rediscounting of bills; (c) extension of seed capital/soft loans; (d) granting direct assistance; (e) providing services like factoring, leasing, etc., and (f) extending financial support to State Small Industries Development Corporations.

During the financial year 1994-95 the paid-up capital of SIDBI was Rs. 450 crore and its reserves were Rs. 500 crore. It had raised Rs. 1,400 crore from bonds and debentures and Rs. 300 crore from deposits. Through borrowings from the GOI, RBI and others, it collected Rs. 6,600 crore. Its other liabilities were Rs. 1,100 crore. Thus, its total resources were Rs. 10,400 crore. The financial assistance sanctioned and disbursed was about Rs. 4,700 crore and about Rs. 3,400 crore, respectively.

At the end of March 1995, the cumulative financial assistance sanctioned and disbursed was about Rs. 16,200 crore and Rs. 12,000 crore, respectively. The SIDBI also decided to join selected nodal banks in promoting separate 'factoring' companies so as to mitigate the difficulties faced by SSI units on account of delayed payments for their sales.

4. (i) National Housing Bank (NHB)

NHB was set up in July 1988 as a wholly-owned subsidiary of the RBI. As the apex agency in housing finance, it seeks to promote sound and effective institutional framework for the supply of finance in the housing sector. To that end, it provides refinance to scheduled commercial banks for housing loans, housing finance companies, Housing and Urban Development Corporation (HUDCO), co-operative housing finance societies, scheduled state co-operative, state land development banks and some other eligible agencies under a variety of special schemes.

At the end of June 1994, the NHB had paid-up capital of Rs. 250 crore and reserves of about Rs. 200 crore. It had got long-term loan of Rs. 175 crore from the RBI from its National Housing Credit (Long-Term Operations) Fund. Besides, it augmented its resources by the sale of bonds and debentures and other loans and advances, all amounting to about Rs. 3,000 crore. Its cumulative disbursements upto June 1994 were Rs. 2,000 crore, of which Rs. 1,630 crore went to the Housing Finance Companies, Rs. 260 crore to the co-operatives and the rest to the commercial banks.

In the field of housing finance, the following two institutions are also important.

(ii) Housing and Urban Development Corporation Ltd. (HUDCO)

Till March-end 1995, cumulatively, HUDCO had sanctioned about Rs. 16,600 crore for nousing projects—less than half of them were for rural areas. Cumulative disbursements were about Rs. 7,000 crore.

HUDCO had raised resources as term loans from the GIC and subsidiaries, the NHB, borrowings and bonds from other sources, raising about Rs. 1,150 crore.

(iii) Housing Development Finance Corporation Ltd. (HDFC)

Cumulatively, as of March 31, 1995, the assistance sanctioned and disbursed by the HDFC was about Rs. 7,000 crore and about Rs. 5,700 crore, respectively.

5. Securities and Exchange Board of India (SEBI).

It was established as a non-statutory Board in April 1988 and accorded statutory status by an Act of Parliament effective March 31, 1992. The SEBI has been vested with wide-ranging powers to oversee constitution as well as operations of mutual funds. Secondly, all stock exchanges in the country have been brought under the annual inspection regime of SEBI for ensuring orderly and healthy growth of the stock market and investor protection. Thirdly, with the repealing of the Capital Issues Control Act in May 1992, SEBI has been made the regulatory authority in regard to the new issue activities of companies. SEBI has issued a series of guidelines covering different aspects of its jurisdiction and responsibility, which is expected to have a significant bearing on the future development of the capital market and also curb the practice of insider trading. Merchant banking has also been statutorily brought under the regulatory framework of SEBI. Merchant bankers now need authorisation of the SEBI to do business.

6. Merchant Banking

Merchant bankers are financial intermediaries between entrepreneurs on the one end and investors on the other. Merchant banking includes a wide range of services. A merchant banker may act as advisor, under-writer and manager for public issues, and also provide bridge loans against these issues. While certifying a project, the merchant banker is expected to ensure that full and accurate disclosures are made in the prospectus and the letter of offer to the public, that the viability of the project has been assessed properly, that under-writers have the capacity to stand by their commitments, etc. From the beginning of 1993, merchant banking has been statutorily brought under the regulatory framework of the Securities Exchange Board of India (SEBI) to ensure greater transparency in the operation of merchant bankers and make them accountable. Also, now no person can act as a merchant banker without obtaining a certificate of registration from the SEBI. Till April 1993 more than 100 merchant bankers had been registered with the SEBI. With expanding financial market and the growth of equity culture among the public, this number is expected to grow further.

7. (i) Credit Rating Information Services of India Ltd. (CRISIL).

This company, set up in 1988, has been promoted jointly by the ICICI and the UTI to provide credit rating services to the corporate sector. Its share capital is held broadly by a large number of banks and financial institutions. Credit rating promotes investors' interests by providing them information on assessed comparative risk of investment in the listed securities of different companies. It also helps companies to raise funds more easily and at relatively cheaper cost, if their credit rating is high. Over time, the operations of CRISIL are on the increase. Upto the end of March 1995, CRISIL had rated more than 1,300 debt instruments issued by 920 companies covering a debt volume of about Rs. 72,000 crore.

The following two more credit rating agencies have come up in recent years:

(ii) Investment and Credit Rating Agency (ICRA)

Cumulatively, till March-end 1995, ICRA has carried rating of 485 debt instruments aggregating about Rs. 18,000 crore;

(iii) Credit Analysis and Research Ltd. (CARE)

Cumulatively, till March-end 1995, CARE had rated 228 debt instruments for a total amount of about Rs. 10,000 crore.

8. Stock Holding Corporation of India Ltd. (SHCIL).

This is a depository institution, sponsored by the seven all-India financial institutions. It commenced operations in August 1988. The SHCIL had been established with the main objective of introducing a book entry system for the transfer of shares and other types of scrips thereby avoiding voluminous paper work involved and thus reducing delays in transfers.

H.2.2. New Financial Instruments

1. Certificates of Deposits (CDs)

The scheme of CDs was introduced in June 1989 to enable commercial banks to raise additional funds from the market through the issue of market paper in the form of CDs of various maturities, typically of 3 months maturity at the short end and of one year at the long end.

Initially, the RBI had fixed a limit for the issue of CDs at 1 per cent of the fortnightly average of outstanding aggregate deposits in fiscal year 1988-89. Later on, this limit was revised upward to 2 and then 3 per cent of comparable deposits in 1989-90 (April-March). This limit was revised again to 5% of the foresaid deposits with effect from April 22, 1991 and yet again to 7% of these deposits with effect from May 2, 1992. The outstanding amount of CDs issued by banks as at March-end 1995 was Rs. 8,000 crore.

The rates of interest for maturity of 3 months had ranged between 12.0 per cent and 13.5 per cent and those for maturity of one year between 9.0 per cent and 15.0 per cent. The interest rates offered on CDs are considered quite high, keeping in view the fact that the CDs are subject to reserve requirements. As a result, holders in the primary market for CDs generally prefer to hold the CDs till maturity and secondary market in them has not developed.

The CDs provide ample flexibility to investors in the deployment of their short-term funds. To enhance this flexibility, banks have been permitted since December 1990 to issue CDs in multiples of Rs. 5 lakhs each, subject to the minimum size of issue to a single investor being Rs. 25 lakhs. They are turning out to be an important source of bulk funds for banks.

2. Commercial Paper (CP)

Another money market instrument introduced recently (Since January 1990) in the country is the commercial paper of companies. Through their issue companies can raise funds. To safeguard the interests of lenders, only companies of the specified minimum size and creditworthiness and above are allowed to issue such paper. The maturity period of CP issued has varied from 3 months to 6 months. Till March 1995, the companies had issued CP worth about Rs. 600 crore and the rates of interest had varied between 14% and 15.5%. Under the revised guidelines, the CP can now be in multiples of Rs. 5 lakhs, subject to the minimum of an issue to a single investor being Rs. 25 lakhs. The secondary market in CP is yet to develop.

REFERENCES

Ackley, G. 1978. *Macroeconomics: theory and policy.* New York : Macmillan.

Banking Commission. 1972. *Report.* New Delhi : Government of India.

Baumol, W.J. 1952. 'The Transactions Demand for Cash: An Inventory-Theoretic Approach'. *Quarterly Journal of Economics,* November, 545–56.

Branson, W.H. 1978. *Macroeconomic Theory and Policy,* 2nd ed. New York : Harper and Row.

Bronfenbrenner, M. and Holzman, F.D. 1963. 'A Survey of Inflation Theory'. *American Economic Review,* September.

Cagan, P. 1956. 'The Monetary Dynamics of Hyperinflation'. In Friedman (ed.). 1956. *Studies in the Quantity Theory of Money.* University of Chicago Press.

Chandler, L.V. 1979. *The Monetary Financial System.* New York : Harper and Row.

Chandler, L.V. and Goldfeld, S.M. 1977. *The Economics of Money and Banking.* 7th ed. New York: Harper and Row.

Chick, V. 1977. *The Theory of Monetary Policy.* Revised ed. Oxford: Basil Blackwell.

Conard, J.W. 1963. *An Introduction to the Theory of Interest.* Berkeley : University of California Press.

Dandekar, V.M. 1986. 'Monetary Policy for Independent Monetary Authority'. *Economic and Political Weekly,* January 25, 169-74.

Datta, B. 1986. 'Monetary Reform'. *Economic and Political Weekly,* January 11, 74-77.

Deaver, J.V. 1970. 'The Chilean Inflation and the Demand for Money'. In Meiselman, D. (ed.) *Varieties of Monetary Experience,* 9–67. Chicago University Press.

Duesenberry, J. 1950. 'Mechanics of Inflation'. *Review of Economics and Statistics,* May, 144–49.

Fiege, E. 1964. *Demand for Liquid Assets : A Temporal Cross-Section Analysis.* Englewood Cliffs : Prentice-Hall.

Fisher. I 1911. *The Purchasing Power of Money : Its Determination and Relation to Credit, Interest and Crises.* New York : Macmillan.

Friedman, M. 1956. 'Quantity Theory of Money — A Restatement'. In Milton Friedman (ed.) Studies in the Quantity Theory of Money. Chicagc : University of Chicago Press.

—. 1959. 'The Demand for Money—Some Theoretical and Empirical Issues'. *Journal of Political Economy,* 327-51.

—. 1961. 'The Lag in Effect of Monetary Policy'. *Journal of Political Economy,* 447–66.

—. 1962. *Price Theory : A Provisional Text.* New York: Aldine. Reprinted. 1970. Ludhiana: Lyall Book Depot.

—. 1966. 'Interest Rates and the Demand for Money'. *Journal of Law and Economics.* Reprinted in Friedman. 1969.

—. 1968 a. 'The Role of Monetary Policy'. *American Economic Review,* March, 1-17.

—. 1968 b. 'Money : Quantity Theory' In *International Encyclopedia of the Social Sciences.* Free Press, 432–47. Reprinted in A.A. Walters (ed.) *Money and Banking.* Penguin, 1973, 36-66.

—. 1969. *The Optimum Quantity of Money and Other Essays.* London: Macmillan.

—. 1970. *The Counter-Revolution in Monetary Theory.* London: IEA Occasional Paper no. 33.

—. 1972. 'Comment on the Critics'. *Journal of Political Economy,* September/October, 906-50.

—. and Meiselman, D. 1964. 'The Relative Stability of Monetary Velocity and Investment Multiplier in the United States, 1897-1958' In Commission on Money and Credit, *Stabilizatin Policies.* Englewood Cliffs : Prentice-Hall.

—. and Schwartz, A. 1963. *A Monetary History of the United States,* 1867-1960. Princeton university Press.

Ghosh, D.N. 1979. *Banking Policy in India.* Bombay: Allied.

Gibson, W.E. and Kaufman, G.G. (eds.) 1971. *Monetary Economics: Readings on Current Issues.* New York : McGraw-Hill.

Government of India, Ministry of Finance, 1993, *Economic Survey* (Annual), 1992-93.

Gupta, S.B. 1971. 'Some Notes on the Short-Run Determination of Income and the Price Level'. (Mimeo.) Delhi School of Economics.

—. 1972 a. 'On the Transactions Demand for Money to Hold'. *Indian Economic Journal,* April-June, 483–96.

—. 1972 b. 'Currency Holding, Mobilisation of Savings and Dangers of

Inflationary Spending'. *Economic and Political Weekly*. September 8, 1877-82.

—. 1972c. 'The Theory of the Real-Balance Effect — A Criticism and a Generalisation'. *Indian Economic Review,* October, 202-15.

—. 1973. 'The Controversy over Differential Lending Rates for Banks: An Examination'. *Indian Economic Review,* April, 16-38.

—. 1974a. 'The Demand and Suply of Loanable Funds: An Accounting Critique of the Traditional Approach'. *Indian Economic Review,* April, 18-35.

—. 1974b. 'Food-Shortage, Demand Pull, and Inflation in India'. In S.L.N. Simha (ed.) *Inflation in India.* Bombay: Vora, 155-72.

—. 1974c. 'Monetary Management in India: An Evaluation'. In J.C. Sandesara (ed.) *The Indian Economy: Performance and Prospects.* Bombay University Press, 266-79.

—. 1974d. 'Credit Policy, Interest Rates, Central Banking and All That: A Comment'. *Economic and Political Weekly,* July 6, 1071-73.

—. 1975. 'Planning Neutral Money for India'. *Indian Economic Journal,* Oct.-Dec., 169-90.

—. 1976a. 'Factors Affecting Money Supply—Critical Evaluation of Reserve Bank's Analysis'. *Economic and Political Weekly,* January 4, 117-28.

—. 1976b. 'Money Supply Analysis: A Reply'. *Economic and Political Weekly,* November 20, 1834-44.

—. 1979. *Monetary Planning For India.* Delhi: Oxford University Press.

—. 1980. 'Credit Planning for India'. Keynote paper delivered at the 63rd annual conference of the Indian Economic Association. Pune. December.

—. 1982. 'Macroeconomic Theory When All Markets Are Interdependent'. *Indian Economic Journal.* Vol. 30(1), 27-48.

Gurley J. and Shaw, E.S. 1960. *Money in a Theory of Finance.* Washington: Brookings Institution.

Hicks, J. 1937. 'Mr. Keynes and the Classics; A Suggested Interpretation'. *Econometrica,* April, 147-59.

—. 1967. *Critical Essays in Monetary Theory.* London: Oxford University Press.

Johnson, H.G. 1962. 'Monetary Theory and Policy'. *American Economic Review,* 335-84. Reprinted in *Surveys of Economic Theory,* Vol. I, 1-55. London: Macmillan.

Kalecki, M. 1937. 'Principle of Increasing Risk'. *Economica*. Revised version as 'Entrepreneurial Capital and Investment' printed in *Theory of Economic Dynamics* (1954). Reprinted in *Selected Essays on the Dynamics of the Capitalist Economy,* 1933–70. (1971), essay 9.

Keynes, J.M. 1923. *A Tract on Monetary Reform.* London: Macmillan.

—. 1936. *The General Theory of Employment, Interest and Money.* London: Macmillan.

—. 1937. 'The Ex-Ante Theory of the Rate of Interest'. *Economic Journal,* 663–79.

—. 1940. *How to Pay for the War.* London: Macmillan.

Kirkpatrick, C.H. and Nixon, F. I. 1976. 'The Origins of Inflation in Less Developed Countries: A Selected Review'. In Parkin, M. and Zis, G. (eds.) *Inflation in Open Economies,* Manchester University Press.

Krishnaswamy, K.S. 1976. 'Some Thoughts on Inflation and Distribution'. *Indian Economic Journal,* October-December, 127–38.

Laidler, D.E.W. 1971. 'The Influence of Money on Economic Activity : A Survey of Some Current Problems'. In G. Clayton, J. Gilbert and R. Sedgwick (eds.). 1971. *Monetary Theory and Monetary Policy in the 1970s.* London: Oxford University Press.

—. 1975. *Essays on Money and Inflation.* Chicago University Press.

—. 1977. *Demand for Money, Theories and Evidence,* 2nd ed. New York: Dun-Donnelley.

—. and Parkin J.M. 1975. 'Inflation—A Survey'. *Economic Journal,* December, 741–809.

Leijonhufvud, A. 1968. *On Keynesian Economics and the Economics of Keynes.* Oxford University Press.

Lindbeck, A. 1963. *A Study in Monetary Analysis.* Stockholm: Almqvist and Wiksell.

Lipsey, R.G. 1960. 'The Relation Between Unemployment and the Rate of Change of Money Wage Rates in the United Kingdom, 1862–1957 : A Further Analysis'. *Economica,* February.

Marshall, A. 1923. *Money, Credit and Commerce.* New York: Kelly (Reprinted, 1965).

Myrdal, G. 1968. *Asian Drama: An Inquiry into the Poverty of Nations.* Harmondsworth: Penguin Books.

Pandit V.N. 1978. 'An Analysis of Inflation in India, 1950–1975'. *Indian Economic Review,* October, 89–115.

Patil, R.H. 1986. 'Monetary Reform: Some Unresolved Issues'. *Economic and Political Weekly,* January 25, 174-77.

Patinkin, D. 1948. 'Price Flexibility and Full Employment'. *American Econoic Review*, Septermber, 543-64. Revised version in *Readings in Monetary Theory*. 1951. New York: Blakiston. 252-83.

—. 1965. *Money, Interest, and Prices*, 2nd ed. New York: Harper and Row.

Phillips, A.W. 1958. 'The Relation Between Unemployment and the Rate of Change of Money Wage Rates in the United Kingdom, 1861- 1957'. *Economica*, New Series, 283-99.

Pigou, A.C. 1943. 'The Classical Stationary State'. *Econoic Journal*. December, 343-51.

Raj, K.N. 1966. 'Price Behaviour in India. An Explanatory Hypothesis'. *Indian Economic Review*. 56 –78.

Raj Krishan. 1979. 'Small Farmer Development'. *Economic and Political Weekly*, May 26, 913-18.

Rangarajan, C. 1985. 'Money, Outrut and Prices'. In *Reserve Bank of India Bullektin*, December , 1037-44.

— 1987. 'The Analytical Framework of the Chakravarty Committee Report on the Monetary System'. In *Reserve Bank of India Bulletin*, September, 702-5.

— and Singh, A. 1984. 'Reserve Money: concepts and Policy Implications for India'. Reserve Bank of India, *Oceasional Papers*, June, 1–26.

Reder, M.V. 1948, 'The Theoretical Problems of a National Wage- Price Policy'. *Canadian Journal of Economics*, February, 46- 61.

RBI. 1961. a. 'Analysis of Money Supply in India—I'. *Reserve Bank of India Bulletin*, July, 1045-67.

—. 1961 b. 'Analysis of Money Supply in India—II'. *Reserve Bank of India Bulletin*, August, 1214-19.

—. 1983. *The Reserve Bank of India : Functions and Working. 4th edition*. Bombay.

—. 1975. *Report of the Study Group to Frame Guidelines for Follow-up of Bank Credit*. (Chairman : P.L. Tandon). Bombay.

—. 1977. 'Money Supply : Concepts, Compilation and Analysis'.

(Report of the Second working Group). *Reserve Bank of India Bulletin*, January. 70–134.

—. 1991 'Growth of Deposits with Non-Banking Companies, 87- 88. *Reserve Bank of India Bulletin*, July, 643–74.

—. 1987. *Statstical Tables Relating to Banks in India*, Bombay.

Report on Trend and Progress of Banking in India, 1989-90. Bombay.

RBI. 1991. *Report on Currency and Finance*, Vols. I and II

—. *Annual Report*. Several issues.

Robertson, D.H. 1938. 'Mr. keynes and Finance : A Note' *Economic Journal*, 314.18.

Saving, T.R. 1971. 'Monetary-Policy Targets and Indicators'. In Gibson and Kaufman. (eds.) 1976.

Schultze, C. 1959. *Recent Inflation in the United States*. Washington : Joint Economic Committee, U.S. Congress.

Singh, Shetty and Venkatachalam. 1982, *Monetary Policy in India : Issues and Evidence*. Supplement to Reserve Bank of India Occasional Papers. June.

Streeten, P. 1972. *The Frontiers of Development Studies*. London : Macmillan.

Timberg, T. and Aiyar, C.V. 1980. 'Informal Credit Markets in India'. *Economic and Political Weekly*, Annual No. 279-302.

Tinbergen, J. 1952. *On the Theory of Economic Policy*. Amsterdam : North-Holland.

Tobin, J. 1956. 'The Interest-Elasticity of Transactions Demand for Cash'. *Review of Economics and Statistics*, August, 241–47.

—. 1958. ''Liquidity Preferences as Behaviour Towards Risk'. *Review of Economic Studies*, February, 65–86.

—. 1965. 'the Monetary Interpretation of History'. AER, June, 464-85.

Trevithick, J.A. and Mulvey, C. 1975. *The Economics of Inflation*. London: Martin Robertson.

Trivedi. M.S. 1980. 'Inflationary Expectations and Demand for Money in India (1951-1975)'. *Indian Economic Journal*, July- September, 62–76.

Vasudevan, A. 1977. 'Demand for Money in India—A Survey of Literature'. *Reserve Bank Staff Occasional Papers*, Vol. 2(1), 58–83.

— 1980. 'Money stock and Its Components in India, 1950–51 to 1979-80 : A Statistical Account'. *Indian Economic Journal*, July-September, 1-17.

INDEX

Acceptance credit, 55
Adjusted high-powered money, 289-90
 360, (*see also* High-powered money)
Aggregate monetary resources (AMR), 16
Agricultural credit, (*see* Credit, sectoral to agriculture)
All India Rural Credit Survey Commitee, 76, 126

Bank
 Credit
  multiplier, 298-300
  supply, theory of, 297-300
  (*see also* Credit)
 deposits
  Changes in composition of, 104-5
  growth of, 104
  inds of, 11-4
  multiplier, 299
  supply, theory of, 297-300
 rate policy, 362-365
Banking
 System in India
 Deficiencies and Reforms, 427-446
Bazar bill rate, 339
Bills
 commercial
  discounting of , 53-5
  meaning and kinds of, 52-5
  rediscounting scheme, 56-8
  usance of, 53
Bill market
 commercial, 52-5
  new scheme, 56-8
  old scheme, 55-6
 treasure, 51-2, 72
Bond market in Keynes' monetary theory, 227

Call money
 market, 48-9
 rate, 49
Cambridge cash-balances
 Theory of demand for money, 181-184
  and Keynes, 190, 229-30
 version of quantity theory of money, 205-12
Capital markets, 44-8, 440-41
Cash balances, nominal versus real, 180-1
Cash credit system, 92, 94-96
Cash reserves
 of banks, 72-3, 91
 ratio (CRR), 91, 375-78
Chakravarty Committee recommendations 406-423
Chit funds, 156-7
Clearing house, 7-8
Commercial banks
 assets of, 94-98
 before independence, 97-8
 branch expansion of, 101-4
 classification of 84-5
 definition of, 82-3
 liquidation and amalgamation of, 100-1
 nationalisation of, 99-100
 regulation of, (by RBI) 100
 services of, 83-4
 staff, productivity and profits of, 104-5
Commercial bank credit, sectoral allocation, 104-114
 to agriculture, 109-113
 as food advances, 110-113
 to industry, 115-6, 110
 to priority sectors, 108-112
 to public sector units, 112-13
 to export, 113-14
 Under IRDP, 111-12

Commercial bank lending
forms of, 96-98 (*see also* Commercial bank assets and Cash credit, system)
reform of, 96-101
Commercial banking, major developments in, since independence, 99-105
Commercial Paper (CP),
Co-operative banks
central (CCBs), 119-20
primary co-operative banks (PCBs), 125-26
primary agricultural credit socienties, (PACSs) 120-169
state (SCBs) 118-9
(*see also* Land development banks)
Co-operative banking system
importance of, 113-15
flow of funds from / to, 117-8
and RBI/NABARD, 76-77, 116, 126-28
size of, 128
structure of , 115-18
Credit
monitraing arrangement (CMA) 369-70
cost of, 42
distinction from money, 19-20
economy 20
end-uses of, 37-9
guarantees, 79-81
inter-borrower allocation of, (*see* Institutional credit)
kinds of, 37-41
meaning of, 19, 20
rationing, 313-14
sources of, 37
supply curve for individual borrowers, 310-13
terms of, 39-41
users of, 39
CRISIL, 445
Credit policy
and goals of economic policy, 358-60, (*see also* Monetary Policy, selective credit controls *and* Credit authorisation scheme)
Credit, sectoral
to agriculture, 76-77, 108-13, 120-9
to industry and exports, 55-65, 77-81 117-19, 125-6, 145-58
to priority sectors, 110-14

Deflator
in Hicks' IS-LM model, 242
in Keynes' monetary theory, 230, 247
in Keynesian theory, 241
Deficit financing, 356-7
Demand-deposit multiplier, 274
Demand for money
Cambridge approach to, 181-84
emprical evidence on, 197-78
and expected rate of change of prices, 197-98
Friedman's theory of, 195-97
and income, 181-84
Keynes' theory of, 184-90
neoclasical theory of, 181-84
and non-money financial asets (NMFA), 189-90
precautionay, 185
and range of substitution of money, 231-2
and rate of interest, 186-90, 194, 196-98
speculative, 185-89
transactions, 191-95
Baumol-Tobin theory of, 194-95
popular textbook explanation of, 191-94
Depost growth, 103
Demand loans, 93
Deposits
and Finance House of India (DFHI) 441-42
with banks, (*see* Bank deposits)
with post offices, (*see* Post office deposits)
Development banks, 129-44
Discount
houses, 55
rate on bills, 53

Equipment Leasing Finance Companies 157-58

Excess reserves, *see* Reserves of banks
Expected rate of change of prices, 197-98 395-98
and demand for money and other financial assets, 196-92, 395-98
and distributin of income and

wealth, 397
estimation of, 397-99
and inflation, 396
and money rates of interest, 246-7, 396-97
and Phillips curve, 401-04
Export finance, 78-9
Export-Import (or EXIM) Bank of India 142

Finance, (*see* Credit)
Finance brokers, 48-9, 65, 169-70
Financial
assets, 21-2, 29-33
intermediaries, 23-4, (*see also* Banks *and* Non-bank financial intermediaries)
intermediation, 26-8
gains from, 24-6
markets, 43-67
system
meaning, 20-1
functions and importance of , 28-37
Foreign
exchange reserves, management and control of, 73-74
Friedman's monetary theory, 212-17
General Insurance Companies, (GICs) 148-49

Gilt-eddged market, 65-6, 72-3
Government bond market *see* Gilt-edged market

Hicks' IS-LM model, 191, 220
High-powered money
definition of, 271
as a dterminant of money supply, see Money supply, theory of
factors affecting, 286-89
policy determination of, 289-92
Hire-purchase Finance Companies, (HPFCs) 156-57
Housing Finance Companies (HFCs) 158
Hundi, 161
Income velocity of money, 204, 208, 210, 239n
behaviour in India of, 221
constancy of, 218-21
independence of money of, 221
as a multiplier

Indigenous bankers, 161-69
Industrial credit, (*see* Credit, sectoral, to industry and exports)
Industrial Development Banks, (IDBs) 131-143
all-India, 131-142
Industrial Credit and Investment Corporation of India (ICICI), 132-33
Industrial Development Bank of India (IDBI), 131-32
Industrial Finance Corporation of India (IFCI), 132
Industrial Reconsruction Bank of India (IRBI), 133
main features and evaluation of, 133-
state level, 140-42
Informal Loan Market, 173-74
Inflation
acceleration of, 395-98
cost-push, 255-56
matrial-cost push, 260
profit push, 259-60
wage push, 256-59
demand-pull
Keynes' inflationary-gap analysis, 251-54
quantity theory of money (QTM) explanation, 254-55
demand-shift theory of, 261
income-shares theory of, 260
and money, 268-69
structural, in LDCs, 264-65
(*see also* Phillips curve)
Inflationary
bias of the Indian economy, 354
expectations, (*see* Expected rate of change of prices) 395-98
Institutitonal credit, inter-borrower, allocation of
financial factors in, 302-14, 313
creditworthiness of borrower, 303
debt-equity ratio, 304-05
income-interest ratio, 305
margin requirement, 309-10
net rate of return, 302-3
repaying capacity of borrower, 319

risk of default, 303-6
security, primary and collateral, 306-9
as institutional proces, 300-310, 313-14
non-financial factors in, 314-15
traditinal theory of, 300-01
Inter-bank call money market, (*see* Call money market)
Interest rates
administered,
deficiencies (equalising and non-equalising), 331-35
Chakravarty
Committee, recommendations on, 412-22
differentials in, 324-31
heterogeneity in determination of, 321-24
see also Rate of interest
Investment
of banks, 91
companies, 153-55
demand function, 231-34
and income, 234-39

Keynes' monetary theory
of employment, 239-40
of income and output, 234-38
and the LDCs, 237, 239
introduction to, 234-36
of the prise level, 240-42
of the rate of interest, 236-40,
criticism of, 229-31
and effectiveness of monetary policy, 228-29
see also Inflation, demand-pull, Keynes' inflationary-gap analysis

Land development banks, 144-45
Law of declining economic quality of IOU's (*see* 'Principle of increasing marginal risk')
Lead bank scheme, 102-03
Lender
of intermediate resort, 48
of last resort, 48
Life Insurce Corporation, 146-48
Liquidity
of an asset, 40-1
of a debtor, 40-1
of old securities, 62-3
trap, 187, 228-29
Loan
companies, 155-56
market, informal, 173-74

M_1 or M_3 ?, 424-26
Managed paper currency standard, 68-69
Managing agency system, 6-1
Marginal efficiency of investment
meaning, 231-32
function, 233
and investment demand function, 233
Marginal productivity of Labour
and Price level, 240-41
Merchant Banking, 444-45
Monetary
authority, government as, 70
data and the RBI policy, 74
distinguished from credit policy, 345
goals of, 348-56
indicators of , 359-60
instruments of control of, 355-71
targets of , 366-9, 433-8
transmission mechanism, 392
Monetarists versus Keynesians, 206, 209, 215
Monetisation,
Money
functions of, 3-6
kinds of, 6-9
market, 179
markets
meaning, 44
organized and unorganised, 44-7
seasonal pattern of, 47
and monetary and credit policy, 46-7
multiplier
determinants of, 286
process, 280-86
theory of, (*see* Money supply, H theory of)
value of, 274
supply
definition of, 270
H theory of, 271-280

mesaures of, 15-8,
Reserve Bank's analysis of , 294-98
Money lenders, 170-73
Moral suasio, 367-68

Narasimham Committee Recomendations, 427-37
National Bank for Agricutural and Rural Development, (NBARD) 143-44
NHB, 443-44
National Industrial Credit (Long-Term Operations) Fund, 77-78
Natural rate of unemployment, 401, 405
Neutral money, 342, 344
and other policy goals, 347-50
New issues market, 59-2
New Financial Developments, 427-37
New Financial Institution and Instrument, 441-45
Nidhis, 157
Non-bank financial intermediaries, 145-158 (*see also* Financial intermediaries)

Open market operations, 356-58
Other deposits of the RBI, 16-7
Other 'Non-Bank Financial Companies (NBFs) 152-53
Overdrafts, 92-3
Over-the-counter market, 63

Participation certificates, 88-90
Payments system, 9-11
Phillips curve
and cost-of-living influence on wages, 399-401
and Indian economy, 344-45
and institutional influences on inflationary process, 404-05
loan run, 400-404
and 'natural rate' of unemployment, 401-404
and price expectations, 401-404
relation and theory, 261-64
shifting, 264. 399-405
Post office deposits, 14-5, 152
Price expectations (*see* Expected rate of change of prices)
Principle of increasing marginal risk, 311
Provident/Pension funds, 151-52

Quantity theory of money, (QTM) 200-223
Cambridge cash-balances approach to, 205-8
adjustment mechanism of, 208-9
appraisal of, 217-23
as a theory of money income, 207-11
as a theory of prices, (P) 211-12, 215-16, (*see also* adjustment mechanism)
Fisher's quantity equation in income form, 203-05
and the commodity market, 385-87
and Keynes, 222
Fisher's transactions approach to, 201-03
Modern QTM, 212-17

Rate of interest
and investment, 231-34
Keynes' theory of, 226-31
loanable funds theory of, 316-21
saving-investment theory of, 226 (*see also* Interest rates)
Real-balance effect, 400-02
Real bills doctrine, 53-4
Regional rural banks, 85-86
Reserve Bank credit
to banks, 288, 361-65
to development banks, 288, 367
to foreign sector, 289
to government, 288
Reserve Bank of India
as banker to government, 70-2
as controller of money supply and credit, 73, 371-384
(*see also* Monetary policy, instrum-ents of control)
and credit
guarantees, 79-81
to 'priority sectors' 109-13
to weaker sections, 79
as currency authority, 68-70
and 'differential interest rate' scheme, 80-81
and exchange management and control, 73-4
and monetary data, 74

and money-supply analysis, 292-96
net non-monetary liabilities of, 289
and promotion
of bill market, 55-8, 76
of commercial banking, 75-6
of co-operative banking, 76, 119-20, 126-28
of export finance, 78-91
of industrial finance, 77-8
of rural (agricultural) credit, 76-7, 126
Reserves of banks
demand for, 272-74
supply of, 277-78
Rural credit, *see* Agricultural credit
Savings
deposits, demand and time liability portions of, 12-5
and financial assets, 30-3
of household sector, 28-33
institutionalisation of, 33
mobilisation of, 33
net domestics, 30

Secondary market in old issues, 62-5
Securities,
listed, 63
primary and secondary, 23, 33
Scheduled Banks-Assets and Liabilities, 85-87
Selective credit controls, 371-73
SEBI, 444
SHCIL, 445
SIDBI, 442-43
SIDCs, 142
Stagflations, 264
State financial corporations, 141-42
State Industrial Development / investment Corporations, (SIDCs) 142-43
Statutory liquidity ratio (SLR), 91, 119, 365
Stock market, 58-62

Tandon study group, recommendations on bank credit, 96-99
Transactions velocity of money, 201-03
Term loans, 93-94
Treasury bills, (*see* Bills, treasury)
Treasury bill market, (*see* Bill Market, treasury)

Unauthorised overdrafts, 70-71
Unit Trust of India (UTI), 149-51
Unregulated credit markets, 159
and black money, 174-75
and credit policy, 175-76

Velocity of money, (*see* Income velocity of money *and* Transactions velocity of money.)

IMPORTANT BOOKS ON ECONOMICS

MICRO ECONOMIC THEORY

K.P.M. Sundharam

M.C. Vaish

The twentieth edition of the book in its compact form covers the syllabi of graduate and post-graduate examinations in economics and commerce. Undoubtedly, the present edition of the book will prove of immense use to the students.

CONTENTS: PART ONE: Introduction • PART TWO: Consumption • PART THREE: Prodution and Cost • PART FOUR: Exchange • PART FIVE: Distribution • PART SIX: Income and Employment • PART SEVEN: Trade Cycles and Growth • PART EIGHT: Welfare Economics • PART NINE: International Trade.

08 196 ISBN-81-219-1682-8 pp. 756

मैद्रिक अर्थशास्त्र

एम.सी. वैश्य

पुस्तक का यह ग्यारहवाँ संस्करण पूर्णत: परिशोधित है । पुस्तक के प्रत्येक अध्याय में व्यापक गुणात्मक तथा परिमाणात्मक परिवर्तन एवं सुधार किए गए हैं। प्रत्येक अध्याय में प्रस्तुत किए गए चित्रों को पुन: बनाया गया है तथा सभी सामग्री को नवीनतम सुधार करने के पश्चात् प्रस्तुत किया गया है ।

विषय सूची: प्रथम भाग: मुद्रा तथा कीमतें • मुद्रा का आविष्कार • मुद्रा तथा अर्थव्यवस्था • मुद्रा के प्रकार तथा कार्य इत्यादि • द्वितीय भाग: चक्रीय उच्चावचन तथा स्थिरता • व्यापार चक्र का अर्थ तथा प्रकृति • व्यापार चक्र के सिद्धान्त • व्यापार चक्र का नियंत्रण • मुद्रा स्फीति • निवेश इत्यादि • तृतीय भाग: बचत, निवेश, ब्याज तथा रोजगार • बचत पूर्ति • निवेश माँग • नकदी अधिमान • ब्याज के सिद्धान्त इत्यादि • चतुर्थ भाग: साख मुद्रा, बैंकिंग, विदेशी विनिमय तथा अन्तर्राष्ट्रीय व्यापार • साख मुद्रा • बैकिंग का विकास • केन्द्रीय बैंक • विदेशी विनिमय दर • विदेशी विनिमय नियन्त्रण • मुद्रा अवमूल्यन • मुद्रा बाजार • पंचम भाग: अन्तराष्ट्रीय वित्तिय संस्थाएं • अन्तराष्ट्रीय मुद्रा कोष • अन्तर्राष्ट्रीय नकदी • अन्तर्राष्ट्रीय पुननिर्माण एवं विकास बैक इत्यादि • षष्ठ भाग: भारतीय मुद्रा तथा बैंकिग • भारतीय मुद्रा का इतिहास • रिजर्व बैंक ऑफ इण्डिया • स्टेट बैंक ऑफ इण्डिया इत्यादि

08198 ISBN:81-219-1710-7 pp.693

ECONOMIC REFORMS IN INDIA—A CRITIQUE

Ruddar Dutt

This book is a compilation work of recently updated articles, written by the author for various publications. The volume has been divided into four parts, each dealing with significant weaknesses in the reform processes initiated in India.

CONTENTS: Part I: Economic Reforms and Related Issues • **Part II:** Balance of Payment Crisis and Debt Trap • **Part III:** Industrial Policy— Industrial Policy (1990) (The Internal Contradictions) • New Industrial Policy (1991)–(The bright and dark spots) • Appendices • Index

08 193 ISBN:81-219-1492-2 pp. 368

PUBLIC FINANCE (Theory and Practice)

K.P.M. Sundharam & K.K. Andley

This book has been primarily written for the graduate and post-graduate students offering Public finance as a subject keeping in view the syllabi of all the Indian Universities. The book is divided into first two parts, the frist part deals with the theory of Public finance and the second part deals with the Indian Finance.

CONTENTS: Part I: Theory of Public Finance • Nature, Scope and Importance of Public Finance • Principle of Maximum Social Advantage • Public Expenditure • Effects of Public Expenditure • sources of Public Revenue • Canons of sound Taxation • Theories of Taxation • Direct and Indirect Taxes • Taxation of Income • Tax on Corporate Income • Capital Gains Tax • Expenditure Tax • Taxation of Wealth or Capital • Death Duty and Gift Tax • Commodity Taxes • Theory of Incidence and Shifting of Taxes • Effects of Taxation • Taxable Capacity and other Taxation Problems • Public Debt • Federal Finance • Fiscal Policy and Economic Activity-I: Advanced Economies • Fiscal Policy and Economic Activity-II: Developing Economies • War Finance • **Part II: Indian Public Finance** • Budgetary Trends and Policy in India • Public Expenditure in India • Public Revenue–Direct Taxes • Public Revenue–Indirect Taxes etc.

08 199 ISBN: 81-219-1741-7 pp. 672

ECONOMETRICS AND MATHEMATICAL ECONOMICS

S.P. Singh, Anil K.Prashar H.P. Singh

The book has been presented for those student who have taken up Econometrics and Mathematical economics as one of their paper at the M.A. level . In this book, all methods are explained and discussed within the simplest framework, and generalizations are presented as logical extensions of the simple cases